Please Please Me
THE BEATLES

■ **GEORGE HARRISON** (lead guitar) ■ **JOHN LENNON** (rhythm guitar)
■ **PAUL McCARTNEY** (bass guitar) ■ **RINGO STARR** (drums)

SIDE ONE

1. **I SAW HER STANDING THERE**
   (McCartney-Lennon)
2. **MISERY**
   (McCartney-Lennon)
3. **ANNA (GO TO HIM)**
   (Alexander)
4. **CHAINS**
   (Goffin-King)
5. **BOYS**
   (Dixon-Farrell)
6. **ASK ME WHY**
   (McCartney-Lennon)
7. **PLEASE PLEASE ME**
   (McCartney-Lennon)

SIDE TWO

1. **LOVE ME DO**
   (McCartney-Lennon)
2. **P.S. I LOVE YOU**
   (McCartney-Lennon)
3. **BABY IT'S YOU**
   (David-Williams-Bacharach)
4. **DO YOU WANT TO KNOW A SECRET**
   (McCartney-Lennon)
5. **A TASTE OF HONEY**
   (Scott-Marlow)
6. **THERE'S A PLACE**
   (McCartney-Lennon)
7. **TWIST AND SHOUT**
   (Medley-Russell)

Recording first published 1963

Pop picking is a fast 'n' furious business these days whether you are on the recording studio side listening out, or on the disc-counter side listening in. As a record reviewer I find myself installed halfway in-between with an ear cocked in either direction. So far as Britain's record collecting public is concerned, The Beatles broke into earshot in October, 1962. My natural hometown interest in the group prevented me taking a totally unbiased view of their early success. Eighteen months before their first visit to the EMI studios in London, The Beatles had been voted Merseyside's favourite outfit and it was inevitable that their first Parlophone record, LOVE ME DO, would go straight into the top of Liverpool's local hit parade. The group's chances of national chart entry seemed much more remote. No other team had joined the best-sellers via a début disc. But The Beatles were history-makers from the start and LOVE ME DO sold enough copies during its first 48 hours in the shops to send it soaring into the national charts. In all the busy years since pop singles first shrank from ten to seven inches I have never seen a British group leap to the forefront of the scene with such speed and energy. Within the six months which followed the Top Twenty appearance of LOVE ME DO, almost every leading deejay and musical journalist in the country began to shout the praises of The Beatles. Readers of the *New Musical Express* voted the boys into a surprisingly high place via the 1962/63 popularity poll ... on the strength of just one record release. Pictures of the group spread themselves across the front pages of three national music papers. People inside and outside the record industry expressed tremendous interest in the new vocal and instrumental sounds which The Beatles had introduced. Brian Matthew (who has since brought The Beatles to many millions of viewers and listeners in his "Thank Your Lucky Stars", "Saturday Club" and "Easy Beat" programmes) describes the quartet as *visually and musically the most exciting and accomplished group to emerge since The Shadows.*

Disc reviewing, like disc producing, teaches one to be wary about making long-term predictions. The hit parade isn't always dominated by the most worthy performances of the day so it is no good assuming that versatility counts for everything. It was during the recording of a Radio Luxembourg programme in the *EMI Friday Spectacular* series that I was finally convinced that The Beatles were about to enjoy the type of top-flight national fame which I had always believed that they deserved. The teen-audience didn't know the evening's line-up of artists and groups in advance, and before Muriel Young brought on The Beatles she began to read out their Christian names. She got as far as John ... Paul ... and the rest of her introduction was buried in a mighty barrage of very genuine applause. I cannot think of more than one other group — British or American — which would be so readily identified and welcomed by the announcement of two Christian names. To me, this was the ultimate proof that The Beatles (and not just one or two of their hit records) had arrived at the uncommon peak-popularity point reserved for discdom's privileged few. Shortly afterwards The Beatles proved their pop power when they by-passed the lower segments of the hit parade to scuttle straight into the nation's Top Ten with their second single, PLEASE PLEASE ME.

This brisk-selling disc went on to overtake all rivals when it bounced into the coveted Number One slot towards the end of February. Just over four months after the release of their very first record The Beatles had become triumphant chart-toppers!

Producer George Martin has never had any headaches over choice of songs for The Beatles. Their own built-in tunesmith team of John Lennon and Paul McCartney has already tucked away enough self-penned numbers to maintain a steady output of all-original singles from now until 1975! Between them The Beatles adopt a do-it-yourself approach from the very beginning. They write their own lyrics, design and eventually build their own instrumental backdrops and work out their own vocal arrangements. Their music is wild, pungent, hard-hitting, uninhibited ... and personal. The do-it-yourself angle ensures complete originality at all stages of the process. Although so many people suggest (without closer definition) that The Beatles have a trans-Atlantic style, their only real influence has been from the unique brand of Rhythm and Blues folk music which abounds on Merseyside and which The Beatles themselves have helped to pioneer since their formation in 1960.

This record comprises eight Lennon-McCartney compositions in addition to six other numbers which have become firm live-performance favourites in The Beatles' varied repertoire.

The group's admiration for the work of The Shirelles is demonstrated by the inclusion of BABY IT'S YOU (John taking the lead vocal with George and Paul supplying the harmony), and BOYS (a fast rocker which allows drummer Ringo to make his first recorded appearance as a vocalist). ANNA, ASK ME WHY, and TWIST AND SHOUT also feature stand-out solo performances from John, whilst DO YOU WANT TO KNOW A SECRET hands the audio spotlight to George. MISERY may sound as though it is a self-duet created by the multi-recording of a single voice ... but the effect is produced by the fine matching of two voices belonging to John and Paul. There is only one 'trick duet' and that is on A TASTE OF HONEY featuring a dual-voiced Paul. John and Paul get together on THERE'S A PLACE and I SAW HER STANDING THERE: George joins them for CHAINS, LOVE ME DO and PLEASE PLEASE ME.

TONY BARROW

PMC 1202

TRADE MARK OF
THE Parlophone Co., Ltd.

LONG PLAY 33⅓ R.P.M.

E.M.I. RECORDS LIMITED
(Controlled by Electric & Musical Industries Ltd.)
HAYES · MIDDLESEX · ENGLAND
Made and Printed in Great Britain

USE
EMITEX
CLEANING MATERIAL
The use of "EMITEX" cleaning material (available from Record Dealers) will preserve this record and keep it free from dust.

The BEATLES
Please Please Me to With The Beatles

Compiled by Bruce Spizer

With additional contributions by

Bill King,
Al Sussman,
Frank Daniels,
Piers Hemmingsen
and other Beatles fans

Copyright ©2023 by 498 Productions, L.L.C.

498 Productions, L.L.C.
935 Gravier Street, Suite 707
New Orleans, Louisiana 70112
Phone: 504-299-1964
email: 498@beatle.net

All rights reserved. No part of this book may be used or reproduced in any form or by any means, or stored in a database or retrieval system without written permission of the copyright owner, except in the case of brief quotations embodied in critical articles and reviews. Making copies of any part of this book for any purpose other than your own personal use is a violation of United States copyright laws.

This book is sold as is, without warranty of any kind, either express or implied. While every effort has been made in the preparation of this book to ensure the accuracy of the information contained herein, the author and 498 Productions, L.L.C. assume no responsibility for errors or omissions. Neither is any liability assumed for damages resulting from the use of the information contained herein.

The Billboard, Cash Box and Record World chart data used in this book was taken from books published by Record Research, including The Comparison Book 1954-1982. Photo credits: Zack Smith Photography (page vi); CBS News Archive (page 78); www.popsiephotos.com (page 91); rowland.sherman@verizon.net (page 93); Rivera Family Collection (page 164); Ketterer Family (page 169); Callaghan Family (page 174); Mitchell Family (page 177); Keystone/Hulton Archive/Getty Images (page 233); Terry O'Neill/Iconic Images (pages 240-241); Norman Parkinson/Iconic Images (pages 244, 245, 249, 250 and 257); and Les Lee/Daily Express/Hulton Archive/Getty Images (page 262). Most of the Canadian images were provided by Piers Hemmingsen. Other items are from the collections of Bruce Spizer, Frank Daniels, Perry Cox, Andrew Croft, Jeff Hoganson and Stephen Spence.

This book is published by 498 Productions, L.L.C. It is not an official product of Universal Music Group, Inc., Capitol Records, Inc. or Apple Corps Ltd.

Print edition ISBN: 979-8-9863190-6-3 US$39.98

Printed in U.S.A.
1 2 3 4 5 6 7 8 9 0

Ask Me Why

I'm often asked why people still care about the Beatles. After all, the group broke up in 1970, over 50 years ago. I answer by first explaining why I and millions of other American youngsters fell in love with the Beatles back in 1964. They were very cool. We were not living in a global community back then. They were from England, an exotic foreign land across the Atlantic Ocean. They had British accents. We learned they grew up in Liverpool, a town most of us had never heard of. And then there was the "radically long" hair. Well, long by comparison to the buzz cuts many of us had, including me. We also liked how the Beatles could mock authority, but did it in such a clever way that the adults didn't realize they were being made fun of. But we knew! And, oh yeah, the music was really good.

So what about today? The internet can take us instantly to anywhere in the world. The fact that they are British is no big deal. And that "radically long" hair they wore in 1964? Once again, nothing special. By today's standards, it's quite tame. As for mocking the establishment, well, the Beatles broke up in 1970. So what's left? A really boring, simple answer: The music.

Yeah, that's right. Great songs played in an exciting style that never grows old. The Beatles music is timeless. Just like the music of Bach, Beethoven, Mozart, Shubert, Louis Armstrong...well, you get the idea.

I'm often asked about my first memory of the Beatles. That dates back to early January 1964. By way of background, I was eight years old and in the third grade at Newman School in New Orleans. I had been listening to the radio since I was two. My first two sentences were: "Daddy, I want an ice cream cone;" and "Mommy, I want a radio." I had two sisters who were seven and eight years older than me. They had a radio in their bedroom, so I wanted one too.

At first, I did not understand that radio stations played records. I thought the groups sang their songs at the radio station and then drove to another station to sing it again for that station. But then I learned that for the most part, the person on the radio was playing records. My sisters even had a few of those.

My radio station of choice was WTIX-AM, the Mighty Six-Ninety. When I got in bed at night, I turned my radio on. I did not need a lot of sleep—five to six hours was about it for me. So I heard a lot of music. I would wake up around five in the morning and listen to disc jockey Uncle Gene, the All-Night Satellite.

As I got older, my sisters got a few more records. I began to move their black and red plaid hatbox-style portable record player into my room. It hummed and had four speeds: 16, 33⅓, 45 and 78 RPM. My favorite of their singles was "Please Mr. Postman" by the Marvelettes. They also had a few records that were given to them by our older cousin Jay, including "Money" by Barrett Strong and my absolute favorite, *The Coasters Greatest Hits* LP. I loved everything about that album. It had incredible songs like "Poison Ivy," "Along Came Jones," "Down In Mexico," "The Shadow Knows," "Charlie Brown," "Yakety Yak," "Young Blood," "Searchin'" and "That Is Rock & Roll." And when I was old enough to read the back liner notes, I learned all about the group and noticed that nearly all of the songs were written by Jerry Leiber and Mike Stoller. The Coasters were my favorite group, until...

Right after we returned to school from Christmas break in 1964, I heard a song on the school bus radio on the way home that sounded both different and exciting. When it was over, the disc jockey said the song was by the Beatles. I did not know who they were. I heard the record again the next afternoon and then began hearing it at night as well. It was being played about every 90 minutes. A week or so later, there were two more exciting songs by the Beatles, "She Loves You" and "Please Please Me." By then I knew the group was from England, which I thought was really cool. And when I learned that the Beatles were going to be on The Ed Sullivan Show, I couldn't wait to get to see the group that had replaced the Coasters as my faves.

My family watched the Sullivan Show that night along with 73 million other Americans. My sisters didn't scream, and my parents didn't get it, but I couldn't take my eyes off the TV screen. I fully absorbed the music. They started with two songs I had not heard before, but I thought both were great. And then it was on to "She Loves You." Later they played both sides of their Capitol single, which had been getting saturation air play on WTIX for about a month.

About a week after the show, my mom agreed to take me to the closest record store, Studio A, just off Harrison Avenue. I couldn't help but notice the street had the same name as one of the Beatles guitar players. I brought a bunch of saved quarters with me to buy *Meet The Beatles!*, but when my mom realized that the cost of the album was about 13 weeks allowance, she bought it for me as a present. When we got home, I played the album, which opened with that great Capitol single. I also recognized "All My Loving" and "Till There Was You" from the Sullivan Show. Every song was great! I particularly liked "It Won't Be Long," "This Boy," "Don't Bother Me" and "Not A Second Time."

I read the liner notes on the back of the album jacket. I immediately noticed that, just like the Coasters, most of the songs were written by two people. But unlike that group, the two songwriters, Lennon and McCartney, were also members of the band. That really impressed me. I wrote my name on the blank line of the store sticker that was attached to the back cover.

My cousin Barry, who was six weeks younger than me and my best friend, got a copy of *Introducing The Beatles*. Between the two of us, we had it covered.

I still have my original copy of *Meet The Beatles!*, which I occasionally play on my Beatles record player that I purchased when I began collecting Beatles memorabilia in the late 1990s. The record player hums like the one from my childhood. And my album cover still has the sticker that reads: **THIS BELONGS TO BR. SPIZER AND CAME FROM *Studio A* OF COURSE!**

Do You Want To Know A Secret

This book is both the seventh and the first installment of my Beatles album series. It is the seventh book published in the series, but the first chronologically. For those of you new to the series, it started with *The Beatles and Sgt. Pepper: A Fans' Perspective*, which was published in 2017 to coincide with the 50th anniversary of the release of *Sgt. Pepper's Lonely Hearts Club Band*. I moved forward with books on *The White Album*, *Abbey Road* and *Let It Be*. I then filled in some gaps with a book covering *Magical Mystery Tour* and *Yellow Submarine* before moving back in the catalog to a single tome on the *Rubber Soul* and *Revolver* albums that also includes the unique Capitol album *Yesterday And Today*.

The Beatles Please Please Me to With The Beatles goes back to the group's early LPs. Because of the brilliance of their later albums, these records rarely receive the recognition they deserve. Yet these albums and their associated singles were responsible for starting Beatlemania in Great Britain, the United States, Canada and other countries throughout the world. In America, Vee-Jay Records changed the title of the *Please Please Me* LP to *Introducing The Beatles*, while Capitol Records reconfigured and changed the name of the group's second album, *With The Beatles*, to *Meet The Beatles!* These U.S. albums appeared in stores within days of each other. In Canada, the group's second album was released first and retitled *Beatlemania! With The Beatles*. Most of the tracks on the first album were released about two months later on an LP titled *Twist And Shout*.

Regardless of their names, these albums contain exciting vocal and instrumental performances by the Beatles of their own compositions and cover versions that are better known than the original versions. They are full of youthful energy and still sound fresh.

Much of the information contained in this book's American chapter comes from my earlier books *The Beatles Records on Vee-Jay*, *The Beatles' Story on Capitol Records* and *The Beatles Are Coming!: The Birth of Beatlemania in America*. Those wanting more details about the Beatles early discs and appearances in America are referred to these books. I could not possibly fit the information contained in those books into a 50-page chapter!

Other primary sources for this book included *The Beatles Recording Sessions* and *All These Years: Tune In* by Mark Lewisohn and *I Want To Tell You, The Definitive Guide To The Music Of The Beatles Volume 1: 1962/1963* by Anthony Robustelli.

I assembled the same team utilized in the previous volumes in this series: Frank Daniels, Al Sussman, Piers Hemmingsen and Bill King. And, of course, the book contains dozens of Fan Recollections of the exciting days of Beatlemania!

On the technical side, Diana Thornton worked her magic to make the book look terrific as always and Kaye Alexander coordinated the interactions with our new printer. Proofreaders for this book included Diana, Frank, Al, Beatle Tom Frangione, Anthony Robustelli and Tom Brennan. In the tradition, my thanks to my family, Sarah, Eloise, Barbara, Trish, Big Puppy and others too numerous and crazy to name.

Finally, to paraphrase the ending credit of those early Bond films, The Beatles Album Series Shall Return with *The Beatles A Hard Day's Night*.

MEET THE AUTHOR!

Bruce Spizer is a native and lifelong resident of New Orleans, Louisiana, who was eight years old when the Beatles invaded America. He began listening to the radio at age two and was a die-hard fan of WTIX, a Top Forty AM station that played a blend of New Orleans R&B music and top pop and rock hits. His first two albums were The Coasters' Greatest Hits, which he permanently "borrowed" from his older sisters, and Meet The Beatles!, which he still occasionally plays on his vintage 1964 Beatles record player.

During his high school and college days, Bruce played guitar in various bands that primarily covered hits of the sixties, including several Beatles songs. He wrote numerous album and concert reviews for his high school and college newspapers, including a review of Abbey Road that didn't claim Paul was dead.

Bruce received his B.A. (in economics), M.B.A. (concentrating in finance and marketing) and law degrees from Tulane University in New Orleans. His legal and accounting background have proven invaluable in researching and writing his books.

Bruce is considered one of the world's leading experts on the Beatles. A "taxman" by day, Bruce is a Board Certified Tax Attorney with his own practice. A "paperback writer" by night, Bruce is the author of 15 critically acclaimed books on the Beatles, including The Beatles Are Coming! The Birth of Beatlemania in America, a series of six books on the group's American record releases, Beatles For Sale on Parlophone Records, which covers all of the Beatles records issued in the U.K. from 1962-1970, and his new series of books on the Beatles albums. His articles have appeared in Beatlefan, Goldmine and American History magazines.

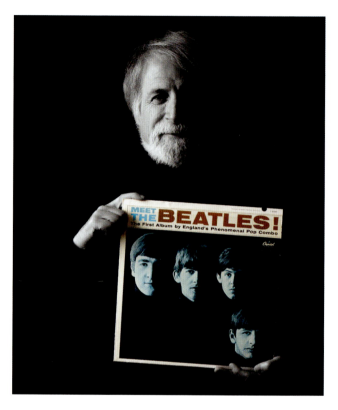

He was selected to write the questions for the special Beatles edition of Trivial Pursuit. He maintains the popular website **www.beatle.net**.

Bruce has been a speaker at numerous Beatles conventions and at the Grammy Museum, the Rock 'N' Roll Hall of Fame & Museum and the American Film Institute. He has appeared on ABC's Good Morning America and Nightline, CBS's The Early Show, CNN, Fox, and morning shows in New York, Chicago, Los Angeles, New Orleans and other cities, and is a frequent guest on radio outlets including NPR, BBC and the Beatles Channel.

Bruce serves as a consultant to Universal Music Group, Capitol Records and Apple Corps Ltd. on Beatles projects. He has an extensive Beatles collection, concentrating on American, Canadian and British first issue records, promotional items and concert posters.

contents

1	The Beatles Please Please Their British Fans	Bruce Spizer
50	Beatlemania! Explodes in America	Bruce Spizer
94	Beatlemania! Invades Canada	Piers Hemmingsen
106	Beyond The Beatles & Beyond The Fringe	Al Sussman
132	The Not-So-Dark Ages of Rock 'n' Roll	Al Sussman
146	An Experiment in the Mad, Mad World of 1963 Film	Frank Daniels
160	Picture Sleeves	
164	Fan Recollections	
178	Getting to Know the Beatles was Different for U.S. Fans	Bill King
180	Covers That Stand Out in the Shop Window	Bruce Spizer
190	The Decca Audition & Commercial Test	Bruce Spizer
202	The June 6, 1962 EMI Session	Bruce Spizer
206	The First Singles Sessions	Bruce Spizer
220	The *Please Please Me* & *With The Beatles* Sessions	Bruce Spizer

Beatles manager Brian Epstein paid EMI to run this full-page ad in the September 27, 1962 edition of Record Retailer using funds from his NEMS (North End Music Stores) retail business. The "Love Me Do" single was issued the following week on Friday, October 5, 1962.

The Beatles Please Please Their British Fans

By the fall of 1962, the Beatles had developed an enthusiastic fan base in their hometown of Liverpool; however, the group would not gain national exposure until the release of their first record on October 5, 1962, a single that paired two original John Lennon-Paul McCartney compositions, "Love Me Do" and "P.S. I Love You" (Parlophone 45-R 4949). The British music trade magazine Record Retailer reviewed the disc in its October 4 issue, noting the single's sales potential: "A new group from the Liverpool area. Their first record but they already have a strong following and this seems to be the strongest outsider of the week." The Beatles would not remain "outsiders" for long.

At the time of the single's release, British music fans kept up with the latest music news in four weekly tabloid-style magazines: Melody Maker; New Musical Express ("NME"); New Record Mirror ("Record Mirror"); and Disc. These mags were printed on non-glossy newsprint paper and cost 6d (a sixpence or tanner; six pennies). Pop Weekly was a glossy 7" x 9½" magazine priced at a shilling (12 pence). Fans could also read about recording artists signed to Columbia, HMV (His Master's Voice), Parlophone, Stateside and other labels under the umbrella of Electrical & Music Industries Ltd. ("EMI") in EMI's monthly publication, Record Mail, sold at record stores for 1d (a penny).

The October 6 Disc reviewed the Beatles debut single, with reviewer Don Nicholl giving it two out of four stars: "THE BEATLES sound rather like the Everlys or the Brooks according to whose side you're on. But in **Love Me Do** they have got a deceptively simple beater which could grow on you. Harmonica backing. **P.S. I Love You** weaves a little Latin into itself as the boys sing a letter ballad of everyday sentiments." [The Everly Brothers were a highly successful American duo whose recordings combined elements of country, pop and rock music with tight vocal harmonies that greatly influenced the Beatles. The Brook Brothers were a British pop duo that had a few hits after they abandoned their skiffle roots to imitate the look and sound of the Everlys.] The magazine also ran a short piece on the Beatles, described as a "rock-slanted vocal-instrumental group." The article noted that the band's demo disc was turned down by EMI, but, upon the recommendation of A&R man George Martin, their debut disc was cut.

The following week Record Mirror ran its review of the single in its October 13 issue: "Harmonica again starts off 'Love Me Do' and then this strangely-monikered group gets at the lyrics. Fairly restrained in their approach, they indulge in some off-beat combinations of vocal chords. Though there's plenty happening, it tends to drag about midway, especially when the harmonica takes over for a spell. Not a bad song, though. Fairly straight-forward group handling of a poorish arrangement for the flip. The song stands up well enough but things don't happen frequently enough to make us interested." [The harmonica reference was not aimed at the Beatles in particular, but rather to recent pop records such as Bruce Channel's "Hey! Baby," Frank Ifield's "I Remember You" and Brian Hyland's "Sealed With A Kiss," which all feature harmonica.] Record Mirror gave the "strangely-monikered group" three out of four bells for its debut single. Neither NME nor Melody Maker reviewed the disc.

The group's debut disc was met with more enthusiasm in Liverpool, where the city's largest evening newspaper, The Liverpool Echo, ran a review under the headline BIG DATE FOR THE BEATLES: "Next Friday, October 5th, will be an important day for that talented Liverpool group THE BEATLES and thousands of young Merseysiders who have become their faithful followers. Parlophone will be issuing the quartet's debut single on that day. On the A side lead vocalists John Lennon and Paul McCartney chant out their self-written lyrics of 'Love Me Do', an infectious medium-paced ballad with an exceptionally haunting harmonica accompaniment which smacks home the simple tune and gives the whole deck that extra slab of impact and atmosphere so essential to the construction of a Top Twenty smasher. There's nothing startlingly distinguished about the simple, repetitive lyrics but a disc like 'Love Me Do' relies more upon punchy, ear-catching presentation and on this score The Beatles come out with flying colours. Flip 'Love Me Do' to hear another, slightly faster Lennon/McCartney number entitled 'P.S. I Love You.' This bright ditty has a tingling Latin taste to it. There's a refreshing do-it-yourself approach to this single by The Beatles. They have written their own material and provided their own vocal performance. I wish these four go-ahead young men the very best of good fortune with their initial Parlophone release." The review appeared in the Off The Record column by Disker, a pen name used by Tony Barrow, who was then writing liner notes for Decca Records. Prior to writing the review, Barrow was paid £20 by Beatles manager Brian Epstein to prepare a press kit for the group. By the end of the year, Barrow quit his job with Decca to become press officer for Brian's NEMS Enterprises at double his former salary.

Liverpool's music magazine, Mersey Beat, covered the Beatles starting with its debut issue dated July 6-20, 1961. That edition published John Lennon's satirical piece "Being a Short Diversion on the Dubious Origins of Beatles" in which John explained how the group got its name: "It came in a vision—a man appeared on a flaming pie and said unto them 'From this day on you are Beatles with an A.'" The second issue reported on the band's Polydor recording sessions with producer Bert Kaempfert in Germany, backing singer Tony Sheridan on "Why," "My Bonny" [sic] and "The Saints," and recording two tracks on their own, the instrumental "Cry For A Shadow" and the John Lennon vocal "Ain't She Sweet." The cover to the January 4, 1962 edition ran a picture of the group under the headline "Beatles Top Poll!" (see page 193). The May 31 issue reported the great news that Brian Epstein had "secured a recording contract with the powerful E.M.I. organization for The Beatles to record for the Parlophone label." The August 23 issue broke the news "Beatles Change Drummer!" and printed the following official (but false) statement from the Beatles: "Pete [Best] left the group by mutual agreement." The article added that the Beatles were flying to London on September 4 to record at EMI Studios. They were to record numbers specially written for the group, which they received from their recording manager, George Martin. The magazine's September 20 edition reported on the Beatles recording session at EMI's No. 2 studio. After rehearsing six numbers and breaking for dinner, the group took 15 takes to get an acceptable music backing for "Love Me Do" before overdubbing the vocals.

The October 18 Mersey Beat listed "Love Me Do" at number one in its Merseyside Tops chart. Although a writer described the song as "rather monotonous," he recognized it was "the type of number which grows on you," stating that, while he was disappointed when he first heard it, he enjoyed it more and more with each play. Reviews of later Beatles releases often contained similar expressions of initial disappointment replaced by admiration after repeated listens. This was due in part to the higher and higher expectations for each new record issued by the group.

Liverpool resident and reporter Alan Smith introduced the group to readers of NME in his article "Liverpool's Beatles wrote their own hit" that ran in the magazine's October 26 edition. Smith indicated that "Love Me Do" was their first disc released on a British label, adding that they were previously with Polydor and "had several discs released on the Continent" with singer Tony Sheridan. Smith noted that during their "brief but eventful career," the Beatles had become fan favorites at Hamburg's Star Club and appeared on shows in England with Little Richard, Bruce Channel, Gene Vincent, Acker Bilk, Kenny Ball and Joe Brown. The boys had written more than 100 of their own songs.

One of the first national journalists to recognize the Beatles potential was Norman Joplin, who penned an article titled "Meet The Beatles" for the October 27 Record Mirror. Joplin wrote that the group had found a style with an unbeatable combination of skiffle and folk, rock and rhythm and blues, with an accent on the blues. They successfully tried their music on audiences in Mersey venues and in Hamburg. After writing about the members of the band, he quoted Cavern Club compère and DJ Bob Wooler: "The biggest thing to hit Liverpool for years…the hottest property any promoter could hope to encounter. Musically authoritative and physically magnetic, the Beatles are rhythmic revolutionaries with an act which is a succession of climaxes." Joplin added, "I think he could be right."

The November 10 Record Mirror contained a report on Little Richard's U.K. tour by reader Graham Knight, who traveled 2,500 miles with the artist. Richard, who was backed only by a drummer, saxophonist and organist Billy Preston, put on action-filled performances throughout the tour. The American singer/pianist had praise for two British groups, the Beatles and Sounds Inc. Little Richard told the Beatles: "I think your record 'Love Me Do' is great. You should come to America and be famous. Please don't be offended, but I think you sound like a coloured group.

Very few white people have that sound. Jerry Lee Lewis and Bobby Darin have it." The article was accompanied by a photograph of the Beatles.

"Love Me Do" entered the Britain's Top 50 chart published by Record Retailer at number 49 on October 11, 1962. That week the top five songs were "Telstar" by the Tornados, "The Loco-Motion" by Little Eva, "Sheila" by Tommy Roe, "It Might As Well Rain Until September" by Carole King and "She's Not You" by Elvis Presley. The Beatles debut disc remained on the charts for 18 weeks, hitting its peak of number 17 twice, first on December 27, 1962, while Elvis held the top spot with "Return To Sender," and then on January 10, 1963. By the time the single was released, Record Mirror no longer compiled its own chart listing, but rather printed the chart prepared by Record Retailer.

The single first appeared in the Melody Maker Pop Fifty on October 27 at number 48. The magazine charted "Love Me Do" for 16 weeks, with a peak at number 21 on January 5 and 12, 1963. Disc published a Top 30 chart each week with listings based as of the end of the previous week. "Love Me Do" debuted at number 28 in the November 10 Disc before moving up one spot to 27 for the next three weeks and peaking at 24 in the December 8 issue in its fifth of six weeks on the charts. NME reported "Love Me Do" for one week at number 27 in its October 26 issue.

Despite respectable chart action, EMI was disappointed with the single's initial sales of about 17,000 units by the end of 1962. It has been speculated that Brian Epstein ordered 10,000 copies of "Love Me Do" to sell through his NEMS stores in Liverpool. While the implication is that Brian did this to run the single up the charts, Tony Barrow believes that Brian hoped to sell the discs based on his belief that the thousands of Liverpool fans who regularly went to see the group at the Cavern Club and who had voted the group number one in the Mersey Beat popularity poll would rush out and buy the single. When sales were not quite up to expectations, Brian and other Liverpool retailers were left with several copies of unsold discs. After the group's popularity spread beyond Liverpool with each successive release, "Love Me Do" sold an additional 100,000 units before its deletion from the EMI catalog in the mid-sixties. Initial pressings of the single had red labels, while later copies were pressed with EMI's newly designed "45 RPM" black labels. Strong sales of the 1982 20th anniversary reissue may have pushed total sales to near 300,000.

Although EMI's Record Mail failed to review the Beatles debut disc in its October 1962 issue, the November issue introduced the Beatles to its readers in an article titled "The Beatles play original rock'n'roll." These were bold words indeed for a British group in 1962. Although nothing more than a repeat of EMI's press release, it provided the Beatles with much-needed national exposure to record buyers. The article opens with a description of a memorable concert performance by the group: "THINGS really happened for The Beatles on December 27, 1960, at a suburban town hall in Liverpool. It was their first important public appearance since their formation in mid-1958 and followed local club and ballroom dates as semi-pros." This is followed by a description of the show written by Bob Wooler in early 1961: "Here again, in The Beatles, was the stuff that screams are made of . . . rugged yet romantic, appealing to both sexes, with calculated naiveté and an ingenious throwaway approach to their music, effecting indifference to audience response and yet always saying 'thank-you.'" This attention-grabbing introduction ends with: "The Beatles, who have achieved their success as singers and instrumentalists, were further described by Mr. Wooler as 'musically authoritative and physically magnetic.' And, after explaining how they had exploded on a jaded scene, he went on to attribute their success to—the 'resurrection' of original-style rock 'n' roll music."

The rest of the article contains short and over-simplified stories of the group's formation, their success in Hamburg, their accompanying Tony Sheridan on his record "My Bonnie" and Brian Epstein's efforts to get the group a contract with a British record company, with the following quote from Epstein: "I went into the HMV Record Shop in Oxford Street to get some tapes transferred to disc. As soon as the people there heard the tapes they advised me to get in touch with George Martin, Parlophone's A&R manager." The article also has brief bios of the members of the band.

The November 24 Record Mirror contained another Norman Joplin article on the Beatles. Paul talked about how the group worked hard to please the audiences, and enjoyed playing R&B numbers such as "Twist And Shout," "Some Other Guy" and "If You Gotta Make A Fool Of Somebody." Paul revealed that the band would soon be recording its next disc, with "Please Please Me" as the favorite. Joplin noted: "It's a more catchy number than 'Love Me Do' which, incidentally, was first performed by the boys in the Holly style. And if their new disc is anything like the first by this high-class rock team, it will certainly please us."

While the Beatles enjoyed regional success in 1962, this quickly expanded the following year. The January 3, 1963 Mersey Beat featured an article by Alan Smith regarding the recording session for "Please Please Me." Smith wrote that the song "has everything, from the hypnotic harmonica sound that came over so well in 'Love Me Do' to the kind of tune you can remember after one hearing. This time the harmonica sounds much bolder, too. It almost jumps out at you. And in the background there's the solid, insistent beat, defying you not to get up and dance." He said he wouldn't be surprised if the single jumped right into the Top Ten. The music industry trade magazine Record Retailer also recognized the single's potential in its January 10, 1963 issue, stating that the group was "destined to be regular chart entries" and that their second record "has chart written all over it and seems sure to do well."

Although NME wrote little about the Beatles in 1962 (two articles and charting "Love Me Do" for only one week), the magazine began what would soon become saturation coverage of the group in its January 11, 1963 issue in its "Keith Fordyce tips all the hits" column. Fordyce's review began sarcastically, but then proved to be spot on: "'Please Please Me' recorded on Parlophone by the Beatles has been publicised as 'the record of the year.' I have just the slightest nagging doubt that, with fifty weeks of releases yet to come this year, it may prove to be a teensy weensy exaggeration! However, this vocal and instrumental quartet has turned out a really enjoyable platter, full of beat, vigour and vitality–and what's more, it's different. I can't think of any other group currently recording in this style. 'Ask Me Why' is really good flipside value. I shan't be in the least surprised to see the charts invaded by Beatles."

The January 11 Record Mirror ran a picture of the Beatles, noting that "Love Me Do" had re-entered the Top Twenty for a third time. This was followed by a review of "Please Please Me": "From the oh-so successful Beatles come this follow-up. It's a high-pitched number with plenty of guts, and good tune, vocalising and some off-beat sounds on the disc. The backing verges on great, while the singing is taken by various members of the team. We reckon its chart chances–it would probably make it even as a first disc. Rather bluesy, fast tempo. Merry little ditty on the flip, with some more off-beat sounds from the team. It's a pleasant rock piece with some great performances again. A good flip, making this into a good all-around disc–one worth buying in fact. There just happens to be some sounds on this that other British groups can't reproduce." The song was given four out of four bells.

In the January 12 Disc, Don Nicholl gave the new Beatles single three out of five stars in his brief review: "'Please Please Me' will undoubtedly please the growing band of fans who are following The Beatles. The boys chant this one briskly to a dark twangy background." While Melody Maker charted "Love Me Do" for 16 weeks in its Top 50 Hit Parade listing, it did not write about the group until its January 26, 1963 issue. The magazine described the Beatles as a "vocal-instrumental group with two discs in the Hit Parade" ["Love Me Do" at 34 and "Please Please Me" at 39] in its radio and television listings, noting that the group would broadcast on Here We Go on Friday, January 25. In the same issue, Janice Nicholls provided these less-than-professional remarks on the new single: "I think it's better than their last record, 'Love me do'—more quality in this one. I think it should do a lot better than 'Love me do.' A lot of people don't like it, but I do."

Up until July 1963, Record Mail ran a column reviewing EMI singles titled "A Record Crop–picked by Ray Orchard." Although Orchard ignored "Love Me Do" upon its release, he acknowledged its success in the magazine's February 1963 issue: "The Beatles crashed into the charts with their first release." He thought the new disc was a much better song, leading him to predict "Please Please Me" would be "an even bigger hit," adding: "The unique sound made by the group, coupled with the lyric and memorable melody make it a 'must.'" He also had praise for "Ask Me Why," calling it another top number. "The lyric features more solo vocal work than usual, and tells of a happy love. A nice hesitation gimmick is well used."

The growing popularity of the Beatles and the favorable response to their second disc prompted Mersey Beat to publish comments and reviews of "Please Please Me" in its January 31 issue. BBC disc jockey Brian Matthew declared: "Visually and musically The Beatles are the most exciting and accomplished group to emerge since The Shadows. In the next few months they will become one of the hottest properties in the music industry." World's Fair magazine wrote: "This young group may soon be challenging The Shadows for top chart honours. Go out and buy 'Please Please Me' now.... This group has every chance of being the big star attraction of 1963." As January 1963 came to a close, critics were beginning to take notice. The Beatles recordings had energy and were full of sounds different from those of their contemporaries. The Beatles could well be the next big thing.

The February 1 NME ran an article by Alan Smith titled "You've pleased–pleased us!–say the Beatles." Smith opened his article with: "Things are beginning to move for the Beatles, the r-and-b styled British group which crashed back into the NME chart this week at No. 17...[with] 'Please Please Me'...written by group members John Lennon and Paul McCartney." Paul admitted that the group had disappointments, "but coming in at 17 has pleased-pleased us." He claimed that he and John had nearly a hundred songs up their sleeves and were writing all the time. They had composed a song, "Misery," for Helen Shapiro to record when she goes to Nashville. Paul added: "It moves along at quite a steady pace." Smith noted that the "clipped Negro sound they achieve...brought them a fantastic following in Germany" and that American rock 'n' roll star Little Richard told him: "I've never heard that sound from English musicians before. Honestly, if I hadn't seen them with my own eyes I'd have thought they were a coloured group from back home." Smith noted that, so far, "only Northern fans and visiting American stars have appreciated their talents," but thought that "Please Please Me" would change everything with the group having a bright future.

"Please Please Me" entered the Record Retailer Britain's Top 50 chart on January 17 at number 45 and remained on the charts for 18 weeks. It peaked at number two on January 31, unable to get past Frank Ifield's third consecutive chart topper, "Wayward Wind." The Beatles single spent seven weeks in the top five, including three non-consecutive weeks at number two. Although "Please Please Me" failed to top the Record Retailer chart, the song reached the coveted number one spot in Melody Maker, Disc and NME (and in the BBC chart, which, at the time, was a compilation of the other charts). The single entered the Melody Maker Pop 50 chart at number 47 on January 19 before reaching its first of two straight weeks at number one on March 2. The record charted for 18 weeks, including six weeks in the top five. "Please Please Me" debuted in NME's Top 30 at number 17 on February 1, working its way to the top for one week on March 1. (That week NME also reported the song's sheet music at number one.) NME charted the record for 11 weeks, including seven in the top five. The February 2 Disc noted that the "sensational Merseyside group" the Beatles had crashed into the Top 30 chart at number nine. By February 23, the single was at number one for two straight weeks. The record remained on the charts for 11 weeks, including six in the top five. On April 13, "Please Please Me" was awarded a silver disc by Disc signifying sales of 250,000 units. By the end of 1963, the single had sold 310,000 copies. Once again, initial pressings had red labels, while later discs had the new black labels.

Word that the Beatles would be recording an album first surfaced in the November 30, 1962 NME in a brief piece titled "BEATLES LP FIXED." NME reported that the Beatles would record their first LP the following month, with most of the numbers being written by members of the group. Parlophone recording manager George Martin was considering taping the group "during a session at Liverpool's Cavern Club." Although the article was uncredited, the source of its information was Alan Smith, who had attended the group's November 26 session during which the "Please Please Me" single was recorded.

Smith's full article on the session ran in the January 3, 1963 Mersey Beat. The journalist took the opportunity to talk to George Martin, who, by this time, was quite enthusiastic about the group. "The thing I like about The Beatles is their great sense of humour—and their talent, naturally. It's a real pleasure to work with them because they don't take themselves too seriously…The Beatles are different. They've got ability, but if they make mistakes they can joke about it. I think they'll go a long way in show business." He thought their sound was something like "a male Shirelles." At the end of the November 30 session Martin told of his tentative plans for a Beatles album: "I'm thinking of recording their first LP at the Cavern, but obviously I'm going to have to come to see the club before I make a decision. If we can't get the right sound we might do the recording somewhere else in Liverpool, or bring an invited audience into the studio in London. They've told me they work better in front of an audience." He further indicated that the songs on the disc would probably all be originals, as John and Paul had written over a hundred songs, but that had yet to be determined. He expressed concern about coming up with an appropriate title because "LPs need a catchy title if they're going to stand out in the shop window."

The February 8 NME reported that George Martin would soon be recording the group's first LP in London. The disc, which might be titled "Off The Beatle Track," would consist primarily of songs written by members John Lennon and Paul McCartney. A live album was also under consideration. Norman Joplin wrote of the Beatles plans for an album in the February 16 Record Mirror, listing "Hold Me Tight," "There's A Place" and "My Misery" as possible titles for inclusion. As for "I Saw Her Standing There," John indicated that George would handle the lead vocal. Lennon told Joplin: "We want to try to make the LP something different. You know, not just all somebody else's songs."

The February 15 NME informed its readers that the Beatles first album, recorded on Monday [February 11], would be named *Please Please Me* after the group's new hit single. That same week Melody Maker ran a short article on the Beatles cutting their first LP that gave fans additional information. The disc would have 14 songs, most of which were composed by the group, and would be rush-released in about three or four weeks. The recording session was one of the shortest ever for an album, lasting only 12 hours.

Readers of the February 22 NME learned even more about the Beatles upcoming album. NME reported that it might feature nine titles written by the group. In addition to the four sides of the first two singles, the LP might include "Misery," "Seventeen" [renamed "I Saw Her Standing There"], "Do You Want To Know A Secret," "Hold Me Tight" and "There's A Place." [All but "Hold Me Tight" made the cut.] The album would include the popular stage numbers "A Taste Of Honey" and "Twist And Shout." Other songs recorded for the album were "Baby It's You," "Anna," "Chains," "Boys" and "Keep Your Hands Off My Baby." [The last song, written by Gerry Goffin and Carole King and recorded by Little Eva, was not recorded for the LP. The Beatles performed the song for the BBC's January 26, 1963 Saturday Club.]

The Beatles got additional coverage in the February 23 Melody Maker in a column by Jerry Dawson. The Beatles told Dawson: "If you want to get ahead–get a sound." The group told of their 4½-month stint in Hamburg where they played seven hours a night, seven days a week. "We learned to live and work together, discovered how to adapt ourselves to what the public wanted–and developed our own particular sound...And as it became obvious that the public liked us, we became more confident–and more polished." When the group returned to England, other groups were trying to copy the then-popular Shadows, but the Beatles had their own sound and soon discovered that Merseyside teenagers liked the Beatles. John emphasized: "But please, please don't copy. Try to be original, as we have done. Play what you like and don't try to be too clever. Keep it simple." Paul added that when the group first played "Please Please Me" to George Martin, it was a bit fussy. Following Martin's advise, they smoothed it out a bit and simplified it with great results. George Harrison advised: "Get your group together and play–and play. Find out what you do best–and go on doing it–but better." Ringo also stressed the importance of practice with a group. The Beatles added: "This isn't a job. It's a dedication." Dawson speculated that this was the real reason for their success.

The Beatles *Please Please Me* album was released in mono on March 22, 1963, with the stereo version hitting stores five weeks later on April 26. Norman Joplin provided a track-by-track review of the disc's ten new songs in the March 30 Record Mirror. "I Saw Her Standing There" is fast, long and loud with a "bluesy backing with the boys singing together" that is good enough to be a single. "The fans can go mad to this one." "Misery" is a medium tempo, plaintive tuneful number that is "one of the best ballads on the disc." It has the "usual distinctive group backing" with "the boys singing in the 'Please Please Me' style." The group's recording of Arthur Alexander's R&B song "Anna (Go To Him)" features a John lead vocal. Joplin added: "The boys harmonise beautifully on the slow blues which works out in a terribly atmospheric way." The Cookies hit "Chains" is "insistent and repetitive, exciting and tuneful" with good guitar work on the backing. The Shirelles' "Boys" has a faster beat with "some great instrumental stuff." The track is "Ray Charles-ish" with a lead vocal by Ringo "who probably has more genuine talent as a blues shouter than the other members of the group." Joplin further described the track as: "Exciting and stimulating with a polish that doesn't usually occur on LP material." "Ask Me Why" and "Please Please Me" (from the second single) close Side One. "Love Me Do" and "P.S. I Love You" (from the first single) open Side Two.

"Baby It's You," considered by many to be the Shirelles' best disc, is gently interpreted by the Beatles and done "well enough not to spoil the enchantment of the song." The boys "Sha-la-la" through the song with John's lead vocal. The slowish ballad has "perhaps more atmosphere than any other track on the LP." George is the lead vocal for "Do You Want To Know A Secret," with the others providing "a little choral support." The song is "tuneful and slightly off-beat." While not outstanding, the song is pleasant enough. "A Taste Of Honey" is the only track on the album with a "trick duet," featuring Paul singing on his own. The song, based on the Lenny Welch vocal version, is "gentle and sweet with a great tune, and a sympathetic backing." "There's A Place" features harmonica and has a "wistful flavour with a definitive beat." Although not a standout track, the song has "plenty of appeal." The Isley Brothers' hit "Twist And Shout" is a "frantic R&B song with plenty of opportunity for shouting and screaming." Taken at a fast tempo, the entire group does "a power of work whipping up a storm on the commercial blues number both vocally and instrumentally." Joplin points out that if you buy this disc, you will own all of the Beatles songs issued to date. He adds that "for a debut LP it's surprisingly good and up to standard" with a number of tracks that "could be issued as singles and maintain the boys' chart standard." The album's good cover picture and excellent liner notes make the package a "worthwhile LP in all senses of the word."

Allen Evans reviewed the Beatles debut LP in the April 5 NME, describing it as: "Fourteen exciting tracks, with the vocal-instrumental drive that has put this Liverpool group way up on the top in a very short time." In addition to the title track and "Love Me Do," the disc included 12 other thrillers, including: John Lennon singing a torrid "Twist And Shout" and the Shirelles' "Baby It's You;" drummer Ringo Starr singing "Boys;" and a "pippin of a duet" of John and Paul McCartney on "Misery." Evans added that George Harrison's lead guitar is "powerfully evident throughout."

The April 20 Melody Maker ran a review of the group's debut Parlophone LP in its album review section authored by Ray Coleman and Laurie Henshaw, who noted that the group was "fresh from their single disc triumphs" and that the Beatles LP "bids well for their future." Melody Maker added: "This Liverpool group is one-up on the batch of pop groups in the country—for their combination of top-class twang and exciting all-stops-out vocal work [that] links into a formidably commercial sound." The Beatles album is "predictably fat-sounding" and "already selling heavily."

Peter Aldersley reviewed the *Please Please Me* album in the April 20 Pop Weekly, calling the disc a "really driving, fabulous L.P. from what is, undoubtedly, the most talented and versatile of all British groups." The Beatles more than fulfilled the promise showed in their hit single, "Please Please Me." The boys "have such life and exactitude; they know what they are doing, and why they are doing it." Aldersley looked forward to "a long, successful future from George, John, Paul and Ringo from Liverpool!" The Beatles coming was "an exciting event" as proved by the album, which treated listeners to "a variety of moods and tempo." The album was also favorably reviewed in the May 1963 debut issue of Beat Monthly, a 7" x 9½" magazine in the same glossy format as Pop Weekly. David Gell proclaimed: "Soundwise, songwise and delivery-way, in fact any way you look at it, it's fantastic!" Showstoppers included "Boys" and a rousing "Twist And Shout." Gell praised George Martin's production and added: "The Beatles have proved that they are here to stay for a long, long time. A hit from start to finish, and a must for your collection."

Richard Attenborough reviewed the album in the May 1963 Record Mail. "These boys look good, sound good, and ARE good—very good. Their sheer professionalism reminds one of the bluesy, coloured groups which abound on the other side of the Atlantic, which is to say that they specialize in a form of group singing far above the majority of British vocal-teams." When adding that to the fact they write ninety percent of the songs they record, you get: "Talent, originality and, as is the case with this LP, unparalleled entertainment value." The tracks on the album varied from "the haunting 'Taste Of Honey'—far and away the best vocal treatment this attractive number has ever been given—to the bluesy 'Boys'...on which the boys sound like a multi-tracked Ray Charles." Attenborough concluded with: "Well, you can never have too much of a good thing!" Record Retailer finally reviewed the album in its May 23 issue, stating that the LP was "destined undoubtedly to be a best seller" and calling it "an insight into the Merseybeat music." The magazine observed: "There is a relentless pressure which is a rare occurrence on British records."

Jack Shelley provided a brief review of the Beatles debut LP in The Observer on June 16, 1963, calling the band "By far the best of the groups from Merseyside." The content was described as "loud, of course, but tuneful too." Shelley felt that 14 tracks was a "strain on their talent," but found that "in such a song as 'A Taste Of Honey' something fresh, and rather touching comes across." He closed by conceding: "They're a hit anyway."

Not only were the Beatles a hit, but so was their debut LP. The *Please Please Me* album entered the Record Retailer Britain's Top 20 LP's chart at number eight on April 4, 1963, while the "Please Please Me" 45 was at number 11 on the singles chart. The top five albums that week were the soundtrack to *Summer Holiday* by Cliff Richard and the Shadows, *Sinatra-Basie* by Frank Sinatra and Count Basie and his Orchestra, the soundtrack to *Girls! Girls! Girls!* by Elvis Presley, *I'll Remember You* by Frank Ifield and the soundtrack to the film *West Side Story*. The Beatles LP moved up to number three for two weeks, and then to number two for two weeks, knocking *Summer Holiday* from the top on May 9. *Please Please Me* held down the number one spot for 30 straight weeks before being replaced by the group's second album, *With The Beatles*, on December 5. The album remained on the charts for 70 weeks during 1963 and 1964, including 31 weeks at number one, 19 weeks at number two, 56 weeks in the top five and 62 weeks in the top ten. The Record Retailer Top LP's chart also ran in Record Mirror.

The Beatles debut album entered the NME Best Selling LPs in Britain chart (listing ten albums) at number nine on March 29. It worked its way up to number one on May 10 and remained at the top for all but one week through November 30 before being replaced by *With The Beatles* the following week. NME charted *Please Please Me* for 61 weeks, including 28 weeks at number one, 22 weeks at number two and 56 weeks in the top five. The album debuted in the Melody Maker Top Ten LP's chart on April 6 at number 10. The disc reached the top on May 4 and remained there for 30 straight weeks before dropping to number two behind *With The Beatles* on November 30. *Please Please Me* spent 20 weeks at number two. Melody Maker charted the album for 64 weeks, including 58 weeks in the top five. Disc did not publish an album chart until late 1965. The album reached sales of 250,000 units by November 30, 1963, earning the Beatles another silver disc.

Norman Joplin's article in the February 16 Record Mirror, "The Beatles New Single & Album," speculated that the next single might be "Hold Me Tight." John commented: "There's a good catchy riff on that one." The March 8 NME informed readers that the Beatles had waxed three more songs, including their next single, on March 4. The April 6 Disc ran a short article, titled "Beatles write again," informing readers that the new Beatles single due out next week [April 11] featured two John Lennon and Paul McCartney compositions, "From Me To You" and "Thank You Girl."

EMI's press release described "From Me To You" as "the most unusual number the Beatles have recorded to date." The April 11 Record Retailer stated that it was even better than the first two singles, calling it a catchy tune with a "good gimmicky vocal performance" and lasting appeal. The magazine added: "Beatle hysteria has never been higher—and this is likely Number One." In the April 12 NME, Keith Fordyce informed readers: "That lively group from Liverpool, the Beatles, have a new one on Parlophone called 'From Me To You.'" Fordyce noted that the singing and harmonizing was good and that there was "plenty of sparkle." He found the lyric to be commercial, but didn't think the tune was as good as on the group's first two singles. "Thank You Girl" was a "steady beat number, but a little bit on the slow side." He told readers they could "safely expect to see this disc in the charts very quickly."

The other magazines reviewed the new single in their April 13 issues. In Disc, Don Nicholl gave the record his coveted DNT designation, making it a Don Nicholl Tip ("really hit records that look like spinning to the top"). He observed that the "Top Twenty seems a pure formality so far as the Merseyside marvels are concerned." He described "From Me To You" as a "lusty beater" and "ballad on the up-tempo with a simple set of words, and some surprising falsetto phrases." He predicted that the group's "mouth-organs, guitars and voices are almost certain to send it to the top." He was less impressed with "Thank You Girl," finding it "more conventional" and noting "but then it's not the selling side, is it?" Record Mirror gave the disc four stars and reviewed it under the headline: "Another huge hit from the Beatles." The single opened with "some smooth group wordless vocalising" leading into a "plaintive fast-ish number with plenty of their distinctive high-pitched sounds and perhaps better vocal work than on their last two discs." The song had "a good catchy tune and some decent lyrics to hold it up." The magazine concluded: "The boys supply themselves with a good beat backing on the number—it should be a number one." The only blemish from the four tabloid-style music weeklies came from Melody Maker's pop singles review team of Ray Coleman and Laurie Henshaw, who were not impressed, running the headline "Below par Beatles…." Their opening salvo reads: "The Beatles have a certain follow-up hit with 'From Me To You'—but if this average song was done by a less prominent group it would mean little." The song is described as an "up-tempo beat number with a just so-so melody" that is "not nearly so outstanding in originality as 'Please Please Me.'" The pair conceded it would be a best-seller, but thought that "the group ought to be able to do something better than this as a follow-up to an instant hit."

DISC
THE TOP RECORD & MUSICAL WEEKLY

No. 264 Week ending April 13, 1963
Every Thursday, price 6d.

INSIDE
BRENDA LEE CONTEST WINNER
pages 6/7

BUDDY HOLLY
page 12

---

8   DISC, April 13, 1963

DISC DATE WITH DON NICHOLL

Top Twenty again? How can The Beatles miss!

The Beatles
From Me To You; Thank You Girl
(Parlophone R 5015)

D.N.T THE Top Twenty seems a pure formality so far as the Merseyside marvels are concerned at the present time. The Beatles' own song - writing members, John Lennon and Paul McCartney, are responsible for both the numbers on the latest release.

"From Me To You" is a lusty beater. A ballad on the up-tempo with a simple set of words, and some surprising falsetto phrases. These mouth-organs, guitars and voices are almost certain to send it to the top.

"Thank You Girl" is more conventional, and its hoarse chanting not so impressive . . . but then it's not the selling side is it?

The Rooftop Singers
Tom Cat; Hey Boys
(Fontana 271702 TF)

D.N.T IT took only a week for "Tom Cat" to prove itself a winner in the States. May take a little longer here, but it should still climb...

rhythm, opens on saxophone, and this unnamed soloist continues alongside brushing drums for a good part of the way. Strings and piano take over lushly for the mid section.

Johnny de Little
Days Of Wine And Roses; Ride On
(Columbia DB 7023)★★★★

WITH the film about to break over here to a large burst of publicity, the Johnny Mercer-Henry Mancini song may happen

RATINGS
★★★★★ — Excellent.
★★★★ — Very good.
★★★ — Good.
★★ — Ordinary.
★ — Poor.

And the really hit records that look like spinning to the top are marked by D.N.T. (Don Nicholl Tip)

which may easily repeat the success it's been achieving in the States. Miss March is just 15, but with a big voice . . . and a big backing too from strings and male chorus.

Wind Up Doll is a slow contrasting ballad sung plaintively.

Cleo Laine
It Looks Like They're In Love; I'm A Dreamer Aren't We All
(Fontana 267270 TF)★★★★

IT Looks Like They're In Love is one of the best new ballads the year has produced, and it has the quality to make it a standard. Written by Mitch Murray and Les Reed, it weds melody and lyric like a double-yoked egg. But believe me there should be no egg-laying about this recording.

Cleo sings the romancer with the effortless flow it demands, and her interpretation could easily see her

back into the parade. It deserves to do so.

The oldie **I'm A Dreamer** opens in whispering fashion to guitar, then goes swinging admirably.

Al Caiola and Ralph Marterie
Acapulco 1922; The Breeze And I
(United Artists UP 1022)★★★★

THE fabulous guitar and trumpet partnership again in some of their long-player tracks. **Acapulco 1922** is a beautifully reminiscent melody trot with xylophone adding its colour to Caiola's brilliant guitar work while Marterie's trumpet soars overhead.

The Breeze And I has that South of the Border touch too, with some glossy unison trumpet sound. A vocal chorus is used sparingly on this half.

A disc that will undoubtedly

send thousands album hunting in a hurry.

Maori Hi-Five
Putti Putti; Seven Canoes
(Columbia DB 7020)★★★

YOU may have seen the Maori Hi-Five on television or stage. Here they come chanting two traditional airs with updated lyrics. Southern seas accompaniment for a cheerful A side. Underneath you'll

FIRST OF MANY?

The fantastic success story of THE BEATLES reached a climax on Friday when their A and R man George Martin presented them with our award of a Silver Disc for sales of more than a quarter-million for "Please Please Me," their second disc which rocketed to the top spot a few weeks ago. Now their third single is out and Don Nicholl reckons it just can't fail.

find an infectious swaying rhythm in Seven Canoes.

Dolores Gray
Mornin' Train; Our Day Will Come
(Philips 326582 BF)★★★★

MADE here with Ivor Raymonde as the musical director, this is a very infectious disc from Miss

Continued on page 9

...shorts...shorts...shorts...shorts...shorts...

WELCOME ANY TIME AT McCURN

My own preference is for the race-along **Blue Grass Express** composed by Lloyd and Kelly McCormick and featuring some of the finest banjo playing I've heard.

LEE CURTIS — Little Girl; Just One More Dance (Decca F 11622)★★★ — If setting Latin tempo for **Little Girl** set by the Harry Robinson orchestra while Lee Curtis sings a simple, not unappealing lyric. Could be some of the femme hearts fluttering. **Just One More Dance** is used romantically with strings and drums with an occasional interjection from the saxes.

WOUT STEENHUIS — Kassian; Minnehaha (Columbia DB 7021)★★★ — If people have decided yet that they can pronounce his name, Wout Steenhuis should be starting to sell well. **Kassian** is the guitarist's two own tunes, both feature his own...

... is a rapid-fire trotter that carries a spell of first-rate net work. **Minnehaha** is at the pace for a good Bossa Nova on the straw.

with some girl voices chiming in for extra colour. Samantha contrasts a rasping instrumental noise against the soft girl voices. Not the Porter song.

DAVID ROSE — Whistle Bait; The Happy Bow (MGM 1197)★★★ — Gimmicky little item used in the new film "The Courtship Of Eddie's Father." David Rose and his orchestra move it down the road with plenty of humour in the string section.

A Rose original **The Happy Bow**, is a picturesque plaything.

SHIRLEY DOUGLAS — Cruel Love; I Never Will Marry (HMV POP 1151)★★★ — Shirley Douglas drifts through **Cruel Love** to a very delicate accompaniment under the direction of Martin Slavin, Chas. McDevitt duets with Shirley on the second half for a wistful folksy effort.

DOROTHY SQUIRES — Bless Your Heart My Darling; Once Upon A Time (Columbia DB 7009)★★ — Dorothy Squires singing a straightforward ballad, seemingly aimed directly at request programmes. On the turnover, the star's own composition is a slow romancer with plenty of dressing from chorus and orchestra.

THE EMBERS — Chelsea Boots; Samantha (Decca F 11625)★★★ — Organ, drums and guitar teaming adroitly and with punchy effect for **Chelsea Boots**. Steady, rocking Latinwork

those who understand what it's all about. **Amor, Mon Amor, My Love** is the better bet for this country. A lush, romantic ballad.

MARILYN KABEL — The P.T.A.; I'm Too Young (Pye N 15518)★★★ — An Ilford girl making her disc debut at the ripe old age of 12, Marilyn Kabel chants a beat number about a meeting of the **P.T.A.** (Parent Teachers Association). Well, Brenda Lee was having hits at 12 I know . . . but I'd like to reserve judgment on this tot.

I'm Too Young is an easy little melody.

VAN DOREN — Piano Medley No. 2 (Decca 11623)★★★ — Pianist Van Doren plays "Wayward Wind," "Loop De Loop," "Island Of Dreams," "Summer Holiday," "The Night Has A Thousand Eyes" and "Rhythm Of The Rain," it's a well-chosen portrait of the pop parade — a happy-go-lucky performance.

SHANI WALLIS — My Heart Cries For You; All Over Again (Decca F 11632)★★★ — A release under Bunny Lewis's Ritz mark. And not the sort of thing you might be expecting to hear from Shani Wallis. Although she's singing the old **My Heart Cries For You**, it is with a snappy modern beat.

All Over Again is a smokey ballad which Shani sings slowly, emotionally—more as you might expect.

CLAUDIO VILLA — La Buffera; Amor, Mon Amor, My Love (Cetra SP 1162)★★★ — **La Buffera** opens dramatically with drums and Villa goes marching in theatrical Italian style. Well sung, but limited in sales I'd say to

TONY VICTOR — Cokey Cokey; Thinking Of You (Decca F 11626)★★ — Extra tracking from Tony Victor who returns to the record scene with a contemporary caper using the old

Hokey-Kokey dance. Cokey Cokey, as it's called here, makes a good fast twister and Victor's gravel voicing is accompanied by organ and drums. Ought to sell.

Think Of You is an up-tempo romancer which the Yorkshire lad handles more than competently. With persistence I'm fairly certain Tony has a good disc future.

THE SHEPHERD SISTERS — What Makes Little Girls Cry; Don't Mention My Name (London HLK 9681)★★ — From the Atlantic label a tinkly song with The Shepherd Sisters singing rather coyly to match. The kind of effort which sets the pop game back about ten years. **Don't Mention My Name** contrasts by whipping up a sturdy beat.

BRYAN KEITH — Sad Sad Song; Mean Woman (London HLU 9707)★★ — Bryan Keith double-tracks mournfully as he sings his **Sad Sad Song**. Quick little beat to the side, but after it's gone . . . I find it's not remembered. **Mean Woman**, with bass guitar and handclapping and girl group rafting for the singer, is drawled in half-talk style.

THE ROCKY FELLERS — Killer Joe; Lonely Teardrops (Stateside SS 175)★★★ — The brisk beat of **Killer Joe** practically picks up your feet and tells them where to go, but the edgy voices of the group will not be to everyone's taste. An almost relaxing twist comes with **Lonely Teardrops** on the reverse.

CYRIL STAPLETON — The Beeje; Golli, Golli (Decca F 11631)★★★ — Cyril's band laying it on the line for dancers with a couple of current

---

The April 13 Pop Weekly awarded the "really fabulous Beatles" a bouquet for "their eagerly awaited second [actually their third] Parlophone single—From Me To You," stating that the "talented Liverpool lads have done it again." The magazine praised the "fascinating use made of ye olde harmonica and solo voice which adds greatly to the overall excitement of the disc." After describing the group as "clean-cut, lively, driving and forever interesting," the reviewer added: "I think The Beatles are, by far and away, the most talented group to come up on the British scene for some time—and if they go on like this they might well be our foremost group!" The single was also favorably reviewed in the May 1963 Beat Monthly. David Gell designated the disc his "gold-plated 24 carat No. 1 cert" and called it a "knock-out number." He added: "A solid beat is laid down from the opening bars by The Beatles' stix-man Ringo Starr and the boys chant the unusual, but oh so hip! lyric and melody." In the May 1963 Record Mail, Ray Orchard proclaimed: "That fantastic, chart-topping, Liverpool group, is set to do it again. Both sides of their latest were composed by half of the team, and present that very special sort of polish and excitement already so well known." "From Me To You" was described as a "bright, happy item, with a lyric that has the boys promising anything and everything the girl might desire, sent with love from me to you," that was certain to top the charts. As for "Thank You Girl," Orchard added: "Harmonica, guitars and bass drive the other number, too."

"From Me To You" entered the Record Retailer chart on April 18 at number 23, one spot behind "Please Please Me." On May 2, "From Me To You" reached the number one spot, knocking out "How Do You Do It?" by Gerry and the Pacemakers. "From Me To You" charted for 21 weeks, including seven weeks at number one and ten in the top five. The single performed similarly in Melody Maker, making its debut at number 19 on April 20 before moving up to one on May 4. The disc charted for 20 weeks, including six at number one and ten in the top five. Disc ran a front page headline on April 20 stating: "The Beatles Come In At Number 10!" with "From Me To You." Two weeks later, on May 4, the headline read "Beatles Take Over Again!" as the single reached the top for its first of five weeks at number one during its 17 weeks on the charts. NME was ahead of the curve, with "From Me To You" making its debut at number six on April 19 and moving up the following week to number one, where it remained for six weeks during its 16-week run. The single also topped the BBC chart. The disc sold 200,000 copies by its seventh day of release. Disc awarded the single a silver disc on May 4 for sales of over 250,000. By the end of 1965, sales were reported at 660,000 units.

By the second week of May 1963, the Beatles had the number one single, "From Me To You," and the number one album, *Please Please Me*. EMI decided it was time to release a Beatles EP (extended play disc). These records typically had two songs on each side of a seven-inch disc that spun at 45 revolutions per minute. EPs were normally packaged in a jacket with a photo on the front and information about the recording artist and/or the selections on the back. The format gave purchasers twice the music of a single for less than double the price and was just over a third the cost of an album. At a time when there were 20 shillings to a pound and 12 pence to a shilling, singles cost 6/8 (6 shillings, 8 pence), while EPs were 10/9 (10 shillings, nine pence) and albums were 32 shillings (one pound, 12 shillings). Record companies often programmed EPs with the best tracks from an album or with hit singles. For those who could not afford an album, the EP was a practical way to get four tracks from an album at an affordable price.

EMI originally planned a summer release for an EP titled *The Beatles' Hits*, which would include the songs from the A-sides of the group's first three singles plus the B-side of the third. But the attention given to the group's *Please Please Me* album, particularly the track "Twist And Shout," prompted the company to program a disc featuring four tracks from the LP. The June 28, 1963 NME reported that EMI was releasing an EP titled *The Beatles No. 1* on July 26 containing songs featuring the group's three vocalists: "Twist And Shout," "A Taste Of Honey," "Do You Want To Know A Secret" and "There's A Place." That same issue ran an article titled "Beatles Make Isleys' Hit," explaining that the Isley Brothers' single "Twist And Shout" had made the NME chart nearly a year after its release due to the Beatles including the song in their stage show and on their album. The article mentioned that Brian Poole and the Tremeloes' new single would be "Twist And Shout." The July 6 Disc also reported on the new Beatles EP featuring "Twist And Shout." Paul told the magazine: "This is typically our sound, and that of Liverpool. It is a natural for The Beatles to record and use in our stage act, and when we do feature it on stage, it seems to be as much a favourite with the audience as it is with us." The July 13 Melody Maker ran EMI's explanation that requests for the Beatles version of "Twist And Shout" had been building up for some time and had "reached such a pitch that a special release was the only answer." In addition, Decca's release of a competing version of "Twist And Shout" by Brian Poole probably played a prominent part in prompting Parlophone to retitle its EP *Twist And Shout* and push its release date up two weeks to July 12. EMI ran an ad for its *Twist And Shout* EP in the July 12 NME.

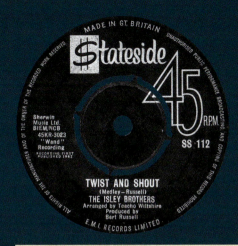

The July 19 NME ran Alan Smith's article "The Twist And Shout Battle Hots Up!" Smith noted that the Beatles were largely responsible for bringing the number to the attention of the public, constantly featuring the song, with "that pounding beat and those bloodcurdling John Lennon screams," since their rise to fame. With "Twist And Shout" only available on the group's *Please Please Me* LP, record fans who could not afford the price of the album began making inquiries and were offered the original Isley Brothers' single, which was still in the Stateside catalogue after being released nearly a year ago. Paul provided the following comments on the Isley Brothers' disc: "When it first came out nobody seemed interested. We all thought it was fab. Everybody else–no go! I suppose people just weren't ready for that kind of music at the time." By mid-1963, everyone was ready for the Beatles "Twist And Shout."

Twist And Shout topped the EP chart published by Record Retailer, the only British magazine to compile a separate EP chart. The record entered the chart on July 18 at number seven and zoomed to number one on July 25, its first of ten straight weeks at the top. After seven straight weeks at number two, it returned to the top on November 21, replacing *The Beatles' Hits*, and remained there for 11 weeks before being replaced by the Rolling Stones' first EP. The *Twist And Shout* EP charted for 57 straight weeks from July 18, 1963, through August 13, 1964, and returned for seven more weeks in 1964. It spent 21 weeks at number one, 44 weeks in the top five and 54 weeks in the top ten. The EP sold so well that the other magazines reported the disc in their singles charts, where it outperformed the less expensive Brian Poole single of "Twist And Shout." The Poole disc peaked in the Melody Maker chart at four, while the Beatles EP peaked at two during its 31 weeks on the chart. Disc charted the EP for 12 weeks, with a two-week peak at number three. NME charted the EP for ten weeks with a two-week peak at four. The July 20 Melody Maker, under the headline "Beatles Blast-off," reported that EMI had orders of 150,000 units for the *Twist And Shout* EP in five days. On August 13, EMI reported that sales had exceeded 250,000 units, making it the company's first EP to break the quarter-million mark. This prompted Disc magazine to award the record a silver disc award on August 24, another first for an EP. By November 22, EMI announced sales of 650,000 units, making it the fourth biggest selling U.K. record of 1963 behind "She Loves You," "I Want To Hold Your Hand" and the Dave Clark Five's "Glad All Over." *Twist And Shout* holds the distinction of being the largest selling EP in British history. Its stunning, energetic cover of the Beatles leaping into the air over a bombed-out area of London was taken on April 25, 1963, by Fiona Adams.

Beatles fans first learned about the next Beatles single in the July 13 Disc in an article titled "It will be Liverpool all the way if these EMI plans for the summer work out!," which was sourced from an interview with George Martin. Nigel Hunter reported: "Word about last week's date at EMI's Abbey Road studios got around, and a horde of fans besieged the place from nine in the morning until eleven at night!" Martin added: "The boys don't really like a lot of people around when they're recording anyway. They're pretty serious about their work." Hunter provided details about the "next single from the fab foursome from Scouseville." The disc, set for release on August 23, featured two Lennon-McCartney songs, "She Loves You" and "I'll Get You." Martin observed that the disc "continues the Beatle tradition of having the words 'you' or 'me' in the titles. I reckon it's their best one yet." Martin admitted: "I'm still a little surprised about a square like me doing these records with the Liverpudlians and getting such satisfying results. I get a great kick out of the sessions...The boys have a skeleton arrangement of sorts ready when we start, and we proceed to put the flesh on the bones from there onwards."

In early August 1963, the first issue of The Beatles Book went on sale. As its title implied, the monthly magazine was devoted entirely to the Beatles. It was published by the man behind Beat Monthly, Sean O'Mahony, who also served as editor of both magazines under the pseudonym of Johnny Dean. Like its sister publication, The Beatles Book was printed on glossy paper and was priced at one shilling and a sixpence. The magazine measured 6" x 8¼". The debut issue's Beatle News page reported on the "Fantastic Demand for 'She Loves You,'" with EMI pressing over 250,000 copies before the single's August 23 release. The magazine informed readers: "John and Paul stayed up until three in the morning only two days before the recording session writing both numbers!!"

The NEMS press release for the single proudly proclaimed: "'She Loves You' is the group's finest slab of audio dynamite to date. It packs a powerhouse rhythm with Ringo's fiercely exciting percussion work to lay down the quick-beat tempo and the voices of Paul, John and George to pump out the lyrics at high pressure." Record Retailer, in its August 22 issue, predicted the song would be a "roaring great hit–a Number One," but said it was debatable as to whether it was as good as "From Me To You." The top side was "another brash, typical Liverpool mixture of vocal and instrumental" that was "the more commercial of two highly commercial performances."

The Beatle News page of the debut issue of The Beatles Book told of the fantastic demand for "She Loves You." The September 1963 Record Mail ran an ad for the new single on its back cover. The front cover featured actor Wilfrid Brambell promoting his *Steptoe and Son* LP from the BBC-TV series and his Parlophone single "Secondhand." Brambell would later play the part of Paul's grandfather in the

Keith Fordyce reviewed "She Loves You" in the August 23 NME. Fordyce admitted one "wouldn't need a remarkable prophet to predict that the new release from the Beatles is going to be another No. 1." The song, its success assured by gigantic advance orders, was a "bright entertaining and catchy sample of the Mersey sound." The flip-side, "I'll Get You," was a "slowish one with a thoroughly commercial lyric." Record Mirror gave the single four bells in its August 24 issue, telling readers: "That noise you hear is the Beatles' newie rushing straight into the charts—an advance order of quarter of a million, for a start." "She Loves You" was "strictly fab, pushed along at precisely the right pace, with a stack of vocal attack." There was a solid instrumental pounding behind the vocal work. The Record Mirror reviewers couldn't "think of anything to have a go about." The flip side, "I'll Get You," was slightly slower and featured "another swingingly commercial slice of Merseybeat." The disc was a "value-for-money coupling," with "She Loves You" destined to attract most of the attention. Their conclusion: "Just clear that Number One spot, that's all."

Don Nicholl titled his DNT review in the August 24 Disc "Watch Out Number One—Here Come Those Incredible Beatles!" Nicholl stated that the Beatles latest release would rip straight into the hit parade. Although their sound was "extremely exciting" on "She Loves You," with "instruments pounding and the boys chanting powerfully," he found it a pity "to waste such energy and rhythmic enthusiasm on such an ordinary song" with a lyric that was "feeble and unimaginative." He "thought a team of such youthful vigour…could afford to set its sights a little higher," adding: "The song's about as ambitious as sitting in an armchair waiting for your pension to be delivered!" Nicholl thought the B-side had better lyrics.

Readers of the August 24 Melody Maker found even more negative comments about the new Beatles single. The magazine canvassed five British disc jockeys about the just-released disc, noting that "She Loves You" was unusually controversial in that it was not universally applauded. David Jacobs found the disc "rather disappointing, probably because one expects so much from [the Beatles]." He didn't feel the new record was up to the standard of the others, not so powerful. Pete Murray had no criticism of the disc, adding that he would be playing it. Brian Matthew expressed his disappointment: "It is the first Beatles record that hasn't knocked me out, and it strikes me they've rested far too much on the success they've already had. This one falls far short of their other discs." He acknowledged that the group went for simplicity of lyrics to appeal to teenagers, but felt they had "carried it to the idiot." Matthew knew kids would buy the disc, but cautioned buyers would be very disappointed. He called it a "nothing record which will be a big success." Alan Freeman disagreed, calling "She Loves You" a great record. It had a wilder sound than "Twist And Shout" and was the best the group had done. He predicted it would sell like mad, but noted: "If the Beatles made a record of themselves snoring for two whole minutes, it would go to No. 1." Jimmy Savile cynically said it had a "great beat, great atmosphere all the way through," but admitted he had not heard it!

That same issue featured the Temperance Seven giving their opinions on hearing the latest discs as part of the magazine's Blind Date feature in which the participants were not told who the recording artists were. The act specialized in authentic jazz dance music of the 1920s, often with a comedic slant. Their Parlophone single "You're Driving Me Crazy" (written in 1930 by Walter Donaldson and recorded that year by Rudy Vallée, Guy Lombardo and others) gave George Martin his first number one as a producer in 1961. The Temperance Seven members' comments on "She Loves You" were in a box titled "Beatles Bashed!" Allan Mitchell said: "It's the Pacemakers without Gerry. I like it except for the woo-hoo parts—that's awful." After Ray Whittam correctly surmised "It's the Beatles," Brian Innes responded: "It's one of the Manchester groups taking off the Beatles." Clifford Bevan was not impressed: "The lyrics are fatuous and erotic. If this is the Beatles, they're heading downwards, although there was something about their other records that was good. They have descended to the general mire." John R.T. Davies added: "Nothing out of the ordinary about this. It made me chuckle, but I didn't like it." John Gieves-Watson deduced: "Once they were distinctive. No longer." Captain Cephas Howard was brief but brutal: "Poor beat stuff, this."

The August 31 Pop Weekly stated that the new single had "all the drive, life and infectious quality of the boys themselves; and, indeed, THE sound!" Although the composition lacked the melodic appeal of their last two hits, "only a fool would predict anything short of another Big Hit for the lads." It was a song that "grows on you the more you hear it." In the September 1963 Beat Monthly, David Gell called the single a "driver which features some fine drum work-outs from stix-man, Ringo Starr." He described "I'll Get You" as another strong side. The record was Gell's "gold-plated and diamond-studded hit of the month."

"She Loves You" entered the Record Retailer singles chart at number 12 on August 29, while the number one song was "Bad To Me," a Lennon-McCartney song performed by Billy J. Kramer with the Dakotas. The following week it moved up to number three before taking over the top spot on September 12. That week the Beatles made British chart history by having the top LP (*Please Please Me*), the top EP (*Twist And Shout*), and the top single ("She Loves You"). After four straight weeks at number one, "She Loves You" spent the next seven weeks at either two or three before returning to the top on November 28. The single's second round at the top ended on December 12, when it dropped to number two behind the Beatles next single, "I Want To Hold Your Hand." All told, "She Loves You" spent an incredible 31 straight weeks on the charts plus an additional two weeks a week after its streak ended. During that time it was number one for six weeks and spent 18 weeks in the top three and 20 weeks in the top five.

The single performed similarly on the other charts. Melody Maker charted "She Loves You" for 31 weeks, including seven weeks at number one, five weeks at number two and 19 weeks in the top five. NME debuted "She Loves You" at number two on August 30, charting the record for 24 weeks, including six weeks at number one, eight weeks at number two and 19 weeks in the top five. The single entered the Disc Top 30 at number three on August 31 before moving up to number one the next week. The magazine charted "She Loves You" for 26 weeks, including five weeks at number one, seven weeks at number two and 19 weeks in the top five. The single also topped the BBC charts.

Due to the strong sales performance of the previous two singles, the *Please Please Me* LP and the *Twist And Shout* EP, EMI's marketing manager recommended an advance production run of 350,000 units, which was well above even the most optimistic forecasts of the day. Managing Director Len Wood balked at the number, but reluctantly agreed to 250,000. It would not be enough as advance orders were double that amount by the single's release on August 23. By October 11, over 750,000 units had been shipped. By November 30, the million mark was passed, and by year's end over 1,300,000 units had been shipped. This number swelled to 1,500,000 by January 31. Disc awarded "She Loves You" a silver disc on September 7, 1963, for sales of 250,000, and later a gold disc for sales of one million units. "She Loves You" was the biggest selling single in British history from 1964 to 1977, when it was topped by "Mull Of Kintyre" by Paul's second band, Wings. Total U.K. sales for "She Loves You" exceed 1,800,000.

The Parlophone promo card for "She Loves You" features a photo taken by Bill Connell on September 19, 1962, in a junk-filled vacant lot at the Bally near the docks of Liverpool.

The chart performance of "She Loves You" was unique in that the single topped the charts for two separate runs eight weeks apart. The song's resurgence on the charts and in sales was caused by a series of momentum-generating events that heralded the birth of Beatlemania on a national scale.

On October 13, 1963, the Beatles appeared on Val Parnell's Sunday Night At The London Palladium, a TV variety show which typically drew an audience of 15 million. It was the British equivalent of America's Ed Sullivan Show. The program exposed the Beatles to a large TV audience throughout Great Britain, which saw the group perform "From Me To You," "I'll Get You," "She Loves You" and "Twist And Shout." Beatles press agent Tony Barrow observed that the London Palladium appearance changed everything. The press noticed that the Beatles attracted screaming fans both inside and outside the theater. The October 14 Daily Mirror headlined "Beatles flee in fantastic Palladium TV siege," writing that 60 policemen fought to hold back a thousand screaming teenagers as the four pop idols made their "getaway" following the show. The Daily Herald reported that "screaming girls launched themselves against the police—sending helmets flying and constables reeling." The Daily Herald would soon describe the hysteria caused by the group as "Beatle Fever!" On October 21, the Daily Mail ran a feature on the group titled "This Beatlemania," while the Daily Sketch headlined its story "Beatles Mania." The following Saturday the November 2 Daily Mirror ran the headline "BEATLEMANIA!" The article, accompanied by pictures of screaming fans, began: "EVERYONE, everywhere is catching it. IT is called Beatlemania. Earlier this week it swept Sweden. Last night it hit sedate Cheltenham...."

Two days after the "BEATLEMANIA!" headline, the group took part in the Royal Variety Performance at the Prince of Wales Theatre in London on November 4, with the Queen Mother and Princess Margaret in attendance. Queen Elizabeth II was pregnant and unable to attend. After playing "From Me To You," "She Loves You" and "Till There Was You," John introduced their closing song: "For our last number I'd like to ask your help. Will the people in the cheaper seats clap your hands. And the rest of you, if you'd just rattle your jewelery. Thank you. We'd like to sing a song called 'Twist And Shout.'" Lennon's cheeky remark was met with laughter in the theater and caught the attention of the press. Although John was mocking the aristocratic audience, it came across as charming. The Beatles popularity expanded beyond their young fans, resulting in renewed interest and sales of their current hit, "She Loves You."

For those unable to attend the exclusive Royal Variety Performance at the Prince of Wales Theatre on November 4, 1963 (and for those who were there but wanted to see it again), ITV broadcast the star-studded show the following Sunday, November 10, at 7:28 PM. The TV Times listed the Beatles and Steptoe and Sons' Wilfrid Brambell and Harry H. Corbett as the top two acts on the program. Marlene Dietrich was placed third in the list of performers.

Encouraged by the phenomenal success of the Beatles *Twist And Shout* EP, EMI made plans for the rapid release of two additional EPs. The August 16 NME and August 17 Disc reported on these future releases. The first EP, set for September 6, would feature "Please Please Me," "From Me To You," "Thank You Girl" and "Love Me Do." [This was the same EP, *The Beatles' Hits*, that was postponed to make way for the rush release of the *Twist And Shout* EP.] The second was scheduled for release in October, featuring "I Saw Her Standing There," "Misery," "Anna" and "Chains."

The Beatles' Hits, released on September 6, 1963, was programmed with "From Me To You" and "Thank You Girl" on Side 1, and "Please Please Me" and "Love Me Do" on Side 2. Although few listeners probably noticed it at the time, the version of "Love Me Do" chosen for the EP was not the hit single with Ringo on drums, but rather the album track with Andy White on drums and Ringo on tambourine. Allen Evans covered the record in his EP column in the September 13 NME, noting that the McCartney-Lennon composed hits were "all spot on, as you know!" EMI's Record Mail gave the EP a big push in its September 1963 issue: "Here are four lads and four songs which need no introduction. The four lads in question, in less than a year, have accounted for mass hysteria, adulation and adoration up and down the country and half way round the world. The four songs have…accounted for close to a million sales. 'Love Me Do' was the boys first release…and was the number which had Little Richard raving when he was over here last year. This made the Top Twenty and paved the way for 'Please Please Me' and "From Me To You.'"

The disc entered the Record Retailer EP chart at number six on September 19, 1963, while the *Twist And Shout* EP was at number one. The following week it moved up to number three, where it remained for five weeks before achieving its first of three straight weeks at the top on October 31. On November 21, it slipped to number two, sandwiched between *Twist And Shout* and *The Beatles (No. 1)*. *The Beatles' Hits* charted for 34 straight weeks plus nine more for a total of 43 weeks, including 19 weeks in the top three, 27 in the top five and 31 in the top ten. Like its predecessor, the EP also made the singles charts. Melody Maker charted the disc for 18 weeks, with a peak at number 14 on December 14. NME charted the record for eight weeks, with a peak of 17 on December 13. Disc reported the EP for 12 weeks, with a peak at number 16 on December 21. The record was awarded a silver disc by Disc on December 14, 1963, indicating sales of over 250,000.

For its third Beatles EP, EMI resurrected its initial title for what became the *Twist And Shout* EP, *The Beatles (No. 1)*. The disc, released on November 1, 1963, was the second EP to pull four tracks off the group's *Please Please Me* LP, once again featuring two Lennon & McCartney originals, "I Saw Her Standing There" and "Misery" (on Side 1), and two covers, "Anna" and "Chains" (on Side 2). *The Beatles (No. 1)* entered the Record Retailer EP chart on November 7 at number ten and peaked at two on December 5 behind *Twist And Shout*. During the 11 weeks commencing on November 14, 1963, and ending on January 23, 1964, the EP charted at number three for ten weeks (it was at number two for the other). During this time the Beatles held down the top three spots on the EP chart with *Twist And Shout*, *The Beatles' Hits* and *The Beatles (No.1)*. Those buying this trio of EPs ended up with 10 of the 14 tracks on the *Please Please Me* LP. *The Beatles (No.1)* remained on the EP charts for 26 straight weeks plus three more for a total of 29 weeks and also made the singles charts. Melody Maker charted the disc for 12 weeks, with a peak at number 19 on December 7. NME charted the record for six weeks, with a peak of 24 on November 23. Disc reported the EP for seven weeks, with a peak at number 18 on November 23. Two years after its release, *The Beatles (No. 1)* reached sales of over 250,000 units and was awarded a silver disc by Disc magazine on November 11, 1965.

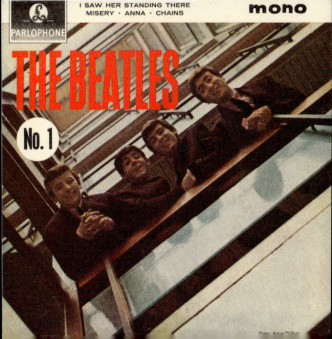

The June 22 Melody Maker reported that the Beatles would be at EMI's London studios on July 1, 15, 29 and 30 to record a new single and material for their second LP. But it wasn't until the September 27 NME that fans learned that a new Beatles LP, *With The Beatles*, was being prepared for late November release. It included "You Really Got A Hold On Me" and Paul singing the Peggy Lee hit "Till There Was You." The seven or eight Lennon-McCartney compositions included one with a solo vocal by Ringo. The September 28 Melody Maker ran a Chris Roberts' story on a Beatles recording session. George Martin reminded Roberts of a "good humoured schoolmaster," letting the boys have their hand to a certain extent, but then he "gently but firmly steers them back into the serious business of recording," in this case two songs for the new LP. Although Roberts did not provide the date of the session or the name of the songs, based on his descriptions, he attended the September 11 evening session where John added a second vocal and George Martin dubbed piano on "Not A Second Time," and the group recorded "Don't Bother Me" with Lennon trying a fuzz box and Harrison asking for a compressor on his guitar "to get a sort of organ sound."

Peter Jones provided a track-by-track review of *With The Beatles* in the November 9 Record Mirror. Jones noted that the Beatles fantastic new LP had a staggering 250,000 in advance orders three weeks before its release. It was the biggest LP advance order in the history of British recording, moving the Beatles to total sales of over three million in just one year. The new album had 14 songs, including seven McCartney-Lennon tunes and one by George Harrison.

Side One opens with "It Won't Be Long," which has John hollering through the lead vocal. The song is good and very loud. The album then changes tempo on "All I've Got To Do," with John taking much of the song solo while Paul "hovers harmonically in the background." "All My Loving" has a "very catchy melody line," with Paul working over the major vocal voices. Jones adds: "John and George operate their tonsils behind. Maybe a trifle 'ordinary' by Beatles standards...but compensated for by some urgent lead guitar from George." Next is George's contribution to the LP, "Don't Bother Me." Jones writes: "George sings it, which is right and proper. He is also double-tracked, which could make it doubly right and proper." The song's background is "enriched by various percussion instruments, including bongo, tambourine and claves." "Little Child" has a John Lennon harmonica at the opening. Paul added piano bits after the main session. The song "swings well and heftily through the mid-instrumental passage."

There is another switch of mood for "Till There Was You." Paul sings this haunting ballad, a biggie in the *Music Man* stage presentation, with a "throaty, appealing sort of delivery." John and George provide "intricate and complex" acoustic guitar work on this "stand-out track." Side One closes with the Marvellettes' "Please Mister Postman." John handles the lead vocal, double-tracked, with "a whole lotta action behind."

Side Two opens with Chuck Berry's "Roll Over Beethoven," which features lots of hand-clapping and George on lead vocal. Paul takes the lead vocal on "Hold Me Tight," a "pretty lively" song with a "heap of mitt-pounding in the background." The Miracles' "You Really Got A Hold On Me" is a "bluesy, draggy piece, with George featured with John." George Martin provides "slabs of pointed piano work." Ringo takes the vocal spotlight on the ravin' "I Wanna Be Your Man," which has flashes of John Lennon on Hammond organ. George takes the lead vocal on the Donays' "Devil In Her Heart," a "nifty tribute" to the American group. "Not A Second Time" has John dual-tracked on lead vocal and more piano from George Martin. The album's closer has John "at his roughest and rawest" vocal on Barrett Strong's R&B classic, "Money." Jones adds: "Paul and George do the answering bits, and the whole thing is a roar-up of the highest order. Big, brash, bright. And, of course, a big favourite of the boys' stage programme."

Alan Smith reported on the album in the November 15 NME in an article titled "Beatles tell the secrets behind their golden tracks." Smith indicated that sales were nearly 300,000 and that he expected that would double. In contrast to their first album, *Please Please Me*, which was recorded in one day, the Beatles spent more time on the new album, enabling the group to polish up their arrangements. George Harrison told Smith some of the songs were incomplete when the Beatles entered the studio, such as missing the middle bit. When George Martin would pop out for a drink, the band would finish the song with "added words and a bit more tune."

Smith thought the highlight of the new LP was the mid-tempo "All My Loving," which had an instantly recognizable melody line. Paul handles the lead vocal, with vocal accompaniment by John and George. "Hold Me Tight" was a Lennon-McCartney original that the group had been playing at Liverpool's Cavern Club for a while. Smith described it as a "gripping track." Because of Ringo's success as the vocalist on "Boys" from the group's *Please Please Me* LP, John and Paul wrote "I Wanna Be Your Man" for him. Smith was impressed. "Ringo handles the insistent rhythm with more polish, in fact, than in 'Boys.' He shows signs of becoming a first-rate beat vocalist." George makes a rare vocal appearance on "Roll Over Beethoven," an out-and-out rocker with the rest of the group adding to the exciting atmosphere by clapping in time. Paul and John handle the vocals on "Little Child." Paul overdubbed piano, and John "dubbed on the Beatles' famous harmonica trade-mark!"

Although most of the album's songs were "wild and up-tempo," the Peggy Lee hit "Till There Was You" provided a distinctive contrast. Paul had been singing the song in the group's stage act for months, with the tune getting a big "plug" at the Royal Command show. The group's interpretation of "Please Mister Postman" was completely different than that of the Marvelettes' version. Other covers included "You Really Got A Hold On Me" and "Devil In Her Heart." George Martin added piano to "Not A Second Time." "Money" was a "wild screamer" from the Hamburg days that the group had "been wanting to record...ever since." Smith added: "And as the last climactic track, it occupies the spot with which 'Twist And Shout' brought the first album to a roaring finish." He called the album a "knock-out" that should even move Beatles-haters. Smith vowed: "If it doesn't stay at the top of the NME LP Chart for at least eight weeks, I'll walk up and down Liverpool's Lime Street carrying a 'I Hate The Beatles' sandwich-board!"

The beatles
RECORD FOR PARLOPHONE

TRADE MARK OF THE PARLOPHONE Co., Ltd.

NEW! AVAILABLE NOVEMBER

PLEASE PLEASE ME
PCS 3042 (STEREO LP)
PMC 1202 (MONO LP)

WITH THE BEATLES
PCS 3045 (STEREO LP)
PMC 1206 (MONO LP)

E.M.I. RECORDS LTD., E.M.I. HOUSE, 20 MANCHESTER SQUARE, LONDON, W.1

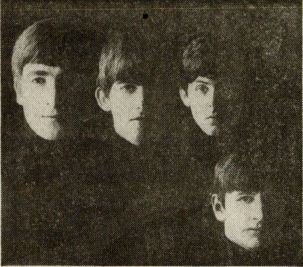

Nigel Hunter gave *With The Beatles* five stars in the November 16 Disc, opening his review with the following words of praise: "Well, folks, this is it. Certainly the album of the year where phenomenally high sales are concerned and also, I suspect, in terms of punch, spirit and general liveliness." He admitted that predicting the success of a Beatles disc was "like saying with confidence that strawberries and cream will be a popular sell-out next summer," adding that, with advance orders heading towards a half-million, "nobody anywhere needs any encouragement from me to get this album." *With The Beatles* had: "the usual unbeatable Beatle mixture. Raucous, uninhibited vocalizing on top of pounding beat and ringing guitaristics, with occasional change in mood and feeling for the utmost contrast."

Hunter picked "Till There Was You" as the album's best track. He was impressed with Paul McCartney's "solo balladeering" on the song from *The Music Man*, finding it a "surprisingly effective track right out of the boys' usual territory and a cert for the charts…if released as a single." He also found the following Side One selections to be "particularly good": The opening shouter ["It Won't Be Long"]; the country "All My Loving" with "nice George Harrison guitar coming through;" "Don't Bother Me" with its Latin beat; and some "blood-tingling" John Lennon harmonica spicing "Little Child."

The second side offered "more strong material in the shape of the pulsating plea to that postman ['Please Mister Postman,' actually the last song on Side One] and the clap-happy 'Roll Over Beethoven' with more Harrison guitar prominent." He noted that George Martin had "used the jiggery-pokery of the recording studio skillfully to enable the boys to double-track for extra effect," and had played piano on "You Really Got A Hold On Me" and the final two tracks ["Not A Second Time" and "Money"]. Hunter ended his review with sage advice that echoed Parlophone's ad for the album (shown on the previous page) that ran in the November 22 NME and the November 23 Disc: "That's it then. All you have to do now is place your order and wait patiently for 14 tracks of great and boisterous Beatledom."

The November 23 Melody Maker described *With The Beatles* as a "great album, with variety of tempo and a raw style that puts the Beatles unmistakably at the top of the beat tree." The magazine picked "All My Loving" as the album's stand-out track, describing it as "jaunty" and "with a haunting quality."

Richard Attenborough's review of the album in the December 1963 Record Mail described the disc as "the LP that everyone has been talking about," pointing out that the album's sales had exceeded the quarter-million mark three weeks before it was released. The disc contained seven Lennon-McCartney originals among its 14 tracks. Attenborough then ran through the songs on Side One. "It Won't Be Long" got the album "off to a rip-roaring start with a powerful vocal from John Lennon." "All I've Got To Do" and "All My Loving" were in a quieter mode, followed by George's "Don't Bother Me." John and Paul joined forces for "Little Child," which led into Paul's solo spot on "Till There Was You." The first side closed with the exciting "Please Mister Postman." Attenborough found the second side just as exciting, but only discussed two tracks. Ringo sang "I Wanna Be Your Man," which also featured John on organ. The album ended with the R&B favorite, "Money." David Gell provided praise for *With The Beatles* in the January 1964 Beat Monthly: "A fab, fab, fab, fab, fab, fab, fab LP. That really is the only way to describe it. From start to finish the Colossus of Liverpool, that is the Beatles, clockbust their way to the topper top. In other words, I love it."

Although The Times (of London) did not review *With The Beatles*, music critic William Mann referenced some of its songs and related single in an article on the Beatles appearing in the newspaper's December 27 edition, naming John Lennon and Paul McCartney as the outstanding English composers of 1963. Mann noted that "This Boy" was "expressively unusual for its lugubrious music, but harmonically it is one of their most intriguing, with its chains of pandiatonic clusters, and the sentiment is acceptable because voiced cleanly and crisply." He added: "But harmonic interest is typical of their quicker songs, too, and one gets the impression that they think simultaneously of harmony and melody, so firmly are the major tonic sevenths and ninths built into their tunes, and the flat submediant key switches, so natural is the Aeolian cadence at the end of 'Not A Second Time' (the chord progression which ends Mahler's 'Song of the Earth')." He wrote that George Harrison's "Don't Bother Me" was "harmonically a good deal more primitive, though it is nicely enough presented." Mann concluded that the Beatles had "brought a distinctive and exhilarating flavour into a genre of music that was in danger of ceasing to be music at all."

The industry trade magazine, Record Retailer, first reported on the new album in its October 17, 1963 issue, telling readers that: "Another huge sales prospect is due shortly from EMI with the release of the second Beatles LP." The album had originally been scheduled for December, but had been moved up to mid-November. The magazine's November 11 issue stated that "The fantastic story of the Beatles goes on," with advance orders for *With The Beatles* exceeding a quarter million, the largest prerelease order for an album in British history. An EMI spokesman stated that "our capacity is being stretched to the limit," with more orders flooding in daily. A week later, EMI told the magazine that the company had taken on additional labor for bagging the record because of the tremendous volume. Although not reported, EMI hired Decca to help press copies of the LP. By the end of November, sales were at 530,000. By the end of January 1964, sales were 885,000. Record Mail later reported that *With The Beatles* had sold over 1,000,000 copies, making it the first LP pressed at EMI's Hayes factory to do so. It would not be the last.

Released on November 22, 1963, *With The Beatles* entered the Record Retailer chart on November 28 at number two behind the group's first LP, *Please Please Me*. The next week it took over the number one spot, where it remained for 13 straight weeks before being replaced for one week by *Please Please Me*. It returned to the top on March 12, 1964, for seven more weeks before dropping to number two behind the Rolling Stones debut album. *With The Beatles* charted for 51 weeks in 1963-1964, including 20 weeks at number one, 12 weeks at number two and 35 weeks in the top five. The album entered the Melody Maker chart on November 30 at number one, where it remained for 22 straight weeks before dropping on May 2, 1964, to number two, where it stayed for 11 straight weeks. All told, the LP charted for 43 weeks, including 38 in the top five. *With The Beatles* debuted in the 10-position NME Best Selling LPs in Britain chart on November 30 at number one, where the disc remained for 21 straight weeks before placing in the second spot for seven straight weeks. The album charted for 39 weeks, including 33 weeks in the top five. NME also included the *With The Beatles* LP in its singles chart for seven weeks, with a peak on December 6 at number 11, the highest ever for an LP on the NME singles chart. Disc, which did not publish an album chart at the time, reported *With The Beatles* in its Top 30 singles chart for seven weeks, showing a peak at number nine on January 4, 1964.

The November 8 NME reported that the Beatles fifth single, set for release on November 29, would contain two John Lennon and Paul McCartney songs, "I Want To Hold Your Hand" and "This Boy." NME added that, as of Wednesday, November 9, advance orders had topped 700,000.

Record Retailer reported on EMI's November 4 announcement that it would be issuing a new Beatles single, which was unexpected as "She Loves You" was still charting at number two. This was part of the ambitious plan of Brian Epstein and George Martin to issue four singles and two albums a year. The new disc would be the fourth single of 1963, while *With The Beatles* would be the year's second LP. The next day, EMI had advanced orders of 500,000. An EMI spokesman told Record Retailer, "This is completely unprecedented." The December 1963 issue of The Beatles Book (No. 5) informed its readers: "No disc company has ever pressed over 500,000 copies of anything before its release." The magazine added that the fantastic demand had to be satisfied even if it took every pressing machine at the EMI factory. Fans were further told that the single had been recorded several weeks ago, but its release was delayed "due to the continued chart-topping by 'She Loves You.'" Two days before its release orders had grown to 940,000. The single became the first British record to have advance orders of over one million before it went on sale.

Derek Johnson wrote in the November 22 NME that the disc was "worth every single one of its fantastic advance orders." Johnson thought the song, which hit him much harder upon first playing than "She Loves You," was "repetitious almost to the point of hypnosis, had an easily memorized melody, and some built-in hand-clapping to help along the infectious beat." The song's "plaintive and much quieter middle eight…proves a mighty effective buffer to this power-packed disc." The excellent "This Boy" was a complete contrast that demonstrated the Beatles versatility. It was a "haunting, soulful ballad with a pounding beat" that was "movingly sung and beautifully harmonized."

The November 23 Disc announced: "Look out top spot…The Beatles' smash-hit new single is here!" Don Nicholl gave his DNT designation to "the disc which is nearly a million seller before it even reaches the counters!" Nicholl wondered what record dealers and Parlophone would do if the Beatles went out of fashion, leading to "shelves stacked high with the disc and the customers saying: 'We've changed our minds.'" He quickly concluded that was not likely to happen, adding that "the new Lennon-McCartney composed coupling is going to delight the group's fans." Although not as wild as its predecessor, "I Want To Hold Your Hand" was a "steady compulsive beater" with a "crisp hand-clapping gimmick" and "identifying falsetto tremble on the end of the title phrase." The flip side "This Boy" was a gentle ballad that provided interesting contrast and struck Nicholl as one of their most thoughtful offerings.

The November 23 Record Mirror ran two reviews of the disc. Peter Jones raved about the new single, assuring readers that the fabulous, fantastic foursome had maintained their standards and that the record was "worth all the fuss and furore." The top side had a "blusey feel to it from the start, with a dominant bass guitar from Paul McCartney plus a heavy, pounding sound which gets the teen tootsies tapping inside a fifth of a second." He went on to say that the song "lends itself to those distinctive bits of falsetto which are included at precisely the right moment. And Ringo creates a whole world of beat-provision at back of the guitar battery. It builds right thru and there's a touch of hand-clapping at the end when one gets the impression the studio firemen were needed to quell the flames." The song was better than "She Loves You" and "Please Please Me" and would "whistle to number one and should be there all over the Christmas and New Year period." "This Boy" was slower and had "clever lyrical content and a tune which again resides in the average 'nut' after just a couple of plays." Jones added: "Vocally, this is very exciting, especially in the middle sections. The harmonies are gentler than in some Beatles productions and there's less instrumental domination." The track proved that the Beatles were effective on slower numbers.

The Record Mirror Pop Disc Jury gave the new release four stars, calling the record one of their best singles to date. It was a "slightly-slower-than-usual number" that "tends to build, and grows on you with each play." The track had a "bluesy guitar-and-drums backing with a plaintive tune running through the whole thing" interrupted by falsetto breaks. "This Boy" was a slow ballad with a good lyric and "the appeal of the boys clearly shining through." The magazine predicted that, although it was not as commercial as the A-Side, "all the fans'll flip this one after a while."

The November 23 Melody Maker contained opinions of three disc jockeys on the new Beatles disc. David Jacobs said the record sounded very good, but thought they should have issued "All My Loving" from the new LP as the single. Pete Murray called the disc a certain number one, but did not think the Beatles records were improving. He found "From Me To You" more musical than "She Loves You," but acknowledged his older age made him prefer "their more melodic treatments," while that might not necessarily apply to younger fans. Alan Freeman believed that "I Want To Hold Your Hand" would not have the impact of "She Loves You," but added it would top the charts. He found the B-side, "This Boy," to be a revelation that showed off the group's talents more that their hit-bound songs.

Record Retailer reviewed the disc in its November 28 issue, calling it: "Well up to standard." "I Want To Hold Your Hand" was described as "typical Beatles material, with tremendous drive and personality." The magazine commented that "This Boy" was a great song that showed the group "in a milder, more sensitive mood."

Peter Aldersley wrote in the November 30 Pop Weekly that with "I Want To Hold Your Hand," the Beatles once again "give us that sound which so many groups have tried to copy, albeit unsuccessfully!" Although the track exemplified the group's perfect teamwork, it lacked "the explosive quality of 'She Loves You,' being much more restrained." Aldersey found that the melody grew on him with each spin, "although on FIRST hearing the disc didn't make the immediate impact of the boys' other ones." He admitted that this was "purely relative," noting that because the single would have "so many successful spins there'll be plenty of time for the tune to grow on the slowest of ears!" Writing in the January 1964 Beat Monthly, David Gell kept it brief and simple: "No review could do credit to the fantastic success of the Beatles. This bounding geary topside and the balladly set of grooves on the lower deck make this a great, great disc."

"I Want To Hold Your Hand" entered the Record Retailer chart at number ten on December 5 while "She Loves You" was topping the charts. The following week the new single moved up to number one, where it remained for five weeks before being knocked from the top by the Dave Clark Five's first big hit single, "Glad All Over." The Beatles "I Want To Hold Your Hand" charted for 21 weeks, including nine in the top ten. The December 7 Melody Maker reported "I Want To Hold Your Hand" at number one in its first week. The disc topped the chart for four weeks and spent nine weeks in the top 10 during its 18-week chart run. The single debuted at number one in the December 6 NME Top 30 chart, remaining at the top for six straight weeks during its 14-week run that included ten weeks in the top ten. The record also debuted at number one in Disc's Top 30, remaining there for five straight weeks during its 15 weeks on the charts, which included nine weeks in the top ten. The single also topped the BBC chart. Disc awarded "I Want To Hold Your Hand" a silver disc on December 7, 1963, for sales of over 250,000. The magazine soon thereafter awarded the single a gold disc for sales of one million units. By mid-January 1964, sales passed the 1,500,000 mark. Total U.K. sales are estimated to be in excess of 1,700,000.

Beatle News

GREATEST EVER "I WANT TO HOLD YOUR HAND" c/w "THIS BOY"

THE BEATLES new single has already smashed a whole lot of new records. No disc company has ever pressed over 500,000 copies of anything before its release.

But the fantastic demand must be met—even if it takes every machine at the E.M.I. factory. The boys actually cut their new one several weeks ago but its release has been delayed due to the continued chart-topping by "She Loves You."

SIR BEATLES

What if they got knighted! After that terrific performance in the Royal Command show anything could happen. Just imagine —Sir John, Sir Paul, Sir George and Sir Ringo. Seriously though, there's lots of speculation as to who are the big Beatles fans in the Royal Family. Most backers go for Princess Margaret and Lord Snowdon being in the lead but they all seemed to go for the beat kings and their kind of music at the show.

SWEDISH GIRLS

"They're great," said Paul,

The December 1963 edition of The Beatles Book (No. 5) referred to the group's new single as the "Greatest Ever." The Parlophone promo card for "I Want To Hold Your Hand" features a photo taken by Dezo Hoffmann on July 2, 1963, at Russell Square Gardens in Bloomsbury, London.

Prompted by the popularity of "All My Loving" from the *With The Beatles* album, EMI prepared a new EP, the group's fourth, with the song as its title track. The disc also contained another number from the LP, the all-out rocker "Money," which NME reviewer Allen Evans described as "noisy vocally and exciting instrumentally." The EP was rounded out with the B-sides to the group's first two singles, "P.S. I Love You" and "Ask Me Why." The *All My Loving* EP was released on February 7, 1964, the day the Beatles landed in New York to kick off their first U.S. visit. The disc entered the Record Retailer EP chart on February 6 at number seven, joining three other Beatles EPs in the top ten: *Twist And Shout* at two; *The Beatles' Hits* at four; and *The Beatles (No.1)* at five. The four would remain in the top ten for ten more weeks. The new EP spent the next two weeks at number two before replacing the Rolling Stones' first EP at the top of the charts on February 27, its first of eight straight weeks at number one. The EP also spent a total of 11 weeks at number two. *All My Loving* remained on the EP charts for 44 weeks, including 27 weeks in the top five and 35 in the top ten. Melody Maker charted the EP in its singles chart for 12 weeks, with a peak at number 12 on February 29. NME reported the disc in its singles chart for six weeks, showing a peak at 13 on February 21. The EP reached sales of over 250,000 units in six weeks and was awarded a silver disc by Disc magazine on March 31, 1964.

In early December 1963, Disc put readers on alert that the Beatles had shattered their own chart-storming record: "December 7, 1963. If you're a Beatles fan—and who isn't—put it down in your diary, for it is the most important date in the 14 month disc history of this fantastic group." The Beatles had six entries in the magazine's singles chart: The top two singles ("I Want To Hold Your Hand" and "She Loves You"); the *With The Beatles* LP at 11; and three EPs. That same week Melody Maker ran the headline "BEATLES hit charts for SEVEN!" The group had the top two singles plus three EPs in the top 20 of the magazine's singles chart. They also held the top two positions in Melody Maker's Top Ten LP's chart. The December 14 Record Mirror, whose chart information was compiled by Record Retailer, showed the total domination of the British record industry by the Beatles. The group held down: The top two spots on the singles chart with "I Want To Hold Your Hand" and "She Loves You;" the top two spots on the LP's chart with *With The Beatles* and *Please Please Me*; and the top three spots on the EPs chart with *Twist And Shout*, *The Beatles' Hits* and *The Beatles (No. 1)*. In discussing the Beatles chart success in the November 23, 1963 Record Mirror, Peter Jones wrote: "Fantastic, isn't it? And it's really only the start of the story, isn't it?" How right he was!

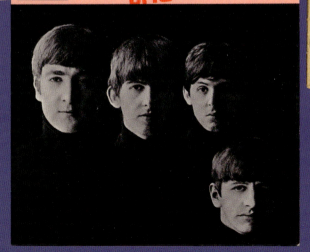

The December 21, 1963 Record Mirror recognized the Beatles as the Stars of the Year, adding that the group "brought freshness, individuality, amiable charm to the scene." The magazine predicted that "when the Final Book of Pop Music is written, they'll be worth several chapters all to themselves."

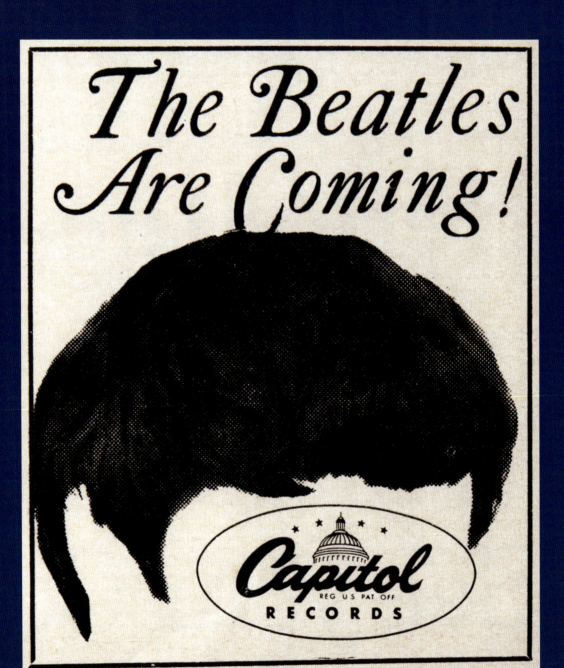

Beatlemania! Explodes in America

The Beatles Are Coming! Those four words appeared in two identical small ads (enlarged image shown on the previous page) in the December 28, 1963 Billboard, which was distributed shortly before Christmas Eve 1963. At the time, most Americans did not know who or what the Beatles were, but that would soon change.

The Beatles Are Coming! Those four words formed the slogan devised by Capitol Records to market its latest signing, the British band with the funny name and the funny hair. At a time when most American males had crew cuts or other short hair styles, Capitol focused on the group's long hair.

The Beatles Are Coming! Those four words were a derivation of "The British Are Coming!" Capitol was comparing the arrival of the Beatles on American soil with the invasion of British soldiers at Lexington and Concord at the start of the Revolutionary War.

One week after the Capitol ad first ran, the December 30, 1963 Evening Sun newspaper in Baltimore issued its own warning: "'The Beatles are coming.' Those four words are said to be enough to jelly the spine of the most courageous police captains in Britain.... Since, in this case, the Beatles are coming to America, America had better take thought as to how it will deal with the invasion.... Indeed, a restrained 'Beatles, go home,' might just be the thing."

But by the time the above editorial was published at the end of 1963, American youngsters were beginning to hear the Capitol single "I Want To Hold Your Hand" on the radio. Within weeks, the song was joined by "She Loves You" on Swan Records and "Please Please Me" on Vee-Jay Records in saturation air play that would soon lead to massive record sales and high chart listings. The albums *Introducing The Beatles* and *Meet The Beatles!* were flying out of record racks and bins. The group's landing at New York's John F. Kennedy International Airport on February 7, 1964, was covered by the New York press and The CBS Evening News With Walter Cronkite. The British Invasion had begun.

But to understand a successful invasion, one must know the background facts that ultimately led to its victorious outcome. During the 1950s and early 1960s (and in previous decades as well), American recording artists had enjoyed tremendous recognition and record sales in Great Britain. London-based Electric and Musical Industries Ltd. ("EMI") had lucrative licensing agreements with RCA Victor and Columbia Records in America. By 1950, over 70% of the company's worldwide catalog consisted of American recordings. In 1952, Columbia terminated its agreement with EMI. Although EMI was able to extend its licensing contract with RCA Victor through 1957, the company knew the agreement could end at that time. To shore up its licensing of American recordings, EMI purchased a 95% interest in Capitol Records in 1955 for $8,500,000.

Capitol was founded in 1942 as an independent record company in Hollywood, California, at a time when the American recording industry was dominated by three companies: Decca, RCA Victor and Columbia. Run by young and aggressive leadership, Capitol experienced remarkable growth and success. By 1952, U.S. News & World Report described how the innovative company had shaken the big three "out of their lethargy with untried concepts in recording, radical departures in merchandising, and revolutionary innovations in sales promotion." Its roster of stars included Frank Sinatra, Nat King Cole, Judy Garland, Peggy Lee, Kay Starr, Benny Goodman, Les Paul & Mary Ford, Dean Martin and Jackie Gleason. EMI's purchase of Capitol more than made up for the loss of Columbia and RCA. Under the leadership of Sir Joseph Lockwood, who became Chairman and Chief Executive Officer in 1955, EMI prospered. By the time the Beatles signed with the company's Parlophone label in 1962, EMI truly was "The Greatest Recording Organization in the World."

For Capitol, its purchase by EMI provided much needed capital to enable it to better compete in the music industry. It also gave Capitol the right of first refusal for the U.S. release of all recordings by EMI artists. For the most part, this arrangement was a one-way street. While EMI enjoyed great success selling records by American artists in England and foreign markets, Capitol was not very successful in breaking British pop acts in America. Capitol's Dave Dexter was assigned the task of reviewing EMI foreign product and determining if the recordings were suitable for the American market. Dexter, whose background was in jazz and R&B, had no appreciation or like for rock 'n' roll.

Dexter rejected most of the British singles sent to him by EMI. And, for the most part, when he advised Capitol to release a British disc, sales were horrendous. In 1956, Capitol issued 15 British singles with total sales of just over 44,000 units. Nearly 40% of the sales (17,214 units) were attributable to a single disc, the novelty tune "Experiments With Mice," recorded by Johnny Dankworth and produced by George Martin. The following year, 1957, saw only a marginal improvement with the release of 20 singles and sales of just over 140,000 discs. This improvement was due primarily to the performance of one song, the instrumental "Swinging Sweethearts" (titled "Skiffling Strings" in the U.K.) by Ron Goodwin, which sold 102,454 copies, giving Capitol its first British hit (charting at number 52).

In 1958, Capitol finally struck gold in the EMI British mine with Laurie London's "He's Got The Whole World (In His Hands)." In the U.K., the Parlophone single peaked at number 12, but in America the spiritual topped the charts and sold over one million copies. London was 13 years old when he recorded the song at Abbey Road. His followup releases failed to capture the magic, although "Joshua" sold 33,083 copies. But this was an exception. Total sales for the other 14 British singles issued that year were less than 28,000 units. The George Martin-produced "Be My Girl" by Jim Dale was a rockabilly-sounding song that charted at number two in England. But when Capitol issued the single, it sold only 297 copies. Cliff Richard was initially marketed as the British version of Elvis. His single "Move It!" was considered by many, including John Lennon, to be the first authentic British rock 'n' roll recording. The disc was a number two hit, and its followup single, "High Class Baby," peaked at number seven. Capitol issued a single pairing the two songs. While Cliff Richard was a rising star in the U.K., the Capitol disc sold only 1,104 copies.

Although Capitol now had a million seller to justify its investment in British recordings, neither of its previous hitmakers could save 1959. Capitol released 17 singles that yielded total sales of only 11,874 units. Laurie London's "My Mother" sold 1,002 copies. Ron Goodwin's records also bombed, with Capitol reporting sales of 2,102 for "Latin Lovers" and minus 202 for "Martians On Parade." That year George Martin wrote to Dave Dexter requesting that he consider releasing a new single that he had produced by Sharkey Todd. Martin explained that Sharkey Todd was a pseudonym of Wally Whyton, former leader of the Vipers Skiffle Group. Martin thought the single "might do very well in the States." Although Dexter followed Martin's advice and issued the record featuring "The Horror Show" and "The Cool Gool," it sold only 171 copies. The label to the A-side stated: "Produced By: Dracula's Mother."

The disastrous sales figures of British discs in 1959 caused Dexter to cut back in 1960, releasing only five singles that had total sales of 4,881 units. The next year would have been a total bust had it not been for two records issued in the later months of 1961. The first six releases had combined sales of 2,080 units. This included a George Martin-produced comedy disc by Peter Sellers and Sophia Loren pairing "Goodness Gracious Me" and "Bangers And Mash" that sold only 186 units, and Helen Shapiro's "Don't Treat Me Like A Child," a number three hit in the U.K. that sold only 101 copies in America. Her next two Capitol singles, both number one hits in England, did relatively better, with "You Don't Know" selling 3,365 copies and "Walkin' Back To Happiness" selling 18,919 units, bringing total 1961 sales up to 24,364. During the first five months of 1962, Dexter issued five British singles that sold a combined 8,039 copies, including Helen Shapiro's "Tell Me What He Said" (4,149 copies) and Mrs. Mills' "Bobbikins" (72 copies).

The recent poor performance of British singles was on Dexter's mind when he received a new batch of discs from EMI in late May or early June of 1962 that included Frank Ifield's "I Remember You" on EMI's Columbia label. He had previously turned down Ifield's "Lucky Devil" and "Gotta Get A Date," which had been moderate hits in the U.K. He had also rejected discs by British teen idol Adam Faith, who had nine top five hits, including two chart-toppers, on Parlophone. When Dexter issued Ricky Stevens' "I Cried For You" in January 1962, the record sold only 125 copies. Dexter may have been turned off by the harmonica on the American pop standard "I Remember You," which he viewed as an R&B instrument having no place in pop, or by Ifield's yodeling of the song's title. Whatever his reasons, Dexter's rejection of this disc would have significant ramifications.

By this time EMI had established Transglobal Music Co., Inc., a New York entity that assisted record companies with the placement of recording masters in the U.S.A., Europe and throughout the world. When Capitol passed on the Ifield single, EMI transferred the single's licensing rights to Transglobal, requesting that the company find an American label to release the disc. Paul Marshall, a New York attorney who was then serving as counsel for EMI and Transglobal, recalls unsuccessfully offering the Ifield master to MGM and other labels before approaching one of his own clients, Vee-Jay Records, a black-owned independent label based in Chicago that specialized in gospel and R&B recording artists. Vee-Jay had recently achieved some success on the pop charts and was looking to expand its reach. The leasing of a hit pop record from England was a low-cost way to move further into the pop market. Vee-Jay released "I Remember You" on VJ 457 in late July 1962. Some copies misspell the singer's first name as "Farnk."

Vee-Jay's successful penetration into the lucrative pop market is evidenced in the October 13, 1962 Billboard Hot 100. The single VJ 456, "Sherry" by the Four Seasons, a group of four male white singers from New Jersey, was in its fifth and final week at number one. And equally significant and nearly as impressive, Frank Ifield's "I Remember You" was at its peak position of number five, demonstrating that Vee-Jay was capable of successfully marketing a British artist in America—something Capitol had been unable to do for years.

Around that time, Dave Dexter received another set of new EMI releases, which included the Beatles first British single, "Love Me Do." Dexter did not like what he heard, later saying: "I didn't care for it at all because of the harmonica sound. I didn't care for the harmonica because I had grown up listening to the old blues records and blues harmonica players...I nixed the record instantly." He didn't want any part of the Beatles. Dexter's rejection of "Love Me Do" did not trigger any reaction from EMI, which did not have high expectations for the Beatles. According to George Martin, the group's name was met with laughs at EMI House and "nobody believed in [the single] at all." Although there was little he could have done, Martin did not bother arguing for the disc's American release.

While the Beatles first single was not issued in the U.S., the Great Britain report in the International Section of the November 24, 1962 Cash Box noted: "A&R manager George Martin sees a bright future for the Beatles – a new vocal instrumental group making their debut on the Parlophone label with their own composition 'Love Me Do.'"

Although there was a lack of enthusiasm for the Beatles debut disc throughout EMI (and to a lesser extent by George Martin), things were different for the band's second single, "Please Please Me." When the Beatles finished recording the song, George Martin told the group: "Gentlemen, you've just made your first number one record." Dave Dexter, however, did not hear it that way. Upon receiving a copy of the record in late December 1962, he quickly rejected the disc, most likely due to its harmonica. This bitterly disappointed Martin, who believed in the record and could not understand why EMI would not order its subsidiary, Capitol Records, to release the disc in America. EMI's explanation that Capitol was completely autonomous did little to reduce the friction between Martin and EMI. Brian Epstein was also frustrated by Capitol's refusal to issue Beatles records.

EMI transferred the rights to the Beatles recordings to Transglobal with the instructions to get the single released in America as quickly as possible. After several labels showed no interest, Marshall offered the song to Vee-Jay, which had success with the previous disc licensed from Transglobal, Frank Ifield's "I Remember You." Under the terms of a January 10, 1963 licensing agreement with Transglobal, Vee-Jay obtained the exclusive right to issue "Please Please Me" and its B-side, "Ask Me Why," in the United States. An important addendum to the agreement gave Vee-Jay the right of first refusal of all Beatles recordings during the five-year term of the agreement, exercisable within 30 days of receipt of the master recordings. Vee-Jay set the release of "Please Please Me" on VJ 498 for February 7, 1963.

Although Vee-Jay's signing of the Beatles in January 1963 did not receive dedicated coverage in any of the American music industry trade magazines, the International News Reports section on Britain in the February 16, 1963 Billboard ran a paragraph on a visit to London by the head of Vee-Jay's international department, Barbara Gardner. The writer of the column, Don Wedge, News Editor of NME, reported that Miss Gardner was on the first stage of her European visit that would take her to France, Holland, Sweden and Switzerland. Wedge further wrote: "In a deal with EMI, Vee Jay will release records made by the Beatles (Parlophone), a promising British vocal-instrumental group which has yet to make a large impact here." As detailed in the previous chapter, the Beatles would soon hit it big in the U.K.

American radio in the early sixties was drastically different than its British counterpart, which was dominated by the British Broadcasting Company ("BBC"). While the BBC played only a bit of pop music on its Light Programme and rarely played records due to needle-time restrictions limiting the amount of music that could be played from records, American radio faced no such rules. Major cities in the U.S. typically had two or three stations broadcasting pop music around the clock. Even small towns often had stations that would allocate part of their air time to pop music. Although some stations were devoted to country, R&B or classical music, many American stations followed a Top 40 format under which the more popular records were played every couple of hours. Unlike today where most stations are limited to a particular genre of music, Top 40 was a wide open format that stressed popularity regardless of style. It was not unusual for listeners to hear rock 'n' roll, folk, adult contemporary singers such as Frank Sinatra and Dean Martin, R&B, teen idols, soul, girl groups, novelty records and an oldie or two all within the span of an hour.

Many stations were independently owned, and even when they were part of a group of stations, local stations normally had full autonomy to program for their own market. Several stations published their own charts (often called "surveys") based on the station's most requested songs and the area's top selling records. Some disc jockeys had large followings that rivaled those of the singers whose records they were playing.

The first DJ to play the Beatles in America was most likely Dick Biondi, who played "Please Please Me" on Chicago's WLS in February 1963. Biondi, who often got together with Vee-Jay president Ewart Abner, recalls receiving a copy of the single in early February. Abner endorsed the 45 with his usual "I feel this could be a big record," and Biondi liked what he heard. WLS program director Gene Taylor added the single to the station's playlist. Biondi may have debuted the song as early as Friday, February 8, during his 9:00 PM to midnight shift. The station's March 8 survey indicates that "Please Please Me" by "Beattles" (misspelled with two "T"s) had been played for three weeks and lists the song at number 40. The March 15 survey features a picture of Biondi and shows the single at its peak and final position of 35. Biondi can be heard announcing the song on a tape recording of his show from February 23, 1963.

Although "Please Please Me" failed to make the national charts published by the industry trade magazines Billboard, Cash Box and Music Vendor (renamed Record World with its April 18, 1964 issue), the song did chart in a few local markets other than Vee-Jay's Chicago home during April and May of 1963. KFXM, the number one station in Riverside and San Bernardino, California, first charted "Please Please Me" at number 41 in its Fabulous 59 survey of April 6, 1963. The song fell off the charts for two weeks before reappearing at number 40 on April 27. The single remained at 40 the following week and then peaked at 38 on May 11, its final of four weeks on the charts. San Francisco's KEWB charted "Please Please Me" for three weeks, with its debut at number 37 on April 20, 1963. The single peaked the following week at number 34 before falling to 40 on May 4. Miami's WQAM reported "Please Please Me" for two weeks at number 47 in its Fabulous 56 surveys of April 27 and May 4. KNUZ in Houston listed the song at number 34 on its May 3 survey. WSPR in Springfield, Massachusetts added the Beatles single to its Successful 70 survey in May 1963 with confirmed listings at 68 and 66. Honolulu, Hawaii's KPOI only assigned numbers to the top ten singles. The station first aired "Please Please Me" on April 22, 1963, and was playing the song through at least mid-May.

HOT NEW RELEASES!

The #2 RECORD IN ENGLAND!!

"THE WAYWARD WIND"
by
FRANK IFIELD
Vee Jay #499

Going Great R&B, C&W & Pop!
Now #13 in London, England!

"PLEASE, PLEASE ME"
by
THE BEATLES
Vee Jay #498

THE **REAL** BOSSA NOVA!

"MIMA"
by
EDDIE HARRIS
Vee Jay #496

THIS IS A MUST!

"HOLD ME CLOSE"
by
RON MARSHALL
MOHAWK #134

"NURSERY RHYMES"
by
NINO & THE EBB TIDES
MISTER PEEKE #123

WLS
The **bright** sound of Chicago Radio

SILVER DOLLAR SURVEY
Chicago's Official Radio Record Survey
MARCH 15, 1963

THIS WEEK			WEEKS PLAYED
* 1.	THE END OF THE WORLD	Skeeter Davis — RCA	9
* 2.	HE'S SO FINE	Chiffons — Laurie	4
* 3.	WILD WEEKEND	Rebels — Swan	9
* 4.	RHYTHM OF THE RAIN	Cascades — Valiant	11
* 5.	WALK LIKE A MAN	Four Seasons — Vee Jay	10
6.	RUBY BABY	Dion — Columbia	11
* 7.	SOUTH STREET	Orlons — Cameo	8
* 8.	OUR DAY WILL COME	Ruby & Romantics — Kapp	9
9.	LINDA	Jan & Dean — Liberty	5
10.	OUR WINTER LOVE	Bill Pursell — Columbia	6
*11.	BLAME IT ON THE BOSSA NOVA	Eydie Gorme — Columbia	6
12.	PLEASE DON'T MENTION MY NAME	Shepherd Sisters — Atlantic	5
*13.	SUN ARISE	Rolf Harris — Epic	6
*14.	IN DREAMS	Roy Orbison — Monument	6
*15.	OUT OF MY MIND	Johnny Tillotson — Cadence	5
*16.	DON'T WANNA THINK ABOUT PAUL	Dickey Lee — Smash	5
*17.	ALL I HAVE TO DO IS DREAM	Richard Chamberlain — MGM	6
*18.	I GOT BURNED	Ral Donner — Reprise	6
*19.	DON'T BE AFRAID LITTLE DARLIN	Steve Lawrence — Columbia	4
*20.	ONE BROKEN HEART FOR SALE	Elvis Presley — RCA	7
*21.	HOW CAN I FORGET	Jimmy Holiday — Everest	6
*22.	YOUNG AND IN LOVE	Dick & Dee Dee — WB	4
*23.	BULE	Jack Reno — Fono Graf	5
24.	LOVE FOR SALE	Arthur Lyman — Hi Fi	6
25.	TELL HIM I'M NOT HOME	Chuck Jackson — Wand	4
*26.	DO THE BIRD	Dee Dee Sharp — Cameo	5
*27.	YOUNG LOVERS	Paul & Paula — Philips	4
*28.	YELLOW BANDANA	Faron Young — Mercury	6
*29.	SAX FIFTH AVENUE	Johnny Beecher — WB	4
30.	PIPELINE	Chantays — Dot	2
*31.	CASTAWAY	Hayley Mills — Vista	5
*32.	MR BASS MAN	Johnny Cymbal — Kapp	4
*33.	ON BROADWAY	Drifters — Atlantic	4
*34.	DON'T SAY NOTHIN BAD	Cookies — Dimension	4
*35.	PLEASE PLEASE ME	Beattles — Vee Jay	4
*36.	PIN A MEDAL ON JOEY	James Darren — Colpix	3
*37.	CAN'T GET USED TO LOSING YOU	Andy Williams — Columbia	2
*38.	SANDY	Dion — Laurie	3
*39.	LITTLE STAR	Bobby Callender — Roulette	5
*40.	PUFF	Peter, Paul & Mary — WB	3

FEATURED ALBUMS
THE END OF THE WORLD — SKEETER DAVIS — RCA
I WANNA BE AROUND — TONY BENNETT — COLUMBIA
GOLDEN HITS — VOL. 2 — BROOK BENTON — MERCURY

Don't miss the fun with

Dick Biondi

9 to Midnight — Monday thru Sunday

WLS • DIAL 890 • 24 HOURS-A-DAY
ABC RADIO IN CHICAGO

This survey is compiled each week by WLS Radio/Chicago from reports of all record sales gathered from leading record outlets in the Chicagoland area. Hear Clark Weber play all the SILVER DOLLAR SURVEY hits daily from 3:00 to 6:30 P.M. *Denotes record first heard on WLS.

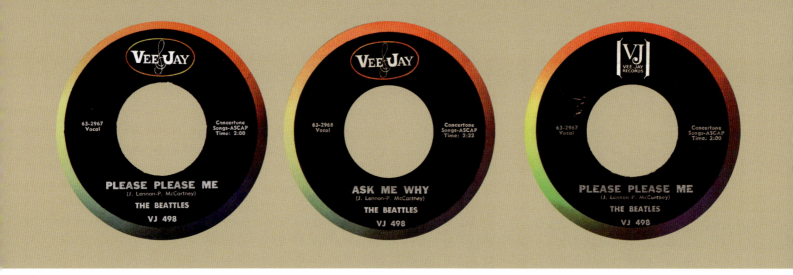

Cash Box reviewed the "Beattles" single in its February 23 issue, with "Please Please Me" receiving a grade of B+ ("very good") and garnering the following endorsement: "There's an air of teen-beat originality to this session by the exciting rocksters and their supporting sound, which includes distinctive harmonica statements throughout." The magazine added that the English import could "prove to be a Top 100 issue." The flip side, "Ask Me Why," was given a B ("good") and the following description: "Teeners also get an original-sounding Latinish romantic pose in this corner." Billboard did not review the disc, but gave "Please Please Me" a Four Star rating (indicating sufficient commercial potential to merit being stocked by dealers) and "Ask Me Why" three stars in its March 2 issue.

The limited air play for "Please Please Me" in a handful of markets prevented the record from being a total stiff. Vee-Jay sold approximately 5,650 copies of the single during the first half of 1963. By mid-year the record had run its course as evidenced by Vee-Jay's claim that only two copies were sold in the last six months of 1963. A limited pressing of the single in 1964 added sales of approximately 1,650 units, raising total sales to 7,310 copies. The initial pressings of the single have labels with the Vee-Jay oval logo and the group's names misspelled as "THE BEATTLES." Later pressings with the group's name spelled correctly as "THE BEATLES" have labels with either the Vee-Jay oval logo or the later Vee-Jay brackets logo.

Vee-Jay chose to exercise its right of first refusal on the Beatles next Parlophone single pairing "From Me To You" with "Thank You Girl." It was issued on VJ 520 during the second half of May 1963.

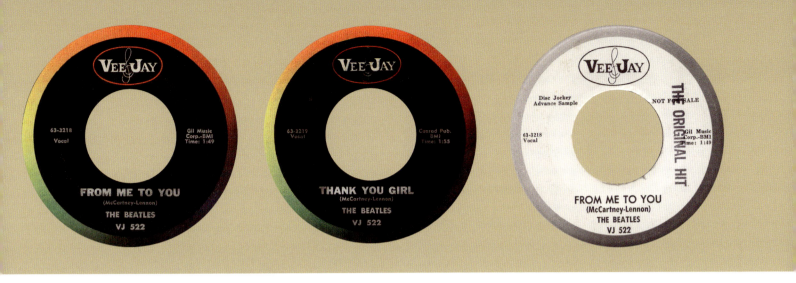

Unfortunately for the Beatles and Vee-Jay, American singer/guitarist Del Shannon released a near-identical-sounding cover version of "From Me To You" a few weeks later. Vee-Jay became concerned that disc jockeys might be more inclined to play Shannon's competing version of "From Me To You" based upon his track record. While the Beatles were virtually unknown in America, Shannon had topped the charts with his million-selling runaway hit "Runaway" three years earlier and had remained on playlists with four subsequent top 40 hits. In ads appearing in the June 8 Billboard and the June 22 Cash Box, Vee-Jay touted the Beatles single as "The Original Hit Version!" In addition, Vee-Jay began stamping "THE ORIGINAL HIT" onto the later promotional copies of the single sent to disc jockeys.

Vee-Jay's educational efforts did not get disc jockeys in most markets to play the Beatles original version of the song. Even WLS in Vee-Jay's hometown of Chicago went with the Del Shannon recording. WLS ignored the new Beatles single and began playing the Shannon disc immediately upon its release. The station charted the record for six weeks, with a peak at number 15 on July 12 and 19, 1963. It was this non-Beatles recording that became the first Lennon-McCartney song (credited to "McCartney-Lennon" on the label) to hit the national American charts. "From Me To You" by Del Shannon entered the Billboard Hot 100 on June 29, 1963, at number 96 and peaked at number 77 during its four-week run. Cash Box also charted the song for four weeks, with a debut at number 86 on July 6, 1963, and a peak at 67 on July 27. Cash Box combined multiple versions of a song into one chart position with artist and label information shown for each disc. The Del Shannon single received the primary listing (indicated by a star), with the Beatles single listed second. Music Vendor charted the Shannon single for five weeks with a peak at number 78.

The radio air play captured by Del Shannon's version of "From Me To You" thwarted the efforts of George Harrison's sister, Louise "Lou" Caldwell, from getting her brother's record played on the radio. By the spring of 1963, Lou was living in Benton, Illinois. Beatles manager Brian Epstein began sending her multiple copies of the Beatles latest releases. By letter dated July 15, 1963, Brian told Lou: "I will really be more than grateful for anything you can do with the records because we are very anxious indeed that their records will eventually 'break' in the States." Lou responded by sending the group's latest disc, "From Me To You," to Bud Connell, the program director of the predominant pop station in near-by St. Louis, KXOK. Connell replied by letter dated July 31, 1963, telling her that it would be difficult for the station to change to the Beatles version because it had been playing the Del Shannon record for quite some time. He added: "It is a shame, however, that your original did not receive promotion in the United States first, because it is a good sound, and on the basis of its past success, would have certainly been a hit in the right country. Perhaps the next release will become Number 1 in the nation...We hope so!"

Although the Beatles version of "From Me To You" failed to make the Billboard Hot 100 or Music Vendor chart and received second billing in Cash Box, the Beatles disc was played in multiple markets. Akron's WAKR charted the single for five weeks with a peak of 13 in July. The disc got to number 8 on WEBC in Duluth, Minnesota in July. Orlando's WHOO charted the song at 44. Chicago's WYNR charted the Beatles disc at 32 for the month of July. The Beatles version fared best on the West Coast in the summer of 1963. KFXM (Riverside and San Bernardino), which had charted "Please Please Me," reported the Beatles second Vee-Jay disc at number 17. The single did even better on rival San Bernardino station KMEN, which published a weekly survey listing a Top Ten and a few dozen "Honorable Mention" songs. KMEN charted the song for nine weeks with a peak at number nine on July 12. Seattle's KJR charted "From Me To You" for seven weeks with a peak at 15 on August 19. KXLY in Spokane charted the song at number 40. San Diego's KDEO survey showed "From Me To You" by "Beetles" at number 13 in mid-August. KRLA in Los Angeles also played the Beatles version of "From Me To You." Dick Biondi, who had spun "Please Please Me" while at WLS in Chicago, had moved to KRLA after being fired by WLS days before the single's release. He may have been involved in the station's decision to play the Beatles disc. "From Me To You" debuted in the station's Tune-Dex survey on July 14 at number 46. The Beatles single charted for six weeks, peaking at 32 on the August 11 Tune-Dex.

This West Coast action led to the Beatles version of "From Me To You" entering the Billboard Bubbling Under The Hot 100 chart at number 125 on August 3, 1963. The following week the record moved up to number 116. Although the magazine's August 17 issue listed the Beatles single as a "Regional Breakout," it dropped to number 124 that week and then sank without a trace.

The June 1 Cash Box listed the record as one of its "Pick of the Week" discs by Newcomers (artists yet to crack the Top 100) and contained the following review: "Artists who are currently riding atop the English charts with 'From Me To You' can do a bang-up sales job this side of the Atlantic with the deck. It's a real catchy cha cha twist romantic novelty that the fellas deliver in attention-getting manner. More of the same top teen sounds on the 'Thank You Girl' portion." The June 1 Billboard gave "From Me To You" a Four Star rating and "Thank You Girl" three stars.

Vee-Jay's second Beatles single sold much better than its predecessor, achieving sales of 3,900 units during May and June of 1963. From July 1 through September 30, the record sold an additional 8,775 copies. After little or no sales during the last quarter of 1963, the single sold 9,451 units during the first three months of 1964. Although Beatlemania was in full swing in America at that time, there was little demand for this single because Vee-Jay issued a new record pairing "Please Please Me" and "From Me To You." In all, VJ 522 sold 22,125 units before experiencing 899 returns, resulting in net sales of 21,226 copies, nearly three times the sales of the first single.

During the summer of 1963, Vee-Jay encountered severe cash flow problems. Its president, Ewart Abner, had taken an estimated three to four hundred thousand dollars of company money to pay personal gambling debts. The company's founders and major owners, Vivian and James Bracken, chose not to press charges and entered into a settlement under which Abner gave up his long-term contract and the company forgave the debt. Vee-Jay was forced to postpone or cancel all new releases for several months as it had no money to pay the factories that pressed its records. Vee-Jay's planned summer release of a Beatles album was canceled. Vee-Jay also failed to send statements or pay royalties to Transglobal, who sent Vee-Jay a telegram on August 8 demanding that Vee-Jay "immediately cease manufacture and distribution of any and all records containing performances of Frank Ifield or the Beattles [sic]."

Transglobal's unilateral termination of its licensing agreement with Vee-Jay meant that Capitol once again had a right of first refusal for the new releases of Frank Ifield and the Beatles. Around that time, Capitol president Alan Livingston started getting calls from EMI about the Beatles. He also began reading about them in the British music press. This prompted him to discuss the Beatles with Dave Dexter at a weekly staff meeting at the Capitol Tower in Hollywood, California. Livingston recalled: "So at one meeting, I said, 'Dex, what about the Beatles? I read a lot about them, they're doing well in London.' He said, 'Alan, they're a bunch of long-haired kids. They're nothing. Forget it.' I said 'O.K.' I trusted Dexter. And I had no interest in British product at that time."

Dexter received copies of Ifield's "I'm Confessin' (That I Love You)" and the Beatles "She Loves You" in mid-August. After listening to both discs, he had faith in one of the songs and arranged for Capitol to place a full-page ad in Billboard promoting his "sure-bet" hit. The other was deemed unsuitable for the American market. Amazingly, Dexter chose "I'm Confessin'" and recommended that Capitol pass on the Beatles for a third time. Dexter's dislike of Lennon's harmonica playing on "Love Me Do" and "Please Please Me" influenced his decision to turn those records down. But "She Loves You" had no harmonica and, ironically, "I'm Confessin'" did. Ifield's previous American success with "I Remember You" prompted Dexter to release the disc. Although Capitol could have issued both singles, Dexter had a bias against the Beatles that would cause him to reject anything the group had to offer.

Dexter's rejection of "She Loves You' in August 1963 shows how out of touch he was. At the very time Dexter was sitting in his office at the Capitol Tower in Hollywood judging the Beatles unsuitable for the American market, the group's previous disc, "From Me To You," was receiving considerable air play in his own backyard on KRLA as a near Top Thirty hit. Dexter's disdain for rock 'n' roll and lack of faith in British product also caused him to reject Gerry & the Pacemakers, Billy J. Kramer with the Dakotas, the Hollies, the Dave Clark Five, the Swinging Blue Jeans, the Animals, Herman's Hermits and the Yardbirds. He did, however arrange for Capitol to release Freddie and the Dreamers' "I'm Telling You Now" on October 3, 1963. The record sold only 105 copies, but became a number one hit when reissued on Capitol's Tower subsidiary in 1965. At first it appeared that Dexter made the right choice with Ifield and the Beatles. While "I'm Confessin'" sold over 70,000 copies and charted at number 57, "She Loves You" initially flopped.

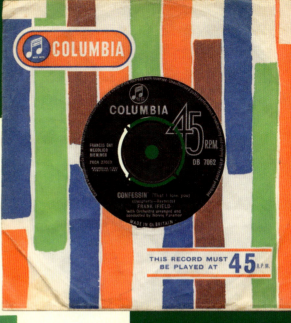

England's #1 Hit Single comes to America— on #5032

CAPITOL RECORDS

FRANK IFIELD

I'M CON- FESS- IN' (That I Love You)

A sure-bet to repeat the success of Frank's first great American Hit, "I REMEMBER YOU"!

By mid-July, George's sister, Lou, became concerned that Vee-Jay was incapable of properly promoting her brother's band and had written Brian Epstein about the company's shortcomings. By letter to Lou dated July 22, 1963, music publisher Dick James acknowledged his understanding that disc jockeys in her area had "experienced difficulty in receiving regular copies [of the Beatles "From Me To You" single] from Veejay Records." James enclosed multiple copies of the disc and expressed his gratitude if Lou could pass the single to the "important DJs" in her locale. Brian sent Lou a letter dated August 23, 1963, informing her that after "going into everything you say very carefully," he had "already instructed persons concerned to change releases of the BEATLES' disc to another label" and assured her that "'She Loves You' will definitely not go out on Vee Jay." After the letter had been typed, Brian hand wrote late-breaking news that: "It's going out on Swan Records PHILADELPHIA." This news was not particularly encouraging for Lou as Swan was not a major label. In fact, Vee-Jay had released many more hit records than the Beatles new label.

Swan was a small independent company based in Philadelphia that began operations in 1957. It was initially owned by Bernie Binnick, Tony Mammarella and Dick Clark, host of American Bandstand, a popular show broadcast nationwide from Philadelphia on ABC-TV. After the U.S. Congress began its investigation in 1959 into the music industry practice of payola, which involved disc jockeys accepting money and other favors to play records, ABC-Paramount president Leonard Goldenson forced Clark to give up his interests in music companies, including Swan, to avoid an appearance of a conflict of interest. In 1963, Binnick heard the Beatles while in London and was aware of the group's growing popularity. EMI and Transglobal were aware of Swan through the leasing of Freddy Cannon recordings by EMI's Top Rank label, which had a number three hit in 1960 with Cannon's "Way Down Yonder In New Orleans." His "Palisades Park" was the first disc issued on EMI's new Stateside subsidiary in 1962. After several companies, including Decca, RCA and Columbia, showed no interest in the Beatles, EMI, through Transglobal, offered "She Loves You" to Swan. Binnick quickly agreed, and Swan entered into an agreement with Transglobal to license the U.S. rights to the single. Due to the Beatles rapidly expanding fan base, EMI insisted on a very restrictive licensing agreement with only a two-year term and limited to the singles format. Swan was not given a right of first refusal; however, a rider to the contract provided that if Swan sold and paid for 50,000 copies of "She Loves You" within four months of release, Swan could license an additional Beatles single. "She Loves You" was issued as Swan 4152 on September 16, 1963.

PER AIR MAIL

Miss L. Caldwell,
113, McCann Street,
BENTON,
Illinois

NEMS ENTERPRISES LTD
DIRECTORS: B. AND C. J. EPSTEIN

24 MOORFIELDS, LIVERPOOL, 2   TELEPHONE CENtral 0793

BE/AT

23rd August, 1963

Dear Louise,

Just very briefly a note to acknowledge your last letter. I am going into everything you say very carefully. I have already instructed persons concerned to change release of the BEATLES' disc to another label. 'She Loves You' will definitely not go out on Vee Jay. More news soon. xx

Yours sincerely,
BRIAN EPSTEIN

Miss L. Caldwell,
113, McCann Street,
BENTON,
Illinois

AIR MAIL

xx It's going out on SWAN Records PHILADELPHIA

Cash Box reviewed the new Beatles single in its September 21, 1963 issue: "The big English hit, by The Beatles, could do big things in this country via the artists' release on Swan. Tune, tagged 'She Loves You,' is a robust romantic rocker that the crew works with solid sales authority. Backing's a catchy cha cha-twist handclapper." That same week Billboard gave "She Loves You" a four-star rating and gave three stars to "I'll Get You."

WIBG in Swan's hometown of Philadelphia issued a weekly survey of the Top 99 Records of the Week. The September 23 chart listed "She Loves You" at 81. On September 28, New York WINS disc jockey Murray the K played "She Loves You" as one of five new singles on his Record Review Board feature, where listeners were told to call in and "Voice Your Choice" for their favorite of the songs. That night "She Loves You" came in third place. Although he played the disc for a week or so, it did not catch on. Dick Clark, who remained friends with Swan's owners, featured "She Loves You" on American Bandstand's Rate-A-Record segment shortly after the single's release. The song averaged a mediocre 73 score. According to Clark, "When the kids saw a photo of the four long-haired lads, they just laughed."

While the Beatles had three number one hits in a row in Great Britain, it was a different story in America. Paul McCartney summed it up best: "'Please Please Me,' flop, 'From Me To You,' flop, 'She Loves You,' flop."

In mid-September, the Beatles took a well-earned and rare two-week break from their busy schedule, with George and his brother, Peter, visiting their sister, Lou, in the States. Although Lou had been unable to get any major station to play Beatles records, she did get WFRX, a small station in West Frankfort, Illinois, to play "From Me Yo You." That summer, 17-year-old Marcia Shafer, whose father owned the station, played the disc on her teen-oriented Saturday Session radio show. In gratitude, George agreed to be interviewed by her on the station. In her high school newspaper, Marcia wrote: "Their music is wild and uninhibited and outsells the world's greatest recording artists, although not one of the Beatles can read music." George purchased several albums and a Rickenbacker 425 electric guitar. He befriended a bass player, Gabe McCarty, and joined his band, the Four Vests, on stage for a brief set at a VFW Hall concert. Upon returning home, George joked that he had been on a reconnaissance mission to determine the Beatles chance of success. His assessment: "I think we can make it; I don't think there's a lot of competition."

Although the promotion copies of the Swan Beatles single had "X" markings on the "She Loves You" side to identify it as the A-side, Dick "The Derby" Smith, music director/disc jockey at WORC in Worcester, Massachusetts, took a liking to the flip side. The station's November 2 "Official Request Survey" listed "I'll Get You" as a song "Ready to Pop the Top." The next week it debuted at number 41 and peaked at 16 on December 21 and 28 during its 11 weeks on the survey. WORC also prepared a chart "Based 100% on Requests." The December 6 survey listed "I'll Get You" at number one, with "She Love You" [sic] at nine. When Beatlemania exploded in America in early 1964 and "She Loves You" became a million-seller, Swan Records presented the disc jockey with a gold record award dedicated to "Dick Smith, America's First Believer." Buffalo's WGR played "She Loves You" in mid-December, charting the song at 50.

The day after the Beatles played the Royal Variety Performance on November 4, Brian Epstein headed to New York. A story in the October 22 Daily Mirror mentioned the trip and quoted him as saying he intended to "start spreading the gospel of the Beatles in the U.S.A." However, Brian's primary purpose of this trip was to promote another one of his artists, Billy J. Kramer. Brian desperately wanted a solo artist star in America and thought Kramer had the potential to develop into a successful cabaret crooner capable of headlining shows in New York and Las Vegas. Kramer's first U.K. single, "Do You Want To Know A Secret," was a number two hit. The follow-up, "Bad To Me," topped the charts. But Kramer's U.S. singles on Liberty Records were largely ignored, although Boston's WMEX charted "Do You Want To Know A Secret" at number 16 and KRLA at 44. Brian hoped that introducing Kramer to the folks at Liberty would prompt the label to push the singer's records and lead to stardom in the States.

The day before Brian's arrival, The New York Times ran a brief and largely unnoticed account of the enthusiastic response the Beatles had received upon their return to London from a tour of Sweden on October 31. The November 4 article stated that the screams of fans at the airport drowned out the whine of taxiing jets. No one suspected that just over three months later the Beatles would receive a similar response in New York. After all, no British music act had ever made a lasting impression in America. But Brian believed in his boys. And thus began Operation U.S.A.

One of Brian's key contacts in New York was entertainment attorney Walter Hofer, who had met Brian through Dick James, the Beatles music publisher and Hofer's friend and client. Although Hofer tried his best to help Brian, his attempt to set him up in a social setting with the right people was a miserable failure. Hofer recalled: "I had a cocktail party for Brian at my house [on Saturday, November 9], invited a slew of people, and very few showed up because who wants an English group and who's interested in an English manager?" Although Liberty's head of A&R, Dick Glasser, flew in from Los Angeles, the company's New York staff didn't show up for the party, disappointing Brian.

Brian's most significant meetings took place at the Delmonico Hotel with Ed Sullivan, host of a popular variety show that aired on Sunday nights on the CBS television network. The meeting was arranged by Peter Prichard, a London theatrical agent working for impresarios Lew and Leslie Grade. Prichard served as Sullivan's talent coordinator for British and European acts. During the summer of 1963, Prichard took Jack Babb, the talent coordinator for The Ed Sullivan Show, to see the Beatles on at least one occasion. Although the Beatles were developing a large following on the British concert circuit and were selling tons of records, the group had yet to become part of the national consciousness. Because no British pop act had ever achieved prolonged success in America, neither Prichard nor Babb gave any consideration to booking the Beatles on Sullivan's show. But that changed in October when Prichard learned that Brian Epstein was going to America. By then, the Beatles had played the British equivalent of The Ed Sullivan Show, Val Parnell's Sunday Night At The London Palladium (see page 32). Prichard called Brian and offered to negotiate a deal for the Beatles to appear on The Ed Sullivan Show. When Brian stated that he wanted to handle the negotiations himself, Prichard told Brian to call him when he got to New York so that he could set up a meeting with Ed Sullivan.

As Brian's plane was heading to New York, Prichard began working on his pitch for Sullivan to book the Beatles. He later called Sullivan to give him a report on the Royal Variety Performance, mentioning the tremendous response the Beatles had received and recommending the Beatles for Sullivan's show. Sullivan seemed interested, but needed an angle to promote the group, which, at that time, was virtually unknown in America. Prichard convinced Sullivan to give the group serious consideration by informing him that the Beatles were the first "long-haired boys" to be invited to appear before the Queen of England (although the Queen missed the show due to her pregnancy). Beatles lore has long held that Sullivan learned of the Beatles by being at London airport when the group returned from its tour of Sweden on October 31, 1963, and being impressed by enthusiastic response. However, that does not appear to be true. Sullivan normally did not leave town when his live show was in production, and no one can confirm Sullivan was in London or even out of New York at that time. The story was most likely a creation by Sullivan's PR team.

Brian met with Sullivan at his suite at the Delmonico Hotel on Monday, November 11. Sullivan was impressed with Brian's presentation and belief in the group. They agreed that the Beatles would appear on Sullivan's February 9, 1964 show live from New York, and the following Sunday on a special remote show broadcast live from the Deauville Hotel in Miami Beach. The second show, which featured Mitzi Gaynor, had already been scheduled. This would give the Beatles a bit of a vacation in sunny Florida. Brian met Sullivan again the next day for a dinner meeting at the Delmonico Hotel's restaurant with Bob Precht, Sullivan's son-in-law and the producer of the show, in attendance. Sullivan told Precht that Brian had a great group of youngsters who were going to be "really big." Although Sullivan often paid between $5,000 to $10,000 for big-name acts, he offered Brian only $3,500 for each show, but agreed to cover the group's transportation and lodging expenses. Precht suggested that in addition to the two live shows, the Beatles should tape a performance for later broadcast. The parties agreed on a payment of $3,000 for the taped segment, bringing the total for the three shows to $10,000.

Although some accounts state that Brian met with Capitol's Brown Meggs and secured a deal for Capitol to release the Beatles future recordings, that does not appear to be the case. Brian's appointment book has no reference to such a meeting, and Meggs did not have the authority to commit Capitol to sign the group.

As Brian headed back to London on November 14, he had much to think about. He had failed to get Liberty Records or anyone excited about Billy J. Kramer, but had booked the Beatles for three appearances on The Ed Sullivan Show. That alone made the trip a success. Operation U.S.A. was definitely gaining momentum. And proof that America was beginning to take notice of the Beatles was on the newsstands the week he headed home. The current issues of Time and Newsweek magazines contained articles in their music sections on the Beatles.

The November 15, 1963 issue of Time titled its story "The New Madness." Time observed: "Though Americans might find the Beatles achingly familiar (their songs consist mainly of 'Yeah!' screamed to the accompaniment of three guitars and a thunderous drum), they are apparently irresistible to the English." The group was described as a "wild rhythm-and-blues quartet" that had sold 2,500,000 records. The story reported that "crowds stampede for a chance to touch the hem of the collarless coats sported on stage by all four of them." Time informed the American public that: "Although no Beatle can read music, two of them dream up half the Beatles' repertory. The raucous, big-beat sound they achieve by electric amplification of all their instruments makes a Beatles performance slightly orgiastic. But the boys are the very spirit of good clean fun. They look like shaggy Peter Pan, with their mushroom haircuts and high white shirt collars, and on stage they clown around endlessly—twisting, cracking jokes, gently laughing at the riotous response they get from their audience. The precise nature of their charm remains mysterious even to their manager."

Newsweek's first Beatles story, titled "Beatlemania," appeared in its November 18, 1963 issue. The magazine reported that the Beatles "wear sheepdog bangs, collarless jackets, and drainpipe trousers" and that "all four sing ... and sing ... and sing." After stating that the "sound of their music is one of the most persistent noises heard over England since the air-raid sirens were dismantled," Newsweek described the music and performances as follows: "Beatle music is high-pitched, loud beyond reason, and stupefyingly repetitive. Like rock 'n' roll, to which it is closely allied, it is even more effective to watch than to hear. They prance, skip, and turn in circles; Beatles have even been known to kiss their guitars. The style, certainly, is their own. 'They don't gyrate like Elvis,' says one young girl. 'They stamp about and shake and, oh dearie me, they just send the joy out to you.'"

The following week (November 23) Billboard and Cash Box ran brief updates on the Beatles in their international sections. Billboard reported: "There's no stopping Britain's hottest disk, stage and TV attraction, the Beatles," noting that advanced orders for its fifth single, "I Want To Hold Your Hand," had topped 700,000. Cash Box told its readers: "The Beatles epidemic continues to sweep the country as more and more people are bitten by the bug. Latest victims, the notoriously staid audience at the Royal Command Performance." Music Vendor ran an extensive page 3 story on the Beatles, duplicating parts of the Time and Newsweek articles. Unaware of the previous records released on Vee-Jay and Swan, the article concluded with: "it is only a matter of time before an American diskery grabs this hot group and brings a little bit of stomping old Liverpool to swinging Tin Pan Alley. It's probably happened already."

On Saturday, November 16, the Beatles played a concert at the Bournemouth Winter Gardens. All three major American TV networks, CBS, NBC and ABC, filmed the boys in action, along with the screaming fans' reactions. Up until September 2, 1963, the network evening news programs ran for only 15 minutes. On that date, the 15-minute Walter Cronkite With The News was renamed The CBS Evening News With Walter Cronkite and expanded to 30 minutes. Mr. Cronkite used the occasion to interview President Kennedy. One week later, NBC's nightly news program, The Huntley-Brinkley Report, followed suit. These two rival programs battled for evening news supremacy. ABC kept its evening news show at 15 minutes until January 1967. The expanded format enabled CBS and NBC to add feature stories to their programs, which up until then were almost exclusively hard news. NBC ran its popular two-hour Today show in the 7:00 to 9:00 AM time slot. The program mixed news with interviews and features. By 1963, CBS had added its 30-minute CBS Morning News With Mike Wallace program to the 10:00 AM Eastern time slot. CBS normally re-ran feature stories from its morning news show on its expanded evening news program. In January 1975, ABC first broadcast its morning news show, which evolved into Good Morning America that November.

The November 22, 1963 British music weekly New Musical Express reported that the American TV crews who attended the Beatles Bournemouth concert were flabbergasted by what they saw. The CBS reporter, Josh Darsa, who was sent there by bureau reporter Alexander Kendrick, told NME's Tony Crawley: "I never thought a British audience could or would react in this way for anyone." Darsa stated that a story on the Beatles would probably run on a morning or evening news program, or both, the following week. William Sheehan of ABC found it "unbelievable and un-British." He thought that the presence of the other TV networks filming there would lead ABC to use its film "pronto." Based on these comments, Crawley wrote that the "three top U.S. TV-networks [were] racing against time, and each other, to be the first to feature Beatlemania on American television." He viewed this as the start of "The big break through to America for the Beatles." But that start would be delayed for about a month. Although ABC's London Bureau was excited about the Beatles, the network's New York office did not share this enthusiasm and did not even run a story on the Beatles in 1963. NBC ran a four-minute story on the Beatles filed by former London bureau chief Edwin Newman on the Monday, November 18 Huntley-Brinkley Report. A few days later, CBS ran its four-minute feature on the Beatles towards the end of its broadcast of The CBS Morning News With Mike Wallace.

Although the Beatles story would normally have been re-run approximately eight hours later on The CBS Evening News With Walter Cronkite, fate intervened. About two hours after Wallace went off the air on Friday, November 22, 1963, three shots rang out in Dallas, striking President Kennedy in the head and causing his death. CBS and the other networks went with non-stop coverage of the assassination, dropping all other news and feature stories.

Although much has been written about how the assassination of President Kennedy played a key role in the Beatles success in America, this connection has been blown out of proportion by those looking for an explanation as to why America's youngsters fell for the group. While the youth of America was initially despondent over the President's death, that did not cause Beatlemania to explode in America. The fact that they were British, had long hair and were cool was certainly a part of it, but the main reason Americans embraced the Beatles in 1964 is the same reason people still do today—the excitement and quality of the music. The Kennedy effect becomes quite tenuous when one looks beyond the United States. The Beatles were popular in Great Britain, Germany, France, Italy, Australia, Denmark, Sweden, the Netherlands, Canada, Japan and several other countries. None of these nations was suffering the trauma of having its head of state assassinated, yet the youth of these countries embraced the Beatles. Did the Beatles lift the spirits of American youngsters? No doubt, but it was not caused by the death of a president. However, as discussed below, the assassination may have indirectly contributed to the group's success in America.

The failure of Swan's "She Loves You" single to attract any attention in America prompted EMI to take back the U.S. rights to the Beatles from Transglobal in mid-October 1963. EMI believed that the facilities and resources of a large record company were needed to properly exploit the Beatles in America. If Capitol couldn't see the group's potential, perhaps Columbia Records would. But Columbia also had no interest. EMI sent Capitol a copy of the Beatles latest single, "I Want To Hold Your Hand," hoping that Capitol would finally agree to release a Beatles disc, but once again, Dave Dexter failed to hear the group's potential and recommended that Capitol pass on the Beatles for a fourth time. Brian Epstein was totally frustrated with Capitol's refusal to release the band's recordings, leading him to take matters into his own hands and no longer rely on EMI. He realized his best shot of getting his boys on Capitol was to take his cause to the president of the company, Alan Livingston.

In an interview with the author in 1999, Livingston recalled: "I'm sitting in my office one day and I got a call from London from a man named Brian Epstein, who I didn't know. I took the call. And he said, 'I am the personal manager of the Beatles and I don't understand why you won't release them.' And I said, 'well, frankly, Mr. Epstein, I haven't heard them.' And he said, 'Would you please listen and call me back.' And I said, 'OK,' and I called Dexter and said, 'Let me have some Beatles records.' He sent up a few and I listened. I liked them. I thought they were something different. I can't tell you in all honesty I knew how big they'd be, but I thought this is worth a shot. So I called Epstein back and said, 'OK, I'll put them out.' Smart man, Epstein, he said, 'Just a minute, I'm not gonna let you have them unless you spend $40,000…to promote their first single.' You didn't spend $40,000 to promote a single in those days, it was unheard of. For whatever reason, I said 'OK, we'll do it,' and the deal was made [in late November 1963]."

On December 4, Capitol issued a press release boldly stating: "Beatlemania, the totally unprecedented musical phenomenon that has turned England tops-turvey this past year will be spread to the United States in 1964. Alan W. Livingston, president of Capitol Records, Inc., announced today that the company has concluded negotiations with Electric & Musical Industries (EMI), Ltd., for exclusive U.S. rights to recordings by The Beatles, the sole cause of the mania. In making the announcement, Livingston said: 'With their popularity in England and the promotion we're going to put behind them here, I have every reason to believe The Beatles will be just as successful in the United States." Capitol's Director of Eastern Operation, Brown Meggs, and Publicity Director, Fred Martin, Jr., were tasked with putting together a massive publicity plan that became known as "the Beatles Campaign." The promotional tools included: a four-page tabloid newspaper titled "National Record News" that looked deceptively legitimate, but was entirely a clever Capitol concoction that was distributed in record stores and schools; "Be A BEATLE Booster!" buttons to be distributed in bulk to store clerks and disc jockeys; and "The BEATLES are coming!" stickers to be distributed en mass and placed "on any friendly surface." (These items are shown on the opposite page.) Capitol also prepared an eye-catching and informative two-page ad and easel-backed cardboard standee (shown on page 81) and an "extremely exciting motion display" (shown on page 89). Capitol set January 13, 1964, as the release date for the single "I Want To Hold Your Hand," with an album to follow in February. But that time-table was pushed forward by a series of events triggered by a decision made by a middle-aged news director/anchorman, Walter Cronkite.

Special BEATLES Issue
NATIONAL RECORD NEWS

"Beatlemania" SWEEPS U.S.

How It All Started

They wore black leather jackets, their hair was untidy and the only way one could tell them apart from characters in a Marlon Brando movie was that they had no motorcycles.

They were the Beatles, but no one knew it. In those days they called themselves a variety of things—The Quarrymen, Moon Dogs or The Moonshiners. It was early 1958, and they spent most of their time playing in the cellar of a friend's home in Liverpool for kicks.

CELLAR CLUB

If there was a turning

What Britain

The Beatlemania phenomenon that began in England last year and is now sweeping the United States, has created a wave of controversy so extensive that psychologists and sociologists are taking a hard clinical look at it. Most adults regard Beatlemania with horror, distaste, even fear and find it easy to blame the Beatles for what they, the adults, feel is a loss of taste and control among young people.

CORBETT SAYS

Anthony Corbett, an English psychologist, called the Beatles as having "a desperately need...

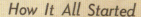

THE BEATLES, four young Englishmen, have become, in just one year, the...

The BEATLES are coming!

Newsweek
SEPTEMBER 23, 1963 25c

The TV News Battle

Walter Cronkite of CBS

On December 10, Cronkite thought it was once again appropriate to run feature stories on the evening news. The past few weeks had been dominated by the Kennedy assassination and other dark topics, so a light-hearted piece on a strange musical phenomenon taking place in England seemed an effective way to close the news broadcast. The four-minute story on Beatlemania showed the Beatles on stage in Bournemouth in front of screaming fans, reporter Alexander Kendrick at the London Beatles Fan Club and reporter Josh Darsa interviewing the group backstage. It also contained a music clip of "She Loves You." Shortly after the show ended, Cronkite got a call from an excited Ed Sullivan requesting: "Tell me more about those...bugs or whatever they call themselves." Cronkite had to check his program sheet for the Evening News broadcast to tell Sullivan that the group was called the Beatles. He added that he would query their guy in London, Alexander Kendrick, to call Sullivan about the group. The next day CBS issued a press release stating that the Beatles would be appearing twice on The Ed Sullivan Show in February.

Marsha Albert, a 15-year-old girl living in Silver Spring, Maryland, saw the Beatlemania story on the CBS Evening News with her family. Marsha liked what she saw and heard, prompting her to write a letter to her local DJ at WWDC. She mentioned the Beatles appearance on the CBS news and asked: "Why can't we have music like that in America?" Disc jockey Carroll James, who had also seen the story, arranged for a friend who was a stewardess with British Overseas Airways Corporation ("BOAC") to bring him a copy of the Beatles latest record, "I Want To Hold Your Hand." On December 17, James had Marsha come down to the station to introduce the song on his radio show. WWDC wisely taped the proceedings for posterity. After James introduces her to his listeners and asks her to introduce "something brand new, an exclusive, here at WWDC," Marsha says: "Ladies and gentlemen, for the first time on the air in the United States, here are the Beatles with "I Want To Hold Your Hand."

After the song ended, James requested that listeners write in to let him know what they thought of the Beatles. But most couldn't wait and began calling the station immediately. According to James, the station's switchboard lit up like a Christmas tree with eager listeners phoning in to praise the song. "I Want To Hold Your Hand" was immediately added to WWDC's playlist and placed in heavy rotation. When Capitol learned that WWDC was playing "I Want To Hold Your Hand" four weeks prior to its scheduled release date, it requested that the song be pulled off the air, but the station refused. Alan Livingston then called New York attorney Walter Hofer, who represented Brian Epstein, and directed Hofer get James to stop playing the record. Hofer called James and sent him a telegram demanding that WWDC "cease and desist" playing the song, but the disc jockey refused. According to Hofer, James told him, "Look, you can't stop me from playing it. The record is a hit. It's a major thing."

Hofer advised Livingston that Capitol would not be able to stop WWDC from playing the record. As Livingston believed this was an isolated situation that would not spread elsewhere, he decided to press a few thousand copies of "I Want To Hold Your Hand" to send to the D.C. area. This strategy might have worked had James not made a tape copy of the song for a disc jockey buddy of his in Chicago, who then played it on his show. Listeners in the Windy City also reacted favorably towards the song. When a St. Louis disc jockey with KXOK played a tape of the Beatles new song, his station was hit with tons of listener requests. With Christmas less than a week away, stations in three major markets were playing "I Want To Hold Your Hand." In addition, tapes of the song were circulating among the nation's disc jockeys. Capitol realized that the genie was out of the bottle and remembered that radio air play was essential for sales. Capitol's job was to get stations to play the Beatles so it made no sense to try to halt air play just because the record's scheduled release was weeks away. Although record companies traditionally did not issue new product during the holiday season, Capitol was beginning to realize that there was nothing traditional about the Beatles. The company pushed up the single's release date to the day after Christmas. Capitol also realized that its initial factory requisite of 200,000 units would be insufficient to meet demand. Word went out to Capitol's factories in Scranton and Los Angeles to step up production by having all pressing machines exclusively manufacture the Beatles 45. Capitol subcontracted with other companies, such as RCA and Decca, to press additional copies of the single. Wanting rockers on both sides, Capitol replaced the U.K. B-side "This Boy" with "I Saw Her Standing There."

"I Want To Hold Your Hand" was released by Capitol on December 26, 1963. Radio station WMCA in New York immediately began playing the song, with WABC and WINS quickly joining in. Kids and teenagers were all on holiday break from school, listening to the radio day and night. There were no video games, home computers or cell phones. No Internet. No Facebook, Instagram, Twitter, YouTube or TikTok. No iTunes or streaming services. To the youngsters of the era, AM radio was their primary form of entertainment. And being out of school gave them the opportunity to go to stores and to buy the record with recently received Christmas and Hanukkah money.

The single exploded up the charts in New York, debuting in WABC's December 31, 1963 survey at number 35 before moving to number one the next week on January 7, 1964. The disc first topped WMCA's survey a week later on January 15. The rest of the nation would soon follow suit with "I Want To Hold Your Hand" topping radio station surveys throughout the country.

All three music trade magazines reviewed "I Want To Hold Your Hand" in their January 4, 1964 issues. Billboard gave the single a Pop Spotlight Review (reserved for discs with the potential to be listed in the Top 50 of Billboard's Hot 100 chart). For the benefit of those who had yet to hear of the Beatles, the magazine stated: "This is the hot British group that has struck gold overseas." The A-side was described as "a driving rocker with surf on the Thames sound and strong vocal work from the group." The flip side was identified by name. Cash Box made the disc one of its Picks of the Week, informing readers: "The Beatles, the boys behind the expression 'Beatlemania,' which is sweeping England and currently receiving endless publicity, bow [debut] on Capitol with the deck that's already #1 in Great Britain." The top side was called "an infectious twist-like thumper that could spread like wildfire here." The engaging flip side contained "more hard-hitting teen stuff." The review ended with: "Boys'll be on up-coming Jack Paar and Ed Sullivan TV stints." Music Vendor listed the single as one of its "Sure Bets," telling readers: "The long-awaited American debut of one of the world's hottest acts. Listen yourself to this amazing sound; it could be #1 in a few weeks." Although Music Vendor had written several articles on the Beatles starting in late November 1963, the reviewer was not aware that Vee-Jay and Swan had already released a total of three singles by the group. However, his prediction that "I Want To Hold Your Hand" could top the charts in a few weeks was spot on.

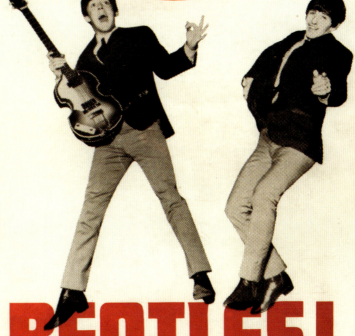

MEET THE BEATLES!

BRITAIN'S "BEATLEMANIA" HAS SPREAD TO AMERICA! On TV: Jack Paar Show (NBC-TV)! Ed Sullivan Show (CBS-TV)! Walter Cronkite News (CBS-TV)! Huntley-Brinkley News (NBC-TV)! Featured in TIME, LIFE, NEWSWEEK & newspapers everywhere! Now <u>hear</u> the performances that have made THE BEATLES the most exciting vocal group in English History!

FIRST CAPITOL SINGLE:
I WANT TO HOLD YOUR HAND
b/w I SAW HER STANDING THERE

FIRST CAPITOL ALBUM:
MEET THE BEATLES!

In Billboard, "I Want To Hold Your Hand" debuted at number 45 on January 18, 1964, before shooting up to three in its second week and topping the Hot 100 chart in its third week on February 1, replacing Bobby Vinton's "There! I've Said It Again" and blocking Lesley Gore's "You Don't Own Me" from hitting number one. The song held down the top spot for seven weeks before giving way to "She Loves You." Things happened even faster in Cash Box, with the song entering the Top 100 at number 80 on January 11 before moving up to 43 the following week, and giving the Beatles their first American number one on January 25. The tune topped the chart for eight weeks before being passed by "She Loves You." The Capitol single entered the Music Vendor Top 100 Pop chart at number 34 on January 18 and, as anticipated by the magazine's January 4 review, became the number one single a week later on January 25. "I Want To Hold Your Hand" remained at the top for nine weeks before falling behind "She Loves You" and "Twist And Shout."

Cash Box published a weekly Radioactive survey of key radio stations in all important markets throughout America to determine, by percentage of those reporting stations, which releases were being added to their playlists for the first time. The survey kept a cumulative total to show the degree of concentration. The January 11, 1964 Cash Box reported that as of January 2, 16% of its reporting stations had added "I Want To Hold Your Hand" to their playlists. The following week the song was added by 43% of the stations, bringing the total to 59%. As of January 16, another 39% had joined in, bringing the total percentage of reporting stations playing Capitol's Beatles single up to 98%.

The flip-side, "I Saw Her Standing There," also received considerable air play. Cash Box's Radioactive chart indicated that 17% of its reporting stations added the song during the week ending January 29. The song was charted by Billboard for 11 weeks, peaking at 14, Music Vendor for 7 weeks, peaking at 29, and Cash Box for one week at 100.

Capitol's first Beatles release was an instant best seller with over 250,000 copies sold in its first three days of release. By January 10, 1964, the 45 had sold over 1,000,000 units, enabling Capitol to obtain RIAA (Record Industry Association of America) certification in time to present the band with a gold record award one month later on February 10. By mid-January, the single was selling 10,000 copies an hour in New York City. The March 28, 1964 Billboard reported Capitol's claim that the record had sold 3,400,000 units. The record went on to sell over 5,000,000 copies.

In early 1964, Swan reissued its "She Loves You" single in an attractive picture sleeve (shown on page 161). Swan's initial 1963 sales of the Beatles single (estimated at about 1,000 units) were so lackluster that the company agreed, when asked by Transglobal, to delete the rider to its licensing agreement that would have given Swan the right to license an additional Beatles single if Swan sold 50,000 copies of "She Loves You" within four months of its release. The agreement to delete the rider was signed by Swan on November 27. Things were different in 1964. By January 10, Swan had orders of 100,000 units. The song entered the Billboard Hot 100 at 69 on January 25. It raced to the number two slot behind "I Want To Hold Your Hand" on February 22 and spent its first of two weeks at number one on March 21. Billboard charted the single for 15 weeks. Cash Box charted "She Loves You" for 16 weeks, including two weeks at number one and four weeks at number two. Its Radioactive chart showed that 50% of its reporting stations added the song by February 1, with an additional 40% the next week to bring its total to 90%. Music Vendor charted the single for 17 weeks, including one week at the top and five weeks at number two. "She Loves You" sold over 2,500,000 copies, but because Swan did not request RIAA certification, the RIAA did not award gold record status. Instead, Swan owners Bernie Binnick and Tony Mammarella (far right in picture below) presented the Beatles with an in-house gold record award at Carnegie Hall on February 12, 1964. The reissued single had black labels.

Like Swan, Vee-Jay took notice of Capitol's publicity campaign for the Beatles and realized its Beatles masters could be converted into gold. Although Transglobal had unilaterally terminated its licensing agreement with Vee-Jay for master recordings of Frank Ifield and the Beatles, Vee-Jay was advised by counsel it could continue to press records with previously issued recordings. For its next Beatles single, Vee-Jay was taking no chances. VJ 581, released in early 1964, combined the A-sides from Vee-Jay's first two Beatles records. While "Please Please Me" was largely ignored when first issued in February 1963, it was an entirely different story the second time around. Vee-Jay shipped 55,000 units to distributors during the first 15 days of January. But then Capitol sued Vee-Jay and obtained a temporary injunction prohibiting Vee-Jay from manufacturing or distributing Beatles recordings. Three different lawsuits would work their way through state and federal courts in Chicago and New York until Vee-Jay and Capitol entered into a settlement agreement on April 1, 1964. Prior to that time, the injunction against Vee-Jay would be in force and set aside several times, disrupting Vee-Jay's ability to manufacture and sell Beatles records. The full story of these lawsuits can be found in the author's books *The Beatles Records on Vee-Jay* and *The Beatles Are Coming!*

"Please Please Me" entered the Billboard Hot 100 on February 1 at number 68. Despite distribution issues resulting from the litigation, the single worked its way into the top ten at number six on February 29. Two weeks later, on March 14, "Please Please Me" reached the number three spot, blocked from the top by "I Want To Hold Your Hand" and "She Loves You." Billboard charted the song for 13 weeks, including seven in the top ten. "Please Please Me" performed similarly in the other trades, peaking at three, with Cash Box charting the song for 14 weeks, including seven in the top ten, and Music Vendor/Record World reporting the song for 12 weeks, including six in the top ten.

Vee-Jay's strategy of splitting its two singles and pairing "Please Please Me" and "From Me To You" on the same disc backfired as the latter song got lost in the slew of Beatles songs racing up the charts in early 1964. "From Me To You" stalled at number 41 in Billboard during its six-week run, and peaked at number 46 in both Cash Box (charting nine weeks) and Music Vendor (charting five weeks). Had the song been separately released as an A-side after the chart dominance of "I Want To Hold Your Hand," "She Loves You" and "Please Please Me" had subsided, it surely would have topped the charts like "Love Me Do" did in May 1964.

Realizing the visual appeal of the Beatles, Vee-Jay prepared a picture sleeve (shown on page 162) to further entice fans into buying the record. Vee-Jay sold over 1,185,000 copies of VJ 581 in 1964. The record was certified gold and platinum by the RIAA fifty years later on July 24, 2014, after its CPA firm audited Vee-Jay sales ledgers presented to the RIAA's CPA by the author.

Vee-Jay packaged a limited number of the promotional copies of the single in a special title sleeve (shown on page 163). The sleeve proudly informs disc jockeys that "Please Please Me" was "The Record That Started Beatlemania." While this may be a bit of an overstatement, the song was the Beatles first big hit in the U.K., topping all but one of the major British charts. The sleeve describes the group as "England's Sensations" and states that the group just did The Jack Paar Show on January 3, 1964. On that program, host Jack Parr showed a film clip obtained from the BBC of the Beatles performing "She Loves You," the song that really started Beatlemania in the U.K. The sleeve also references the group's upcoming February 9 and February 16, 1964 live appearances on The Ed Sullivan Show. (At the time the sleeve was prepared in early January 1964, Sullivan had not yet decided on when he would broadcast the Beatles third performance on his show, which was to be taped in New York after the dress rehearsal.) Vee-Jay also reminds disc jockeys that the Beatles were featured in three prestigious magazines: Time [November 15, 1963]; Newsweek [November 18, 1963]; and Life [December 13, 1963]. These references to the spread of Beatlemania in America give this special title sleeve historical importance. The sleeve's significance, combined with its limited production, has made this one of the most sought after and valuable Beatles 45 sleeves.

Although Vee-Jay had intended on issuing a Beatles LP in the summer of 1963 titled *Introducing The Beatles*, the album was cancelled when the company encountered financial difficulties. Prior to the disc's cancellation, Vee-Jay had taken several steps towards the album's release, including the preparation of mono and stereo masters, the manufacture of the metal parts to press the vinyl discs, the shipping of the metal parts to three regional pressing plants, the preparation of the film to print the front cover slicks and the printing of 6,000 front cover slicks. Based on the 1963 documents regarding the album, Vee-Jay was expecting sales of under 6,000 units for its Beatles LP, which made sense since the group's "Please Please Me" single had only sold 5,650 copies at that time.

Although Vee-Jay had Universal Recording Corporation cut a reference acetate duplicating the 14-track Parlophone *Please Please Me* LP, the company decided to trim the LP down to the American standard of 12 songs to save on royalty payments (see page 233). As "Please Please Me" and "Ask Me Why" had already appeared on a Vee-Jay single that was not a hit, Vee-Jay dropped those songs from the lineup. The album did include the songs on the Beatles first U.K. single, "Love Me Do" and "P.S. I Love You," which was not issued in the United States. The running order of the LP was left the same except for the deletion of the two songs.

Vee-Jay corporate minutes from a January 7, 1964 Board of Directors meeting indicate that the label knew its legal rights to release the album were questionable (because Vee-Jay had failed to exercise its right of first refusal by releasing the album within 30 days of receipt of the master recordings). However, Vee-Jay's cash flow problems necessitated taking the calculated risk of releasing Beatles recordings even if the company had to pay in a year or two if it lost its legal battles with Capitol. The album was released three days later on Friday, January 10, 1964. Invoice summary sheets indicate that 79,169 mono and 2,202 stereo copies of *Introducing The Beatles* were shipped to distributors during the first 15 days of January before Capitol obtained its injunction prohibiting Vee-Jay from manufacturing or distributing Beatles records. Another lawsuit, brought by Capitol's music publishing company, Beechwood Music, Inc., which owned the U.S. publishing for "Love Me Do" and "P.S. I Love You," resulted in a court order prohibiting Vee-Jay from issuing those songs. To get around that issue, Vee-Jay reconfigured the album by dropping the songs and replacing them with "Please Please Me" and "Ask Me Why."

Cash Box and Billboard reviewed *Introducing The Beatles* in their February 1 issues. Cash Box observed: "All America has succumbed to Beatlemania and this package of vocal-instrumental stylings by England's number one rock group on Vee Jay is sure to get maximum sales and deejay activity." The magazine added that "the boys with the wagging wigs lash out with forceful treatments of 'I Saw Here Standing There,' 'Chains' and 'Baby It's You' and nine others geared for top teen approval." Distributors and record dealers were told to "Watch it move out." Billboard noted that no matter the record label, the Beatles "are about the hottest thing around the pop scene these days." The LP was "another strong example of their exciting driving sound" and one that "can do its share of business." The magazine listed the same tracks as Cash Box plus "Twist And Shout."

Introducing The Beatles debuted in the Billboard Top LP's chart on February 8 at number 59. Billboard charted the album for 49 weeks, including 15 weeks in the top ten and nine weeks at number two, unable to pass Capitol's *Meet The Beatles!* LP. Cash Box charted the Vee-Jay LP for 34 weeks, including 14 in the top ten and seven at its peak position of number two. Music Vendor/Record World charted the album for just over 30 weeks, including 11 weeks in the top ten and five weeks at number two. On March 18, Music Vendor became the only one of the big three trade magazines to chart *Introducing The Beatles* at number one. Based on surviving Vee-Jay documents, the album had net sales of approximately 1,304,316 mono and 41,910 stereo units. The album was certified gold and platinum by the RIAA on July 24, 2014, based on documents provided by the author. The stereo album was heavily counterfeited in the late sixties and seventies. As a result, fake copies of the record significantly outnumber the genuine 1964 LP.

After planning its first Beatles single, Capitol was faced with the task of programming its own album introducing the Beatles to America. Although Dave Dexter had turned down the Beatles four times, it was his job as head of foreign product to program the LP. Dexter based Capitol's first Beatles album on the group's second and current British LP, *With The Beatles*, but with a few alterations. While Capitol wisely decided to use the same striking front cover photo, the company gave the picture a bluish tint and changed the name of the album to *Meet The Beatles!* For economic reasons, the disc would only have 12 tracks, so some songs on the U.K. album would be deleted from the lineup.

Dexter, following the conventional wisdom in America that hit singles make hit albums, opened the album with both sides of the group's Capitol single, "I Want To Hold Your Hand" and "I Saw Her Standing There," even though neither was on *With The Beatles* and the latter had been on the group's first LP, *Please Please Me*. The next song is "This Boy," the B-side to the U.K. single "I Want To Hold Your Hand." Following the opening rockers with "This Boy" was brilliant programming, as the ballad effectively slows down the pace of the album and showcases the beautiful vocal harmonies of John, Paul and George. The last three songs on the first side are the first three songs from Side One of *With The Beatles*, "It Won't Be Long," "All I've Got To Do" and "All My Loving." Side Two opens with the next three songs from the British LP, namely George Harrison's "Don't Bother Me," Lennon-McCartney's "Little Child" and the Peggy Lee arrangement of the Broadway show tune "Till There Was You." The final three songs are the remaining Lennon-McCartney originals from the British disc, "Hold Me Tight," "I Wanna Be Your Man" and "Not A Second Time." It was the perfect album to introduce the Beatles to America. With one exception, all of the album's songs were written by members of the group, enabling Capitol to exploit the band's songwriting abilities. The one cover tune, "Till There Was You," was a song even parents could enjoy. As for the five covers of American songs dropped from *With The Beatles,* they would be issued by Capitol three months later on *The Beatles' Second Album*.

Capitol planned on issuing its first Beatles album in mid-February, but moved the release date up to January 20 when it decided to rush release its single. However, the January 18 Billboard reported that by January 10, Alan Livingston ordered the immediate release of the its Beatles LP due to "pressure too great for us to hold back any longer." Liberty Music advertised in the Sunday, January 12, New York Times that *Meet The Beatles!* was available for purchase.

The three trade magazines reviewed *Meet The Beatles!* in their January 25 issues. Billboard praised the group and the record: "The Beatles are the hottest act to hit the disk business in years. Their single 'I Want To Hold Your Hand' is already a smash in two weeks, and this album, released just three weeks before their first visit to America for two appearances on the Ed Sullivan show, should reap plenty of big action. The hit single is here along with 'I Saw Her Standing There,' 'It Won't Be Long,' 'This Boy' and others. Set should move fast." Cash Box wrote that the Beatles, riding high with their current single, "unleash their potent vocal and instrumental talents full-blast" on their premier U.S. album. The magazine added that the "swingin' British group turn in outstanding renditions of 'This Boy,' 'All My Loving,' 'Little Child,' and their current chart-rider," and predicted: "Disk should pull loads of loot." Music Vendor doubled-up on its coverage. First, the magazine designated the disc an "ALBUM HIT," showing its cover and adding: "After only one week of selling like a single, the LP from the phenomenal British group shows up at 34. Further sales are indicated." The LP was separately reviewed under the "Sure Bets" designation: "Good Grief! Looks like the bug (natch!) has bitten and has taken a good hold over here, too. By this time a good many people have heard and bought 'I Want To Hold Your Hand' (It's #1 this week) and perhaps an equal number will go after this album. Sort of reflex buying. Some people say it's their hair (see the album cover), others their sound, but whatever it is, The Beatles have got it. Other numbers are 'This Boy,' 'All I've Got To Do,' 'All My Loving,' 'Little Child' and 'I Wanna Be Your Man.' Zounds, what sounds!" AM radio, normally limited to singles, broke protocol and played tracks from the LP.

Meet The Beatles! debuted at number 92 in the Billboard Top LP's chart (then top 150 albums) on February 1, 1964. Two weeks later the album replaced *The Singing Nun* at the top, where it remained for 11 weeks before being replaced by *The Beatles' Second Album*. Billboard charted the album for 71 weeks, including 17 in the top five and 21 in the top ten. Cash Box published both Monaural (top 100 albums) and Stereo (top 50 albums) charts in 1964. *Meet The Beatles!* topped the Monaural list for 11 of its 41 weeks on the chart and the Stereo for five of its 28 weeks. The album topped the Music Vendor/Record World charts (top 100 albums) for ten of its 38 weeks on the chart. Capitol initially hoped to sell 250,000 copies of its Beatles album. At the time, rock albums were not normally big sellers. A few of Elvis Presley's albums had sold in excess of a million units, but those were either Christmas, greatest hits, sacred or movie soundtrack LPs. Neither of the King's first two rock 'n' roll albums hit sales of a million.

But *Meet The Beatles!* exceeded all expectations. From the start, it was selling like a single, reaching sales of 400,000 units one week after its official release date of January 20. By the time the Beatles stepped off the plane in America, the LP had easily met the benchmark for an RIAA gold record award for an album with sales of over $1,000,000. On February 10, 1964, Alan Livingston, the president of the company that turned the Beatles down four times, presented the group with RIAA-certified gold record awards for "I Want To Hold Your Hand" and *Meet The Beatles!* at the Plaza Hotel in New York. The March 28, 1964 Billboard reported sales for "I Want To Hold Your Hand" at 3,400,000 units and *Meet The Beatles!* at 3,650,000. Incredibly, the album was outselling Capitol's Beatles single. The RIAA later certified sales of five million units, making the album 5x Multi-Platinum.

"The Beatles are Coming!" became "The Beatles are Here!" on February 7, 1964, one year to the day that Vee-Jay released the group's first American single, "Please Please Me," to general indifference. One year later, the Beatles were greeted by over 3,000 teenagers who had skipped school to welcome their heroes as they deplaned from Pan American Airways Flight 101, a Boeing 707 named Clipper Defiance. Film of the group's arrival was broadcast on The CBS Evening News With Walter Cronkite. On Sunday, February 9, the Beatles debut appearance on The Ed Sullivan Show attracted an audience of 73 million. That Monday, the Beatles held a press conference, received gold record awards for their Capitol single and album and attended a cocktail party for the press at the Plaza Hotel. On Tuesday, the group took the train to the nation's capital and played their first concert in America at the Washington Coliseum in front of over 8,000 screaming fans. After returning to New York City by train the following day, the Beatles played two sold-out shows at Carnegie Hall. The next day they flew to Miami for some vacation time and to appear again on The Ed Sullivan Show, this time broadcast live from the Deauville Hotel in Miami Beach on February 16.

Although the death of President Kennedy did not directly cause Beatlemania to explode in America, it played an indirect role. By the end of 1963, the press had grown weary of reporting on the assassination and other depressing events. The Beatles provided a break from the somber news. In the February 11, 1964 New York Daily News, Anthony Burton observed: "It's a relief from Cyprus and Malaysia and Viet Nam and racial demonstrations and Khrushchev. Beset by troubles all around the globe, America has turned to the four young men with the ridiculous haircuts for a bit of light entertainment." By keeping the Beatles in the news, the press helped fuel Beatlemania.

During his November stay in New York, Brian hired independent promotion man Bud Hellawell to handle the American promotion of his artists. Hellawell played an unsung but important role in promoting the Beatles and keeping Brian informed of the excitement generated by the Beatles. He sent disc jockeys a special packet of promotion materials that included the singles "I Want To Hold Your Hand," "She Loves You" and "Please Please Me," encouraging stations to play all three songs. This contributed to the trio of songs topping the charts in several cities. After running into Sid Bernstein in a New York City deli and being told by Sid of his interest in the Beatles, Hellawell arranged for Brian to call Sid, which led to Sid booking the Beatles to perform at Carnegie Hall, giving the group added credibility.

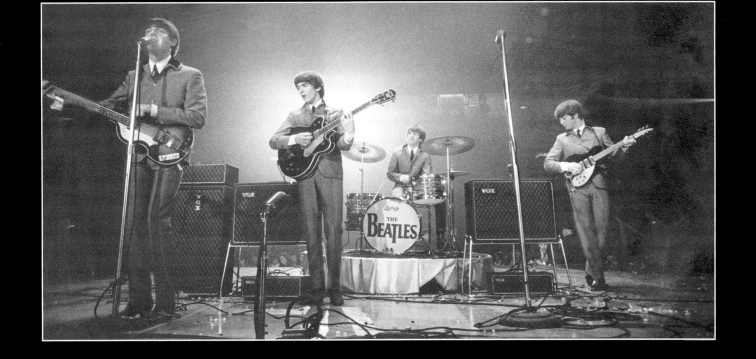

On February 21, the Beatles flew back to New York for their return to London. For this flight, Pan Am temporarily changed the name of Clipper Defiance to Clipper Beatles; however, "defiance" accurately described what had transpired. The Beatles had defied their doubters and history by becoming the first British recording artists to conquer America. They were aided by a fortuitous series of events, starting in late summer 1963 when the CBS television network decided to expand its evening news program from 15 to 30 minutes, which enabled Walter Cronkite to run a feature story on the Beatles on December 10, which was seen by 15-year-old Marsha Albert, who wrote to WWDC, whose DJ Carroll James obtained and played a British pressing of "I Want To Hold Your Hand" on December 17, which led to an enthusiastic response that forced Capitol to push up the release date of the single to the day after Christmas, which generated saturation radio air play and massive record sales that started Beatlemania in America. In addition to "I Want To Hold Your Hand," disc jockeys across America began playing Swan's reissued "She Loves You" disc and Vee-Jay's reconfigured "Please Please Me" single. Americans flocked to the record stores not only to buy the singles, but also to purchase the albums *Meet The Beatles!* and *Introducing The Beatles*. By the time of their arrival in America, the Beatles were already a national sensation. The Ed Sullivan Show provided the exclamation point to **BEATLEMANIA!**

Beatlemania! Invades Canada
by Piers Hemmingsen

Canada's membership in the British Commonwealth was an important factor in the country succumbing to the music of the Beatles months before the U.S. did. Canadian music fans could read about the latest pop artists via imported copies of British music weeklies such as Melody Maker and New Musical Express ("NME"). In addition, Capitol Records of Canada began releasing Beatles singles from the start, albeit with delayed release dates.

A few copies of the Beatles first U.K. single, "Love Me Do," arrived in Canada prior to the disc's Canadian release. Winnipeg radio station CKY played the Beatles single on its Sunday morning program Music From Around The World, most likely on November 11, 1962. Ray Sonin, a Londoner who previously wrote for Melody Maker and NME, emigrated to Canada in 1957. He began hosting a Saturday radio program on Toronto's CFRB, Calling All Britons. Sonin obtained a copy of "Love Me Do" and broadcast the song on either December 8 or 15, 1962. George Harrison's sister, Louise, who was then living in Canada, received a copy of the single as a Christmas present from her mother.

Paul White, national promotion manager for Capitol of Canada, began releasing pop singles by EMI artists in early 1962. In January 1963, he received another stack of singles from EMI. According to White: "One evening, as I was getting bored again listening to all these 45s, 'Love Me Do' slipped out of its sleeve and plonked onto the turntable. I thought, 'My God, that's different!' I thought it was different because, although the guys were definitely singing a simple lyric, they seemed to be happy doing it, compared to the guys on the other 50 records I'd heard that week. So...I thought, 'I've definitely got to release this record.'" White did not obtain the master tape, but rather had the songs dubbed from the U.K. single for release as Capitol of Canada 72076 on February 18, 1963. He praised the single in Capitol's weekly promotional flyer, The Sizzle Sheet, dated February 22, 1963: "Give this disc a couple of spins and you'll be hooked! This is an English record and a recent top 20 disc over there. Don't neglect this side!"

THE SIZZLE SHEET
FAST TALK ABOUT HOT Capitol Records SINGLES

FROM THE DESK OF Paul White   NO: 21   WEEK ENDING FEBRUARY 22nd, 1963

CAPITOL SINGLES ARE THE HIT SINGLES!

We've a big list of HOT PROSPECTS this week, but first let me keep you abreast of our current established hits. The following records are on almost ALL charts:-

1. YOU'RE THE REASON/Bobby Darin/4897
2. GREENBACK DOLLAR/The Kingston Trio/4898
3. LET'S TALK ABOUT LOVE/KEEP AWAY FROM OTHER GIRLS/Helen Shapiro/72062
4. SING A LITTLE SONG OF HEARTACHE/Rose Maddox/4845

THESE ARE THE NEXT SMASH HITS!
****

NOTHING GOES UP/NAT COLE/4919 -- This seems to be the side, and initial reaction is tremendous. Already a housewives' favourite.

THE WAYWARD WIND/FRANK IFIELD/72077 -- Dealers in Canada seem to be following the pattern set in England. They are ordering stock in quantity and the disc has only just been released. This is going to be No. 3 for Frank!

ETERNALLY/THE CHANTELS/72078 -- Oh Boy -- This R & B side just has to score! The hit-making group have come up with their best effort to date -- it's headed right for the top!

LOVE ME DO/THE BEATLES/72076 -- Give this side a couple of spins and you'll be hooked! This is an English record and a recent top 20 disc over there. Don't neglect this side!

SUN ARISE/ROLF HARRIS/72059 -- Action a-plenty for the Australian hit-maker. Big in the States -- a real chart item!

I WILL FOLLOW YOU/FRANCK POURCEL/4916 -- What more can I say? This side (under the title "Chariot") is currently No. 3 in Italy and France. It's been proven in two countries -- next stop -- a high place on Canadian charts.

LAUGH AND THE WORLD LAUGHS WITH YOU/JACK SCOTT/4903 -- Hefty action for Jack Scott in Manitoba -- the rest of you are missing out here -- it's the best Jack has done for Capitol. Why not re-audition???

JANIE/DANNY COUGHLAN/72068 -- This Canadian artist is starting to break through in Ontario. Chart action with CFPL-LONDON, CKLB-OSHAWA is just the start. If you give this CANADIAN artist the play he deserves you'll find your station has a hit on your charts!!!

There they are 8 .... I repeat 8 - fabulous reasons why Capitol Records are setting the pace in 1963 with singles. You'll be hearing more from me about these discs as they c-r-a-s-h onto the surveys.

White continued hyping the single in subsequent editions of The Sizzle Sheet. The March 1 Sizzle Sheet claimed that the Beatles disc was starting to gain sales attention. The next week he listed "Love Me Do" as one of the "Choice Up-And-Coming Sure Shots." In the March 15 Sizzle Sheet, he included the single as one of the "Hot Singles To Watch--And Play." White promoted the single because he "liked the group's fresh new sound." Sandy Gardiner reviewed the record in the March 2 Ottawa Journal: "Another British group sure to crawl into the charts here with their debut disc are **The Beatles**, John, Paul, George and Ringo are their names, 'Love Me Do' the beat number, and it ranks a chart place." Despite White's efforts and Gardiner's praise and prediction, most Canadian disc jockeys ignored the disc. A rare exception was Montreal's CFMB, whose program director added "Love Me Do" shortly after its release. The single debuted at number 42 in the station's February 27 Collegiate 63 Easy Listening Survey and charted for two more weeks with a peak at 40. The record also received a few spins on CFPL in London, Ontario. Without air play, the disc was doomed, reaching sales of about 170 units of the 1,000 copies pressed.

Paul White kept his eyes on the British music magazines throughout 1963 and noticed that the Beatles second Parlophone single, "Please Please Me," was a Top Five hit by mid-March 1963. White scheduled an April 1 release for the disc as Capitol of Canada 72090, once again having the songs dubbed from the British single and mastered at RCA Victor's Toronto studios. As was the case with the prior Beatles disc, White had about 1,000 copies pressed at RCA's Smiths Falls, Ontario pressing plant. The April 5 Sizzle Sheet touted the new single, informing readers that "Please Please Me" was now number one in England and that a few Canadian stations were reporting "great listener reaction." After adding that the song was a "Pick Hit" with CKOC in Hamilton and a "Wax to Watch" on the Dick Williams show on CFPL in London, Ontario, he alerted disc jockeys: "Don't lose sight on this one." The following week's Sizzle Sheet stated that CFPL listed the song at 40 with "good teen reaction." The single did even better in the Silver Dollar Survey issued by CFGP in Grand Prairie, debuting at number 34 in the April 20 chart and moving up to 27 the following week. Despite the initial positive reaction to "Please Please Me," the Beatles second single was another disappointment. White joked that the disc "became a zinc record and sold about 180 copies," though actual sales may have approached 500 units. Because both Beatles singles sold poorly, Capitol of Canada gave little to no consideration towards issuing the group's debut album, *Please Please Me*.

That, however, did not discourage White from releasing the Beatles third single, "From Me To You," as Capitol of Canada 72101 on June 17, 1963. He praised the disc and the group in the June 21 Sizzle Sheet, reporting that the record had topped the British charts, telling readers: "This group HAS IT and this disc could be a No. 1 in Canada too!" Oddly enough, competition from Del Shannon's cover version of "From Me To You" on Quality 1545 may have helped the record's sales. In the July 5 Sizzle Sheet, White told disc jockeys: "We're having a battle with Del Shannon but so far it's anybody's hit." Radio stations in Winnipeg, Calgary and Vancouver pitted the Beatles own version of "From Me To You" against Del Shannon's cover version in "battle of the bands" contests during early evening programming when young listeners were supposed to be doing their school homework. Disc jockeys asked the kids to call in to the station and vote for their favorite version. Del Shannon had the edge given his established track record with several prior Canadian hits. Winnipeg's CKY charted both versions of the song for 12 consecutive weeks. It was truly a battle. July Sizzle Sheets listed stations that were playing the Beatles disc, with CKDH in Amherst, Nova Scotia reporting the Beatles disc at number nine and CJQC in Quebec at eight. To ensure availability in the competition with the Shannon disc, Capitol pressed a second run of 1,000 copies. White encouraged disc jockeys to go with the Beatles in the August 2 Sizzle Sheet: "Sales are satisfactory but without more chart listings, we could lose out to Del Shannon. The Beatles are worth the spins--and they'll make it big in Canada yet!" His bold prediction in early August would come true before the end of the year, but "From Me To You" would not be the record to break the Beatles in Canada. Sales during the summer of 1963 were approximately 500 units. White also issued "How Do You Do It" by Gerry and the Pacemakers and "Do You Want To Know A Secret" by Billy J. Kramer.

Although there were pockets of early bird Canadian Beatles fans in Canada in 1963, centered primarily in Montreal, the Upper Ottawa Valley, Toronto and London, Ontario, Capitol of Canada was disappointed by the poor sales for the first three Beatles singles. According to White: "The president of the company finally said to me, 'Why are you releasing these records? They're all stiffs!' I said, 'Quite frankly, I like them. This group is dynamite, plus they're selling zillions in England and they can't all be wrong.' He said, 'I'll give you one more chance, but then get on something different.'"

When "She Loves You" rocketed to number one on the British charts two weeks after its release in August 1963, Paul White believed that the record could do the same in Canada. He had the songs from the new Parlophone single dubbed and mastered for release as Capitol of Canada 72125, once again playing it safe with a press run of about 1,000 singles. Realizing he was out on a limb with his Canadian bosses by releasing another disc by a group that had three strikes, White's Sizzle Sheet for September 13 boldly declared: "FLASH...Next week we're rushing you the new single by THE BEATLES..."SHE LOVES YOU"--Why RUSH???...Because it's No. 1 in the U.K. after TWO WEEKS..." The new Beatles single was in stores during the week of September 16, making it the first Beatles single to be issued in Canada within a month of its British release. White continued to push the Beatles in the September 20 Sizzle Sheet, with an extensive paragraph on the group and a request to "give this record the VIP treatment it deserves."

Despite White's efforts, it took a few months for "She Loves You" to catch on. However, a few Ontario stations were early birds in charting the song. Oshawa's CKLB charted the single at number 26 on its September 27 survey. The record debuted at 50 on the October 22 survey of CKWS in Kingston and moved up to 34 the next week. When White realized that the initial pressing of "She Loves You" would soon sell out, he arranged for EMI to send a tape of the single to Capitol's Canadian offices. Subsequent pressings of the disc were made from this tape. By mid-December, CFPL reported "She Loves You" at number one. The single soon worked its way up to the top of Toronto's CHUM Hit Parade, charting for 22 weeks. By the end of February 1964, Capitol had shipped 150,000 copies of the single. It would sell about 250,000 units. White proudly recalled: "'She Loves You' landed in every major Canadian record chart, becoming a huge seller, and taking the three previous releases along with it, so all four hit the charts."

Capitol sent 5" x 7" promo cards of the Beatles, identified as "Exclusive Capitol Recording Stars," to DJs along with the 2nd pressing of "From Me To You." The company later prepared an 8" x 10" glossy photo version for DJs, the press and fans.

After "She Loves You" began showing signs of success, White lobbied Capitol to release the group's second LP, *With The Beatles*. Based on a November 9 Ottawa Journal article by Sandy Gardiner (the opening of which was placed on a Capitol promotional card), White retitled the LP *Beatlemania! With The Beatles*. He altered the front cover by adding enthusiastic quotes about the group from Gardiner, Alan Harvey and Time and Newsweek magazines. The November 22 Sizzle Sheet boldly stated "'Beatlemania' Invades Canada," with White adding: "BE WARNED--"BEATLEMANIA IS GOING TO TAKE OVER CANADA in the same way it captured Great Britain and Europe." He explained that stations were airing "She Loves You" and that newspaper and magazine coverage had created such a demand for Beatles material that Capitol contacted EMI on Monday, November 17, and quickly received permission to release the Beatles new LP. The jacket was ready and discs were being pressed for a Friday, November 22, release (although the LP would not appear in most stores until the following Monday, November 25). Capitol was rush-releasing two tunes from the album, "Roll Over Beethoven" and "Please Mister Postman," on a single (to help promote the LP). White told disc jockeys "you ain't heard nothing yet!," warning them not to fall behind exploiting the Beatles in their area.

Capitol issued its *Beatlemania!* LP in mono only as Capitol of Canada T6051. It ran an ad in the November 26 Toronto Telegra proclaiming "Beatlemania Sweeps Canada" and promoting the album: "It's WILD! the MOST! you'll STOMP, JUMP 'N SHOUT to the wild…SOUND OF THE BEATLES (Britain's rave singing group). Included: 8 original songs, 6 new versions of favourite Rhythm 'n Blues numbers. GET YOUR LP NOW! at your Capitol Record Dealer." Capitol distributed 8" x 6" promotional cards (with Gardiner's article under the headline "BEATLEMANIA! INVADES CANADA") to record dealers and distributors. The extracted article describes Beatlemania as a disease spreading throughout Britain, Europe and the Far East, and references two popular TV doctors of the sixties, Ben Casey and Dr. Kildare. CHUM charted the LP for 23 weeks in its Top 5 LP chart, including five weeks at number one. The album sold 194,000 units.

The "Roll Over Beethoven" single's release was postponed due to the surging sales of "She Loves You," but then was issued on December 9 due to consumer demand. CHUM charted the single for 16 weeks, with a peak at number two behind "She Loves You." The "Roll Over Beethoven" single sold over 110,000 copies in Canada. After Beatlemania hit south of the border, 350,000 copies were imported into the United States.

Capitol prepared 8" x 6" cards to promote its *Beatlemania! With The Beatles* LP under the headline "BEATLEMANIA! INVADES CANADA." The Davis Agency, a chain of stationary stores that also carried records, ran an ad for the album (shown left) in the January 16, 1964 edition of the Ottawa Journal.

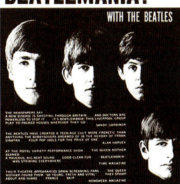

Beatlemania Will Get You If You Don't Watch Out!

Beatlemania? The dizzy disease nobody wants to be without.
Cause? The Beatles — 4 shaggy-headed young Britishers .. who aided and abetted by Capitol Records, blithely destroy the myth about British reserve.
Symptoms? Quadruple vision, Tendency to scream in ecstasy at sight and/or sound of Beatles. Mad desire to dance with gay abandon or by yourself.
Cure? None. Who wants to be cured?
Catch Beatlemania at The Davis Agency. Beatle down to your nearest Davis Agency Record Department and announce in proudly ringing tones that you have come to be infected. Listen to "Beatlemania" in our convenient listening booths but, as Mr. Borge would say, don't dance unless you absolutely have to. Be the first one on your block to catch Beatlemania — the disease you can't afford to be without.

203 Sparks Street
Billings Bridge Plaza
Carlingwood Plaza
All Three Stores Dial 236-7444

Davis Agency Stores Are Open Until 9 p.m. Every Friday

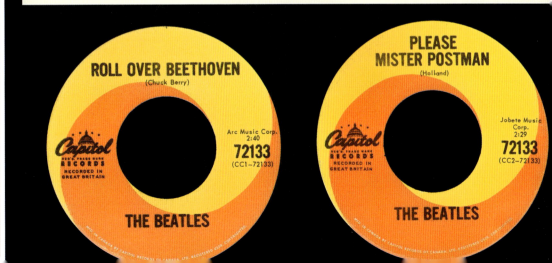

Capitol of Canada followed up its unique "Roll Over Beethoven" single by releasing the same single as its U.S. parent company, "I Want To Hold Your Hand" b/w "I Saw Her Standing There." After CHUM began playing the U.S. single in early January 1964, Capitol of Canada moved up its release date to January 11, although most stores did not have sufficient copies of the single until later in the month. The A-side became the Beatles second Canadian chart-topper. CHUM began listing the single as "Hold Your Hand/Her Standing There" in its Hit Parade survey, which charted the single for 17 weeks, including six weeks at number one. The single sold 290,000 copies in Canada.

Less than a month after releasing *Beatlemania! With The Beatles*, White convinced Capitol of Canada to issue another Beatles LP, this time featuring songs from the group's first U.K. album, *Please Please Me*. News of the planned LP was announced on CHUM on December 23, 1963, by the president of the Ontario Beatles Fan Club, Trudy Medcalf, who had been given the information by Capitol's Toronto office. Because the "Please Please Me" Canadian single had sold poorly, White decided to name the album after the title track from the Beatles hit British EP, "Twist And Shout." With "She Loves You" moving up the charts, White added the song to the lineup, along with the previous single, "From Me To You." This meant that the *Twist And Shout* LP would contain the A-sides to the Beatles first four singles, along with the B-sides to the first two discs. To get to 14 tracks, White dropped the opening song, "I Saw Her Standing There," which was the B-side to "I Want To Hold Your Hand," and the second track, "Misery." Side One opens with "Anna" and has the same running order as the British LP through "Love Me Do," which is followed by the side's closing track, "From Me To You." Side Two picks up with "P.S. I Love You" through "Twist And Shout," ending with "She Loves You." The LP's striking front cover has the same exciting photo of the Beatles jumping into the air over a bombed-out London structure that graced the jacket of the British *Twist And Shout* EP. Capitol added a pink banner with the album's title in white and a box promoting the presence of the current hit single, "She Loves You."

The *Twist And Shout* LP was officially released in mono only as Capitol of Canada T6054 on February 3, 1964; however, record stores were selling and advertising the album by Friday, January 31. By the end of February, Capitol had shipped 130,000 units. The album would go on to sell over 250,000 copies. CHUM charted the album for 17 weeks, including ten weeks at number one.

Capitol prepared 5⅞" x 3¾" cards to promote its Beatles catalog. The front side (below left) features a Dezo Hoffman photo and the front cover to the *Twist And Shout* LP. The back lists the company's Beatles albums and singles with text in English and French. The company ran an ad promoting the new LP and the group's Ed Sullivan Show appearances on the back of a Montreal CKGM survey. Capitol also prepared an attractive 22" x 8¾" in-store promotional poster for *Twist And Shout*.

Paul White used the January 24, 1964 Sizzle Sheet to tell DJs the obvious: "Beatlemania Spreading Like Wildfire!" White observed that the Beatles meant more to teenagers than Elvis "in that they reflect something of themselves... mischievous rebels, enjoying themselves." "She Loves You" was now number one at CHUM (Toronto), CKY (Winnipeg), CKLC (Kingston), CHIQ (Hamilton), CFOS (Owen Sound), CFRS (Simcoe), CHEX (Peterborough) and CHUB (Nanaimo). "Roll Over Beethoven" was number one on CKEY (Toronto). In Toronto, the Beatles held down the top two singles ("She Loves You" and "Roll Over Beethoven") and number one album (*Beatlemania!*) at CHUM, whose weekly survey had a circulation of 108,000. The following week, White listed "I Want To Hold Your Hand" as the "Smash of the Week." The song was number one at CFAC (Calgary), CFUN (Vancouver), CJCA (Edmonton), CKRC (Winnipeg), CFPL (London), CFCO (Chatham) and CHOK (Sarnia). White claimed the single was on 99% of the charts and predicted it would be number one the following week in every major area in Canada. On February 7, the day the Beatles arrived in New York, White wrote: "Beatles So Hot--They're Scorching the Hit Parade!" Beatlemania was the "biggest thing to happen in the history of Show Biz...the Record Biz—and Anybody's Biz!" He listed 11 stations that had "She Loves You" at one and 17 stations with "I Want To Hold Your Hand" at the top. Both songs were at two or three if not number one. (White provided chart information of cities throughout Canada because there was no national Canadian chart at that time.) He plugged the Beatles appearances on The Ed Sullivan Show, which was a top five show in Canada.

By the end of February 1964, the invasion was complete. White informed his readers in the February 28 Sizzle Sheet that Capitol of Canada had shipped over 800,000 units of Beatles records ("wowie!!"). The breakdown was: *Twist And Shout* LP (over 130,000); *Beatlemania!* LP (over 120,000); "I Want To Hold Your Hand" (almost 200,000); "She Loves You" (150,000); and "Roll Over Beethoven" (110,000). Although not listed, the first three singles were now selling in much larger numbers. Their approximate Canadian sales would grow to: "Love Me Do" (75,000); "Please Please Me" (80,000); and "From Me To You" (80,000). White announced that due to overwhelming public demand [fueled by the Beatles playing the song on the Sullivan Show], "All My Loving" would be the next Beatles single, due for release on March 9. The flip side would be "This Boy," a song that had not been available on an album or single in Canada. He added that advance dealer orders had already made the single a hit. The "All My Loving" single would sell over 200,000 copies in Canada. In addition, 300,000 copies were imported into the United States.

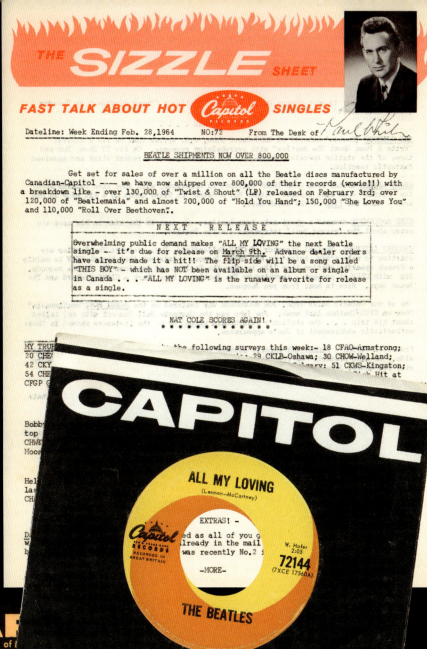

Beyond The Beatles & Beyond The Fringe
by Al Sussman

There's an old proverb, often said to be a Chinese curse, that goes: "May you live in interesting times." In the 20th century, there were rarely times as "interesting" as October 1962. That month, James Meredith became the first black student to attend the University of Mississippi. Astronaut Wally Schirra completed the U.S. space program's then-longest mission with six orbits of the earth aboard Sigma 7. The revolutionary Second Vatican Council, presided over by Pope John XXIII, convened in Rome. War broke out between Red China and India. And the world came closer than it ever has to thermonuclear war when the United States and the U.S.S.R. faced off over the Soviet installation of nuclear missiles in Cuba. At the same time, pop culture triggered seismic explosions that are still being felt today.

James Meredith's enrollment at Ole Miss on October 1, 1962, took place despite the defiance of Mississippi Gov. Ross Barnett, whose vow that the university remain segregated led to riots that left two dead. It took the force of the federal government, in the form of 30,000 troops, to restore order, protect Meredith and enable him to deal a blow to white supremacy. The success of Wally Schirra's nine-hour Mercury mission on October 3 gave the National Aeronautics and Space Administration ("NASA") the confidence to proceed with a full-day mission in 1963. On October 11, Catholic bishops and invited church dignitaries gathered at St. Peter's Basilica for the opening of the Second Vatican Council called by Pope John XXIII, who saw the need for an update of church doctrine. Consisting of four sessions that ran through December 1965, Vatican II sought to bring the church into the modern world while retaining continuity with its past. On October 20, Chinese troops entered disputed territory on its border with India, leading to a one-month war ending with a cease-fire after territorial gains by China. On October 22, President Kennedy ("JFK") addressed the nation on the build up of Soviet nuclear missiles in Cuba. He understood the risks of his aggressive response, including a naval blockade, telling the nation: "The cost of freedom is always high—but Americans have always paid it. And one path we shall never choose, and that is the path of surrender or submission." The Cuban Missile Crisis ended with the removal of the missiles and a U.S. pledge not to invade Cuba.

Newsweek

NOVEMBER 5, 1962 25c

SHOWDOWN
'The Cost of Freedom Is Always High...'

Newsweek

OCTOBER 8, 1962 25c

SPECIAL ISSUE

The Space Age

By the time the crisis ended at month's end, the first troops of a pop culture invasion from England had landed in America. On October 3, *Stop The World — I Want To Get Off*, directed by and starring Anthony Newley, with music and stage play by Newley and Leslie Bricusse, debuted at New York's Shubert Theatre after playing over a year in London's West End. On October 27, *Beyond The Fringe*, a satirical comedy revue at the head of England's "satire boom," starring Peter Cook, Dudley Moore, Alan Bennett and Jonathan Miller, arrived on Broadway at the John Golden Theatre after runs in Edinburgh and the West End going back to August 1960. Waiting in the wings was Lionel Bart's musical *Oliver!*, which would debut on Broadway in early 1963. And, while America knew nothing of it yet, October 5 saw the U.K. release of *Dr. No*, the first film treatment of Ian Fleming's books featuring British secret agent 007, James Bond, starring Scottish actor Sean Connery. And that same day, EMI's Parlophone label released "Love Me Do" c/w "P.S. I Love You," the first single by a rock band from Liverpool called the Beatles.

Five days earlier, Johnny Carson began a nearly thirty-year tenure as host of The Tonight Show on NBC-TV in New York. Across the country in Hollywood, California, Capitol Records released the first album by the Beach Boys, *Surfin' Safari*, named for the Hawthorne, California band's Top 15 hit single. And the first transcontinental baseball World Series began on October 4 at Candlestick Park between the San Francisco Giants and the New York Yankees. By that time Boeing 707 jets had cut the flight time in half from eight to four hours. The jet-age and space-age had arrived.

Indeed, on November 2, physicist John W. Mauchly, a co-designer of the early massive electronic digital computers, spoke before the American Institute of Industrial Engineers and, according to the New York Times, predicted that, "in a decade or so," everyone would have access to their own personal computer, complete with "exchangeable wafer-thin data storage files to provide inexhaustible memories and answer most problems." Mauchly further predicted: "There is no reason to suppose the average boy or girl cannot be master of a personal computer." The Times article was headlined, "Pocket Computer May Replace Shopping List." In the meantime, the Atlas supercomputer, the first computer system to do multiprogramming, though with just 576 KB of storage, would be dedicated that December at the University of Manchester. In February 1963, an inventor named Luther Simjian received a patent for his "Bankograph," a primitive optical reader for banking transactions that presaged the age of automated banking.

In the November U.S. midterm elections, the Democrats strengthened their majorities in the Senate and House of Representatives, and 30-year-old Ted Kennedy was elected to the Senate seat from Massachusetts vacated by his brother Jack when he was elected President two years earlier. Ted Kennedy would serve as a liberal lion of the Senate until his death in 2009. Meanwhile, the man JFK defeated for the presidency in 1960, Richard Nixon, was defeated again, this time by California Gov. Pat Brown in the state's gubernatorial election. The next day, Nixon lashed out at the media, declaring it is his "last press conference," adding: "You won't have Nixon to kick around anymore."

The next day, Eleanor Roosevelt, widow of President Franklin D. Roosevelt ("FDR") and a major world figure in her own right, died at age 78. At her funeral in the Roosevelts' hometown of Hyde Park, New York, four Presidents shared the same pew — FDR's successors Harry Truman and Dwight Eisenhower, President Kennedy and (while no one could have imagined it) his successor, Vice-President Lyndon Johnson. The following July, JFK would meet another future President, 16-year-old Bill Clinton, at an American Legion Boys Nation event at the White House.

On November 24, another major component in the British "satire boom" emerged with the debut on BBC-TV of That Was The Week That Was, a satirical look at the week's events written, produced and directed by Ned Sherrin and hosted by 23-year-old David Frost. The series would run for just over a year, but what a tumultuous year that was for Britain (and the world). A less-sharp-edged American version, also hosted by Frost at the outset, debuted in January 1964. Its regular cast included Buck Henry and Alan Alda. The show featured satirical songs written by Tom Lehrer.

The U.S. Embassy in Tokyo was the site on November 28 of the marriage of Japanese avant-garde artist Yoko Ono to fellow artist Anthony Cox, two days after Ono's future husband, John Lennon, had recorded the Beatles first big U.K. hit single, "Please Please Me," which topped most of the British charts.

On November 27, the first Boeing 727 three-engine jet airliner was rolled out from its hangar in Seattle, just over two months before its first flight and a little over a year before Eastern Airlines would put the 727 into commercial service. Two days later, Britain and France signed an agreement to develop the Concorde supersonic airliner.

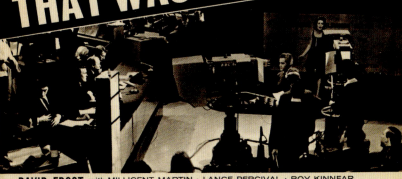

On December 14, the U.S. spacecraft Mariner 2 flew within 21,000 miles of the planet Venus and became the first space probe to transmit data from another planet. The data showed Venus to have a surface temperature of around 900 degrees Fahrenheit, making it inhospitable to human life. Meanwhile, on Earth, Leonardo da Vinci's classic painting The Mona Lisa arrived in the United States for the first time on December 19, to be put on display at the National Gallery in Washington, D.C. in January and, in February, at the Metropolitan Museum of Art in New York.

The coldest winter of the 20th century in Great Britain began with a blizzard on December 29. The so-called "Big Freeze of 1963" would last more than two months through early March, making for difficult traveling for a Liverpool rock 'n' roll band on its first season of touring outside of Northern England. Indoors, on December 30, a BBC-TV play called *Madhouse on Castle Street* featured one of the first television performances of the soon-to-be civil rights anthem "Blowin' In The Wind" by its young composer, Bob Dylan.

1963 would be the year that the battle over civil rights became a daily part of the national conversation. The year's first salvo was fired on January 14 with the inauguration of Alabama's new governor, George C. Wallace. In his inaugural address, Wallace declared: "I draw the line in the dust and toss the gauntlet before the feet of tyranny, and I say 'segregation now, segregation tomorrow, and segregation forever.' Let us send this message back to Washington, that from this day we are standing up, and the heel of tyranny does not fit the neck of an upright man."

President Kennedy heard the message and was initially cautious about treading into the civil rights struggles lest he anger the Southern state Democrats. But on June 11 he went on national TV and radio to announce that he was sending Congress a sweeping civil rights bill, which would reach Capitol Hill on June 19. Most of his inner circle was against pushing for civil rights legislation, but his brother, Attorney General Robert Kennedy, lobbied hard for the legislative tack and even helped craft JFK's speech. The President framed the struggle for equal rights for black people in moral, rather than political or judicial terms: "The heart of the question is whether all Americans are to be afforded equal rights and equal opportunities, whether we are going to treat our fellow Americans as we want to be treated…It is as old as the scriptures and is as clear as the American Constitution."

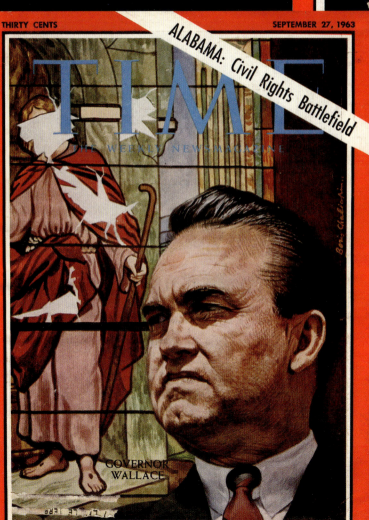

Progress and setbacks preceded Kennedy's June 11 speech. In late January, Harvey Gantt, a black student, peacefully entered the previously all-white Clemson University in South Carolina. On April 3, Southern Christian Leadership Conference volunteers began their campaign against segregation in Birmingham, Alabama. Nine days later, the campaign's leader, Rev. Dr. Martin Luther King, Jr., was arrested for "parading without a permit." On April 16, Dr. King released his Letter From Birmingham Jail, which became one of the seminal documents of the civil rights movement. As the protests and boycott of segregationist businesses in the city moved into high gear, hundreds were arrested, with police dogs and fire hoses used to repel the demonstrators. Film of the violent scenes aired on the nightly network news reports, horrifying much of the nation. Finally, on May 10, a settlement was reached under which leading business owners promised access to lunch counters, etc., and to hire more blacks for clerical and sales jobs.

On the day of Kennedy's speech, Gov. Wallace tried to block two black students from enrolling at the University of Alabama, but backed down when faced with the threat of arrest and the federalized Alabama National Guard. A few hours after the speech, civil rights activist Medgar Evers was assassinated outside his home in Jackson, Mississippi.

That summer plans were made for a massive event, the March on Washington for Jobs and Freedom, set for August 28. Although the Kennedy White House feared a possible race riot, the march was remarkably peaceful, attracting a multi-racial crowd of over 250,000. The march was highlighted by speeches from nearly all of the movement's leaders and musical performances by Bob Dylan, Joan Baez, Peter, Paul and Mary, Marian Anderson and gospel music legend Mahalia Jackson, who exhorted Dr. King to "tell them about the dream, Martin." Indeed, the movement's spiritual leader gave a memorable day its most unforgettable moment–King's "I Have a Dream" speech. After the march, movement leaders went to the White House for a meeting with JFK, who hoped the peaceful march would forge momentum for the civil rights bill. One post-march comment proved prophetic. Rev. Abraham Woods remarked: "Everything has changed. And when you look at it, nothing has changed. Racism is under the surface, and an incident could scratch it, can bring it out." Sure enough, on September 4, the bombing of a black household in Birmingham sparked a racial disturbance, followed by the killing of four young black girls in the Sunday morning bombing of the Sixteenth Street Baptist Church in Birmingham on September 15. The struggle would continue...

Newsweek

SEPTEMBER 2, 1963   25c

The March on Washington

Newsweek

SEPTEMBER 30, 1963   25c

BOMBING IN BIRMINGHAM

Another social movement was just starting to emerge as 1963 began. In mid-February, a new book authored by journalist Betty Friedan, *The Feminine Mystique*, was published and reawakened the American feminist movement, which had largely faded into the background after women were given the right to vote in 1920 by the 19th Amendment to the U.S. Constitution. In *The Feminine Mystique*, Friedan focused on the housewife-mothers of the 1950s and early '60s, who she found to be unhappy and feeling unfulfilled. The best-selling book sold a million copies. A year after its publication, teenage pop singer Lesley Gore would have a Top Five hit single with what became an early anthem of liberation for young girls and women (albeit written by two men), "You Don't Own Me." Some three years after *The Feminine Mystique* debuted, Friedan would co-found the National Organization for Women ("NOW"), which would accelerate the growth of second-wave feminism in the U.S. in the second half of the decade.

Early February saw two interesting, if then little-noticed, pop culture events. On February 7, Chicago's Vee-Jay Records released the second U.K. single by the Beatles, "Please Please Me," which would soon top several charts in Britain. Four days later, The French Chef, hosted by cookbook co-author Julia Child, debuted on Boston public television station WGBH. The series would run for nine years and be the inspiration for a pair of 21st century series.

On March 5, one of country music's great stars and an artist who would be a major influence on future generations of female country singers, Patsy Cline, was killed at age 30 in a plane crash in Camden, Tennessee, as she was returning to Nashville from a charity concert in Kansas City, Kansas. Killed in the same crash were country stars Hawkshaw Hawkins and Cowboy Copas and their manager, Randy Hughes, who was piloting the plane.

With the New York World's Fair a little over a year away, construction began on March 6 on the Fair's symbol, the Unisphere, a 120-foot Earth globe that remained an attraction two decades into the 21st century, along with the 58-story Pan Am Building (now called the MetLife Building) at 200 Park Avenue in midtown Manhattan, which opened the next day. On April 22, President Kennedy keyed "1964" on a new touch-tone telephone to begin a countdown to the Fair's opening. JFK told a crowd at Flushing Meadow Park on that phone line that "three hundred and sixty-six days from today, I plan to attend your opening." Seven months later, fate would tragically intervene.

Almost exactly a year after the nationally televised fatal beating of welterweight boxing champion Benny "Kid" Paret, featherweight champion Davey Moore met a similar fate at the hands of Sugar Ramos in a March 21 title bout at Dodger Stadium in Los Angeles. Unlike Paret, who never regained consciousness after being knocked out by Emile Griffith, Moore collapsed in his dressing room less than an hour after the fight and died four days later. The deaths of two boxing champions from in-the-ring beatings in the space of a year renewed calls for the abolition of boxing. Bob Dylan, by then in the social commentary phase of his career, wrote a song on the subject called "Who Killed Davey Moore?" Another piece of social commentary by young Dylan, "Talkin' John Birch Paranoid Blues," became a source of controversy in mid-May when CBS network censors refused to allow Dylan to perform the song for what would have been his first appearance on The Ed Sullivan Show, thus causing Dylan to cancel his appearance. Dylan's breakthrough album, *The Freewheelin' Bob Dylan*, was released by CBS' Columbia Records in the last week in May.

March 21 was also the day that British Labour Party Member of Parliament George Wigg asked the British government to hold hearings on whether Prime Minister Harold Macmillan's War Secretary, John Profumo, had "behaved inappropriately" with a 20-year-old London call girl named Christine Keeler, which Profumo denied the next day before the House of Commons. Thus began the U.K.'s biggest story of 1963, save for the rise of the Beatles. By the time the scandal climaxed in October, just as Beatlemania was taking over the British press' front pages, Macmillan had resigned due to illness, though he was not involved in the scandal.

The Profumo scandal had everything the Fleet Street press loved, especially in the wake of the success of the first Bond film *Dr. No* – sex, espionage and the secret lives of public figures. Profumo had indeed had an affair with Keeler while she was still a teenager, as had Soviet naval attaché Yevgeny Ivanov. Both had met Keeler through a London osteopath/socialite, Dr. Stephen Ward, who had taken Keeler and her more flamboyant friend, Mandy Rice-Davies, under his wing. Ward was perceived by the authorities to be a high-class pimp who was soon charged with a series of immorality offenses and put on trial that summer, with both Keeler and Rice-Davies testifying against him. Before he was convicted, though, Ward took a fatal overdose. Profumo resigned his position in the Macmillan government on June 5, with The Times (of London) calling his lies "a great tragedy for the probity of public life in Britain."

Later in June, the House of Commons debated Profumo's resignation, with Labor opposition leader Harold Wilson attacking Macmillan and his Conservative government for not identifying the security risk in Profumo's association with Ward, who was portrayed as a Soviet agent due to his association with Ivanov. But, by late September, after a summer of sensationalist "revelations" in the Fleet Street dailies, a government report declared that Profumo was guilty of an "indiscretion," but there had been no security leaks owing to the affair. On October 10, Macmillan, fearing he had cancer, resigned as prime minister and was succeeded by Sir Alec Douglas-Home. Fittingly, that same day, *From Russia With Love*, the second Bond film, opened in U.K. theaters. A year later, though, the Conservatives would be narrowly voted out and Wilson would become prime minister (earning him a name-check in George Harrison's "Taxman"). Following his resignation, Profumo devoted himself to charitable work. He was later awarded a CBE in 1975 and declared a national hero by Margaret Thatcher.

While the Profumo/Keeler soap opera was beginning to pick up press coverage in America, a new TV soap opera, General Hospital, premiered on ABC-TV on April 1 and went on to reach the 15,000-episode milestone just a bit over 59 years later. A week after the debut of General Hospital, *Lawrence Of Arabia* won the Best Picture Oscar at the 35th Academy Awards ceremony, with Anne Bancroft winning Best Actress for *The Miracle Worker* and Gregory Peck awarded Best Actor for *To Kill A Mockingbird*.

On April 10, the same day that the U.S. nuclear submarine Thresher sank near Cape Cod, killing 129 naval and civilian personnel, far-right-wing U.S. General Edwin Walker escaped injury when a rifle shot was fired at his home in Dallas, Texas, already a hotbed of extremist politics. Not much attention was paid to the attack on Walker until the same rifle was later alleged to have been used in another shooting in Dallas that November.

On May 15, the Mercury phase of NASA's manned space program climaxed with Air Force Major Gordon "Gordo" Cooper's flight on Faith 7, which set a new American record for orbits of the Earth (22) and time in space (34 hours, 19 minutes). This was the last U.S. solo manned mission. NASA would now move on to Project Gemini, the first American two-man mission, which would launch nearly two years later.

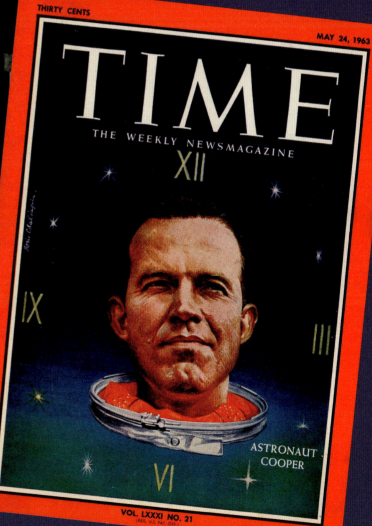

In October, NASA introduced its third group of astronauts, including two members of what would be the first manned mission to the moon in 1969, Buzz Aldrin and Michael Collins. Within days after the final Mercury mission, Soviet cosmonaut Valery Bykovsky completed 82 orbits and nearly five days in space aboard Vostok 5, while Vostok 6, launched two days after Vostok 5, was helmed by the world's first female human space traveler, Valentina Tereshkova. It would be almost exactly 20 years before another female, American astronaut Sally Ride, would go into space. In September, in a speech before the United Nations General Assembly, President Kennedy proposed a joint U.S./U.S.S.R. mission to the moon. The Soviet response via Pravda was that the idea was "premature." Indeed, no joint space projects between the two superpowers would happen until the mid-1970s.

Less than a year after the Cuban Missile Crisis and with relations between the U.S. and the U.S.S.R. still very tense, President Kennedy, sensing that Nikita Khrushchev was interested in better U.S.-Soviet relations, held out a rhetorical olive branch to the Soviets in a commencement speech on June 10 at American University in Washington, D.C. Titled "A Strategy of Peace," Kennedy announced that the U.S. would agree to negotiations on a nuclear test ban treaty and was willing to unilaterally suspend all atmospheric testing as long as all other nations did the same. Framing relations between the two superpowers in human terms, Kennedy remarked: "For, in the final analysis, our most basic common link is that we all inhabit this small planet. We all breathe the same air. We all cherish our children's future. And we are all mortal." On June 20, Washington and Moscow authorized a hotline for better communications than had existed during the missile crisis. By early August, the U.S., the U.K. and the Soviets had signed a Partial Nuclear Test Ban Treaty that would go into effect on October 10, close to a year after the missile crisis. But all this tentative cooperation between the two superpowers exacerbated the ideological split between the Soviets and Red China, which accused the U.S.S.R. of making "unconditional concessions and capitulation to the imperialists," according to The People's Daily, the Chinese Communist newspaper. China's public criticism of the U.S.S.R. began with the Russian withdrawal of missiles from Cuba, which China viewed as "submission to the U.S. nuclear blackmail." The Chinese viewed the Nuclear Test Ban Treaty as a "joint Soviet-U.S. plot to…deprive China of nuclear weapons." Although China was still viewed as a "Paper Dragon," Newsweek warned that with a growing population and the later obtainment of nuclear armaments, "the Chinese dragon could be breathing real fire."

Newsweek

AUGUST 5, 1963 25¢

A TRUCE IN THE COLD WAR?

Newsweek

NOVEMBER 25, 1963 25¢

RED CHINA: A Paper Dragon?

On June 23, President Kennedy arrived in Europe for what turned out to be the final foreign trip of his administration and of his life. In West Germany, Kennedy delivered his memorable "Ich bin ein Berliner" speech before some 120,000 people near the Berlin Wall. His trip to Ireland became a hauntingly poignant visit to the land of his ancestors, where even the steely JFK was visibly moved by the reception he received. Kennedy then visited England and Italy, where he met with Pope Paul VI in Vatican City before heading back to America.

Meanwhile, the civil war in Vietnam, which most Americans were barely aware of, was continuing to deepen, as was American involvement, which had slowly been growing since 1961. However, as 1962 came to a close, the war in Vietnam was still an international news story. There were 11,000 uniformed Americans in South Vietnam, but they were there only in advisory or support positions, providing logistics with helicopters and air cover with fighter jets. Less than 50 Americans had been killed in action. The day after Kennedy's June 10 American University speech, a 65-year-old Buddhist monk immolated himself at a major intersection of South Vietnam's capital, Saigon, to protest the treatment of Buddhists by South Vietnam's U.S-supported but corrupt government of President Ngo Dinh Diem. Associated Press photographer Malcolm Browne took a Pulitzer Prize-winning photo of the burning monk. The negative blow back from that may have been the flashpoint for the Kennedy administration's growing disenchantment with the Diem government. Secretary of State Dean Rusk recognized it was a "dirty, untidy, disagreeable war" with no end in sight. By August, JFK's old political opponent Henry Cabot Lodge, Jr. had been appointed the new U.S. ambassador to South Vietnam and tried unsuccessfully to get Diem and his equally corrupt brother, Ngo Dinh Nhu, to resign and leave the country. Not helping matters was the arrival in the U.S. in early October of Nhu's wife for a speaking tour, during which she aimed increasingly incendiary charges at the Kennedy administration. Publicly, Kennedy said that the progress of the war was up to the people of South Vietnam and all the U.S. could do was act as military advisors, which had been the American role for some two years. Behind the scenes, though, Washington was heavily lobbying for a coup d'etat to oust Diem by South Vietnamese generals, which finally happened on November 1, climaxed by the bloody execution of Diem and Nhu, which shocked Kennedy. He had been looking for a way out of the deepening morass that wouldn't jeopardize his re-election chances and was looking to withdraw about 1,000 of the U.S. "advisory" troops by the end of the year and be out of the war entirely by the end of 1965.

Despite the calls that spring for the abolition of boxing, a heavyweight championship bout was still one of the glamor events in sports and, on July 22 in Las Vegas, Sonny Liston defended his championship by repeating his first-round knockout of former heavyweight champion Floyd Patterson from the previous September. But the highlight of the evening was the appearance of the loquacious young contender from Louisville, Kentucky, Cassius Clay. Clay, the light-heavyweight gold medalist at the 1960 Rome Olympics, was the talk of boxing with his speed, brash style and predictions of the round in which he'd knock out his opponent. After Liston quickly dispatched Patterson, he pointed at Clay in a ringside seat and said, "You're next, big mouth!" A Liston-Clay title match was signed that fall and ultimately scheduled for the following February 25 at Miami Beach's Convention Hall.

What had been a triumphant summer for President Kennedy took a tragic turn in early August with the premature birth of his second son, Patrick Bouvier Kennedy, who developed infant respiratory distress syndrome and died just 39 hours into life. For First Lady Jacqueline Kennedy, it was her third loss of a child, following a miscarriage in 1955 and a stillborn baby girl in 1956, before the healthy, if difficult, births of Caroline and John, Jr. Early that autumn, during a therapeutic getaway trip to Greece, Jackie would first meet Greek shipping magnate Aristotle Onassis.

In what came to be known as Britain's Great Train Robbery, a gang of 15 men robbed a Royal Mail train traveling from Glasgow to London of 2.6 million pounds in the early morning hours of August 8. Other than the train driver, who was hit on the head with a metal bar, no one was injured and most of the gang was apprehended within days, though most of the money was never recovered. But, coming in the middle of the Profumo scandal, the Great Train Robbery was another black eye for British authorities, along with providing abundant material for That Was The Week That Was. The robbery lived on in pop culture. Two 1965 feature films, the Beatles *Help!* and the fourth James Bond film, *Thunderball*, contained references to the Great Train Robbery.

With a seeming thaw in relations between the U.S. and the Soviets, the possible passage of a civil rights bill, a relatively strong economy and a general feeling of hope for the future, Americans had every reason to feel optimistic on the Friday morning before Thanksgiving....

November 22, 1963. At around 1:35 PM, Eastern time, Walter Cronkite, anchor and managing editor of the CBS Evening News, was eating his lunch in front of the United Press International teletype machine when the bell sounded for a major news story. Clattering up the machine was a bulletin from UPI's White House correspondent Merriman Smith that three shots had been fired at President Kennedy's motorcade in downtown Dallas. With the tube-driven TV cameras needing to be warmed up before he could go on the air from the CBS-TV newsroom, Cronkite dashed for a sound booth. The CBS News Bulletin slide appeared on screen and Cronkite interrupted the soap opera As The World Turns at 1:40 with Smith's bulletin and further word that Kennedy may have been seriously, perhaps fatally, wounded by the shooting.

Most Americans were unaware that JFK, looking toward his re-election campaign in 1964, was in Texas to smooth over a feud within the state's Democratic party and hopefully woo voters in the right-wing hotbed of Dallas. In a city not considered a major media market, news was sketchy at best, mainly coming from telephones commandeered at Parkland Hospital, where Kennedy and Texas Gov. John Connally had been rushed, with nothing coming from most White House personnel save for a terse "He's dead" from Secret Service man Clint Hill. Then, other sources such as the Roman Catholic priests who had given Kennedy las rites also confirmed that he had died, as had CBS' Dan Rather. Approximately an hour after reading the initial bulletin, Cronkite announced: "From Dallas, Texas, the flash apparently official, President Kennedy died at one PM Central Standard Time, two, Eastern Standard Time, some 30 minutes ago." He bit down on his lip and checked the time on the clock to keep his emotions under control.

For Americans with first-hand memories of November 22, 1963, and the three days following, what they recall are images. The grim-faced new President Lyndon Johnson, making his first public statement that evening from Andrews Air Force Base. JFK's rocking chair being moved out of the White House in the rain on Saturday. The televised murder of the accused assassin, Lee Harvey Oswald, on Sunday morning in the basement of Dallas' city jail. The brilliant sunshine in Washington, D.C. on Sunday as Kennedy's casket was taken to the Capitol to lie in state. The hushed silence from the quarter of a million people who journeyed to Washington to pay their respects and walk past the coffin in the Capitol rotunda. The majesty of the state funeral procession on Monday. Young John Kennedy Jr.'s salute to his father's flag-draped coffin after the funeral on his third birthday. The heartbreaking solemnity of the burial at Arlington National Cemetery

The headline on the front page of the New York Daily News on Tuesday morning, November 26, was "LIFE GOES ON" as Americans returned to work and school. Not everyone, of course, had mourned the President's death. There were anecdotal reports of schools in the South where students cheered the news of the assassination, a reflection of the attitude that Kennedy was an elitist liberal who was soft on communism and had no business interfering in the racial policies of Southern states. But, overall, young people considered JFK to be a hero, and his murder left a huge psychic wound. Indeed many baby boomers of that era view November 22, 1963, as a generational demarcation line, that nothing was ever quite the same as it was that morning. Perhaps that's why so many still associate the loss of Kennedy with the breakthrough of the Beatles in America, even though several weeks passed between November 22 and "I Want To Hold Your Hand" taking off in many markets in the first days of January 1964.

Nonetheless, after a somber Thanksgiving, life did return to a semblance of normalcy in early December. On December 3, the Second Vatican Council closed after passing several revolutionary changes to the Roman Catholic liturgy, including changing the language of the Mass from Latin to the local language, turning the altar around, with priests facing their congregation and more participation in the Mass by the congregation, which in turn affected worship in other religious denominations. That same day, the United Nations Security Council unanimously condemned the policy of apartheid practiced by the Republic of South Africa.

December 7 marked TV's first use of videotaped "instant replay" in the telecast of the annual Army-Navy Game, thanks to CBS Sports director Tony Verna rewinding the tape of a touchdown by Army quarterback Rollie Stichweh (the Navy quarterback that day was 1963 Heisman Trophy winner Roger Staubach) and immediately playing it back, with play-by-play announcer Lindsey Nelson reminding viewers that they weren't seeing another Army touchdown.

Less than a month into his presidency, Lyndon Johnson signed the first legislative bills of what he would soon call his "Great Society" programs. The Higher Education Facilities Act authorized $1.2 billion in loans and grants to private universities for construction, creation of new community colleges and graduate schools and student aid. The Clean Air Act was one of the U.S.'s first and most influential modern environmental laws to reduce and control air pollution.

On December 12, Kenya, a British colony in East Africa, became the 35th African country to achieve independence. On December 20, for the first time since the Berlin Wall went up over two years earlier, citizens of West Berlin were allowed one-day passes to travel over to the East side of the Wall for the Christmas holidays, under an agreement between the governments of East and West Germany. By the time the wall was closed again on January 5, 1.3 million West Berliners had crossed to visit relatives in the East. The holiday open period was repeated in 1964 and 1965, after which the Wall was closed until the reforms in the Fall of 1989 that brought an end to the Wall.

In a brief, somber ceremony on Christmas Eve morning attended by Sen. Ted Kennedy, New York City changed the name of Idelwild Airport in Queens to John F. Kennedy International Airport. The ceremony was held at the airport's International Arrivals Building. The next major event there would be a far more boisterous one on February 7, 1964.

January 1964 was the start of a presidential election year. The heavy favorite for the Republican nomination, Sen. Barry Goldwater of Arizona, officially entered the race on January 3, just hours before Jack Paar gave the Beatles their first prime-time TV exposure in America. The next day, Pope Paul VI became the first Roman Catholic pontiff to fly in an airplane, the first to leave Italy since 1809 and the first ever to visit the Holy Land.

On January 11, Surgeon-General Luther Terry released the first government-mandated report on the effects of tobacco smoking. The report had been commissioned two years before by JFK, a cigar smoker with a wife who was a chain cigarette smoker, as we found out years later, and several of the scientists who contributed to the report were smokers. The report found a definite connection between smoking, heart disease and emphysema, that cigarette smoke was the main cause of chronic bronchitis and, bottom line, there was a direct link between smoking and lung cancer. In 1962, 41,000 Americans died from lung cancer and another 15,000 from chronic bronchitis and emphysema while 1963 had been the seventh consecutive year of record cigarette consumption in the U.S. The report didn't eradicate cigarette smoking and, nearly a quarter of the way into the 21st century, far too many people were still cigarette smokers, but it did lead to a leveling off in smoking and directly led to warning labels on cigarette packs and, in 1971, a ban on cigarette advertising on TV and radio.

While there had been long-running, very successful Broadway shows in the recent past (*Oklahoma* and *South Pacific* in the 1940s, *My Fair Lady* in the 1950s), the era of the Broadway mega-hit began with the opening on January 16 of *Hello, Dolly!*, starring Carol Channing. Later in the decade, *Hello, Dolly!* would set the record for first-run performances on Broadway, but that record would last for just a few months before being eclipsed by *Fiddler on the Roof,* which opened in September 1964. Late March saw the opening of *Funny Girl*, the musical story of comic actress Fanny Brice that launched Barbra Streisand to major stardom. And, a year after its Broadway debut, *Oliver!* was still a hit show, with its cast booked for what looked to be an eventful edition of The Ed Sullivan Show on February 9.

Readers of the Sunday New York Times woke up to a futuristic sight on January 19, a scale model of the 110-story "twin towers" that would be the centerpiece of New York City's World Trade Center ("WTC") in lower Manhattan, which was announced the day before as a joint project of the Port Authority of New York and New Jersey. The WTC wouldn't be completed for about a decade. Seeing the picture of that scale model, which looks almost identical to the eventual actual Twin Towers, is unsettling, given their tragic destiny. Then, on February 6, Great Britain and France announced plans for a joint project that would be the first railway tunnel under the English Channel. What would become known as the Channel Tunnel, or "Chunnel," wouldn't open until 30 years later, in 1994.

In the aftermath of a second military coup in South Vietnam, passage of the 24th Amendment to the Constitution (prohibiting poll taxes for voting in federal elections) and another U.S.-Cuba kerfuffle, this time over the American seizure of four Cuban fishing boats, the arrival of the Beatles in America was the perfect palette cleanser, making The CBS Evening News With Walter Cronkite that Friday evening, February 7. That set up what would be the then-highest-rated TV program that Sunday night when 73 million people tuned in to The Ed Sullivan Show to see what Beatlemania was all about. The next week 72 million watched the Beatles perform on the Sullivan Show broadcast live from the Deauville Hotel in Miami Beach. Then, on February 23, Americans watched the Beatles for a third time on The Ed Sullivan Show, though the group's performance had been video-taped on February 9 after the dress rehearsal for the live evening broadcast. For a group that was on the fringe in October 1962, they sure shook up the world. A brash young boxer would soon do the same. And by 1967, the Beatles would be beyond the fringe.

Thank you for your recent request for tickets to THE ED SULLIVAN SHOW & REH. FOR FEB. 9, 1964 We appreciate your interest and are sorry to tell you that so many ticket requests already have been received that we are unable to send you any at this time.

Ticket Bureau, CBS Television Network
485 Madison Avenue, New York 22, New York

February 9, 1964 **Sunday** Evening

8:00 ⑦ ⑨ ⑩ **ED SULLIVAN**—Variety
England's rock 'n' rolling Beatles make their American live TV debut, and 30 policemen will be on hand in case a "Beatle-Mania" reaches the riot pitch—as it has in England. Other scheduled guests include "Oliver!" star Georgia Brown and the show's youngsters singing "Consider Yourself" and other "Oliver!" tunes, and Tessie O'Shea of Broadway's "Girl Who Came to Supper." Ray Bloch orchestra. (Live; 60 min.)

8:30 ② ⑥ ⑫ **ARREST AND TRIAL**
"People in Glass Houses." A pair of bandits take an expectant mother hostage when they commandeer a squad car for their escape. Script by Antony Ellis. Kirby: Roger Perry. Egan: Chuck Connors. Anderson: Ben Gazzara. Miller: John Larch. Harris: Don Galloway. (90 min.)

Guest Cast
Frieda Jennison .... Katherine Crawford
Coley Mitchum .... Dennis Hopper
Frank Vose .... Henry Silva
Handley .... Ken Lynch

④ ⑤ ⑱ ㉟ **GRINDL**—Coca
"Dial G for Grindl." Grindl is mistaken for a professional killer. Grindl: Imogene Coca. Foster: James Millhollin.

Guest Cast
Olive York .... Gloria Grahame
Harold York .... Tod Andrews
Riddle .... Gregory Morton
Operative G .... Douglas Henderson

9:00 ④ ⑤ ⑱ ㉟ **BONANZA**—Western
[COLOR] "The Cheating Game." A stranger tells Laura Dayton that she will receive a large sum from her late husband's insurance. Adam: Pernell Roberts. Ben: Lorne Greene. Sheriff: Ray Teal. Little Joe: Michael Landon. (60 min.)

Guest Cast
Laura Dayton .... Kathie Browne
Ward Bannister .... Peter Breck
Peggy Dayton .... Katie Sweet

⑦ ⑨ ⑩ **JUDY GARLAND**
Tonight Judy gives a one-woman concert, singing three songs—"Liza," "Lorna's Song" and "Happiness Is Just a Thing

10:00 ④ ⑤ ⑱ ㉟ **NBC WHITE PAPER**

CUBA: THE MISSILE CRISIS

"... It shall be the policy of this Nation to regard any nuclear missile launched from Cuba against any nation in the Western Hemisphere as an attack by the Soviet Union on the United States, requiring a full retaliatory response upon the Soviet Union."
—President John F. Kennedy,
Oct. 22, 1962

[SPECIAL] Probably we have never been closer to nuclear war than in October 1962. The point of conflict: Russian missile sites in Cuba.
In chronicling those tense days, producer Fred Freed has called on two men who were in on the Administration's planning from the start. McGeorge Bundy and Theodore Sorensen, both top Kennedy aides, recall the development of the incident from the moment U-2 photos of the missile bases were developed. Each recounts how strategy was worked out in the series of high-level meetings at the White House.
But the final decision was President Kennedy's. On Oct. 22, he went before the Nation on TV. His plan: to stop the shipment of offensive weapons to Cuba, alert our armed forces and our allies, and call a meeting of the UN. Chet Huntley narrates. (60 min.)

Two nights after the Beatles third Ed Sullivan Show appearance, boxing heavyweight champion Sonny Liston stepped into the ring at Convention Hall in Miami Beach for a second defense of his championship, this time against Cassius Clay, who had ramped up his verbal attacks on Liston since the match was signed in the fall of 1963. Most experts predicted not only would Liston quickly knock out Clay, but that Cassius might be seriously hurt by Liston. When the Beatles were in Miami Beach for their second Ed Sullivan Show appearance, an overture was made to Liston's camp for a photo op, but jazz fan Liston wanted nothing to do with the British rock band. So they ended up at Clay's camp, where he played them as straight men for his in-the-ring shtick.

At the weigh-in on the morning of the fight, Clay appeared to have finally bought into all the hype about Liston. Cassius carried on, his blood pressure reading was sky-high and gave every impression that he was scared to death. The boxing commission was ready to cancel the fight but Clay's trainer, Angelo Dundee, convinced them that he could settle his fighter down and have him ready for the fight. When Clay's handlers got him out to their car and Dr. Ferdie Pacheco took his pulse and blood pressure, it was absolutely normal. Clay had done his first major rope-a-dope, making Liston think he was in the room with a crazy man, often an Achilles heel for bullies.

That night, unlike most of Liston's opponents, Clay used his exceptional speed to elude Liston's powerful punches. His quick, slashing jabs opened up a mouse under Sonny's left eye in the second round. Then, Liston injured his shoulder futilely swinging at Clay. Except for a scary fifth round, after liniment rubbed on Liston by his cornermen got on his gloves and then into Clay's eyes, the challenger was totally in command. Once his eyes cleared for the sixth round, Clay went on the offensive against the bloodied, suddenly slow-footed Liston. At the end of the round, Liston went back to his corner and, moments later, spit out his mouthpiece and, in what became a metaphor for futility, he quit on his stool. Clay, noticing Liston's actions, ran to the center of the ring with his arms raised in the air and shuffled his feet. He then faced the press and repeatedly yelled "I am the greatest!" and "I shook up the world!" He had just become the youngest boxer to take the title from a reigning heavyweight champion. Two days later, Cassius confirmed he had been a member of the Nation of Islam for the past five years. On March 6, Nation of Islam leader Elijah Muhammad announced that he had given the young champion a Muslim name: Muhammad Ali.

The Not-So-Dark Ages of Rock 'n' Roll

by Al Sussman

The sixteen-month period starting with the British release of the Beatles first single on October 5, 1962, through the group's arrival in America on February 7, 1964, has improperly been considered a part of rock 'n' roll's dark ages. This myth received traction starting in the late sixties, when the emerging American rock press first began to look back at the less-than-two-decade history of rock 'n' roll. In 1969, broadcaster/documentarian John Gilliland debuted a radio series on the music and its antecedents called The Pop Chronicles. Episode 20 of the series was called "Forty Miles of Bad Road," named for a 1960 instrumental hit by twangy guitar king Duane Eddy. In this episode, Gilliland labeled the period from 1958-59 until the American breakthrough of the Beatles as "rock 'n' roll's dark ages."

Prior to Beatlemania infecting the American music industry, American pop music enjoyed tremendous success not only in the United States, but also in Great Britain and Canada. The British charts of the fifties and early sixties were frequented by American records and cover versions by British artists of American songs. British record companies recognized the attraction towards anything American, and began adding special designations to the labels of discs featuring American artists. London Records incorporated the phrase "American Recordings" into its logo on these singles, while Oriole added the word "American" below its logo. About a year after purchasing Top Rank International, EMI phased out the label and replaced it with Stateside.

But the trans-Atlantic exchange for the most part flowed only in one direction. While American artists such as Elvis Presley, Chuck Berry, Little Richard, Jerry Lee Lewis and Buddy Holly were household names in the U.K., no British artist had any sustained success in America. British teen idols Cliff Richard, Billy Fury, John Leyton and Adam Faith all failed to make any significant impact on the American charts. There were, of course, occasional exceptions. Capitol Records had a chart-topping million-seller in 1958 with Laurie London's "He's Got The Whole World (In His Hands)." But that was a spiritual song sung by a 13-year-old boy, who never came close to duplicating his initial success.

  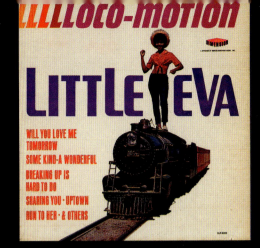

More typical was Jim Dale, whose "Be My Girl" (produced by George Martin) was a rockabilly-sounding song that charted at number two in England. When Capitol issued the single in America in 1958, it added the words "English Rock 'N' Roll" to the label (see page 53). This designation impressed no one, with the record selling a measly 297 copies.

But Gilliland 's condemnation of the music of the late fifties and early sixties was not aimed at the British Isles. As an American DJ on Los Angeles' KRLA, he focused on the American music of the period, describing it as a time dominated by novelty records, dance ditties and lightweight teen idols. But by October 1962, the times they were a-changin'.

Oh sure, there were novelty tunes such as Bobby "Boris" Pickett's "Monster Mash," which topped the Billboard Hot 100 for the two weeks before Halloween 1962. And there were a slew of dance hits, including Chris Montez's "Let's Dance," which charted at No. 4 for two weeks in October and got to No. 2 in England. Montez would be part of a British package tour in May 1963 with the Beatles and fellow American Tommy Roe, who had a No. 2 hit with "Sheila" in mid-September (No. 3 in the U.K.). Little Eva was still telling us to do "The Loco-Motion," which had topped the charts in late August and would nearly do the same in the U.K., stopping at No. 2 in late October. The song was written by the Brill Building songwriting team of Gerry Goffin and Carole King. In addition to singing backing vocals on the song, King had a No. 3 U.K. hit that month with "It Might As Well Rain Until September." Jimmy Clanton's "Venus In Blue Jeans" (No. 7) and Marcie Blane's "Bobby's Girl" (No. 3) were pop confections that were significant hits that fall. The songs became hits in the U.K. through cover versions by Mark Wynter and Susan Maughan.

  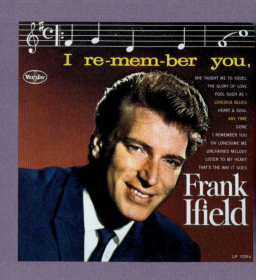

Meanwhile, in Chicago, a black-owned R&B/gospel label took aim at the lucrative pop market by releasing discs by white artists. Vee-Jay Records entered into an agreement with Bob Crewe's production company, Genius, Inc., to release recordings by a long-struggling doo-wop vocal group from central New Jersey that had just cut a killer track with Crewe titled "Sherry." By the time the group recorded the song, they were known as the Four Seasons (named after a New Jersey bowling alley). The group then consisted of lead singer Frankie Valli, singer/keyboardist Bob Gaudio (who wrote "Sherry" and many of the group's other hits), singer/guitarist Tommy DiVito and bass singer/bass guitarist Nick Massi. Led by Valli's soaring falsetto voice, doo-wop backing vocals and exciting rhythm track, "Sherry" quickly topped the charts in mid-September and remained there for five weeks. Because the disc was issued on Vee-Jay, many black program directors thought that the song was recorded by a black vocal group, helping the song top the Billboard Hot R&B Sides chart. The song peaked at No. 8 in the U.K. The group's follow-up singles, "Big Girls Don't Cry" and "Walk Like A Man," followed the same formula as "Sherry" and were equally successful. Unlike many American artists, the Four Seasons continued to have hits during and after the British Invasion.

Frank Ifield, a British native who had spent much of his life in Australia, had his first big hit in the summer of 1962 with "I Remember You," a World War II–era ballad. The single, fueled by a bluesy harmonica and Ifield's mixture of smooth vocalizations and yodeling, topped the U.K. charts for seven weeks. The Beatles even added the song to their stage show. When Vee-Jay issued the disc in the U.S., it went all the way to No. 5. Although Ifield had three more number one hits in the U.K., he was a one-hit wonder in the States.

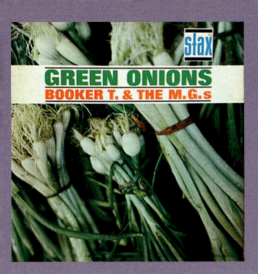  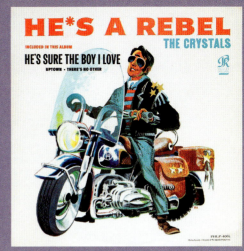

The two R&B labels that would have the most success crossing over to the mainstream audience were well-represented that October. Memphis' Stax Records had a six-week Top 10 hit with "Green Onions," an instrumental by the Stax house band for its string of soul music classics later in the decade, Booker T. & the M.G.s. Meanwhile, in Detroit, the Motown family of labels (Tamla, Gordy, Motown) was gaining momentum on the way to becoming the dominant black music company of the decade, with Mary Wells' "You Beat Me To The Punch" a Top 20 hit, as was the Marvelettes' "Beechwood 4-5789," and the Contours' dance-floor workout "Do You Love Me" reaching No. 3 by the end of October. Marvin Gaye, backed up by the core of Martha & the Vandellas, had his debut Top 10 R&B hit with "Stubborn Kind of Fellow," which peaked at No. 49 in the Billboard Hot 100. And the Isley Brothers, who would have a good run of success at Motown later in the decade, had their first Top 20 pop hit with a song called "Twist And Shout." The song instantly became a beat group favorite in England despite not even reaching the U.K. Top 40.

A year after Phil Spector debuted his Philles Records, the label gained its first No. 1 hit by the beginning of November 1962 with "He's A Rebel," credited to the Crystals but actually sung by the popular backup vocal group the Blossoms and its big-voiced, gospel-trained lead singer, Darlene Love. "He's A Rebel" was written by the already accomplished singer/songwriter Gene Pitney, who reached No. 2 with his own "Only Love Can Break A Heart" the same week that "He's A Rebel" reached the top of the charts. Similarly, Neil Sedaka, at that point the most successful singer/songwriter of the Brill Building crew, followed up his summertime No. 1 hit "Breaking Up Is Hard To Do" with "Next Door To An Angel," which debuted on the charts in October and reached the Top Five by mid-November.

 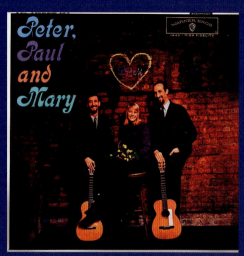 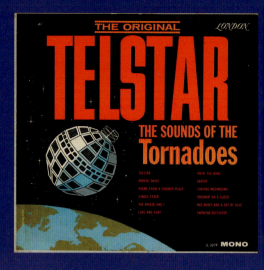

Cameo/Parkway, the Philadelphia-based label that sparked the early '60s dance craze with Chubby Checker's version of "The Twist" in 1960, was still on a hit-making roll with the October debuts of the Orlons' "Don't Hang Up," the very underrated Dee Dee Sharp's third Top 10 hit of the year, "Ride!," and Chubby Checker's Caribbean-flavored "Limbo Rock." And the King of Rock 'n' Roll was still a major presence on the pop scene. Elvis Presley had already had three Top 20 singles that year, and his fabulous "Return To Sender" would spend five weeks at No. 2.

The new, socially relevant brand of folk music gained its first No. 1 album late in October with the debut LP by Peter, Paul and Mary. The album's first single, their version of Pete Seeger's "If I Had A Hammer," reached the Top 10 in mid-October, just before the Cuban missile crisis. The Kingston Trio, who had kicked off the modern folk era in the late '50s, reached the Top 25 with Seeger's anti-war anthem "Where Have All The Flowers Gone." The Rooftop Singers topped the pop chart early in 1963 with a modern folk arrangement of the country blues "Walk Right In." Peter, Paul and Mary's album ended the 14-week run at the top of the album chart for Ray Charles' revolutionary melding of soul and country, *Modern Sounds In Country And Western Music*.

Starting In October, an instrumental with a space-age sound, courtesy of producer Joe Meek and performed by a band called the Tornadoes, topped the U.K. charts for five weeks. Titled "Telstar" after the pioneering American communications satellite launched in July 1962, the single would be released in America on British Decca's London label. "Telstar" topped the final Billboard Hot 100 for 1962, becoming the first number one hit for a British group.

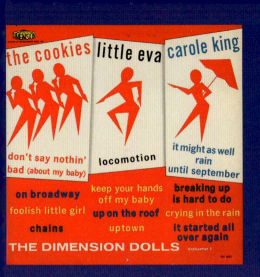  

Musical variety was a major component of Top 40 radio in the 1960s, as contrasted with the fragmented, genre-segregated contemporary hit radio of the 21st century. In the fall of 1962, along with the pop/rock and R&B hits of the day, one could hear classic pop ballads like Tony Bennett's "I Left My Heart In San Francisco" and Sammy Davis, Jr's "What Kind Of Fool Am I?," Stan Getz & Charlie Byrd's bossa nova instrumental "Desifinado" and the debut hit "The Lonely Bull" by a mariachi-style instrumental combo then known as the Tijuana Brass featuring Herb Alpert.

"Up On The Roof" was a classic Brill Building tune from Gerry Goffin and Carole King. The superb production by Jerry Leiber and Mike Stoller, and Rudy Lewis' wonderful lead vocal for the Drifters, made for a No. 5 hit and an ageless pop record. Goffin and King were on a major hit-songwriting roll as 1962 gave way to '63. Little Eva had a No. 12 hit with "Keep Your Hands Off My Baby," while the Cookies, also on Dimension Records, scored with "Chains" (No. 17) and "Don't Say Nothin' Bad (About My Baby)" (No. 7). Pop crooner Steve Lawrence topped the charts in January 1963 with their "Go Away Little Girl," following the Top 10 success in the U.K. of the song by Mark Wynter. Weeks later, Lawrence's wife, Eydie Gorme, had a Top 10 hit with "Blame It On The Bossa Nova," written by another husband-wife Brill Building songwriting team, Barry Mann and Cynthia Weil, with vocal backing by the Cookies.

Leiber and Stoller racked up another major hit as producers in January with "Tell Him" by a New York–based group called the Exciters, which reached the Top Five on the pop and R&B charts. The song was written by legendary '60s producer/songwriter/record company head Bert Berns (as Bert Russell), who also wrote "Twist And Shout."

  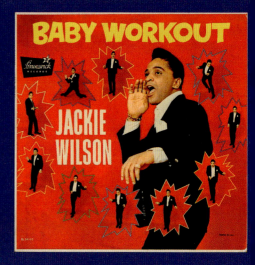

The last No. 1 LP of 1962 was one that would be doomed to the dustbin of history. Vaughn Meader was a musician-turned-comedian who collaborated with writer/producers Bob Booker and Earle Doud on an album gently parodying President John F. Kennedy (portrayed by Meader) and his family. When *The First Family* was released in November, it became the fastest-selling album to that point in time, selling over a million copies in its first two weeks. It topped the charts for 12 weeks, won the Grammy Award for Album of the Year and spawned a *Volume Two*, which reached the album Top Five in 1963. But it all came to an end on the afternoon of November 22, 1963, with the assassination of President Kennedy. Meader's comedy bookings were canceled and both his *First Family* albums were pulled from stores. Although he tried moving forward with non-Kennedy material, the public still associated him with JFK.

Even with the musical changes already in motion, the teen idols of the late '50s/early '60s were still having success in early 1963, as were typical teen love songs, as exemplified by Bobby Vee's "The Night Has A Thousand Eyes," Dion's cover of the mid '50s Drifters R&B hit "Ruby Baby," Paul & Paula's "Hey Paula" (No. 1 for three weeks in February) and Ruby & the Romantics' "Our Day Will Come," which topped the charts late in March. R&B continued to be a potent presence on the pop charts. Motown gained momentum with Mary Wells' "Two Lovers" and the Miracles' Smokey Robinson–penned "You've Really Got A Hold On Me" each reaching the pop Top 10. Johnny Thunder's "Loop De Loop" peaked at No. 4, while "Mr. Excitement," Jackie Wilson, hit the Top Five in April with "Baby Workout." The Drifters scored a Top Ten hit with "On Broadway," a haunting R&B classic written by Barry Mann, Cynthia Weil, Jerry Leiber and Mike Stoller. The Leiber-Stoller-produced track features a unique-sounding guitar solo by Phil Spector.

  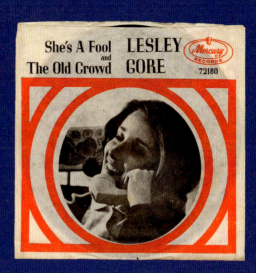

During February and March, everyone was listening to the rhythm of the falling rain in a song by the Cascades, a group from San Diego, California. "Rhythm Of The Rain" became a No. 3 hit in the U.S. and reached No. 5 in the U.K. The song, written by group member John Gummoe, opens and closes with the sound of a thunderstorm, with the singer believing that the falling rain is telling him he's been a fool for losing the only girl he cared about. The track included top L.A. session players such as Hal Blaine on drums, Carol Kaye on bass and Glen Campbell on guitar, and features a celeste (the keyboard instrument played by George Martin on "Baby It's You"). BMI ranked the song at No. 9 in its 1999 list of the Top 100 Songs of the Century to receive radio or TV air play in America. Country singer Skeeter Davis crossed over to the pop charts with her No. 2 song of lover's angst, "The End Of The World." Peter, Paul and Mary scored a No. 2 with "Puff, The Magic Dragon," a fantasy song about loss of innocence (not drugs).

But 1963 will always be remembered as the year of the girl groups and girl singers. In April the Orlons were at No. 3 with their ode to Philly's "South Street," and the Bronx-bred Chiffons were at the top of both the pop and R&B charts with one of the all-time girl group classics, "He's So Fine." By month's end, 15-year-old Little Peggy March had become the youngest female singer to top Billboard's pop chart with "I Will Follow Him," which had been previously released by Petula Clark in the U.K. and U.S. in 1962, but did not chart in either country. In June, a 17-year-old high school junior from Tenafly, New Jersey, Lesley Gore, spent two weeks at No. 1 with her Quincy Jones–produced tale of teen angst, "It's My Party." She would have two more Top Five hits in 1963 with the follow-up "Judy's Turn To Cry" and "She's A Fool." Her late 1963 single "You Don't Own Me" would stall at No. 2 behind "I Want To Hold Your Hand."

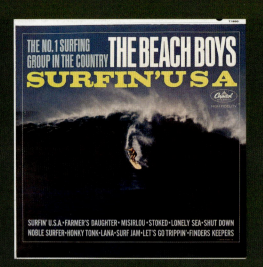  

In May, Jimmy Soul topped the charts for two weeks with "If You Want To Be Happy," a party-atmosphere song based on the calypso song "Ugly Woman." That month also saw the arrival of the Beach Boys as the Four Seasons' primary competition among U.S. groups. With Brian Wilson now the group's songwriting/producing guiding spirit, the Beach Boys reached No. 3 with their Chuck Berry–derived surf anthem, "Surfin' U.S.A.," with subsequent singles "Surfer Girl" and "Be True To Your School" reaching the Top Ten. All three featured quality B-sides that also charted: "Shut Down" (No. 23); "Little Deuce Coupe" (No. 15); and "In My Room" (No. 23). At a time just before rock groups became big album sellers, the Beach Boys' *Surfin' U.S.A.* LP charted at No. 2, while their *Surfer Girl* album peaked at No. 7. The *Little Deuce Coupe* LP stalled at No. 4 in 1964 as *Meet The Beatles!* leapfrogged to the top of the charts.

1963 would also see the rarity of two foreign-language No. 1 hits in the U.S. The first came in June with a record titled "Sukiyaki" for the English-speaking audience, but was actually called "Ue o Muite Aruko" or "I Look Up When I Walk." This was a 1961 single by Japanese pop singer Kyu Sakamoto. Sometime in 1962, British Pye Records executive Louis Benjamin heard the song several times during a visit to Japan. He bought the record and brought it home to England. Pye then released an instrumental of the song, now called "Sukiyaki," by U.K. trad-jazz hitmaker Kenny Ball, which became a U.K. Top 10 hit. Then, a disc jockey at a radio station in Pasco, Washington, began playing Sakamoto's original. Audience reaction was swift and very positive. "Sukiyaki" began getting major airplay in Washington state and Capitol Records (does this scenario sound familiar?) picked up the record's distribution rights and released a U.S. single. By the middle of June, "Sukiyaki" was the No. 1 single in the U.S. for three straight weeks.

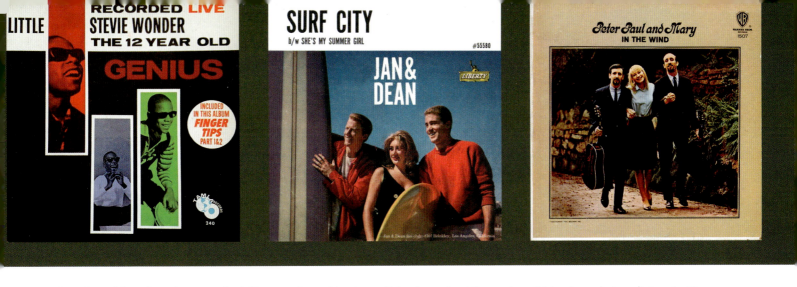

Proof positive that the so-called "forty miles of bad road" had reached its end could be heard via a listen to Top 40 radio in the summer of 1963. The girl groups and female singers were still dominant with Motown's Martha & the Vandellas' "Come And Get These Memories" (followed at summer's end by "Heat Wave"), the Chiffons' Goffin-King-written "One Fine Day," the Crystals' Spector-produced "Da Doo Ron Ron," the Angels' late summer No. 1 "My Boyfriend's Back," Barbara Lewis' "Hello Stranger" and Doris Troy's "Just One Look." A 13-year-old musical wunderkind called Little Stevie Wonder had his debut hit for Motown, "Fingertips - Part 2," a three-week No. 1 in August. The Essex, an R&B group made up of active Marines, had a two-week No. 1 in July with "Easier Said Than Done." Out of Chicago, Major Lance had a major pop/R&B hit with "The Monkey Time," written by Curtis Mayfield, while the Miracles kept the kids dancing with "Mickey's Monkey." The California duo of Jan Berry and Dean Torrance (Jan & Dean) scored with their take on the 1940s pop hit "Linda" (written for Paul's future wife, Linda Eastman) and the surf anthem "Surf City," co-written by Berry and Brian Wilson. And doo-wop had its last major revival that summer with the Tymes' "So Much In Love," the Classics' "Till Then" and Randy & the Rainbows' "Denise."

Peter, Paul and Mary reached No. 2 in August with the summer's civil rights anthem, Bob Dylan's "Blowin' In The Wind," while Trini Lopez hit No. 3 with Pete Seeger's "If I Had A Hammer." In October, the trio's version of Dylan's "Don't Think Twice, It's All Right" reached the U.S. Top 10, and the LP from which it was released, *In The Wind,* leaped to the top of Billboard's album chart, dislodging the group's resurgent debut album from No. 1. Peter, Paul and Mary had what was then a rarity for an act—the top two albums in the U.S. It would happen again just four months later.

141

 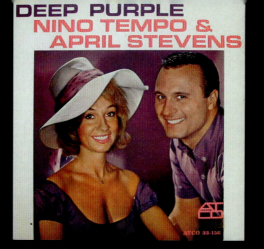 

The summer climaxed with two classic girl group records. There was the Jaynetts' moody and mysterious "Sally, Go 'Round The Roses," said by some to be the first "psychedelic" hit. At the other end of the spectrum was one of the greatest examples of Phil Spector's "wall of sound," the Ronettes' classic debut hit "Be My Baby," which never reached No. 1 on Billboard's Hot 100, spending three weeks in October at No. 2 behind… "Sugar Shack."

"Sugar Shack" was a pleasant little record about a guy trying to woo a waitress that topped the charts for five weeks and became Billboard's No. 1 single of 1963. It was recorded by Jimmy Gilmer and the Fireballs, who were produced by Norman Petty, Buddy Holly's former producer. Petty had the Fireballs provide instrumental backing on unreleased home recordings by Holly following his death. The strange keyboard heard on "Sugar Shack" is a Hammond Solovox, a 1940s electronic instrument. On New Year's Eve, 1963, a DJ played "Sugar Shack" as the year's No. 1 song. Afterwards he added: "That's their No. 1. Here's mine." He then played the Drifters' "On Broadway."

"Sugar Shack" was one of six straight No. 1 records, running from late September of 1963 through January 1964, that were pretty far removed from rock 'n' roll and helped to create the myth that it took the Beatles to reinvigorate the American pop scene. Bookending this string of number ones were two big band/crooners–era tunes updated slightly by Bobby Vinton, "Blue Velvet" and "There! I've Said it Again." "Sugar Shack" was knocked from the top by the brother-sister team of Nino Tempo and April Stevens' update (complete with harmonica) of the 1930s hit "Deep Purple." This was followed by Dale & Grace's version of the late '50s country song "I'm Leaving It Up To You."

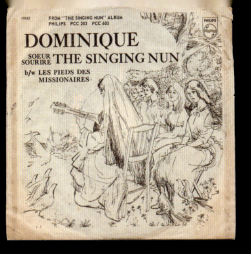  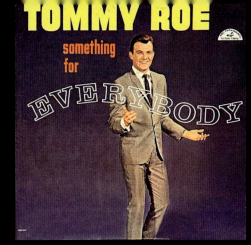

The second foreign-language song to top the singles chart was No. 1 for the last four weeks of the year. "Dominique" was recorded by a Belgian nun and singer/songwriter named Jeannine Deckers, known within her Dominican order as Sister Luc Gabriel and professionally as the Smiling Sister and, in America, The Singing Nun. "Dominique" was a Belgian-language tribute to the Dominican order's founder Saint Dominic that became an international sensation, reaching the Top 10 in the U.K. and topping the charts in Australia, New Zealand, Argentina, Venezuela, South Africa and Canada, as well as the U.S. The Sister appeared on The Ed Sullivan Show in early January of 1964, just over a month before the Beatles, and then pretty much faded into pop culture history, save for a 1966 movie called *The Singing Nun*, starring Debbie Reynolds, which the Sister dismissed as "fiction." Deckers would leave the order in 1966. She and a longtime female companion would end up taking their own lives in March 1985. Bizarrely, Kyu Sakamoto, who had 1963's other foreign-language U.S. No. 1, would die just over four months later in the crash of Japan Air Lines Flight 123, which killed 520 of the 524 aboard a doomed Boeing 747.

Even with the success of "Dominique" through December, there was still rock 'n' roll on the charts in those final weeks of 1963 and a couple of previews of what lay just ahead. A British duo called the Caravelles, and Tommy Roe, who had toured with the Beatles the previous spring in the U.K. when their star was just starting to rise, each reached No. 3 that month. The Caravelles' "You Don't Have To Be A Baby To Cry" was a wistful, country-flavored tune, but Roe's "Everybody" was a rave-up rocker on which he tried to capture the essence of the new sounds coming out of England. Both were booked as opening acts for the Beatles first American concert at the Washington Coliseum.

143

And then there were "Louie Louie" and "Surfin' Bird." Written and originally recorded in 1958 by Richard Berry, "Louie Louie" became a popular number with bands in the Pacific Northwest in the early '60s. Idaho's Paul Revere & the Raiders recorded the song earlier in 1963, and then it was covered by an Oregon garage band called the Kingsmen. With a driving beat and slurred vocals that soon got the attention of politicians looking for smutty lyrics that weren't there, "Louie Louie" topped radio surveys in New York, Boston and elsewhere. Billboard placed the song at No. 2 for six weeks, first behind "Dominique" and then "There! I've Said it Again." "Surfin' Bird" was actually a medley of two tunes, "Papa-Oom-Mow-Mow" and "The Bird's The Word," by the popular surf-rock band the Rivingtons, covered by a band from Minneapolis called the Trashmen. "Surfin' Bird" raced up the charts and had reached No. 4 by the end of January and appeared to be headed for No. 1. But then…

After turning down the Beatles four times, Capitol Records finally agreed to release the Beatles latest single, "I Want To Hold Your Hand," in mid-January 1964. After a copy of the British single was played on WWDC and excited listeners throughout the Washington, D.C. area, Capitol rush-released the disc the day after Christmas. In 1964's first week, the song entered New York's WABC's survey at No. 35. By January 7, it was No. 1, with the station's primary competition, WMCA, placing it at the top a week later. Cash Box placed "I Want To Hold Your Hand" at the top of its singles chart on January 25, making the single the first national chart topper for a rock record by a British band. By the first week in February, it topped the Billboard Hot 100, with reissues of "She Loves You" and "Please Please Me" quickly climbing the chart along with British female song stylist Dusty Springfield's "I Only Want To Be With You."

  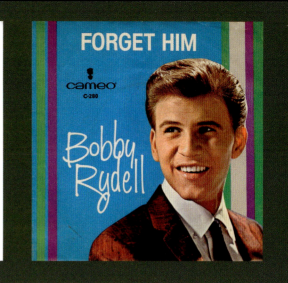

While "I Want To Hold Your Hand" was in its second and third week at No. 1 on WABC, the No. 2 song was "Forget Him," teen idol Bobby Rydell's biggest hit in America since 1960s "Volare." The record was actually about a year old, recorded in England in February 1963 and reaching the U.K. Top 15 that spring. "Forget Him" was originally released in the U.S. that fall as a bonus single tucked into a Rydell album of hits of '63 on Cameo/Parkway. The single took off in the final weeks of 1963 and peaked nationally the same week that "I Want To Hold Your Hand" topped Cash Box's singles chart. "Forget Him" was written and produced by Tony Hatch, who already had a long resume of hit credits in the U.K. but was hardly known in America. On October 16, 1964, Hatch produced a session with British pop singer Petula Clark during which she recorded his new composition "Downtown." They continued to work together, with Clark having more hits than any other female vocalist of the British Invasion. For Bobby Rydell, though, the Beatles and the rest of the British acts would make the youth of America forget him. He would not crack the Top 40 again.

In the early morning hours of February 7, 1964, just hours before the Beatles were scheduled to arrive at the newly renamed John F. Kennedy International Airport in New York, Bob Lewis, the disc jockey known as "Bob-A-Loo," was doing his overnight show on WABC and giving numerous plugs to that afternoon's coverage of the Beatles arrival, to be anchored by the station's nighttime DJs Scott Muni and Bruce Morrow (known as Cousin Brucie). But, as was his custom, Lewis was playing a lot of oldies. On this particular night, he focused on late '50s/early '60s doo-wop hits. It was almost as if Lewis subconsciously knew that a page of music and pop culture history was hours away from being turned and he was giving a final bow to the music that was about to be deemed out of fashion.

An Experiment in the Mad, Mad World of 1963 Film

by Frank Daniels

The top films of 1962 included an adaptation of the Broadway show *The Music Man*, which featured a lovely song "Till There Was You" that was already part of the stage show of an obscure British group by the time of the film's release. There was a drama about Helen Keller's blind tutor, *The Miracle Worker*, and a romantic comedy starring Cary Grant and Doris Day, *That Touch Of Mink*. For those seeking exotic adventure mixed with comedy, there was *Hatari!*, a John Wayne movie filmed in East Africa that featured a delightful Henry Mancini tune, "Baby Elephant Walk." *The Longest Day* was an epic war movie about the D-Day invasion at Normandy. Then there was *Lolita*, an exploration into the relationship between an older college professor and a young teenage girl. In *The Man Who Shot Liberty Valence*, James Stewart and John Wayne tell the western drama that explains the film's title. *Experiment In Terror* was a shocking thriller in which an asthmatic murderer terrorizes a bank teller by trying to force her to steal $100,000 from her bank. The film's dramatic conclusion features a chase through San Francisco's Candlestick Park where, five years later, a now-famous British group would play their last paid concert.

The period from October through December 1962 starts with an important British film debut. Opening on October 5, the same day the Beatles released their first single, "Love Me Do," *Dr. No* was the first big-screen appearance by James Bond. The low-budget spy thriller initiated the adventure/spy drama genre that is still popular today (as is James Bond). Although the October 1962 issue of EMI's Record Mail did not review "Love Me Do," the magazine praised *Dr. No* from its dazzling opening credit titles to its ending, calling it a thrilling and superb picture. The movie began with the viewer staring at Bond through the barrel of a gun. He fires, and blood fills the screen. If that sequence is familiar, it is because that opening became a trademark of the Bond films. The James Bond theme music that debuted in *Dr. No* later influenced Ken Thorne's instrumental music for the Beatles second film, to the point where some of it was attached to the beginning of the title song, "Help!," on the American soundtrack album.

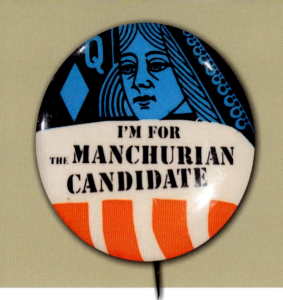 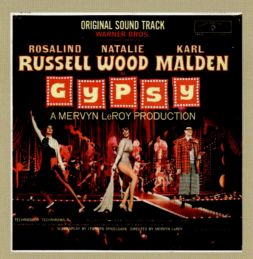 

Frank Sinatra had appeared in over three dozen movies by 1962, but *The Manchurian Candidate* had a different air about it than any of his previous films. Far from *Pal Joey* or *Young At Heart*, the spy film is about a real worry of the Cold War: what if Communist China found a way to put their supporters into office in the United States? Even worse, what if they brainwashed someone into doing their bidding? Dr. Robert Jay Lifton's book about Chinese brainwashing techniques, *Thought Reform and the Psychology of Totalism*, had only been out for a year. People who read that book made it a pattern for describing the techniques of persuasion that cults used. In this movie, Frankie learns first-hand what those techniques are! Director John Frankenheimer was nominated for a Golden Globe Award. Angela Lansbury, who superbly plays the villainous mother of a sleeper agent, won a Golden Globe for Best Supporting Actress and was nominated in the same category for an Academy Award.

What Ever Happened To Baby Jane? was a psychological horror film starring Bette Davis and Joan Crawford, two acclaimed actresses nearing the end of their careers. Davis was nominated for a Best Actress Academy Award. Another Broadway adaptation, *Gypsy,* was a critical and financial success. The musical film features Rosalind Russell, Natalie Wood and Karl Malden, and the songs "Everything's Coming Up Roses" and "Let Me Entertain You."

Cinerama was a widescreen film process that originally projected images from three synchronized 35mm projectors onto a huge, curved screen. Due to logistics and expenses, only a few true Cinerama three-lens feature films were made. *How The West Was Won* was an epic western with a star-studded ensemble cast narrated by Spencer Tracy.

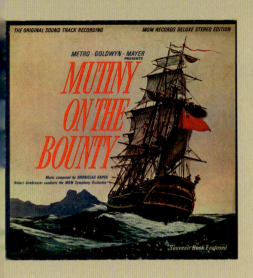  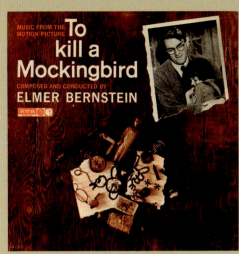

Mutiny On The Bounty was shot with a competing wide-screen format, Ultra Panavision, which used 70mm cameras and 65mm Eastmancolor film for projection on 70mm systems or reduced to 35mm prints for theaters that did not have the larger projectors. But while *How The West Was Won* was a financial and critical success, *Mutiny On The Bounty* and star Marlon Brando's performance were panned by filmgoers and critics alike, costing MGM millions.

Every now and then, a period film captures the hearts of people around the world. Such was *Lawrence Of Arabia*, featuring Peter O'Toole and Alec Guinness. The Academy nominated the movie for ten Oscars, awarding it seven, including Best Picture. The film also earned six Golden Globe Awards. It earned $37,500,000 in the U.S. and a similar amount worldwide; adjusted for inflation, that's $365,000,000 in 2022 dollars. In 1962 and 1963, few viewers realized that director David Lean deliberately centered the movie around a relationship between two gay men. "[Homosexuality] does pervade it, the whole story, and certainly Lawrence was very if not entirely homosexual," he said. The 222-minute film was shot in Ultra Panavision and featured an award-winning score by Maurice Jarre.

Released at Christmas, *To Kill A Mockingbird* featured Gregory Peck as the heroic Atticus Finch, an attorney going up against the norms of racism in Alabama during the 1930s. In the book (and the movie), birds are somewhat symbolic. Since mockingbirds harm no living creatures, it is a sin to kill a mockingbird; that is, to kill or destroy an innocent. A much later movie, *Deeds*, mentions a character from *To Kill a Mockingbird*: Boo Radley, the reclusive neighbor. This demonstrates the pervasive influence that the movie and book have had over the years.

1963 certainly did not disappoint moviegoers. Jack Lemmon, already a master of comedy, delivers some of his best work alongside Shirley MacLaine in *Irma La Douce*, produced, directed and co-written by Billy Wilder, with a score by Andre Previn. Lemmon portrays an honest cop surrounded by prostitutes. He winds up rescuing a woman from her pimp, but in order to help her give up her profession, he adopts the persona of Lord X. Things really get crazy when Lord X is murdered. Oh, boy. I don't want to spoil the ending for you; watch the film!

Sylvia Syms and June Ritchie starred as club hostesses in the somewhat risqué movie, *The World Ten Times Over*, which was released two years later in the U.S. as *Pussycat Alley*. William Hartnell plays the role of Syms' father, a man who seems estranged from his daughter. Variety described his performance as "unworldly." Although the magazine meant that word differently, on November 23, 1963, Hartnell became the first of many actors to play the role of The Doctor in the BBC series *Doctor Who*. The show quickly became part of British society (and later worldwide). So much a part of society was *Doctor Who* that two years later the time-traveling Doctor views footage of the Beatles from an April 1965 episode of Top Of The Pops. Upon hearing the group perform "Ticket To Ride," The Doctor's companion, Vicki, says they are marvelous, but adds she didn't know the Beatles played classical music. Ironically, the rest of that performance was wiped from the television archives, so only the brief clip from *Doctor Who* remains.

One of the year's movies tells the fictionalized story of how John F. (Jack) Kennedy came to be labeled a war hero. Young Kennedy had a history of illness, and in 1940, the Army rejected him because of his ailments, including VD and back problems. His father, Joe Kennedy, convinced the head of Naval Intelligence to allow a Boston doctor, rather than a Navy doctor, to certify Jack's health. As a result, Kennedy entered the Navy as ensign in 1941. When he later asked for leave to obtain back surgery, the Navy doctors rejected his request, so Kennedy wound up at Northwestern University in Midshipman's School. Lt. Cmdr. John Duncan Bulkeley spoke to the school about how his PT-boat squadron had sunk Japanese ships. His stories inspired students to sign up for PT training. Reportedly, Joe Kennedy explained to Bulkeley how young Jack ought to command a PT boat to advance his political career. Jack was in.

After completing training, Jack was sent to the Solomon Islands, commanding PT-109. The PT boat was in bad shape, but Kennedy's crew made it seaworthy. Early in the morning of August 2, 1943, PT-109 found itself on a combat mission. Kennedy's crew did not hear radio warnings that Japanese destroyers were heading in their direction. Suddenly, an enormous destroyer appeared in the night heading right for them. Jack spun the wheel to turn his ship toward the enemy, but its engines failed. The destroyer rammed the boat, splitting it and killing some of the crew. Kennedy ordered the rest to abandon ship. Minutes later, the fires that had engulfed the boat died down, and the crew returned to the boat temporarily. Jack saved the life of one man who was in the water helpless and burnt. Their goal at this point was to make it to a small island, an exhausting swim that took them five hours. A few days later, the stranded crew ran out of food, so they relocated to another island. On August 8, they were rescued and returned to base, where two reporters heard the story and wrote of the dramatic rescue. In 1944, author John Hersey wrote the story like a novel, and it was published in the June 17 New Yorker. Hersey's account, titled "Survival," made Kennedy into a hero. It was peppered with language like: "In spite of his burden [carrying an injured man], Kennedy beat the other men to the reef that surrounded the island." Hersey avoided talking about why and how the collision occurred, instead focusing on how the men survived. Joe Kennedy convinced the magazine to allow Reader's Digest to publish a condensed version that focused on his son, helping to get Kennedy elected for Congress two years later.

Americans embraced the heroic telling of the story of their president in the June 1963 film *PT 109*, starring Cliff Robertson. They laughed along with Jack at the parody LP, *The First Family,* and would purchase Kennedy memorial albums after his death in November. Jack was more than a president to them; he was like a member of the family.

In *Flipper*, a young boy rescues an injured dolphin and treats the animal as if it is part of his family. The 1963 film had a catchy theme song and led to sequels and a TV series that ran for three seasons starting in September 1964.

But animals are not always friendly. On August 18, 1961, the Santa Cruz Sentinel reported that "a massive flight" of birds had swarmed the shore at 3AM, waking people as they began "slamming against their homes." Eight people reported being bitten. The article concluded by stating that "a phone call came to The Sentinel from mystery thriller producer Alfred Hitchcock from Hollywood, requesting that a Sentinel be sent to him." This real-life event (caused by the birds' consumption of toxic algae) became the basis for Hitchcock's horrifying film, *The Birds*. The master of suspense put the events of that night together with the basic structure of Daphne duMaurier's novella (also called *The Birds*), creating a horror film with no neat ending. Although the protagonists manage to survive and leave the area, the film gives no reason for the avian attack, demonstrates at the end that the birds are still outraged at something, and provides no indication that there is any safe place. Showing both adults and children in danger, the movie kept people at the edges of their seats.

Always at the edges of their seats were fans of Elvis Presley. In '62-'63, Elvis released three movies: *Girls! Girls! Girls!*; *It Happened At The World's Fair*; and *Fun In Acapulco*. The King of Rock and Roll played a fishing guide who sings, a crop-duster pilot who sings, and a former circus performer who...sings. None of the movies was particularly striking, but Presley was still releasing hit singles, and the movies gave his fans the opportunity to watch him sing them.

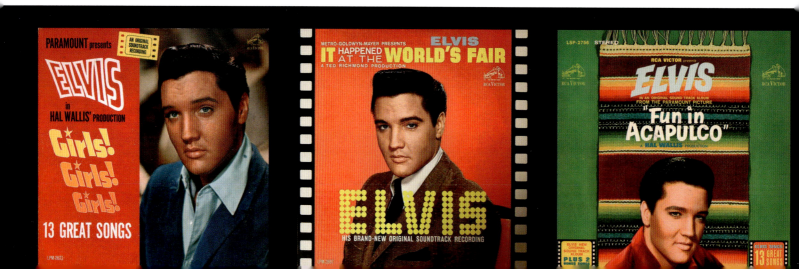

Presley had stopped touring after he was drafted into and entered the Army in 1957. His induction prompted the creation of a hit musical. The title character was to be called Ellsworth, but that was later changed to Conrad Birdie, a parody of Conway Twitty, whose 1958 hit "It's Only Make Believe" had some listeners assuming it was sung by Elvis using a pseudonym. The play, *Bye Bye Birdie*, was adapted into a movie starring Dick van Dyke, who played the lead character on Broadway, and Jesse Pearson as Conrad. Also noteworthy was Ann-Margret's appearance as Kim. In fact, the producers altered the movie to increase the size of her part. She went on to act with Elvis himself in 1964. The producers thought it would be interesting to have Elvis portray Conrad; however, Col. Tom Parker, Elvis' manager, thought that doing so would put Elvis in the ridiculous position of playing a parody of himself. To see rock 'n' roll musicians act as parodies of themselves in a film, the public would have to wait until 1964. Meanwhile, "We Love You, Conrad" would be adapted by the Carefrees into "We Love You, Beatles" in early 1964. Another song from *Bye Bye Birdie*, "Hymn For A Sunday Evening," paid homage to Ed Sullivan. Less than a year after the film's debut, that once-obscure British group would be seen coast to coast with America's favorite host by 73 million people.

Another fun movie for teenagers in 1963 was *Beach Party* starring former Mouseketeer Annette Funicello and teen idol singer Frankie Avalon. *Beach Party* was so successful for American International Pictures that they signed Funicello to a multi-year contract. By 1965, she had been to every sort of party on every beach in the world – including an appearance with the Beach Boys. *Beach Party* was the huge hit that spawned the beach movie craze, and API got involved just in time to experience great success. If you'd like to join a beach party, this might be the one!

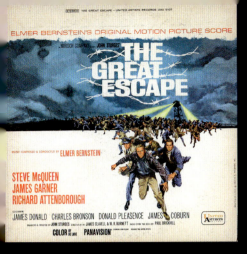 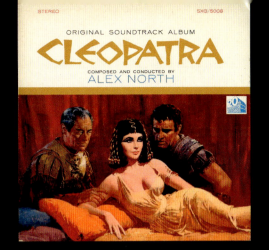 

If you'd rather escape from it all, then you should watch *The Great Escape*. Chances are, if you enjoyed action/adventure movies in the 1960s, this was one of your favorite films. As an American soldier, Steve McQueen winds up in a prison camp alongside James Garner, Charles Bronson, Donald Pleasance, James Coburn, David McCallum and other stars. Based on the true story of a dramatic escape from a real German stalag, the movie follows British and American soldiers through the ups and downs of trying to find a way out. Once they get out, they need a way to escape from Germany. They start clipping wire and digging, and, for a while, the Nazis always seem to foil their plans. Then they decide to make one really big escape – one that is sure to be noticed everywhere. Most of them will be killed, but those who do make it out can spread the word about their brave attempt. Notably, McQueen's own efforts include a daring motorcycle chase that features jumping the cycle over fences. The characters are three-dimensional, and by the time the escape comes, the moviegoer is cheering for all of them to make it home. Do they make it? Well, you'll need to watch the film to find out.

If you enjoy historical movies, but Nazis are not your bag, 1963 had plenty for you – in the form of *Cleopatra* (starring Elizabeth Taylor and Richard Burton, with Rex Harrison, Roddy McDowall and Martin Landau) and the Arthurian legend *Sword In The Stone*. The former is an epic film, beginning with Julius Caesar and concluding with the title character's death. The latter was an animated film from Walt Disney Studios, whose cast included Sebastian Cabot and Alan Napier (who later played Alfred on the Batman TV series). General reception for *Sword In The Stone* was mixed, while *Cleopatra* was universally praised, receiving nine Oscar nominations and winning four.

For those who appreciate an ensemble cast but prefer comedy over the war drama that was *The Great Escape*, then possibly the greatest movie of all time is the zany madcap adventure called *It's A Mad, Mad, Mad, Mad World*. The movie became the very definition of "cult classic." Beginning only with the true legend that the original "roadshow" version of the movie (lasting 202 minutes) has not been seen since 1963, that there were several trimmed versions of the movie since then, and that some actors had their entire appearances cut, we discover that we have on our hands a movie that can be – and has been – dissected every which way since it came out. It may be the case that more people have examined the details of *Mad, Mad World* than have looked at the Beatles movies…and that's saying something.

The basic idea is simple: master thief, Smiler Grogan, has just finished fifteen years in prison for a robbery that he committed. Free at last, he is going to retrieve the money, but as he is speeding along a roadway out in the middle of nowhere, disaster strikes, and he winds up "sailing right out there" through the guardrail and down an embankment. Several cars full of people stop to see if they can help. Grogan (Jimmy Durante) begins explaining himself to them. Dentist Melville Crump (Sid Caesar) begins by trying to help: "I'm a dentist. Do you think you're hurt real bad?" Grogan, badly injured, responds: "Is he kiddin'?" Truck driver Lennie Pike (Jonathan Winters) wants to get him to a hospital, but it's too late. Grogan responds with the deal of a lifetime for those lucky people: "You move me, I'll break up in little pieces, but what a deal! There's this dough, see? There's all this dough: 350 Gs." The money is in Rosita Beach State Park, and where is it? "Buried under this…under this big W. You'll see it! You'll see it under this – under this big W. You can't miss it: a big…a big W."

So, the movie begins with Grogan telling them about all that money to split amongst themselves anyway they see fit. They just have to get there. Referring to himself as "everybody's friend," Grogan soon kicks the bucket – literally, and the group finds themselves wondering if the guy's story is true. We meet characters played by Ethel Merman, Milton Berle, Dorothy Provine, Buddy Hackett, Mickey Rooney and Edie Adams. After they cannot determine how to use mathematics in a way that gives everyone a fair share, they each take off – headed for the treasure. Unknown to them, the police are watching them, headed by Captain T. G. Culpepper (Spencer Tracy, in his best comedic role).

Along the way to find the case full of money, they encounter a great number of nutty people, some of whom wind up becoming part of the group and seeking the treasure. These include Dick Shawn, Eddie Anderson ("Rochester"), Peter Falk, Jim Backus, Joe E. Brown, Barrie Chase, William Demarest, Andy Devine, Selma Diamond, Norman Fell, Stan Freberg, Leo Gorcey, Marvin Kaplan, Buster Keaton, Don Knotts, ZaSu Pitts, Carl Reiner, the Three Stooges, Jack Benny, Jerry Lewis and quite a few others. As the group was filming, it seemed that everyone wanted to appear in it – at least in a cameo role. In every scene, people just pop up, and the viewer thinks, "Hey. Isn't that--?"

Some of the group take to the air, while others race on the ground. Every time someone comes up with a brilliant plan, it seems to be thwarted. The pace is fast, but the movie was so long that it breaks for an intermission. Before it is over, buildings are demolished and people are nearly electrocuted, blown up, crashed in airplanes, thrown from high buildings...and we do find the money. You can only ever see a movie "for the first time" once, so if you haven't seen it, get out there and find out what comedy in 1963 was all about.

Charade combined romance, comedy, mystery and suspense in the style of Alfred Hitchcock's lighter fare. Cary Grant and Audrey Hepburn are superb in the lead roles backed by Walter Matthau, James Coburn and George Kennedy. The film's score is by Henry Mancini. Other comedies included films by Jerry Lewis (*The Nutty Professor*) and the Three Stooges (*Around The World In A Daze*). Those seeking monsters got two for the price of one in the Japanese production of *King Kong vs. Godzilla*.

157

If your name happened to be John Lennon, you might have preferred to watch *Le Mépris*. This was a French art film in the New Wave school that tells a story about a playwright who is asked to rework the script to director Fritz Lang's adaptation of *The Odyssey*. The playwright's wife, played by Brigitte Bardot, suspects that her husband may be cheating on her. She tells him that she no longer loves him. Hoping to keep her, he invites her to join him in Capri for the filming. The movie serves as a commentary on the film industry, with the filmmakers arguing about trivial details. Bardot expresses her contempt for her husband (*Contempt* is the English title of the film) because he has been using her to strengthen his relationship with the film's producer. Everyone essentially leaves, and Lang keeps working on his movie. In a bit of on-target irony, the American co-producers of *Le Mépris* wanted to see something more sensual from Bardot, so director Jean-Luc Godard shot a separate introductory scene – realizing that the addition of the scene actually helped make the film's case about the relationship between creators and movie executives.

Our excursion into the mad, mad world of 1963 film began in earnest on October 5, 1962, with the British release of the initial James Bond film, *Dr. No*. One year later, at least in the U.K., James Bond was back with his second film, *From Russia With Love*, which premiered in London on October 10, 1963. The film's theme song was written by Lionel Bart (who wrote the book, music and lyrics for the stage musical *Oliver!*), performed by Matt Monro (whose single release of *From Russia With Love* peaked at number 20 on the U.K. charts) and produced by George Martin. American audiences would have to wait until April 1964 to see the film.

Back in Merry Ole England, the end of November 1963 saw the British premiere of a short film that would truly prepare the way for 1964. This was a simple documentary about the goings-on around one concert performance from one British band at one venue: the ABC Ardwick Theatre in Manchester. For those who hadn't yet witnessed Beatlemania first-hand, *The Beatles Come To Town* was essential viewing. There is a sense to which the short film both explains history and prophesies the future. Featuring excerpts of several Beatles songs, the film from British Pathé captures a moment in history. It marked a transition from one level of greatness to a higher one, as though something "really big" was about to happen. Of course, like James Bond, it happened first in England. But America and much of the world would soon follow.

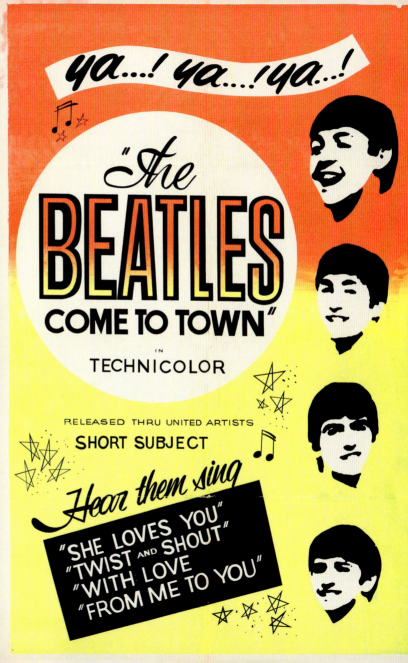

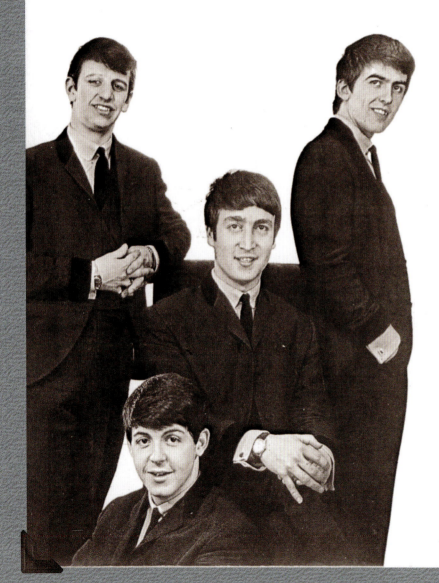

THE RECORD THAT STARTED "BEATLEMANIA"

ENGLAND'S SENSATIONS

JUST DID
JACK PAAR SHOW
(JAN. 3)

COMING UP
ED SULLIVAN
(FEB. 9 & FEB. 16)

FEATURED IN TIME, LIFE, NEWSWEEK

THIS IS THE RECORD THAT STARTED IT ALL

PLEASE, PLEASE ME
AND
FROM ME TO YOU
BY
THE BEATLES

VEE-JAY RECORDS

VJ-581

(PROMOTION COPY)

FAN RECOLLECTIONS

It was Sunday, February 9, 1964. It started out just like any other Sunday afternoon. I was an eleven-year-old kid living in Brooklyn, New York. Like so many other Sundays, my Mom and Dad loaded me and my sister into the car, and we headed up to 99th Street and Park Avenue to visit my dad's parents and sister, who lived in the projects. My dad's sister, Iris, who we affectionately called Titi (aunt in slang Spanish), had never married and loved spoiling me and my sisters. On that particular Sunday, Titi took me and my sister to Korvette's, a discount department store. Once there, Titi brought me to the record section and said, "I'm getting you this," handing me a record with four guys on the cover. I'd heard one of the songs listed on the jacket, "I Want To Hold Your Hand," a few times on the radio with my friends and I thought it was okay. But Titi was adamant, and it wasn't like I was gonna say, "No thanks."

I can still remember sitting on the living room floor of my grandparent's apartment when Titi put the album on their console, which had a TV, radio and record player.

I'm sure I recognized "I Want To Hold Your Hand" and liked the next two songs, but the thing I remember most was hearing John Lennon singing "It won't be long, yeah," and me freaking out. By the time the song was over, I knew it was the coolest thing I'd ever heard, and those very dramatic, half-shadowed faces on the front cover of *Meet The Beatles!* were suddenly mystery men who I wanted to get to know. With each song, the music just got better and better. Now I was staring at the back side of the album with an inset photo of the four hanging out in their boots. They looked like real friends, like a real band, and made it seem like making music together was fun. They had an attitude, and I was digging it.

But I still didn't know what was about to happen that night—that these guys were going to be on The Ed Sullivan Show—until Titi told me after we'd listened to the album. It was the reason she'd bought it for me, she said. After dinner and dessert, we all gathered in front of the TV console, three generations of us in that tiny apartment, and heard Ed Sullivan say: "Ladies and gentlemen, the Beatles...." And there they were, mystery men no longer. *Wow*, I thought, back on the floor next to my grandmother's caged birds, my eyes glued to the TV screen. The confidence, the joy, the cohesiveness, the girls going wild...*I want to be just like those guys*.

Back home, I got my dad's Spanish nylon-stringed guitar and posed next to my *Meet The Beatles!* album jacket. Like me, the neighborhood kids saw on The Ed Sullivan Show how cool those guys were—and how the girls went wild. So we set up the drums and managed to put a little PA system together. We even eventually had a name—Population 4—which we thought was super clever because, you know, there were four guys in the band: my cousin Vinny on lead guitar; Daryl Leoce on drums; Joel Leoce on rhythm guitar; and me on bass, vocals and sax (although I initially played my dad's Spanish guitar).

Unfortunately the only thing that Population 4 had in common with the Fab Four was that there were four of us. After playing in a series of bands and doing session work primarily on sax, I hit the big time, not as a member of my own rock 'n' roll band, but as a sideman. Don't feel sorry for me. In addition to becoming the sax player for Billy Joel, I got to play with three of those mystery men.

I met John Lennon at the Record Plant, a New York recording studio, where I was playing my horn and cleaning up garbage. He was one of those mystery men on the back of that first Beatles record my Aunt Iris had bought me all those years before. The man who, more than any other, made me want to be a rock 'n' roller. There I was, in Studio C, with the man who put color in my rock 'n' roll world. The meeting led to my adding a new sax part on "Imagine," one of my favorite songs of all time, and being on stage with John as he played the song, along with "Slippin' And Slidin'," to track for his participation in the 1975 television show A Salute To Sir Lew Grade.

In 1995, Ringo was putting together his third All Starr Band for a tour when Clarence Clemons, the larger-than-life saxophone player from Bruce Springsteen's E Street Band, had to back out. Ringo needed another sax player, so I got to be a sideman in a band of stars: Billy Preston, Randy Bachman, Mark Farner, Felix Cavaliere, John Entwistle and Zak Starkey. I ended up being the band's Musical Director, a job I have held through various versions of the All Starr Band to this day.

In 2010, Joe Walsh asked if I could put together a band for Paul McCartney to surprise Ringo on stage for his seventieth birthday. As Musical Director, I helped Paul remember "Birthday," which he hadn't played in years.

So while I never got to be *just like those guys*, I'm feeling pretty good as a sideman and looking forward to the next show wherever it may be. It's gonna be great.

Mark Rivera (extracted from his book *Sideman*)

I turned 14 in January of 1964, and was blessed beyond compare. My dad was a doctor, and one of his patients worked for CBS, the same network that broadcast The Ed Sullivan Show. This person knew that the doctor's daughter was crazy about the Beatles, and was able to find this lucky lady one ticket to the show! I felt I won the lottery when I was given a ticket to the afternoon dress rehearsal of the Sullivan Show on February 9. But I wasn't going to wait until Sunday to see the Beatles!

On Friday, February 7, when the Beatles arrived in NYC, I cut afternoon classes and ran to the Plaza Hotel to see them arrive. It was quite cold outside, but so many fans had the same idea that we were just one big fan frenzy waiting for their arrival. The flashing police car lights told of their arrival – and in a flash, they were all inside the hotel. But they were HERE. In NEW YORK CITY!

Sunday could not come soon enough. That afternoon would be my first chance to SEE and HEAR the Beatles. I had butterflies in my stomach as I clutched my precious ticket for The Ed Sullivan Show afternoon dress rehearsal. There were throngs of girls outside of the TV studio as I made my way to the ticketholder's line. I was one of just 728 members in the audience. To say I was restless was an understatement. And then I heard Ed Sullivan say: "Ladies and gentlemen, THE BEATLES!"

I was seated in the balcony looking down on the group. As Paul started with "All My Loving," I was ecstatic, mesmerized, elated and jumping with excitement and joy all at the same time. And a sound came out of my voice I never had experienced before. This was Beatlemania! "Till There Was You" and "She Loves You" followed. My heart was pumping hard. The first set was over in a flash, giving me time to catch my breath and continue to be in this ecstatic state. In the last part of the show, we were treated to "I Saw Her Standing There" and "I Want To Hold Your Hand." It was wonderful, my first of many encounters with John, Paul, George and Ringo. But wait, there was more!

After Sullivan completed the hour's show, we were treated to another wonderful dose of the Beatles, who were brought back with a different set to tape their third week's show. This time John let loose with "Twist and Shout," "Please Please Me" and "I Want To Hold Your Hand." I know some of my screams are on that precious tape, as now I just couldn't control myself. I don't know why, it just happened. It was on that day that I vowed to travel to meet John, Paul, George and Ringo in England as soon as I graduated from high school in three years. That special day was the birth of BeatleTripper.

Leslie Samuels Healy a/k/a Beatle Tripper

Despite having just turned nine years old the day before, I clearly remember what happened on the night of February 9, 1964. The Ed Sullivan Show was a staple of my family's regular Sunday night television viewing in Kewanee, Illinois. But this night the experience was going to be very different. I had heard "I Want To Hold Your Hand" on the local radio station a few days before. The music struck me as being very different from anything I'd heard before. It was almost indescribable, but was vibrant, catchy, and joyous. I liked it immediately. But it wasn't until I saw the Beatles for the first time on The Ed Sullivan Show that I got the full sense of what the Beatles were all about. Their enthusiasm, their look, their "long" hair (which of course my parents had to comment on) and of course their music, made a huge impression on me. I and millions of other Americans got the first glimpse of what would soon become known as "Beatlemania." I've spent the nearly 60 years since that night as a die-hard Beatles fan and collector. Needless to say the night of February 9, 1964, changed my life.

Michael Rinella

It was Tuesday night, January 7, 1964, new survey night on WABC in New York, the fastest-growing Top 40 radio station in the U.S. I was ostensibly doing my eighth grade homework but, at 8:00 PM, the station's prime-time disc jockey, Scott Muni, would be playing the top seven songs on the new survey.

8:00 PM came and Scottso began playing the top seven. The Singing Nun's "Dominque," the dominant record of the last weeks of 1963, was down to No. 6 while the Murmaids' "Popsicles and Icicles" had dropped to No. 7. Everything else hadn't moved except for the previous week's No. 1 song, the Kingsmen's "Louie Louie," which had dropped to the second spot. Instead of doing my homework, I was wracking my brain trying to figure out what the new survey topper was. The jingle trumpeting the No. 1 song played...and I heard a record that I had never heard before. It came roaring out of the tiny speaker and, to ears accustomed to the American pop/rock of the day, it sounded like something from another planet. WABC's new survey topper had leaped there from No. 35 the previous week. It was a group called the Beatles (?????) and a song called "I Want To Hold Your Hand."

Many people have said that their first listen to that song changed their lives, that it was the greatest, most different record they had ever heard. My reaction was quite different...negative. It was just TOO different. How did it become the No. 1 song so quickly? When I got back to school the next day and girls were going crazy for this group that they had never heard of a week earlier, I just rejected it all as just a lot of hype. But it got worse as January progressed. Within days, Dan Ingram, WABC's great afternoon drive-time DJ, was playing THREE records by these Beatles at 5:00 PM every afternoon. "I Want To Hold Your Hand" had been joined on the station survey by "She Loves You" and "Please Please Me." Soon, they began playing the B-sides, something pretty much unheard of in Top 40 radio and, even more unprecedented, tracks from the group's new LP, *Meet The Beatles!*

But I kept up my resistance, convinced that this was some plot, or payola, or something. All I knew about this group was that they were from England and had long hair, probably like beatniks. By the start of February, I knew that the Beatles were coming to America to appear on The Ed Sullivan Show. I saw my first pictures of them on the TV news when they arrived at Kennedy International Airport and then at the Plaza Hotel. I was struck by how ordinary they looked, not at all like the carefully styled teen idols of the day. They were more...real.

That Sunday night, for the Beatles' live American debut, I went in with a "okay, Beatles, show me how good you are" attitude and, unlike millions of kids my age, I wasn't really moved. They were...just okay, certainly not worth all of the pandemonium going on that night. The following Sunday night, February 16, was a different story. There were the Beatles, playing close together on a stage in a hotel ballroom with a sound mix that unintentionally emphasized Paul McCartney's bass and Ringo Starr's drums, what came to be rock 'n' roll's greatest rhythm section. That began to get to me, and then Paul, George Harrison and John Lennon gathered around one microphone and sang "This Boy." To a 14-year-old who had listened to a lot of group harmony records over the last few years, I thought this was VERY cool. I kept up a faltering wall of resistance for another week but the pre-taped third Beatles Sullivan Show appearance, highlighted by a rousing "Twist and Shout," finally won me over. That next week, I went out and got those three singles. I was able to honestly say that it wasn't the rampant Beatlemania that won me over but the quality and magnetism of the Beatles own performances. And I haven't regretted it for six decades.

Al Sussman

I was eleven when the Beatles first appeared on Ed Sullivan. The following morning a student passed around her copy of *Meet The Beatles!* during our school bus ride. Holding the coveted cover, I was enthralled by the half-lit faces and long hair on the front and the cool photo on the back. The Beatles exuded suave fashion from head to toe. Then a neighbor let me borrow his album for a few glorious days. I was taken with its freshness. Its aural accessibility spoke to me unlike any music before, sparking a moving, engaging and profound awakening in me. Nashville Top Forty stations WKDA and WMAK provided generous plays of Beatles tunes, including often-requested album cuts like "All My Loving" and "This Boy."

Soon our school bus rides elicited spontaneous sing-alongs of the Beatles catalog. Gone were the silent, somber bus rides that followed President Kennedy's assassination. We quickly learned the lyrics by repetition. Those joyous afternoons of gleeful singing of Beatles tunes continued throughout the spring. One enterprising bus rider sold packs of Beatles chewing gum cards, which I bought with lunch money. *Meet The Beatles!* opened new horizons of wondrous melodic experience, embraced with contagious, childlike delight as "our music."

Bruce Weaver II

I remember my Mom handing me a copy of *Meet The Beatles!* and telling me: "Don't tell your father!" Like many young silly fans, I wrote all over the back cover with my funny comments about the songs, none of which I would be willing to share because they're too embarrassing! I later wrote the names of my first band members next to the names of the Fabs on the back cover photo. Ironically, I put my name next to John, and 13 years later in 1977 I ended up playing the rhythm guitarist (John) in the original Broadway cast of BEATLEMANIA!

Joe Pecorino

I was three and a half years old when my parents bought *Meet The Beatles!* for me. They were pretty hip considering they were already in their early 30s when the Beatles came to America. They decided their first-born son should have Beatles music. I had a small Pinto Pony spring horse. My parents would play *Meet The Beatles!* and watch me bounce up and down and all around to the music over and over and over again! My 92-year-old Dad still recollects this to this day!

David Paine

After we saw the Beatles on the Sullivan Show, my mother bought me the Swan "She Loves You" single and a mono Capitol *Meet The Beatles!* album. My favorite tracks became "Don't Bother Me" (starting me on the road to being a Harrison fan), "I Wanna Be Your Man" (loved the organ riffs) and "I'll Get You" (starting a trend of listening to B-sides). My father got a 45 of "I Want To Hold Your Hand" played by Arthur Fiedler and the Boston Pops! He would introduce classical music-loving visitors to "Symphony in B" and enjoy their reactions when they recognized the song.

Mark Zutkoff

It was extremely cold that Monday on the playground at Mary Queen Of The Universe grade school in St. Louis, Missouri, the day after The Ed Sullivan Show featuring the Beatles. It was all that the kids were talking about, that group from England that wants to hold your hand! My second grade classmate, Billy Taylor, had one of those Russian-type winter hats with fur inside. He turned it inside out and immediately had a Beatles haircut. A group of girls started screaming and chasing him across the schoolyard! From then on, I wanted to be a Beatle, just like millions of kids all around the world!

Hank Charles Hanewinkel, Jr.

I was 11 when I saw the Beatles on The Jack Paar Show in January 1964, a month before The Ed Sullivan Show. Being out of school for Christmas vacation, I was allowed to stay up late. Of course my parents made fun of their look and music. I first heard *Meet The Beatles!* when my parents went to visit friends who had a son about my age. We were allowed to play the album in the basement so the adults weren't disturbed upstairs. I had to wait to save up to buy my own copy and every Beatles record after that. It was the start of a lifetime of fandom.

Robert Jakubiec

I was 10 years old and in the fifth grade when the Beatles were on Ed Sullivan for the first time. We had only one TV in the house. I was the oldest of the three children, so I advised my brother, sister and parents that the TV was mine on February 9th. We all watched. It was spectacular. I remember the "Sorry, girls, he's married" caption when they showed a close-up of John. After the show, my Dad said, "I'll give them about three months." To this day, I don't know whether he meant their career or my love for them, but, either way, he was wrong!

Susan Gagne

My earliest recollection of "She Loves You" and *Meet The Beatles!* go back to when I was only three years old. The memories are strong due to my dad, Ron, being an RCA record plant pressman in Rockaway, New Jersey [shown at work left]. I still own our black and white label Swan promo 45 of "She Loves You" from September 1963 and our Capitol LP, although they are well worn. My dad would press Beatles records during his workday, and we were listening to them together that evening. This meant me and my younger brother Ken got to hear them well before most of the country.

My dad worked at RCA from 1963-1968. He passed away 16 years ago; however my mother Ann Marie (also an RCA employee for a short time) and I had fun reminiscing about those days just prior to me submitting this fan recollection. As with many people, hearing a Beatles record today takes us back to specific times in the 1960s, in my case my very early childhood. These memories include not only listening to those records in the house as a family, but also hearing them in the car with the radio tuned to WABC.

Mike Ketterer

It was an early January morning in 1964. I was 11 years old and sitting on my bedroom floor listening to singles on my little red metal record player, playing discs by Johnny Mathis, Bobby Vinton and the Beach Boys. My mother shouted from the kitchen for me to come in right away. When I got there, she had the transistor radio going and told me to listen to "that new group from England." WHYN in Springfield, Massachusetts was playing "She Loves You." I was immediately hooked. I had never heard anything like those "yeah, yeah, yeah" and falsetto "wooooo" sounds. The song set the stage for my becoming a real Beatles and music fan and collector as the British Invasion continued.

It was such an important moment in my life. My mom knew how special the Beatles came to be for me over the years well into adulthood. I'm 70 now. I included that very story in her eulogy more than 15 years ago. Love you, Mom! The music is still playing.

Keith J. O'Connor, Sr.

I first met the Beatles on a local TV newscast. The sportscaster had to fill in some time and showed a clip of a musical group causing "great excitement" in England. It was a grainy black and white performance of the Beatles singing "From Me To You." Soon after, "I Want To Hold Your Hand" swamped the airwaves on Atlanta's WPLO and WQXI. I watched the Ed Sullivan performances in awe with all of America in February 1964.

The first album I bought was *Meet The Beatles!* I played my new LP on the family Motorola until the grooves wore smooth. I sang along to "I Want To Hold Your Hand," danced wildly to "I Saw Her Standing There" and loved the harmonies on "This Boy," the "Yeah, Yeah, Yeah"s on "It Won't Be Long" and George's "Don't Bother Me." There was even a song to make my parents believe in Beatlemania: "Till There Was You."

The Beatles literally stopped me in their tracks. I still have my first album as proof that I was there when the Beatles began their quest to conquer the world two and a half minutes at a time.

Tommy Archibald

I was 13½ years old and in eighth grade in February 1964. On Friday, February 7, word was racing around school that a great new group would be on Ed Sullivan on Sunday. My parents and I tuned in as we always did. As Sullivan uttered those famous words, "Ladies and gentlemen, the Beatles!," the audience began screaming. When they hit "All My Loving," I was smitten. The next Friday I purchased a mono version of *Meet the Beatles!* I consider it the greatest "song" of all time because it encapsulates everything about the early Beatles and why we came to love them. I am still in wonder of the magic of the Beatles and how they mesmerized the world.

Janet Redick

As an eight-year-old living in Southampton, England in January 1963, my first Beatles recollection was hearing "Please Please Me" on the radio, which became my hook to my obsession with the group. My father bought me my first single, "From Me To You," and the *Twist And Shout* EP (as he could not afford their debut LP). When the Beatles appeared on Sunday Night At The London Palladium and the Royal Variety Performance, these shows were way past my bedtime, but my parents woke me up to see the Beatles performances and put me back to bed when they were done. For Christmas 1963, they bought me my first album, *With The Beatles*, which contains my favourite Beatles song, "Not A Second Time." I still have the album (well played) with the back sleeve marked with the price of 32 shillings!

Andrew Phillips

I was a fan from the moment I first heard "I Want to Hold Your Hand" in late December 1963. I was playing touch football with a group of friends out on the street. I was so taken by the song's unique sound and incredible energy that I had to stop the game and walk over to the transistor radio that sat playing on the hood of a nearby car to just listen.

One month earlier, John F. Kennedy, the youthful and witty president who had given young people such hope for the future, had been assassinated, and grief hung like a dark cloud over the entire country. But in that one moment on a chilly, cloudy day in December, the sounds coming from that radio broke through the gloom like a blast of summer sunshine.

One month later I went to a party, and as I walked in the door, that same amazing song was playing on the stereo. Only this time when it ended, I heard "One, two, three, FOUR!!!," the high-energy count-in to "I Saw Her Standing There," followed by "This Boy," "It Won't Be Long" and on and on, all Beatles songs I'd never heard before! I sat there mesmerized, listening and staring at the four partially eclipsed faces in Robert Freeman's iconic album cover photo.

The very next day, I took a bus to Eclipse Music in downtown Paterson, New Jersey to buy my very first vinyl album, *Meet the Beatles!*

David Fox

Like so many others, I was introduced to the Beatles on February 9, 1964. We only had one TV in our house. On Sunday nights we were all together, often watching Walt Disney on TV. I remember this particular Sunday night, my brother, who was 3 years older than me, begging our parents to let us watch Ed Sullivan so he could see the Beatles. He kept telling them: "Everybody in school is going to be watching this. Everybody wants to see the Beatles, even Robert." I had no idea what he was so excited about, but, like any young brother wanting to copy his big brother, I started yelling "I want to see the Beatles too." So we all ended up watching Ed Sullivan.

I still remember the excitement of watching their performance and thinking "this is the greatest thing I've ever seen and heard." Afterwards, my brother informed me of what he knew about the group. The next day we asked our mother to buy us a copy of "I Want To Hold Your Hand." Shortly after that I got the *Meet The Beatles!* album, starting my lifelong passion of music and record collecting which continues to this day.

Robert G. Robbins

Being born on a Native American reservation in South Dakota was about as far from anything showbiz as you could get in 1964. That winter had been harsh and dark. Drudgery set in with scarce light during those long days. My brother Larry, 10 years older, somehow heard about a band named the Beatles that would be appearing on The Ed Sullivan Show that weekend. My brother was my hero, but I wanted to see Disney that night as it would feature "The Scarecrow Of Romney Marsh."

With only one black and white TV, we tossed a coin and he won. What happened that Sunday evening reverberated from New York City to our little town in Sisseton, South Dakota. We felt alive as their music could be felt to our core. We sat stunned, but inside we could feel our dull black and white world had flipped a switch to color.

The winter seemed to quicken and Beatles music was everywhere. It lit a fire within that still burns today. This year marks almost 50 years in the broadcasting and music business for me. It may not have happened if it had not have been for that fateful flip of the coin. Thanks, Larry.

Jon Erdahl

In October of 1963, I was 13 years old and living in Victoria, British Columbia, Canada. I was lying in bed on a school night listening to my transistor radio under the covers in the dark to my favorite rock 'n' roll radio show on CKWX hosted by Hall of Fame Disc Jockey Red Robinson. At the time, one of my favorite singers was Del Shannon. I had a couple of his 45s and had just been told by a friend that Del had a new record out called "From Me To You." That night I heard the song on the radio. I liked it, but thought it sounded a little different for Del with the harmonies.

The next week I went to our local department store, Eatons, and purchased Del's "From Me To You" on the Quality label. When I got home and played it, I thought it sounded different from what I had heard on the radio. I soon learned that I had actually heard the Beatles version of "From Me To You" that night. The sound was so different that I have never forgot the first moment I heard the Beatles.

Bob Dalziel

I was born in communist Poland in 1968 and being a teenager meant for me limited access to western music. But a friend of my parents had *With The Beatles*, having worked in U.K. That LP, "It Won't Be Long" especially, started it all for me. My mates didn't know what I was talking about. None of them knew the Beatles. I liked the hits of the day as well, but the energy in this 1963 recording was phenomenal. I didn't feel it in the contemporary artists' songs. All this was in 1981, and I was saddened to hear Lennon was shot dead the previous year. That news had escaped me. But life in a communist country was different to the West (and the U.S. especially). I went on to listen to all the other albums, then solo material, and now I'm in a Bruce Spizer Beatles book!

Jakub Kaleta

As beginner music collectors in the USSR in the late 1980s, we did not have much choice album-wise. We had to deal with so-called custom compilations on the Melodia label for the East European market. We had no idea what *Please Please Me* or *With The Beatles* was. There was a compilation album called *A Taste Of Honey*. It was a collection of songs from the group's early albums. Of course, we did not know that at the time. The album cover had four Beatles 1968 images taken from *The White Album* portraits, and the title was a cover song. It was a really bizarre combination, but it was one of the only two Beatles albums available on Melodia at the time. The other was *A Hard Day's Night*. The Melodia albums sound really good.

Nowadays, the *A Taste Of Honey* compilation is quite rare. I am glad my parents bought it for us, giving us a little more taste of western music.

Yaakov Edisherashvili

"Schi lafs ju, jeh, jeh, jeh" was the first line I heard from the Beatles. At least that's how I would have written it in 1964, as I had just started school and was learning how to read and write in German. Those words and accompanying sounds of "She Loves You" stuck in my seven-year-old head. My conservative parents didn't like any of that "Jeh, jeh, jeh" sound from a boy group with long hair, so I continued to listen to Swiss folk music or German "schlager" until the release of the irresistible "Hey Jude."

Years later I bought the Beatles single "Sie Liebt Dich," which was "She Loves You" sung in German. It was quite strange hearing the Beatles sing in German with British accents, but way better than when I heard myself singing Beatles songs in English on my tape recorder with my Swiss accent!

Marcel Reichmuth

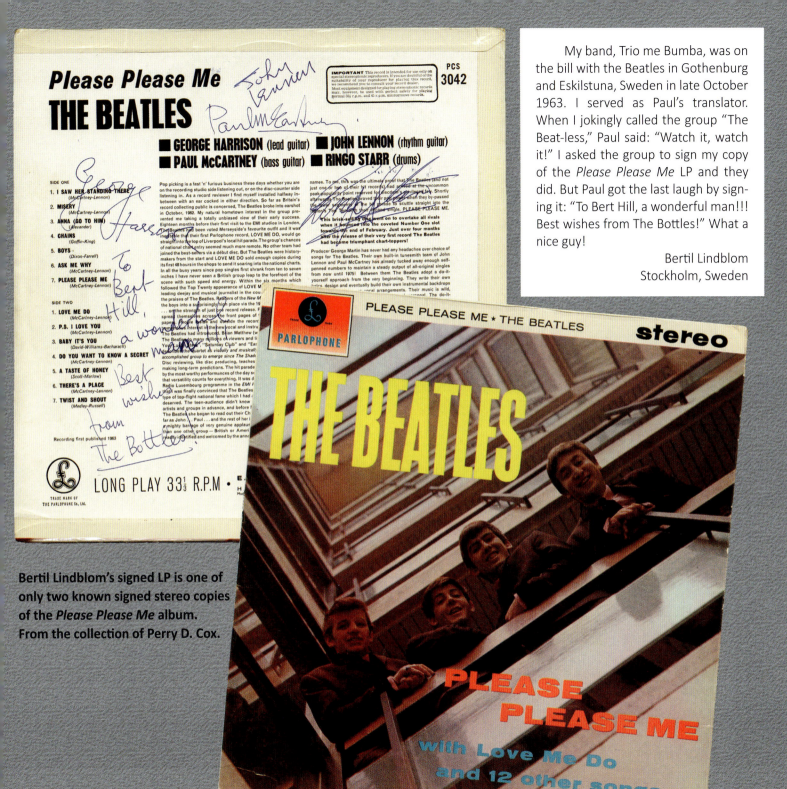

My band, Trio me Bumba, was on the bill with the Beatles in Gothenburg and Eskilstuna, Sweden in late October 1963. I served as Paul's translator. When I jokingly called the group "The Beat-less," Paul said: "Watch it, watch it!" I asked the group to sign my copy of the *Please Please Me* LP and they did. But Paul got the last laugh by signing it: "To Bert Hill, a wonderful man!!! Best wishes from The Bottles!" What a nice guy!

Bertil Lindblom
Stockholm, Sweden

Bertil Lindblom's signed LP is one of only two known signed stereo copies of the *Please Please Me* album. From the collection of Perry D. Cox.

I had never heard "She Loves You" until the Beatles first appearance on Ed Sullivan. Of the five songs played that night, that song stood way out front. What was it? The minor chords? The "yeah, yeah yeah's"? The "oooooo's"? To this day, I can't figure it out. But I wasn't the only one. Within days of the Beatles appearance on Ed Sullivan, the school bus I rode every day to elementary school chose that song to sing out loud as we neared our destination. The entire bus. Loud and proud. And this went on for quite some time. It still gives me chills.

Martin Horn

Growing up in the Bronx I remember my mother purchasing *Meet The Beatles!* for me and seeing them on the Sullivan show. After playing the album about 100 times, I was walking on Southern Blvd. and saw a violin bass in the window of a store. I started begging my mother to please, please purchase that bass for me! My mother, a resourceful woman, told me: "Honey, I cannot buy it for you since it's electric. If you play the wrong note on the instrument you will get electrocuted and die!" With a broken heart, I said, "OK mommy, I understand."

Henry Ordosgoitia

I was diagnosed with Beatlemania at age seven, brought on by The Ed Sullivan Show. That week I broke into my little bank and set off for Jordan Marsh to get a copy of *Meet The Beatles!*, the first record I ever bought myself. I played it endlessly on a portable Decca record player with a tone arm that must have weighed about five pounds. It still sounds pretty good, considering. *Meet The Beatles!* is the cornerstone of my large record collection, and I'm sure I've played it far more times than any other record.

My mom said when I wasn't listening to the record, I was frequently singing "I Want To Hold Your Hand." That may well be what I'm belting out in the photo [shown left] from my eighth birthday that summer of 1964, ukulele in hand, as I savored gifts including a swatch of Beatles wallpaper, a Beatles paperback book, a Mattel six-shooter, and buried under the new Beach Boys and Dave Clark Five albums, a copy of *Introducing The Beatles*. A real Beatles Birthday Bash!

Patrick Callaghan

Beatlemania crept like a cat into my life starting in 1963. I loved British artists in the early sixties like Cliff Richard, the Shadows and Helen Shapiro. My favourite American artists were Del Shannon and Roy Orbison. DJ Red Robinson on CFUN in Vancouver had a "Battle Of The New Sounds" feature, and in the last weeks of June he ran "From Me To You" by Del Shannon versus the Beatles. Del won hands down. His version first charted at the end of June. The following week the survey listed "From Me To You" by Del Shannon paired with the Beatles.

Each week I bought a Beatles 45 – "From Me To You," "Please Please Me" and "Love Me Do." I played both sides of each disc over and over every day. In September I bought "She Loves You." WOW!

I heard that Capitol was releasing an album called *Beatlemania! With The Beatles* on November 22, 1963. I ordered it and could not wait! Unknown to me, Capitol pushed the release date back to November 25. When November 22 came around, I hoped they would have my LP. But that day John Kennedy was shot. Everyone was so upset and saddened that we were let out of school early. I went to the store on my way home to get my album. I was lucky. They gave me my copy early rather than hold it. I took it home and played it all weekend as the TV was dominated by the Kennedy shooting. The record distracted me. That was it, I was hooked on the Beatles.

When the Beatles were on Ed Sullivan, my brother and I set up his camera for each of the shows and took great still pictures off the TV. We rushed the film to the store each week to get the pictures printed. I then took prints to school and took orders from girls for copies of the prints. We sold hundreds of dollars worth of prints, which was then a lot of money. I was forever trapped into buying their releases. The record store got me a Capitol promotional photo. I still follow the Beatles today.

Owen Coppin

I was five years old in February 1964. One Sunday evening, I heard my 13-year-old sister screaming wildly. I followed the sound into the living room and saw her on her knees, hiding her head and screaming at our TV. I was wondering what was happening. She turned, saw me standing there, grabbed my arm, pulled me down and said: "Watch!" I fell down and watched the Beatles singing on The Ed Sullivan Show. I still remember!

Michelle Burke

I remember when I was five, my mother played *Meet the Beatles!* every afternoon on our living room record player while I tried to nap in the next room. That wasn't easy! I still have that record, which is the best compilation of their early stuff. I have since bought another version of the vinyl, a cassette and the Capitol CD reissue.

Mark A. Winters

I was living in a small community in Vermont and had just turned four years old when the Beatles hit the U.S. I remember being in the record department of the store known as Harry's. There were about ten record bins, with all of them containing nothing but copies of *Meet The Beatles!* That, not the music or the fans, is what I most vividly recall about the Beatlemania era in the U.S.

Russell Belding

My first taste of the early Beatles music came in the late 1970s when I received my uncle's 1964 copy of *Introducing The Beatles*. The scratchy old vinyl spoke loud and clear to me, mixing catchy harmonies with rock and roll. Songs from this album came to life for me through the Beatles cartoons that I avidly watched on TV as my love for the band grew. I still treasure that album, which brings back memories of my childhood Beatlemania.

Dr. Jennifer Sandi

My thirteenth birthday and Bar Mitzvah were a few weeks after the February 9 Beatles appearance on The Ed Sullivan Show. Since my parents knew I was a huge fan for all of one whole month, they did me a great kindness. Rather than waiting for my personal big day, they gave me my present early in anticipation of that fateful broadcast–a miraculous, small reel-to-reel tape recorder!

It was a Sony with 3-inch reels operating at 1⅞ IPS–terrible quality, but what did a 13-year-old know? So, on that historic Sunday night, my parents and two younger brothers congregated in our living room around our black and white TV. I was hunched nearest to the set clutching the microphone by its short cord. I distinctly recall my dad mocking their hair saying they looked like girls, with his comments committed to tape by his annoyed teenage son. For years the tape was a prized possession, but when I left for college, I lost track of the tape. Thankfully, the DVD release of the Sullivan shows in 2003 restored my memories, but not my father's critique.

Ken Sall

Nothing was ever the same in my life after watching the Beatles on Ed Sullivan. As a 10 year old, the following day at school we girls could not wait for recess. We met at the swing set on the playground to discuss and rehash every detail of the exciting Ed Sullivan shows. The discussions were amazing and unbelievable. Every birthday party, slumber party, summer camp, school, Halloween and Christmas for the next six years with my little friends were all Beatle records, cards, books, clothes, costumes, posters and decorations. It has never stopped in 59 years and counting which led me to a great love for the Beatles and a Beatles Record Collection. To think, this obsession all started one Sunday evening, February 9, 1964, with a fabulous Ed Sullivan show on a black and white TV set.

Polly Hewitt, Life-long Beatle Girl

One of my earliest memories is watching the Beatles on Ed Sullivan on February 9, 1964, when I was four years old. I was lucky that my parents had tuned in. It affected me profusely. The moment that sent me over was when they started "She Loves You" after the relatively calmer "Till There Was You." I had never heard screams like that. I had never seen people who looked like that or sounded like that. Everything was so different about them. It was electrifying even to a four year old. We watched the Sullivan shows for the next two weeks, and the Beatles were on both times. I took this to mean they were regulars on the show! Thus, I was crestfallen when we tuned in to Ed Sullivan on March 1, 1964, and they were not on! My guess is there were a lot of other junior Beatles fans who felt the same on that day as I did!

Scott Shea

I, like millions of others, got into the Beatles through their first appearance on The Ed Sullivan Show…in 1993! I was 12 years old and had just started playing the drums. One night my parents and I watched a videotape of The Very Best Of The Ed Sullivan Show. The clip of the Beatles performing "I Want To Hold Your Hand" was an absolute game-changer. Their music, their look and their screaming fans seemed so fresh, so different and so fun! I quickly forgot that this B&W footage was almost 30 years old.

My fandom was instant and invigorating. I liked playing the drums, but studying Ringo made me *love* playing the drums. I already loved music, but Beatles music gave me a love for life. I devoured all of the albums, books, articles and videotapes I could find on the Fab Four. I made a lot of friends through our mutual love of the Beatles. It was magical, and it's still inspiring. I now perform and record music professionally–a dream I first had watching the Beatles on The Ed Sullivan Show (on tape in 1993).

John Roccesano

Late 1963 through early 1964—a crazy time to be alive for a nine year old. A bigger house, President Kennedy's assassination and news of the Beatles and their new record, "I Want To Hold Your Hand," which grabbed me by the throat that December and hasn't let go since!

I had been begging my mom for the album *Meet The Beatles!* We went to the local record shop to pre-order, then came back later in January to get it. So exciting! The album still has my name and the order number scribbled in pencil on the back cover. I played the heck out of it, but back then the only record player was in the living room, so everyone probably got sick of it pretty quickly.

The above photo contains much of what I remember: my freshly grown Beatles haircut, the album proudly displayed, a guitar I actually learned how to play, my little sister joining in the excitement, and Dad with newspaper raised, oblivious to it all. Seems like yesterday. Later that year, my mom and her best friend drove their combined nine kids in one station wagon to Detroit for the Beatles Labor Day concert at Olympia Stadium. The coolest moms.

John Mitchell

Due to the large number of fan recollections submitted for this book, we were unable to fit them all in! For additional fan recollections, go to www.beatle.net/fr/please for a free supplement download of more, along with a place to post your own recollections. (Note: the free supplement is already included in the digital edition.)

Getting to Know the Beatles was Different for U.S. Fans

by Bill King (from the Listening to The Beatles series on beatlefan.com)

Even some 25 years after the Beatles U.K. album releases became the international standard, they still seem foreign to me.

I didn't own albums called *Please Please Me* and *With The Beatles* when I was young.

The U.S. equivalent of the *Please Please Me* LP was Vee-Jay's *Introducing The Beatles*. I didn't get a copy of *Introducing* for a couple of years, but the Hopewell girls a couple of houses up from us had it, and I remember spending quite a few afternoons on the couch in their living room listening to the album.

I still remember my initial response to its cover photo: Ugh. It was tinted so that the Beatles looked like they had reddish hair that was kind of greasy.

Likewise, my introduction to most of the tracks on *With The Beatles* was through Capitol's *Meet The Beatles!* I got that for Easter 1964 (yes, my brothers and I actually got Easter presents from our parents). Contrary to *Introducing*, the cover of this one was a moody, magnificent masterpiece with that unforgettable portrait of the Fab Four printed in a bluish black ink.

I remember my brothers and I standing in front of my mother's portable suitcase stereo. We spent hours engaged in what later would become known as "air guitar," silently miming the words because we didn't want to interfere with the music.

In those early days of our Beatlemania, my parents were our source of records as our weekly allowance didn't really allow for purchasing much more than a vanilla Coke or ice cream, or two comic books (12 cents each plus a penny tax) at the neighborhood drug store.

In fact, my father bought my very first Beatles recording — the single of "I Want to Hold Your Hand" b/w "I Saw Her Standing There" — without ever being asked to do so! And, just about every time Mom went downtown in 1964, she returned with yet another Beatles single on what at the time was a bewildering assortment of labels (Capitol, Vee-Jay, Tollie, Swan).

I didn't actually get my own copies of the original *Please Please Me* and *With The Beatles* LPs until I was in college!

Please Please Me was an odd listening experience for me. I had heard most of its songs as singles and B-sides, or on the *Introducing* album or the 1965 LP *The Early Beatles* after Capitol got back the rights to the tracks from Vee-Jay.

The same was true for *With The Beatles*, which has nine tracks in common with Capitol's *Meet The Beatles!* but differs in significant ways.

It wasn't until these albums were issued on CD in the late 1980s (when the U.K. releases became the international standard) that I really spent much time listening to them.

I guess you could say I never "bonded" with these albums.

I listened to them again as part of the box of stereo remasters issued on 09/09/09, but I found the reissues really didn't work to the advantage of the first two albums, which were recorded in primitive twin-track and have that weird stereo separation with the voices coming out of one speaker and the instruments out of the other.

When my then-teenage daughter decided to download the remastered Beatles to her iPod (remember those?), she chose mono for those albums for which it was available. And, I have to say, I find the mono versions of the first two albums a more enjoyable (or, at least, less distracting) listening experience.

All that aside, you'd be hard-pressed to find a more terrific opening track for a debut album than "I Saw Her Standing There" on *Please Please Me*. From Paul McCartney's "one, two, three, fah!" on, it's sheer joy and exuberance, and rightfully a classic that still gets baseball fans singing along.

If I were to try and pretend to be a critic hearing the album for the first time ever, two hallmarks of the young band that I'd note would be the harmonica and, more importantly, the group harmonies and backing vocals. The latter are absolutely superb throughout.

The other notable thing about the Beatles debut album is that it didn't just focus on the two main singers; all four members got their shot at lead vocals. I somehow doubt many producers/A&R people would allow that on the first album by a new act nowadays.

Highlights from the first album, besides the opening track, are "Chains" (with that wailing mouth organ and that quintessential mix of voices), the first single's "Love Me Do" and "P.S. I Love You" (which benefit from being presented in mono, since the original stereo masters were lost), "Baby It's You" (love those "sha-la-la-la-la" backing vocals), "Do You Want to Know a Secret?" (a fine vocal by George Harrison), and, of course, John Lennon's throat-ripping performance of "Twist and Shout," a cover that the Beatles made their own.

As for *With The Beatles*, the main problem for American first-generation fans is that it's sort of disorienting because it's like someone took the terrific *Meet The Beatles!* album, shaved off three of its strongest tracks ("I Want to Hold Your Hand," "I Saw Her Standing There" and "This Boy") and stuck in a bunch of cover versions. It's a fine album, but, let's face it, the Capitol configuration beats it hands-down.

Still, *With The Beatles* is a definite advance from the first collection, with more variety in sound and material. The exuberant "It Won't Be Long," with its "Yeah! Yeah!" call-and-response bit (one of several tracks on the album to make use of that Beatles trademark), is another fantastic album opener.

The other highlights for me are the instant McCartney classic "All My Loving"; the nice arrangement of his Broadway cover, "Till There Was You"; another great cover in "Please Mister Postman" (wonderful backing vocals); the chugging backing and great harmonies of "Hold Me Tight" (a remake of a tune that didn't make the cut for the first album, the liner notes inform); another fine cover by Lennon on "You Really Got A Hold On Me"; Lennon's moody, distinctive piano-driven "Not A Second Time"; and still another great Lennon cover in "Money (That's What I Want)."

The rest of the album is really good, too, with "Little Child" a joyous romp and "Don't Bother Me" an interesting songwriting debut for Harrison (though his lead vocal is way too echoey). The cover "Devil In Her Heart" is the weakest track because it's not a very good song.

Still, I have to confess: I have never really gotten used to the British versions of the Beatles first two albums. In my mind's ear, I keep expecting to hear "Hold Me Tight" after "Till There Was You," not "Please Mister Postman." And "I Wanna Be Your Man" after "Hold Me Tight," not "You Really Got A Hold on Me."

Hey, to my ears, "Please Mister Postman" and "You Really Got A Hold on Me" don't even belong on the same album with those numbers!

Covers That Stand Out in the Shop Window

Beatles Recording Manager George Martin understood that it took more than producing great music to sell albums. In November 1962, he told NME/Mersey Beat reporter Alan Smith that "LPs need a catchy title if they're going to stand out in the shop window." Albums also needed an attention-grabbing cover to catch the eye of shoppers. Finally, the album jacket needed liner notes touting the virtues of the recording artist, songs and music to get the shopper to part with his or her 32 shillings, nearly five times the cost of a single.

Martin's initial idea for the album title of the group's first album was *Off The Beatle Track*, a pun on the expression "off the beaten track," appropriately describing the Beatles and their style of music. For the album cover, the group was to be pictured at the London Zoo by the insect house. This idea was abandoned when the zoo's director objected.

In mid-January 1963, Martin arranged a photo session with British theatrical photographer Angus McBean, who took standard portraits of the group at his Endell Street studio in Covent Garden. The group wore their new brown velveteen suits with pink shirts. While the pictures were pleasant enough, none had the eye-catching appeal that would make the cover stand out in a shop window. A photo from the session was, however, used for the cover of *The Beatles' Hits* EP (see page 35) and the U.S. album *Introducing The Beatles* (see page 183), although the image is flipped on the latter.

After another uninspired photo session, this time at EMI House in Manchester Square, London about a week later, McBean returned to EMI House in February. According to McBean: "As I went into the door I was in the staircase well. Someone looked over the banister. I asked if the boys were in the building, and the answer was yes. 'Well,' I said, 'get them to look over [the rail], and I will take them from here.'" McBean lay flat on his back and shot a few pictures with his standard portrait lens of the group looking down at him over the rail. The upper floors in the stairwell behind the group added an interesting geometric effect. It would be the first of a series of innovative and imaginative covers to grace the Beatles albums. Alternate shots from the session were used for *The Beatles (No.1)* EP (see page 35) and the compilation albums *The Beatles 1962-1966* and *The Beatles 1967-1970*. Apple included two more outtakes in the CD booklet to the *Please Please Me* remaster issued in 2009.

The album's front cover features McBean's stairwell shot with "THE BEATLES" above the group in tall yellow block letters. The lower portion of the cover has "PLEASE PLEASE ME" in red block letters and "with Love Me Do and 12 other songs" in smaller blue letters.

The back cover fulfilled its objectives of informing shoppers of the contents of the album and providing information on the group and its members. The top has the album's title and the group's name. The band is identified, in order, as George Harrison (lead guitar), John Lennon (rhythm guitar), Paul McCartney (bass guitar) and Ringo Starr (drums). The left side has the album's lineup, with all original compositions credited to "McCartney-Lennon" (as is the case with the label credits). The bottom has the Parlophone logo, LP speed, EMI information and a plug for EMITEX record cleaning material.

The back cover has entertaining and informative liner notes written by Tony Barrow, who previously wrote liner notes for Decca Records before being hired by Brian Epstein to work for NEMS.

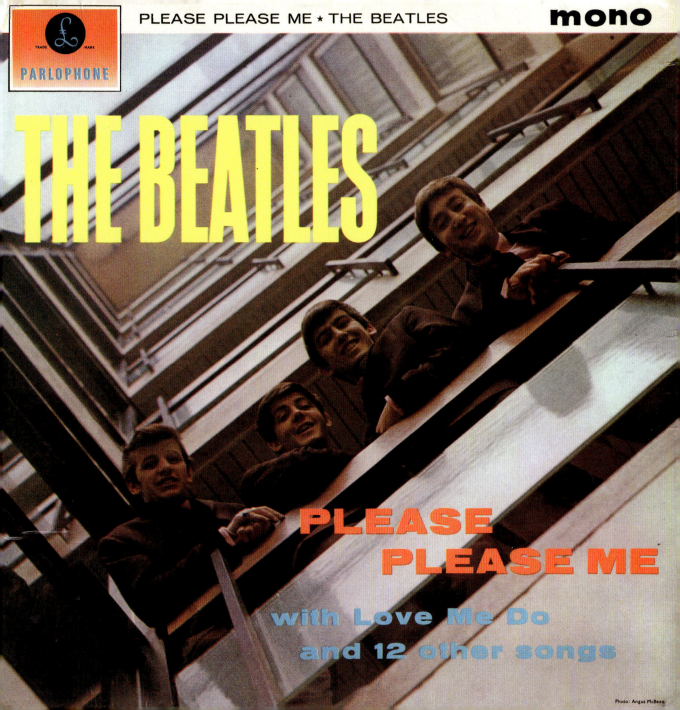

Barrow starts his notes with: "Pop picking is a fast 'n' furious business these days whether you are on the recording studio side listening out, or on the disc-counter side listening in." After praising the group he emphasizes the songwriting abilities of John and Paul by claiming that the pair "has already tucked away enough self-penned numbers to maintain a steady output of all-original singles from now until 1975!" He focuses on the group's do-it-yourself approach, which was not the norm at the time: "They write their own lyrics, design and eventually build their own instrumental backdrops and work out their own vocal arrangements. Their music is wild, pungent, hard-hitting, uninhibited . . . and personal. The do-it-yourself angle ensures complete originality at all stages of the process." He closes with brief descriptions of the songs.

Vee-Jay originally planned on issuing its version of the Beatles *Please Please Me* LP in the summer of 1963. The company dropped the songs "Please Please Me" and "Ask Me Why" to get down to the American standard of 12 songs. The album was titled *Introducing The Beatles* as it would indeed introduce the band to America.

Vee-Jay was sent a picture of the Beatles from Angus McBean's mid-January 1963 photo session with the group wearing their new matching brown velveteen suits with pink shirts. The company cut the photo off at the bottom and flipped the image (most likely by mistake). The group's name is towards the top in red block letters, with "introducing..." above in white and "England's No.1 Vocal Group" below in white uppercase letters. Vee-Jay had 6,000 front cover slicks printed by Coburn & Company in June or July 1963, but no covers were assembled that summer as the album was canceled.

When Vee-Jay decided to issue the LP in January 1964, it was unable to locate the liner notes it had previously received from EMI. Because EMI had terminated its licensing agreement giving Vee-Jay the right to issue Beatles recordings in the United States, Vee-Jay could not ask EMI to resend the notes. To save time, Vee-Jay used the artwork from one side of its new inner sleeve advertising "Other Fine Albums of Significant Interest" on Vee-Jay. The initial covers prepared for the LP feature this colorful set of mini-album covers and are known as "Ad Back" covers. When the company fabricating the covers ran out of these back cover slicks, Vee-Jay told the company to construct covers with a blank white slick. Only a small number of these "Blank Back" covers were manufactured. Most of the covers have a simple design on the back with the new VJ brackets logo and LP title at the top followed by the album's song titles in separate columns for each side. These covers initially included the songs "Love Me Do" and "P.S. I Love You," but later replaced those two songs with "Please Please Me" and "Ask Me Why" when Vee-Jay was forced to drop those songs from the album after being sued by Capitol's music publishing company, Beechwood Music, Inc.

Although the title to the Beatles second British album was rather pedestrian, the cover to *With The Beatles* was neither dull nor boring. It was totally different from the covers of the time. Once again, the Beatles had an album jacket that would stand out in shop windows and demand attention in the record racks and bins.

The album's distinctive cover portrait was taken by Robert Freeman at the Palace Hotel in Bournemouth, England, while the group was in town for a six-night stand at the Gaumont Cinema starting on August 19, 1963. At the time, Freeman was 27 years old and primarily known as a jazz photographer. His idea was to create a half-shadow image of the faces of the group. The lighting was the natural light coming through a window. Freeman photographed the group wearing black turtlenecks against a dark background. The black and white film used by Freeman gave the photo a grainy effect. His use of a 180 mm telephoto lens compressed the boys into a tight group shot. In his book THE BEATLES a private view, Freeman states that because the band had to fit into the square shape of the album cover, he chose not to put them all in a line, but rather put Ringo in the lower right corner "since he was the last to join the group." The printing of the British jacket, particularly the first press run, turned out much darker than anticipated, creating an image of, in Freeman's words, "four white faces in a coal cellar." When EMI used the photo for the cover of its *All My Loving* EP, the picture was printed lighter, revealing the group's turtleneck shirts (see page 49).

While the Beatles were excited about the portrait, Brian Epstein had to be persuaded to present it to EMI. The conservative record company found the cover humorless and expressed concern, wanting to project happy Beatles to happy fans. Fortunately, the Beatles prevailed.

The front cover has a large white banner above the portrait. The Parlophone logo and the album title appear in black on the left side. The right side has "mono" or "stereo" in black.

The top of the back cover has the album's title and the group's name. Once again, the band is identified, in order, as George Harrison (lead guitar), John Lennon (rhythm guitar), Paul McCartney (bass guitar) and Ringo Starr (drums). The left side has the album's lineup, with all original compositions credited this time to "Lennon-McCartney." The bottom has the Parlophone logo, LP speed, EMI information and a plug for EMITEX record cleaning material.

The back cover contains Tony Barrow's informative liner notes. Barrow states that: "The Beatles have repeated the successful formula which made their first 'Please Please Me' LP into the fastest-selling album of 1963. Again they have set eight of their own original compositions alongside a batch of 'personal choice' pieces selected from the recorded repertoires of American R. & B. artists they admire most."

Barrow then describes the songs and provides information on the singers and instruments used on the recording. He writes that the album gets off to a "rip-roarin' start with John's powerful treatment of IT WON'T BE LONG." He describes George's guitar solo on "All My Loving" as superb and an intriguing feature of the song. "Don't Bother Me" is a "fairly fast number with a haunting theme." He writes that "Till There Was You" went down extremely well at the Cavern and that "Roll Over Beethoven" has been "one of the most requested items" at recent concerts. "You Really Got A Hold On Me" has a wild, relentless vocal by John and George.

Barrow notes that Paul describes "Money" as a "really big screamer" that often led to the same "overwhelming response" as "Twist And Shout." The song has "John shouting the raw lyrics with tremendous force and feelings." He concludes: "MONEY makes a completely worthy climax to this knockout programme. Hope it doesn't leave you too breathless to flip back to Side One for a repeat-play session WITH THE BEATLES."

 **with the beatles**

The front cover to Capitol's first Beatles album uses the same Robert Freeman black and white portrait as *With The Beatles*. A December 16, 1963 telegram from London to Capitol's Ray Polley indicates that the 12-inch film positives for the front cover slick to the album were sent to the Capitol Tower by airmail on December 10. Capitol received the package on or about December 16.

Capitol apparently thought that the title *With The Beatles* lacked impact and would mean nothing to the American audience who had yet to be introduced to the Beatles. At that time, Capitol had no way of knowing that Vee-Jay had earlier titled its album *Introducing The Beatles* or that Vee-Jay would soon resurrect its plans to issue the LP. Capitol may have considered naming its LP *Introducing The Beatles!* Imagine the confusion that would have caused. But, as fate would have it, Capitol chose *Meet The Beatles!*

The simple but effective cover for *Meet The Beatles!* was designed by Capitol art department head George Osaki. The portrait of the band has a blue tint not present on the darker all black and white British cover. The Capitol logo and the phrase "HIGH FIDELITY" appear in white in the upper right corner of the photo. The top part of the cover has a thin-lined white box containing the album's title and brief text. "MEET" appears above "THE" in the left side of the box. Both words are in blue block letters. "BEATLES!" is usually either tan or brown, although it is dark olive green in some later slicks.

The text on the front cover below the title describes the record as "The First Album by England's Phenomenal Pop Combo." Although *Meet The Beatles!* primarily contains songs from the Beatles second British LP, Capitol thought it was releasing the first American album by the group. Unbeknownst to Capitol in December 1963, Vee-Jay would release its *Introducing The Beatles* album on January 10, 1964, ten days ahead of the Capitol LP. As the Vee-Jay album contains 12 of the 14 songs from the Beatles first British LP, Capitol's claim that *Meet The Beatles!* was the group's first album was totally incorrect. It was, however, the first *Capitol* album by the Beatles. And, as far as Capitol was concerned, that made it the first.

The back cover is dominated with text about Beatlemania. At the top in large bold black print are the words: "You've read about them in Time, Newsweek, The New York Times. Here's the big beat sound of that fantastic, phenomenal foursome: MEET THE BEATLES!" The left column below the album's title contains information about the group's overseas success, a list of events that are best described as evidence of Beatlemania and the following description of their music: "The foursome—John Lennon, 23, George Harrison, 20, Ringo Starr, 23, and Paul McCartney, 21—write, play and sing a powerhouse music filled with zest and uninhibited good humor that make listening a sensation-filled joy. It isn't rhythm and blues. It's not exactly rock 'n' roll. It's their own special sound, or, as group leader Lennon puts it, 'Our music is just—well, our music.'"

The right column lists the titles and times of the songs and contains additional text about the instruments played by the group and the vocalists on most of the songs. This information is taken from Tony Barrow's liner notes to *With The Beatles*. As the first three songs on the Capitol album are not on the British LP, no information is provided for those songs. The liner notes also inform the reader that: "The Beatles all hail from Liverpool, a seaport city which, because its sailing men bring in the latest hit singles from America, is the hippest pop music spot in England. They wear 'pudding basin' haircuts that date back to ancient England, and suits with collarless jackets which they've made the latest rage."

The lower right quadrant of the album's back cover has a Dezo Hoffmann photo of the group with the names of the members of the band printed below. The lower portion credits the cover photo to Robert Freeman. Most later back covers have "Produced by GEORGE MARTIN," while earlier covers do not.

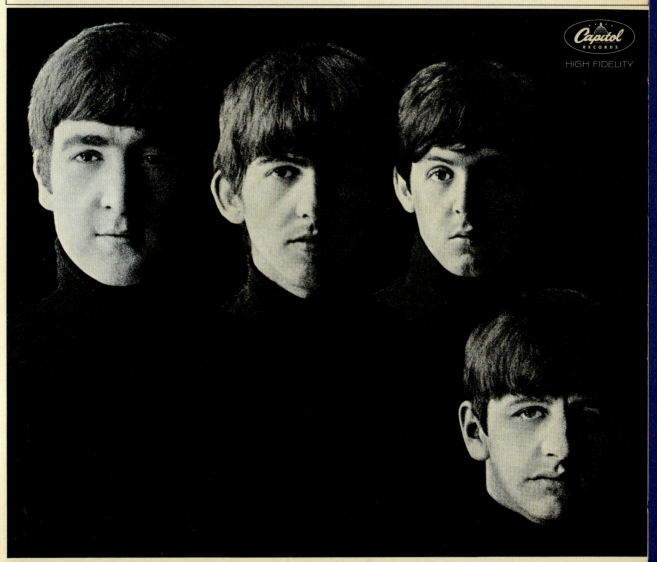

In the early 1960s, the notes on the back covers of LPs and EPs were considered an important part of the marketing of the disc. Because records were bought in stores, the notes were another way to influence shoppers to part with their money and buy the LP or EP.

Tony Barrow wrote the liner notes to the Beatles first three albums and to seven of the eight EPs that had liner notes. By the time the *Help!* album was issued in August 1965, the practice had stopped. Liner notes were not needed to help sell a Beatles record.

For the *Twist And Shout* EP, Barrow notes that the disc's four songs are from the Beatles *Please Please Me* LP, which has topped the top album charts for "umpteen weeks." He adds that "Do You Want To Know A Secret" became a number one hit for Liverpoplian Billy J. Kramer. Barrow states that the EP is "designed to pass the audio spotlight very fairly from Beatle to Beatle, exposing four contrasting facets of the quartet's vocal and instrumental ingenuity." The disc's opening track, "Twist And Shout," is an "all-action, all-raving rocker." John's wild, compelling interpretation of the song has become a "show-stopping highspot of the foursome's stage act!" Barrow adds: "John must have built himself a set of leather tonsils in a throat of steel to turn out such a violently exciting track!" On "A Taste Of Honey," Paul's "clear, sturdy voice turns it into a haunting piece of atmosphere balladeering. On "Do You Want To Know A Secret," George "tempers his vocal delivery with an intriguing blend of warmth and wistfulness." For "There's A Place," Ringo's "percussive pressure" make the song an infectious beat number.

Barrow opens his liner notes for *The Beatles' Hits* with a bold statement: "The four numbers on this EP have been selected from The Lennon & McCartney Songbook. If that description sounds a trifle pompous perhaps I may suggest that you preserve this sleeve for ten years, exhume it from your collection somewhere around the middle of 1973 and write me a very nasty letter if the pop people of the 70s aren't talking with respect about at least two of these titles as 'early examples of modern beat standards taken from The Lennon & McCartney Songbook.'" He adds that the Beatles, as successful songwriters and "golden-touch recording artists," have "combined themselves so brilliantly in the all-around, do-it-yourself versatility of a single singing/playing/composing unit." After writing about the chart success of the songs on the EP, he closes with: "P.S. In case you still doubt my opening paragraph prophesy, you should know that Messrs. Lennon & McCartney have written enough songs to keep them in singles and album from now until 1973 even if their composing talent were to wither and die in the immediate future!"

The liner notes to *The Beatles (No. 1)* open with Barrow observing that: "Each time I settle down to pen a set of paragraphs for the sleeve of another new Beatles release, I am able to recall fresh sets of honours and triumphs which have come the way of this fabulous foursome in the brief 'tween-discs spell. Every Beatle-cut disc adds to the outfit's greatness by topping the charts." After describing the success of the group's first LP and EP, Barrow adds: "They seem to have achieved so much during this first stand-out year that, short of getting themselves a Fan Club branch on the moon* or something equally incredible, I doubt if there are many more strengths for them to go on from or to!" The asterisk refers to a footnote providing the address of the Official Beatles Fan Club for "earth dwellers." The notes close with brief descriptions of the four songs.

Barrow used the liner notes for the *All My Loving* EP to heap praise upon the group. "**John...Paul...George...Ringo.** Names which meant little or nothing eighteen months ago. Today there is an almost legendary magic about John and Paul and George and Ringo. The very mention of any one sends sharp shivers of excitement down the spines of young girls. The names belong to four vigorous-voiced, multi-talented artists who have the 1964 pop music world spread out about their stomping feet. The four command a kingdom of gold and silver trophies. They rule supreme from the hit parade heights. They dominate the thoughts, moods and hearts of a million devoted fans. They fascinate many more millions of long-range admirers from every walk of life and every living generation. They have pioneered and cultivated a dozen different trends in teenage fashions and musical notions. They have altered the course of their contemporary segment of show business history. They are, with less than eighteen months of national importance behind them, amongst the most sensational successes the entertainment world has ever known. They are, in one meaningful word, Beatles.

"The Beatles abhor the contrived, venerate the unconventional. They are what every young girl would have the boy next door to be. They have made the phrase 'pop idol' obsolete. John...Paul...George...Ringo. Four forceful personalities backed by rare and genuine talent."

In December 1963, EMI considered releasing an EP containing both sides of the Beatles latest singles, "She Loves You" and "I Want To Hold Your Hand," both of which had earned golden disc status with sales of over one million units. Although test pressings and labels for *The Beatles' Golden Discs* were prepared, the EP was canceled. No art work or liner notes for the EP are known to exist.

The Decca Audition & Commercial Test

On January 1, 1962, the Beatles, then consisting of John Lennon, Paul McCartney, George Harrison and Pete Best, entered a British recording studio for the first time—Decca Studios at Broadhurst Gardens, West Hampstead, London. The band, accompanied by road manager Neil Aspinall, unloaded their amplifiers and instruments from the van and set up in Studio 2. The group's amplifiers, which worked fine in the clubs, gave off a humming sound that made the equipment unsuitable for studio recording. The session's balance engineer, Mike Savage, brought in some studio amplifiers for the band to plug their guitars into. Pete was directed to set up his drum kit behind isolation screens to prevent the sound of his drums from bleeding over to the vocal microphones.

The Decca session was the result of manager Brian Epstein's December 1961 meetings in London with representatives from England's two largest and most prestigious recording organizations, EMI and Decca. Brian met with EMI's general marketing manager, Ron White, who agreed to take the group's "My Bonnie" single (with the Beatles as the backing band for Tony Sheridan) to the company's top artist and repertoire (A&R) men. None were impressed.

Brian's meeting with Decca, however, was more productive. The company's sales manager, Sidney "Steve" Beecher-Stevens, told Brian that he would push the group's application through Decca's Artistes Department. Although there were no guarantees, Brian was told he would soon receive information on an audition for the Beatles.

On December 13, Mike Smith, who had recently been promoted to Decca's A&R staff, accompanied Brian to see the Beatles perform an evening set at the Cavern Club in Liverpool. Smith was amazed by the crowd's reaction to the group and told Brian that he would arrange for the Beatles to come to London for a studio test. Although the Beatles had impressed Smith in a live setting, he needed to find out if the group could be effectively captured on disc.

The Beatles busy schedule made it difficult for the group to hold practice sessions, but it did keep them sharp. In addition to one-off concerts at the Tower Ballroom and the Casbah Coffee Club, the Beatles played the Cavern nine more times, including an evening show on December 30. The following day Neil Aspinall drove the group down to London. After the Beatles celebrated New Year's Eve in Trafalgar Square, they headed back to their hotel beds confident that they would soon be Decca recording artists.

The next morning the Beatles set up and were ready to go on time, but had to wait until Mike Smith arrived. Although Smith was the producer of the session, he later admitted: "I made no attempt to produce anything. I just collected what they were doing." His lack of involvement would have a negative effect on the recordings. The Beatles had only minimal studio experience from their Hamburg sessions backing Tony Sheridan for German producer Bert Kaempfert. They could have used some guidance and encouragement.

Although artists at commercial tests normally recorded anywhere from two to five songs, the Beatles went through 15 songs during morning and afternoon sessions. Because the group did not have time for a proper practice before the session, they played highlights from their Cavern stage show, which was a mix of rock 'n' roll, country and western, R&B, humorous tunes, show tunes, contemporary hits and Lennon-McCartney originals. As was the case with their live performances, John, Paul and George each contributed lead vocals. Surprisingly, John only sang lead on four songs, while George also sang four and Paul sang seven. Three of the songs were Lennon-McCartney compositions that had recently been added to their Cavern set list. While the 15 songs showed how versatile the Beatles were, the failure to include several rockers led to a relatively unexciting batch of recordings.

Overall, the Beatles gave a sub-par performance, suffering from a bit of nervousness and missing the Cavern crowd to feed off of. John sounds tentative at times. Paul sounds nervous and self-conscious. George's singing is fine; however his guitar playing is inconsistent, ranging from excellent to a bad solo or two. Pete had trouble keeping time and failed to generate any excitement. Engineer Mike Savage was savage in his assessment of Pete: "You could pick up a better drummer in any pub in London. If you've got a quarter of a group being average, that isn't good. The drummer should be the rock, and if the rock isn't good then you start thinking 'No.'" Mike Smith summed it up: "They weren't very good and seemed overawed by the situation."

Despite these problems, the Beatles were expecting Decca to sign them. According to Pete, Smith thought it would be "dead easy" for the Beatles to get a contract, but that it was up to his supervisor, Dick Rowe. Pete also recalls Smith being impressed with two of the group's original tunes, "Love Of The Loved" and "Hello Little Girl." In the Liverpool Echo, Tony Barrow reported: "Decca disc producer Mike Smith tells me that he thinks the Beatles are great...and he is convinced that his label will be able to put The Beatles to good use."

The Beatles would have to wait until early February to learn of Decca's decision. Brian was summoned to Decca for a lunch-time meeting. Although there are conflicting accounts of who was there and what was said, Brian, in his autobiography, *A Cellar Full Of Noise*, quoted Rowe as saying: "Not to mince words, Mr. Epstein, we don't like your boys' sound. Groups of guitarists are on their way out."

Although Rowe may or may not have uttered those words, it was Rowe who sealed the Beatles fate. Mike Smith had recently auditioned another group, Brian Poole and the Tremeloes, who, unlike the Beatles, were from London, were members of the Musician's Union, had upper-crust management and owned high-quality equipment. Smith was looking for a band that he could both record for their own records and use the members as session musicians. Being from Liverpool, the Beatles could not fulfill the secondary role as session players. In addition, Brian Poole and the Tremeloes had performed better in the studio than the Beatles. Smith had decided on signing Brian Poole and the Tremeloes, but really wanted both bands. Rowe did not give Smith that luxury. Rowe told Smith he could only sign one of the groups, so Smith was forced to pass on the Beatles.

Epstein, understandably upset over his boys being turned down, pushed back at the decision, telling Decca that his boys were "going to explode" and one day be "bigger than Elvis Presley." Rowe, impressed with Brian's strong belief in his boys and not wanting to upset a record store owner who sold a lot of Decca product, made Brian an offer. Rowe recommended that Brian contact Tony Meehan, a young and rising star on Decca's A&R staff, about producing the Beatles on an outside deal for about 100 pounds. The Beatles would pay Meehan to produce the session, and Decca would release the record. Although Brian could have afforded to finance the Beatles first record and was tempted to take Decca up on the offer, he decided against it. Brian did not want a producer who did not believe in his boys and viewed the session as another paycheck. He sent Decca a letter thanking them for the offer, but turning it down and falsely claiming the Beatles were offered a contract by another company.

The failed Decca audition did, however, lead to the Beatles being offered a contract by another record company, Decca's biggest competitor, EMI, who had previously turned the Beatles down a few months earlier. As Decca had no plans for the Beatles and wanted to remain on good terms with Brian, the company gave Brian a tape of the session, which Brian had with him when he later met with Robert Boast, manager of the HMV (His Master's Voice) record store on London's Oxford Street. Boast listened to the tape and suggested to Brian that he have the songs cut onto 10-inch 78-RPM acetates. The store's disc cutter, Jim Foy, was impressed with the group's sound and the original compositions. Foy arranged for Sid Coleman, general manager of Ardmore & Beechwood, a British joint-stock company owned by EMI and named after Capitol Records' music publishing subsidiaries, Ardmore Music Corporation and Beechwood Music Corporation, to come down from his office on the top floor of the building to the cutting room to hear the songs. Coleman wanted the publishing rights to the Lennon-McCartney songs for his company and agreed to help Brian get a recording contract for the Beatles. He played an acetate of one of the original tunes, "Like Dreamers Do," to his assistant, Kim Bennett, who took a liking to the song. Bennett pushed Coleman to play the disc for EMI's A&R men, but no one showed any interest. However, as detailed in the next chapter, the persistence of Bennett and Coleman would later pay off.

The Beatles failure to pass their Decca audition turned out for the best. For had Dick Rowe allowed Mike Smith to sign the Beatles, the group would have been produced by Mike Smith rather than George Martin. To save money, Decca may have used the January 1 recordings for the Beatles first two singles, which might have been "Love Of The Loved" c/w "The Sheik Of Araby" and "Hello Little Girl" c/w "Besame Mucho." Neither disc would have attracted much attention outside of Liverpool. And, although John and Paul might have gone on to write better songs, without George Martin's input and guidance, "Love Me Do" would not have been rearranged, and "Please Please Me" may have remained a slow, bluesy number in the style of Roy Orbison rather than developing into an exciting rocker.

Despite the Beatles great talent, they might not have taken England by storm had they not worked with Martin. And without the Beatles breakthrough, London's record companies may not have signed other beat groups, sticking instead with solo artists who had failed to catch on in America. There might have been no British Invasion to influence a whole generation of American musicians and future musicians. Dick Rowe's foolish decision was clearly a blessing.

Money (That's What I Want)

Recorded: January 1, 1962 (Decca Studio 2)

Producer: Mike Smith
Engineer: Mike Savage

John: Lead vocal; rhythm guitar (Rickenbacker Capri)
Paul: Backing vocal; bass guitar (Hofner)
George: Backing vocal; lead guitar (Gretsch Duo-Jet)
Pete: Drums (Premier kit)

The Beatles added "Money (That's What I Want)" to their set list in 1960. The song was recorded in 1959 by Barrett Strong, a pianist/singer working with producer and Motown founder Berry Gordy, at Gordy's Hitsville studio in Detroit. Although Strong would later gain fame as a songwriter (teaming with Norman Whitfield on classics such as "I Heard It Through The Grapevine," "I Wish It Would Rain," "Cloud Nine," "I Can't Get Next To You," "War," "Just My Imagination" and "Ball Of Confusion," with its line "The Beatles new record's a gas"), he did not get credit for "Money." That was claimed by Gordy and Hitsville receptionist Janie Bradford, who recalled: "Mr. Gordy was playing piano, and he had this riff going. We stood there and just kept writing and throwing out lyrics and improving on the melody, and the whole thing came together." Strong always insisted that he came up with the piano riff and helped with the words.

The track was recorded with Strong on lead vocal and piano, Benny Benjamin on drums and Brian Holland on tambourine, joined on guitar by Eugene Grew (a 21-year-old white male) and possibly James Jamerson on bass. The backing vocals were provided by the Rayber Voices, who most likely included Raynoma Gordy, Brian Holland, Robert Bateman, Sonny Sanders and Gwendolyn Murray.

The single was originally issued on Gordy's Tamla label (Tamla 54027) in August 1959. When reissued in March 1960 on Anna 1111, the record received wider distribution and became the first Motown hit, reaching number 23 in the Billboard Hot 100 during its 17 weeks on the charts. It also spent 21 weeks on the Billboard Hot R&B Sides chart, including six weeks at number two.

In the U.K., "Money" was licensed by Decca Records for release on its London label, which issued American master recordings obtained from labels such as Chess, Imperial, Atlantic, Specialty, Essex and Sun. By the late fifties, the label's logo had changed to London American Recordings. "Money" was released in the U.K. as London 45-HLU 9088 in April 1960. (Future Motown/Tamla recordings would be issued in the U.K. by Fontana, Oriole and Stateside.)

"Money" did not chart in the U.K., but garnered plenty of attention with its driving beat, memorable riff, soulful vocals and admission of placing money above all else. Singer Ted Taylor of the Liverpool beat band King-Size Taylor and the Dominoes claims that the Beatles (then the Silver Beatles) added the song (and others) to their stage show after seeing them performed by his group.

Although this R&B classic was most likely one of the highlights of the Beatles stage show, the Decca recording is disappointing. John's lead vocal is tentative, never finding its groove and lacking any real excitement. George and Paul pound out the song's catchy riff with serviceable support from Pete.

The Beatles would later record a vastly superior version of "Money" for their second Parlophone LP, *With The Beatles*. Prior to that EMI session, the group performed "Money" six times for the BBC, the first of which was recorded on May 21, 1963, and broadcast May 25 on Saturday Club.

Memphis, Tennessee

Recorded: January 1, 1962 (Decca Studio 2)

Producer: Mike Smith
Engineer: Mike Savage

John: Lead vocal; rhythm guitar (Rickenbacker Capri)
Paul: Bass guitar (Hofner)
George: Lead guitar (Gretsch Duo-Jet)
Pete: Drums (Premier kit)

The Beatles love of American singer/guitarist Chuck Berry made the addition of "Memphis, Tennessee" to their stage show inevitable. The song was written by Berry, who claimed he recorded the song by himself at home singing lead and playing guitar. Berry overdubbed two additional guitar parts, and Jasper Thomas added drums. The song was issued as the B-side to "Back In The U.S.A." on Chess 1729 in early June 1959. Although "Memphis" failed to chart, "Back In The U.S.A." peaked at number 37 during its eight-week run in the Billboard Hot 100 and at number 16 during its seven weeks on the Billboard Hot R&B Sides chart. The single was released in the U.K. on London 45-HLM 8921 in July 1959. Neither side charted at the time (although a 1963 single issued by Pye International pairing "Let It Rock" and "Memphis, Tennessee" peaked at number six).

Paul recalls listening to the London single in the summer of 1959: "I remember learning 'Memphis' up in John's bedroom—it had the greatest guitar riff ever. It killed us!"

PAGE 4   MERSEY BEAT   JAN. 4-18

MERSEY BEAT POPULARITY POLL

RESULTS

1. The Beatles
2. Gerry and the Pacemakers
3. The Remo Four
4. Rory Storm and the Hurricanes
5. Johnny Sandon and the Searchers
6. Kingsize Taylor and the Dominoes
7. The Big Three
8. The Strangers
9. Faron and the Flamingos
10. The Four Jays
11. Ian and the Zodiacs
12. The Undertakers
13. Earl Preston and the T.T.'s
14. Mark Peters and the Cyclones
15. Karl Terry and the Cruisers
16. Derry and the Seniors
17. Steve and the Syndicate
18. Dee Fenton and the Silhouettes
19. Billy Kramer and the Coasters
20. Dale Roberts and the Jaywalkers

SURVEY

There has been tremendous interest in the "Mersey Beat Popularity Poll" and we were pleased at the response we recieved in voting forms. Fortunately only one or two forms were disqualified as they did not conform to the rules.

That the first four groups were most popular was a foregone conclusion all signs have indicated their popularity; the crowds that flock to their performances, the regularity of their bookings, the letters and requests for photographs and news concerning them. Of the four the Remo Four are acknowledged to be the best instrumental group on Merseyside, and the Beatles have been regarded as a top group about 1961,

MERSEYSIDE'S OWN ENTERTAINMENTS PAPER

MERSEY BEAT

CRANES
The name for Records, Amplifiers Transistor Radios Also Pianos and Organs
HANOVER STREET, LIVERPOOL 1
Telephone: ROYal 4714

Vol. 1 No. 13

NEMS
WHITECHAPEL AND GREAT CHARLOTTE STREET
THE FINEST RECORD SELECTIONS IN THE NORTH
Open until 6-0 p.m. each day
(Thursday and Saturday 6-30 p.m.)

JANUARY 4-18, 1962   Price THREEPENCE

Beatles Top Poll!

FULL RESULTS INSIDE
Cover photograph by Albert Marrion

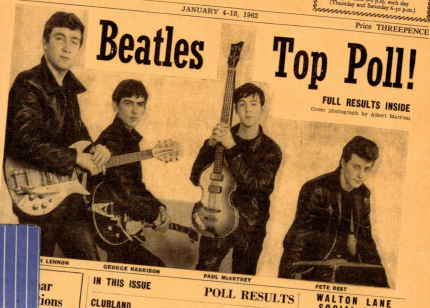

JOHN LENNON   GEORGE HARRISON   PAUL McARTREY   PETE BEST

IN THIS ISSUE

	POLL RESULTS	
CLUBLAND	3 JACK O' CLUBS 3 N.U.R. No. 5 SOCIAL CLUB 7 ODD SPOT OPENS	
PERSONALITIES	2 ALEX POWER 2 BERT DONN 2 TOM HARTLEY 7 JOHNNY SANDON	
JAZZ	6 LEO RUTHERFORD 8 MERSEYSIDE JAZZ	
FEATURES	2 EDITORIAL 5 NEMS TOP TEN	
ALSO	2 ARTISTES DIRECTORY 3 CLASSIFIED ADVERTISEMENTS 5 MERSEY ROUNDABOUT	

PEAK PROMOTIONS
WISH ALL READERS A HAPPY NEW YEAR
See these fabulous groups in 1962 at
HOLYOAKE HALL
BLAIR HALL
COLUMBA HALL, WIDNES
BILLY KRAMER AND THE COASTERS
THE SORRELS
THE SILHOETTES
THE SENIORS
THE M.I.5

WALTON LANE SOCIAL CLUB
Proprietor: Mrs. Ada Taylor
THE PULSE OF CLUBLAND
ALWAYS A WELCOME FOR MEMBERS AND FRIENDS

N.U.R. No. 5 Social Club
DEANE ROAD, LIVERPOOL
Secretary: Mr. J. Guigan
THE HAPPY CLUB
ONLY THE BEST IS GOOD ENOUGH FOR OUR MEMBERS AND FRIENDS

MERSEYSIDE CLUBS ASSOCIATION
Headquarters:
Walton Lane Social Club
THE BEST AUDITION SERVICE ON MERSEYSIDE
OPEN TO ALL BONA FIDE CLUB REPRESENTATIVES
Every Sunday 1-30 p.m. to 4 p.m.
Secretary: Mr. S. McGorian

A few days after the Beatles January 1, 1962 Decca audition, Mersey Beat magazine announced in its January 4-18 issue that the Beatles had topped its popularity poll. The cover identified Paul by his pseudonym created by John: Paul McArtrey.

John handles the lead vocal on the group's Decca recording of "Memphis" with care, seeming more concerned about enunciation than belting out the rocker. The track is bolstered by George mimicking Berry's swinging guitar riffs and Paul's steady bass. Pete provides a steady beat, but little else.

The Beatles performed "Memphis" five times for the BBC. The first, with Pete on drums, was also part of the group's first performance for the BEEB, captured live at the Playhouse Theatre in Manchester on March 7, 1962, and broadcast the next day on Teenager's Turn. The remaining four versions are from 1963. The July 10 recording made at London's Aeolian Hall was broadcast on the July 30 Pop Go The Beatles and appears on Apple's *Live At The BBC* album issued in 1994. The September 7 performance at the Playhouse Theatre in London was broadcast on October 5 and is on the 2013 collection *On Air–Live At The BBC Volume 2*.

Three Cool Cats

Recorded: January 1, 1962 (Decca Studio 2)

Producer: Mike Smith
Engineer: Mike Savage

George: Lead vocal; lead guitar (Gretsch Duo-Jet)
John: Backing vocal; rhythm guitar (Rickenbacker Capri)
Paul: Backing vocal; bass guitar (Hofner)
Pete: Drums (Premier kit)

The Beatles recorded three songs by the Coasters for Decca, demonstrating their appreciation of the comedic aspects of the American R&B vocal group's recordings produced by Jerry Leiber and Mike Stoller. "Three Cool Cats" was written by Leiber-Stoller and recorded by the Coasters on March 17, 1958. It was released as the B-side to "Charlie Brown" on Atco 6132 in January 1959. "Charlie Brown" charted for 15 weeks in the Billboard Hot 100, including three weeks at number two, and for 12 weeks in the Billboard Hot R&B Sides chart, also with a peak at number two. Its humorous flip-side, "Three Cool Cats," did not chart. The disc was issued in the U.K. on London 45-HL-E 8819, with the A-side peaking at number six.

George is the lead vocalist on the group's Decca recording. John and Paul provide the song's intricate and at times silly backing vocals, such as John's differing pseudo accents for his solo line, "Hey man, save one chick for me!" All do an admirable job, although those familiar with the Coasters' recording will miss the bass vocal. The Beatles add vocal ad-libs at the end of the song.

As is often the case with Beatles, the group takes the song at a faster tempo than the original recording it is covering. The song's instrumental break is weak, with George's rockabilly-influenced solo being a poor substitute for King Curtis' smooth saxophone solo on the Coasters version. "Three Cool Cats" is one of five tracks from the Decca session included on 1995's *Anthology 1*.

Searchin'

Recorded: January 1, 1962 (Decca Studio 2)

Producer: Mike Smith
Engineer: Mike Savage

Paul: Lead vocal; bass guitar (Hofner)
John: Backing vocal; rhythm guitar (Rickenbacker Capri)
George: Backing vocal; lead guitar (Gretsch Duo-Jet)
Pete: Drums (Premier kit)

"Searchin'" was the A-side to the Coasters' double-sided smash single on Atco 6087 released in March 1957. The song, written and produced by Jerry Leiber and Mike Stoller, was recorded on February 15, 1957. The Coasters' raw yet flawless vocals are brilliantly backed by an exciting instrumental track dominated by Mike Stoller's rollicking piano and Ralph Hamilton's simple but powerful bass. "Searchin'" charted for 26 weeks in the Billboard pop charts, peaking at number three. The single's flip side, "Young Blood," stayed on the Billboard pop charts for 24 weeks, with a peak a number eight. The combined single held the number one spot on the Billboard R&B Best Sellers in Stores chart for 12 weeks. Released in England in June 1957 on London 45-HL-E 8450, "Searchin'" charted for one week at number 30 on September 28, 1957.

Paul recalls how the group obtained a copy of the single: "A rumour reached town one day that there was a man over the hills who had the record 'Searchin'' by The Coasters. Colin [Hanton], the drummer with John's skiffle group, knew him and so there was a great trek to find the man, and indeed we found him. And relieved him of it. It was too big a responsibility for him to keep. We couldn't return it. We just had to have it; it was like gold dust." Both songs were added to the stage show of the Quarrymen and remained in the group's repertoire when they became the Beatles. According to Paul, "Searchin'" was a "big number with the Beatles; we always used to do it at the Cavern."

Paul handles the lead vocal on the Decca audition recording, trying his best to sound like a black American singer. He changes the lyrics during the verses with the call-out of famous detectives. The Coasters' Billy Guy sings: "Well Sherlock Holmes, Sam Spade got nothing, child, on me/Sergeant Friday, Charlie Chan, and Boston Blackie." Paul sings: "Well now Charlie Chan, Simon Slade got nothing, child, on a-me/Sergeant Friday and-a Peter Gunn well I'll ooh let 'em be." John and George provide the "Gonna find her" backing vocals, with John singing the bass notes "like a" followed by George's falsetto "Bulldog Drummond." Having no piano player, the Beatles backing features John and George strumming away (though Harrison's solo is weak). As was typical of British mixes in the early sixties, Paul's bass, so dominant in the Coasters' recording, is buried in the mix. The track features some of Pete's most active drumming.

The Decca audition recording of "Searchin'" is on *Anthology 1*; however, the song's five-second instrumental opening is edited out. The Beatles, with George singing lead, recorded "Young Blood" at the BBC Paris Theatre in London on June 1, 1963, for broadcast on the June 11 Pop Go The Beatles.

Besame Mucho

Recorded: January 1, 1962 (Decca Studio 2)

Producer: Mike Smith
Engineer: Mike Savage

Paul: Lead vocal; bass guitar (Hofner)
John: Backing vocal; rhythm guitar (Rickenbacker Capri)
George: Backing vocal; lead guitar (Gretsch Duo-Jet)
Pete: Drums (Premier kit)

"Besame Mucho" was written in 1940 by Consuelo Velazquez, a Mexican pianist and songwriter who was 19 when she wrote the song, whose title translates to "Kiss Me Much." It was first recorded by Emilio Tuero. The tune's English lyrics were written by Sunny Skylar, who left the song's Spanish title unchanged. The most popular recording of the song with English lyrics was by Jimmy Dorsey & his Orchestra, with solo vocals by Bob Eberly and Kitty Kallen. Released as the B-side to "My Ideal" (with Eberly as solo vocalist) on Decca 18574 in late 1943, "Besame Mucho" topped the Billboard Best Selling Retail Records chart for seven weeks starting March 4, 1944.

The Beatles interest in recording "Besame Mucho" came from Paul's fascination with the Coasters' arrangement of the song. "With 'Besame Mucho' by the Coasters, it's a minor song and it changes to a major, and where it changes to a major is such a big moment musically. That major change attracted me so much."

The Coasters recorded the song in 1960 at a session produced by Jerry Leiber and Mike Stoller. Bass singer Will "Dub" Jones provides the lead vocal, backed by the group's "Besame, besame" backing vocals. The recording, which runs over four minutes long, was issued in two parts on Atco 6163. "Besame Mucho (Part 1)" peaked at number 70 during its three-week run in the Billboard Hot 100 in May 1960. The disc was issued in England on London 45-HLK 9111 as part of the label's American Recordings series.

The Beatles arrangement of the song is considerably different from and faster than the Coasters' recording. It drops the repeating "Besame, besame" backing vocals and adds a "Cha-cha-boom" vocal that starts and ends the song. John and George provide backing and harmony vocals. The Decca recording of "Besame Mucho" features some of the group's best vocal work from the session. George's flawless strumming and guitar licks propel the song from start to finish. "Besame Mucho" is the only song played by the Beatles at both their Decca audition and first EMI session.

The Sheik Of Araby

Recorded: January 1, 1962 (Decca Studio 2)

Producer: Mike Smith
Engineer: Mike Savage

George: Lead vocal; lead guitar (Gretsch Duo-Jet)
John: Vocal interjections; rhythm guitar (Rickenbacker Capri)
Paul: Vocal interjections; bass guitar (Hofner)
Pete: Drums (Premier kit)

"The Sheik Of Araby" was written in 1921 by Harry B. Smith, Francis Wheeler and Ted Snyder. Its lyrics were inspired by the 1921 silent film *The Sheik* starring Rudolph Valentino. The song quickly became a Tin Pan Alley hit and a jazz standard. Instrumental versions by Club Royal Orchestra and Ray Miller both charted at number three in 1922. The Beatles may have been aware of the Spike Jones (novelty) and Fats Domino (R&B) recordings of the song, but their version is based on a 1961 performance of the song by Joe Brown and the Bruvvers that George Harrison saw on TV.

George handles the lead vocals on the Decca recording, which is included on *Anthology 1*. It is an upbeat rocker that comes across as a mad novelty tune, complete with John and Paul's "Not arf!" vocal interjections. While the song may have gone over well at the Cavern with John and Paul making funny faces for the crowd, this studio version just seems strange.

Sure To Fall (In Love With You)

Recorded: January 1, 1962 (Decca Studio 2)

Producer: Mike Smith
Engineer: Mike Savage

Paul: Lead vocal; bass guitar (Hofner)
John: Harmony vocal; rhythm guitar (Rickenbacker Capri)
George: Lead guitar (Gretsch Duo-Jet)
Pete: Drums (Premier kit)

"Sure to Fall (In Love With You)," written by American singer/guitarist Carl Perkins with Bill Cantrell and Quinton Claunch, was recorded in December 1955. While most of the Perkins songs performed by the Beatles were rockabilly, this one is pure country. Carl sings lead, joined by his brother Jay on harmony vocal on some of the lines to the verses. Sun initially planned to release the song as the follow-up to "Blue Suede Shoes" on Sun 235; however, only DJ copies were pressed. "Sure To Fall" was finally released on *Dance Album Of Carl Perkins* (Sun LP 1225) in 1957. The Beatles learned of the song when the album was released in England as London HA-S 2202 in 1959.

The *Dance Album Of Carl Perkins* would be the source of several other Perkins songs for the group. John was initially the lead singer on "Honey Don't," but by mid-1964, Ringo took over and is the song's vocalist on the group's fourth album, *Beatles For Sale*. George is the lead singer for "Everybody's Trying To Be My Baby," which was added to the set list in 1961 and is also on *Beatles For Sale*. Pete Best sang "Matchbox" until he left the group in August 1962, at which time John took over. Ringo sings lead on the Beatles EMI recording of the song. The Beatles performed "Your True Love" and "Blue Suede Shoes" as part of their stage show.

Paul is the lead vocalist on the Decca recording of "Sure To Fall," singing the middle eight on his own. Unlike the Carl Perkins recording, Paul is joined on harmony by John on all of the lines of the verses. George perfectly mimics Carl Perkins' guitar on the track, and Pete does a decent job on drums.

The Beatles performed "Sure To Fall" four times for the BBC. The first recording, made at the BBC Paris Theatre in London on June 1, 1963, and broadcast on the June 18 Pop Goes To The Beatles, is on *Live At The BBC*. The second BBC performance, recorded at London's Aeolian Hall on September 3, 1963, and aired on the September 24 Pop Go The Beatles, is on the 2013 collection *On Air–Live At The BBC Volume 2*. The last two recordings were broadcast in 1964.

Crying, Waiting, Hoping

Recorded: January 1, 1962 (Decca Studio 2)

Producer: Mike Smith
Engineer: Mike Savage

George: Lead vocal; lead guitar (Gretsch Duo-Jet)
John: Backing vocals; rhythm guitar (Rickenbacker Capri)
Paul: Backing vocals; bass guitar (Hofner)
Pete: Drums (Premier kit)

"Crying, Waiting, Hoping" was written by American singer/guitarist Buddy Holly. He recorded the song alone in his Manhattan apartment on December 14, 1958. After Holly's death on February 3, 1959, producer Jack Hansen obtained the tape of the song and five other tracks. Hansen hired studio musicians and the Ray Charles Singers to enhance the home recordings for release. The overdub session for "Crying, Waiting, Hoping" took place at Coral Records Studio A on June 30, 1959. The song was released as the B-side to "Peggy Sue Got Married" on Coral 9-62134 on July 20, 1959. The disc was issued in the U.K. on Coral 45-Q 72376 on August 28, 1959. The single did not chart in the U.S., but "Peggy Sue Got Married" peaked at number 13 in the U.K.

George does a fine job on both his lead vocal and guitar solo, which faithfully follows Don Arnone's solo on the released single. John and Paul provide effective backing vocals. The Beatles recorded the song at the BBC Paris Theatre on July 16, 1963, for broadcast on the August 6 Pop Goes The Beatles. This performance is on *Live At The BBC*.

To Know Her Is To Love Her

Recorded: January 1, 1962 (Decca Studio 2)

Producer: Mike Smith
Engineer: Mike Savage

John: Lead vocal; rhythm guitar (Rickenbacker Capri)
Paul: Backing vocal; bass guitar (Hofner)
George: Backing vocal; lead guitar (Gretsch Duo-Jet)
Pete: Drums (Premier kit)

"To Know Him, Is To Love Him" was written by Phil Spector, who pulled the title from the epitaph on his father's tombstone, "To Know Him Was To Love Him." (Ben Spector, who was born in Ukraine, immigrated to New York and died in the Bronx on April 20, 1949, and is buried at Beth David Cemetery in Elmont, NY.)

The song's melody is lifted from the opening line to the standard "When The Red Red Robin (Comes Bob, Bob, Bobbin' Along)," written in 1926 by Harry Woods. Spector recorded the teenage ballad with his group, the Teddy Bears, who consisted of Spector, lead singer Annette Kleinbard and Marshall Leib. In addition to writing the song, Spector, who was only 18 years old at the time, arranged and produced the recording. After Kleinbard sang her lead vocal backed by Spector on guitar and Leib on piano, the trio added backing vocals. Sandy Nelson was then recruited to overdub drums. The session took place at Gold Star Studios in Hollywood, California.

"To Know Him, Is To Love Him" was released as Dore 503 in early September 1958. The single debuted at number 88 in the Billboard Hot 100 on September 22 and spent its first of three weeks at number one on December 1 during its 23 weeks on the charts. The disc was released in England on London HLN 45-8733 as part of the label's American Recording series in December 1958, and peaked at number two in 1959 during its 16 weeks on the charts.

The Beatles added the song to their stage show in 1960 with the gender-altered title "To Know Her Is To Love Her." John sang the lead, with Paul and George providing backing vocals. According to Paul, the song represented the first time the group did a three-part harmony. "We learned that in my dad's house in Liverpool."

The tempo of the Decca recording is a bit too fast for the pretty ballad. Although John's vocal sounds sweet, he misses an opportunity to bring the song home on the bridge. Rather than adding excitement by belting out the lyrics, John sings in a softer tone. As was the case with "Crying, Waiting, Hoping," the Beatles recorded the song at the BBC Paris Theatre on July 16, 1963, for broadcast on the August 6 Pop Goes The Beatles. This performance is also on Live At The BBC.

Phil Spector went on to become one of the top record producers of the early and mid-sixties, best known for his famous "wall of sound" that turned pop records into mini-symphonic operas. His early hits included: the Crystals' "He's A Rebel" (#1 U.S. and #19 U.K.), "Da Doo Ron Ron" (#3 U.S. and #5 U.K.) and "Then He Kissed Me" (#6 U.S. and #2 U.K.); and the Ronettes' "Be My Baby" (#2 U.S. and #4 U.K.). Spector met the Beatles in late January 1964 at a London party thrown for the Ronettes, and was on the plane with the Beatles when they flew to New York on February 7, 1964, for their first American visit. After producing John's "Instant Karma" single in early 1970, Spector was hired to re-produce the "Let It Be" album. He later produced albums for John and George.

Till There Was You

Recorded: January 1, 1962 (Decca Studio 2)

Producer: Mike Smith
Engineer: Mike Savage

Paul: Lead vocal; bass guitar (Hofner)
John: Rhythm guitar (Rickenbacker Capri)
George: Lead guitar (Gretsch Duo-Jet)
Pete: Drums (Premier kit)

"Till There Was You" is from the 1957 hit Broadway show The Music Man, with book, music and lyrics by Meredith Willson. The play won five Tony Awards, including Best Musical. The song came to Paul's attention through an older cousin, Betty Danher Robbins, who played him Peggy Lee records such as "Fever" and "Till There Was You." Paul learned to love ballads, recalling: "I could never see the difference between a beautiful melody and a cool rock 'n' roll song."

Peggy Lee's recording of the song was from Latin A La Lee, an album of show tunes with Afro-Cuban rhythms and jazz-influenced, breezy arrangements by Jack Marshall. The 1960 LP was released in the U.S. and U.K. as Capitol (S)T 1290.

In England, "Till There Was You" received additional attention when it was included on a four-song EP from the album and later released as a single (Capitol 45-CL 15184). The song charted at number 30 in the spring of 1961. It was this single that Paul's cousin probably played for him. (At that time, Paul was not aware that the song had been featured in the Broadway show The Music Man, which would not be released as a film until the summer of 1962.)

The Beatles added "Till There Was You" to their set list in 1961. The song was most likely performed early in the Decca audition, with the Beatles coming across as nervous and insecure. Paul seems overly concerned with his enunciation, adding a hard "k" sound to the end of "music" and floating to a high pitch that led John to later say "he sounded like a woman." George messes up his guitar solo and Pete has trouble keeping a steady beat.

The show tune was a regular feature of the Beatles early stage shows and, like "Besame Mucho" and "To Know Her Is To Love Her," is on Live At The Star Club, recorded in Hamburg in late December 1962. The Beatles performed "Till There Was You" seven times for the BBC. The first three recordings of the song (the first was recorded on June 1, 1963, at BBC Paris Theatre, London, and aired on the June 11 Pop Goes The Beatles) predate the July 30, 1963 EMI session that produced the version released on With The Beatles.

September In The Rain

Recorded: January 1, 1962 (Decca Studio 2)

Producer: Mike Smith
Engineer: Mike Savage

Paul: Lead vocal; bass guitar (Hofner)
John: Rhythm guitar (Rickenbacker Capri)
George: Lead guitar (Gretsch Duo-Jet)
Pete: Drums (Premier kit)

"September In The Rain" is a pop standard with music by Harry Warren and lyrics by Al Dubin. It first appeared in the 1937 film *Melody For Two* sung by James Melton. Guy Lombardo & His Royal Canadians brought the song to the top of the charts for four weeks in 1937 with Guy's younger brother, Carmen, providing vocal accompaniment. The George Shearing Quintet, led by blind British pianist Shearing, issued a jazz instrumental version of the song that became an international million seller in 1949.

The Beatles added "September In The Rain" to their stage show in 1961 as a cover of jazz-blues singer and pianist Dinah Washington's version of the song. The single, issued in the U.S.A. on Mercury 71876, peaked at number 23 in the fall of 1961. EMI's release of the single on Mercury 45-AMT 1162 peaked at number 35 in December 1961.

The Beatles Decca recording of "September In The Rain" opens with Paul's count-in: "One, two, two, zippy-do, hey!" This count-in, as well as the song itself, is a far cry from McCartney's exciting "One, two, three, faaa!" count-in on "I Saw Her Standing There" that would later open the Beatles first album, *Please Please Me*. Paul can't seem to make up his mind whether to sing the tune as a rocker or as a crooner. Although the band tries to rock on, they don't seem to take the song seriously, and are hampered by Pete's drumming. The track ends with a bit of musical ad-libbing.

Take Good Care Of My Baby

Recorded: January 1, 1962 (Decca Studio 2)

Producer: Mike Smith
Engineer: Mike Savage

George: Lead vocal; lead guitar (Gretsch Duo-Jet)
Paul: Backing vocals; bass guitar (Hofner)
John: Rhythm guitar (Rickenbacker Capri)
Pete: Drums (Premier kit)

The Beatles and/or manager Brian Epstein apparently thought it was important for the Decca audition to demonstrate that the band could cover current hits. In addition to performing Dinah Washington's "September In The Rain," the group played Bobby Vee's "Take Good Care Of My Baby."

Vee, like the Beatles, idolized Buddy Holly. At 15 years of age, the singer/guitarist formed a band with his brother and a friend. On February 3, 1959, he was looking forward to seeing Holly, Dion and the Belmonts, Ritchie Valens, and J.P. Richardson, known as the Big Bopper, in concert in his home town of Fargo, North Dakota. When he came home from school on his lunch break, he learned that there had been a plane crash in the early morning that had taken the lives of Holly, Valens, Richardson and the pilot. After learning through Fargo's KFGO radio station that the promoter was looking for a local group to add to the bill, Vee volunteered his group, who learned several Buddy Holly songs for the show.

"Take Good Care Of My Baby" was written by Carole King and Gerry Goffin. The song was originally recorded by Dion, who decided not to release the track as a single (although it later appeared on the singer's *Runaround Sue* LP). While meeting with music publisher Don Kirshner of Aldon Music at New York's Brill Building, Vee's producer, Snuff Garrett, heard King's demo of the song. Garrett knew the tune would be perfect for Vee, but thought that it needed an attention-grabbing introduction. Garrett met with King and worked out the song's slow opening lines: "My tears are falling, 'cause you've taken her away/And though it really hurts me so, there's something I've gotta say."

"Take Good Care Of My Baby" was recorded by Vee at a 1961 session with Barney Kessel, Tommy Allsup and Howard Roberts on guitar, Clifford Hills on bass, Robert Florence on piano, and the legendary Earl Palmer on drums. Sid Sharp arranged the strings and the Johnny Mann Singers provided the backing vocals. The song was released on Liberty F-55354 on July 20, 1961. The single charted for 15 weeks and topped the Billboard Hot 100 for three weeks starting on September 18, 1961. The single was issued in the U.K. on London 45-HLG 9438 and peaked at number three in late November (although the song topped the NME chart on December 1).

The Beatles Decca audition recording features George capably handling the lead vocals, backed by Paul on the "Take good care of my baby" lines. While the performance doesn't generate the excitement of the Beatles stage show, it demonstrates that the group could play the hits of the day.

Love Of The Loved

Recorded: January 1, 1962 (Decca Studio 2)

Producer: Mike Smith
Engineer: Mike Savage

Paul: Lead vocal; bass guitar (Hofner)
John: Rhythm guitar (Rickenbacker Capri)
George: Lead guitar (Gretsch Duo-Jet)
Pete: Drums (Premier kit)

"Love Of The Loved" was one of three Lennon-McCartney originals recorded at the Decca audition. Paul recalls writing the song in 1959 on his Zenith acoustic guitar and during a late night walk back to his home in Allerton. The song's middle eight (bridge) is similar to that of "To Know Him, Is To Love Him."

The Decca recording features a nervous Paul McCartney on lead vocal. He adds a hard "k" sound each time he sings the word "look" as in "Each time I look."

Although Mike Smith was impressed with this song, George Martin did not find it suitable for the Beatles. Martin did, however, produce a trumpet-dominated jazzy arrangement of "Love Of The Loved" for Cilla Black's debut disc in the summer of 1963 at a session attended by Paul. The single, released as Parlophone R 5065 on September 27, 1963, peaked at number 35.

Hello Little Girl

Recorded: January 1, 1962 (Decca Studio 2)

Producer: Mike Smith
Engineer: Mike Savage

John: Lead vocal; guitar (Rickenbacker Capri)
Paul: Harmony and backing vocal; bass guitar (Hofner)
George: Backing vocal; lead guitar (Gretsch Duo-Jet)
Pete: Drums (Premier kit)

John considered "Hello Little Girl" to be his first complete song. His 1957 composition grew out of the Cole Porter standard "It's De-Lovely" from the 1936 Broadway musical *Red, Hot And Blue*, originally sung by Ethel Merman and Bob Hope. John was fascinated by the song, whose lyrics included: "It's delightful, it's delicious, it's de-lovely/I understand the reason why/You're sentimental, 'cause so am I." In discussing the tune's influence on "Hello Little Girl," John joked that the words were: "You're delightful, you're delicious and da da da. Isn't it a pity that you are such a scatterbrain."

Two American big bands had hit records with "It's De-Lovely," with Leo Reisman's recording charting at number seven in late 1936, and Eddy Duchin topping the charts in early 1937. John remembers a connection to the song with his mother, Julia. "It's all very Freudian. She used to sing that one. So I made 'Hello Little Girl' out of it."

The Beatles recorded a home demo of the song in early 1960 with John and Paul on electric guitars. The lyrics were different, and the song had a definite Buddy Holly feel to it.

The Beatles Decca recording has all the trappings of the early Merseybeat sound. John and Paul provide their best Everly Brothers harmony during the verses. John sings lead on the bridge, backed by Paul and George. The 1:40 track has a pleasant sound and ends with interesting chord changes. This performance is on *Anthology 1*.

George Martin produced the Fourmost's version of the song on June 3, 1963, with the Beatles in attendance. Two weeks later, Martin had Gerry and the Pacemakers record the song. The Fourmost version, released as Parlophone R 5056 on August 30, 1963, peaked at 19. The single was released in the U.S. on Atco 6280 in November 1963, but did not chart.

Like Dreamers Do

Recorded: January 1, 1962 (Decca Studio 2)

Producer: Mike Smith
Engineer: Mike Savage

Paul: Lead vocal; bass guitar (Hofner)
John: Rhythm guitar (Rickenbacker Capri)
George: Lead guitar (Gretsch Duo-Jet)
Pete: Drums (Premier kit)

Paul recalls: "'Like Dreamers Do' was one of the first songs I wrote and we tried it out at the Cavern." The tune dates back to 1959 when Paul was just seventeen.

The Beatles Decca audition features a solo vocal by Paul, who sounds unsure of himself, reaching for notes and never getting comfortable. This performance is on *Anthology 1*.

The Applejacks recording of the song was arranged by Mike Leander, who later arranged "She's Leaving Home," and produced by Mike Smith, producer of the Beatles Decca session. Released as Decca F 11916 on June 5, 1964, the disc charted at number 20. The U.S. single on London 9681 did not chart. Although the song is not one of Paul's best, "Like Dreamers Do" would play a part in the Beatles obtaining a recording contract with EMI.

The June 6, 1962 EMI Session

The Beatles first entered EMI Studios in St. John's Wood, London, early on the evening of June 6, 1962. (The studio would not be known as Abbey Road Studios until several years after the Beatles *Abbey Road* album immortalized the studio.) The band's lineup that June remained John Lennon on rhythm guitar, Paul McCartney on bass, George Harrison on lead guitar and Pete Best on drums. Prior to the session, the members of the group became EMI recording artists by signing a contract with the Parlophone Company Limited of Hayes in the County of Middlesex on June 4, 1962. Accordingly, they would be paid Musicians Union rates for the session. Although George Martin would be evaluating how the band performed in the studio, he was hoping that the Beatles would record at least two songs suitable for release as the group's debut single.

Prior to obtaining their recording contract with Parlophone, the Beatles had been turned down by EMI's Columbia and HMV labels, Decca, Pye, Oriole, Philips and Ember. As detailed in the previous chapter, Decca came closest to signing the Beatles, going so far as to give the group an audition/commercial test on January 1, 1962. Brian Epstein had the songs that were taped by Decca at the session transferred to 78-RPM acetates, which led to a meeting between Brian and Sid Coleman, general manager of EMI's Ardmore & Beechwood music publishing company. Coleman's assistant, Kim Bennett, liked the Lennon-McCartney song "Like Dreamers Do," and encouraged Coleman to get the Beatles a recording contract with EMI to obtain the publishing for the group's original compositions for their company. Although none of EMI's A&R men were impressed, Coleman and Bennett refused to let it go.

Bennett came up with the idea of asking EMI's managing director, Len "L.G." Wood, if Ardmore and Beechwood could pay for the cost of the record. Coleman liked the plan, realizing that the cost of recording a self-contained group would be minimal, would give their company the copyrights on two original songs for 50 years, and might even lead to royalties from record sales. Although Wood was sympathetic to their request, he told Coleman that they should limit themselves to publishing and let EMI handle the records.

But then fate once again intervened for the Beatles. George Martin, head of EMI's Parlophone label, had upset L.G. Wood during contract negotiations by demanding that EMI pay him royalties on record sales over and above his salary. Wood refused, and when Martin threatened to quit over these terms, Wood held firm, forcing Martin to drop his demand. Wood's frustration with Martin grew when he learned that Martin was having an affair with Judy Lockhart, Martin's secretary. Fortunately for Martin, he was good at his job and respected by Sir Joseph Lockwood, Chairman of the Board of EMI. Wood could not fire George Martin, but soon found a way to put the troublesome head of Parlophone in his place.

When Sid Coleman again approached Wood about allowing Ardmore & Beechwood to pay for a record by the Beatles to get the publishing for "Like Dreamers Do" and the group's other original tunes, Wood refused, but then got the idea to order George Martin to sign and record the Liverpool group. Martin had previously met with Brian on February 13, 1962. At the meeting, Brian apparently played and gave Martin one of the two-sided 78-RPM acetates made from the Decca audition tape: "Hello Little Girl" (with "John Lennon & The Beatles" and the songwriters credit "Lennon, McCartney" added to the label along with the song title); and "Till There Was You" (with the artist listed as "Paul McCartney & The Beatles"). As Martin would later recall, he wasn't "knocked out at all." Being one of EMI's A&R men, he may have previously heard "My Bonnie" and most likely would later hear "Like Dreamers Do."

However, one thing remained constant—George Martin was not impressed with the Beatles and had no interest in recording the group. But, because his affair with his secretary had come to the attention of L.G. Wood, he was being forced to work with the Beatles. Although Martin's assistant producer Ron Richards and EMI engineer Norman Smith knew the reason Martin had agreed to record the Beatles, the group had no idea of the strange set of circumstances that had led them to EMI's Studio Two.

On the afternoon of the June 6 session, George Martin was still wondering who to designate as the group's lead singer. He was envious of the success that Norrie Paramor had achieved for EMI's Columbia label with Cliff Richard and the Shadows. So would the Liverpool group with the funny name be John Lennon and the Beatles or Paul McCartney and the Beatles?

Martin asked his staff producer, Ron Richards, to handle the session. To Martin, the Beatles were a band that he had been forced to sign sight unseen. In addition, Richards was more familiar with rock 'n' roll than Martin. He would, however, be at EMI that evening to check in on the group and the session.

Richards was assisted by balance engineer Norman Smith and tape operator Chris Neal. Technical engineer Ken Townsend was at the studio to assist with the set up of the group's equipment.

Upon their arrival, the Beatles and Neil Aspinal brought the band's equipment into Studio 2. The EMI staff was caught off-guard by the group's appearance. Smith, who was in the upstairs control room, couldn't help looking down into the studio. Townsend recalls: "They dressed a bit differently and all had what we thought was very long hair. They had broad Liverpool accents. We didn't have many people from Liverpool recording at Abbey Road."

The session was recorded on both mono and twin-track tape machines; however, as soon as the group began to play, the engineers realized they had to deal with the poor shape of the group's equipment, particularly Paul's bass amp, which was unsuitable due to its rattling and rumbling. Smith and Townsend improvised and created a bass rig by soldering an input jack to a preamp and combining it with an amp and a large Tannoy speaker taken from Echo Chamber No. 1. They tied a string around John's amplifier to prevent it from rattling. After resolving these problems, the EMI staff was ready to record the group with the hope that the recordings would be of sufficient quality to pull two songs for the band's debut single.

Prior to the session, Brian sent George Martin a list of songs in the Beatles repertoire, including a medley of "Besame Mucho," "Will You Love Me Tomorrow" and "Open (Your Lovin' Arms)." Paul was lead vocalist on the original songs "P.S. I Love You," "Love Me Do," "Like Dreamers Do," "Love Of The Loved" and "Pinwheel Twist," along with "If You Gotta Make A Fool Of Somebody," "Till There Was You," "Over The Rainbow," "Your Feet's Too Big," "Hey! Baby," "Dream Baby," "September In The Rain" and "The Honeymoon Song." John had the originals "Ask Me Why" and "Hello Little Girl," along with "Baby It's You," "Please Mister Postman," "To Know Her Is To Love Her," "You Don't Understand Me," "Memphis, Tennessee," "A Shot Of Rhythm And Blues," "I Wish I Could Shimmy Like My Sister Kate," and "Lonesome Tears In My Eyes." George's songs were "A Picture Of You," "The Sheik Of Araby," "What A Crazy World We're Living In," "Three Cool Cats," "Dream," "Take Good Care Of My Baby" and "Glad All Over" (the Carl Perkins song).

Although no one remembers which or how many songs the group rehearsed before the tapes rolled, documents indicate that four songs were recorded: "Besame Mucho," "Love Me Do," "P.S. I Love You" and "Ask Me Why," in that order. As Richards selected "Besame Mucho" as the first song, he most likely thought it would have the most commercial appeal. And, because he instructed the group to perform the track with a solo McCartney vocal, Richards may have been leaning towards calling the group Paul McCartney and the Beatles. Richards most likely knew that at least one Lennon-McCartney song would be needed for the single to appease EMI's Ardmore and Beechwood music publishing company.

After completing "Besame Mucho," the Beatles moved on to "Love Me Do." While no one was impressed with the group's performance of the Latin standard, balance engineer Norman Smith thought enough of "Love Me Do" to direct tape operator Chris Neal to fetch George Martin from the EMI canteen to get his thoughts. Martin liked the song's raw harmonica sound, but had concerns about the arrangement. He took control of the session, reassigning the vocal on the "Love me do" refrain that ended each verse from John to Paul because John's harmonica playing prevented him from actually singing the word "do." Martin also had the group increase the tempo of the song, which originally had more of a bluesy sound. These would be the first of many suggestions Martin would make over the years.

"Love Me Do" fully exposed a glaring weakness in the band. Although Pete Best was popular with the group's fans, he could not provide the Beatles with the strong studio drumming needed for their sound. His performance on the song is weak, particularly in the middle eight where it sounds like he falls off the bridge. George Martin and Ron Richards took notice, with Martin telling Brian that although Best could remain the drummer for live appearances, a session drummer would replace him for studio recordings. By the time the Beatles returned to EMI in September, Pete Best had been replaced by Ringo Starr, one of Liverpool's top drummers.

The tape from the session survives, but only two songs have been released as of the publication of this book: "Besame Mucho" and "Love Me Do." These historic recordings were first released in 1995 on *Anthology 1*. As for "P.S. I Love You" and "Ask Me Why," neither Martin nor Richards nor Norman Smith were impressed. Smith's recollection of the latter part of the session was rather blunt: "It was twenty minutes of torture–they made a dreadful sound! And then they came up to the control room."

Once in the control room, they met with Martin and the engineers to listen to the playback. Afterwards, Martin lectured them about recording equipment and techniques as the group sat silently. When he finished talking, he asked the group if there was anything they didn't like. George Harrison took a long look at Martin and said, "Yeah, I don't like your tie!" His wisecrack broke the ice, and the Abbey Road personnel were then treated to the Beatles at their entertaining best. Although none of the songs recorded that day was deemed suitable for release, the exploratory session marked the beginning of the group's successful union with George Martin.

Besame Mucho

Recorded: June 6, 1962 (EMI Studio 2)

Producer: Ron Richards
Engineers: Norman Smith; Chris Neal

Paul: Lead vocal; bass guitar (Hofner)
John: Rhythm guitar (Rickenbacker Capri)
George: Lead guitar (Gretsch Duo-Jet)
Pete: Drums (Premier kit)

The first song recorded by the Beatles at their June 6, 1962 session at EMI Studios was "Besame Mucho." The Beatles had previously played the song at their January 1 Decca audition (see previous chapter for details about the composition and the Beatles studio performance). Although the Beatles arrangement of the tune featured John and George backing vocals, including the pair joining Paul on the bridge and the "Cha-cha boom!" refrains, Ron Richards decided to slow the tempo and make the song a solo showcase for Paul McCartney. However, Richards did allow Paul to sing "Cha-cha boom!" to open the song and between the first and second verses. The song was recorded in one take, which fades before its end, so it is not known if Paul ended the tune with another "Cha-cha boom!" Paul sounds a bit more relaxed than he did for the Decca session.

While the Beatles dutifully followed Richards' directions to play "Besame Mucho" as a solo Paul performance with a slowed tempo, the group reverted to its own arrangement when they were recorded by the BBC before a live audience at the Playhouse Theatre in Manchester on June 11, 1962. The high energy beat and "Cha-cha boom!" group vocals were back in full force to the delight of an enthusiastic teenage crowd that included a group of fans bussed in from Liverpool. This performance was broadcast on the June 15 radio program Teenager's Turn/Here We Go.

Love Me Do

Recorded: June 6, 1962 (EMI Studio 2)

Producers: Ron Richards; George Martin
Engineers: Norman Smith; Chris Neal

Paul: Lead vocal; bass guitar (Hofner)
John: Lead vocal; harmonica
George: Rhythm guitar (Gretsch Duo-Jet)
Pete: Drums (Premier kit)

The Beatles were nearing the end of their residency at Hamburg's Star-Club in May 1962 when they learned from Brian Epstein that he had secured them a recording contract with EMI. Following their manager's directive to rehearse new material, John and Paul resurrected and revamped what they perceived to be one of the best of their early collaborations, "Love Me Do." The song was primarily written by Paul in 1958. It was an acoustic number in the key of A that had a Buddy Holly–style arrangement.

By 1962, the Beatles had broadened their musical horizons. They were listening to and performing songs by American girl groups. This exposed them to the Shirelles and their producer, Luther Dixon, who also wrote some of their hits. They added tracks by Motown/Tamla artists, such as Barrett Strong, the Marvelettes, and Smokey Robinson and the Miracles. They savored songs by great songwriting teams such as Jerry Leiber & Mike Stoller and Gerry Goffin & Carole King. They were influenced by the rhythm and soul sounds of the Isley Brothers and the soulful blues of Arthur Alexander. And they were impressed with American records utilizing harmonica, such as James Ray's "If You Gotta Make A Fool Of Somebody" and Bruce Channel's "Hey! Baby." These American artists and their records influenced John and Paul's original compositions and arrangements.

The simple lyrics of "Love Me Do" were left alone: "Love, love me do/You know I love you/I'll always be true/So please love me do." They were augmented by an equally simple bridge: "Someone to love, somebody new/Someone to love, someone like you." The group lowered the song's key from A to G and slowed its tempo, giving the song a bluesier sound. And, most important, John decided to add harmonica to the arrangement, hoping that the Beatles would "be the first British group to use harmonica on record."

The harmonica would have a huge impact on the song and the Beatles career. It was the song's raw harmonica that caught the attention of George Martin in a positive way at their EMI commercial test. The instrument would be featured on the A-side of the Beatles first three singles and on the B-side of their third and fourth singles. However, Capitol's Dave Dexter would pass on the Beatles first two singles due to his dislike of John's harmonica playing.

Pete also contributed to the arrangement of "Love Me Do," but his literally off-beat idea negatively impacted the song and his place in the Beatles. For the song's bridge, Pete suggested that he pick up the tempo with a "skip beat" that never sounded quite right.

"Love Me Do" was the first of the Lennon-McCartney originals recorded at the June 6 session. As such, Ron Richards most likely thought it was the best of the three group compositions. It was during the recording of this song when George Martin entered the control room on the recommendation of balance engineer Norman Smith. Martin was attracted to the harmonica, but realized that the song's arrangement needed tweaking. Although John and Paul sang most of the song in harmony, each verse ended with John singing the line "Love me do" by himself as he began playing his harmonica.

Martin descended the stairs from the control room to the studio floor and, according to Paul, explained the problem to the group: "Wait a minute, there's a crossover there. Someone else has got to sing 'love me do' because you're going to have a song called 'Love Me *Waahhh*.' So, Paul, will you sing 'love me do'?" Paul was not prepared for his new solo spot, getting a case of "screaming hee-begeebies." McCartney's nervousness led to what he describes as a noticeable shake in his voice. Martin also recommended the group increase the tempo, making the song less bluesy and more pop.

While these modifications improved the song, nothing could save Pete's erratic drumming, which was particularly noticeable when he switched to his "skip beat" at the start of the bridge. This rendered the song totally unsuitable for release and most likely sealed his fate. When the other members of the group learned that Martin had told Brian that Pete would need to be replaced by a professional studio drummer for recordings, this removed any doubt that Pete needed to go.

The Beatles recorded four takes of the song, with only Takes 1 and 4 being complete. A reference lacquer was cut from Take 4, which was deemed the best. This lacquer was used for *Anthology 1*.

When the Beatles returned to EMI three months later in September to record their debut single, Pete had been replaced by Ringo Starr. The group would record two different versions of "Love Me Do." One ended up as the A-side of their first single, and the other was on their first LP.

P.S. I Love You

Recorded: June 6, 1962 (EMI Studio 2)

Producers: George Martin; Ron Richards
Engineers: Norman Smith; Chris Neal

Paul: Lead vocal; bass guitar (Hofner)
John: Backing vocal; rhythm guitar (Rickenbacker Capri)
George: Backing vocal; lead guitar (Gretsch Duo-Jet)
Pete: Drums (Premier kit)

"P.S. I Love You" was written primarily by Paul in response to Brian's request that the Beatles rehearse new material for their upcoming EMI recording session. The song, which was most likely started after the band rearranged "Love Me Do," took about a week to complete. Paul's lyrical inspirations for the song were most likely "Soldier Boy" by the Shirelles and "I'll Be Home" by Pat Boone.

The group recorded five takes of the song, though Take 2 was a false start and Take 3 broke down. A lacquer was cut from Take 1, which was deemed the best performance of the song.

The Beatles later recorded "P.S. I Love You" on September 11, 1962. It became the B-side to their first single, "Love Me Do."

Ask Me Why

Recorded: June 6, 1962 (EMI Studio 2)

Producers: George Martin; Ron Richards
Engineers: Norman Smith; Chris Neal

John: Lead vocal; rhythm guitar (Rickenbacker Capri)
Paul: Backing vocal; bass guitar (Hofner)
George: Backing vocal; lead guitar (Gretsch Duo-Jet)
Pete: Drums (Premier kit)

John wrote "Ask Me Why" in March 1962. His inspiration for the song was "What's So Good About Good Bye" by Smokey Robinson and the Miracles. The Beatles had been playing "Ask Me Why" in concert for a few months prior to the session, facilitating their ability to complete the song in one take.

Shortly after the June 6, 1962 EMI session, the Beatles were taped by the BBC in front of a live audience at the Playhouse Theatre in Manchester on June 11 for broadcast on the same June 15 Teenager's Turn/Here We Go program during which the group also played "Besame Mucho" and "A Picture Of You." The Beatles recorded "Ask Me Why" on November 26, 1962, for the B-side to their second single, "Please Please Me."

The First Singles Sessions

Going into the Beatles first EMI session on June 6, 1962, Brian Epstein was confident that it would lead to the group's first single being issued in July 1962. With John wanting the Beatles to be the first British group to have harmonica on their record, they most likely were hoping that "Love Me Do" would be the debut disc.

And while George Martin wanted that session to produce two tracks suitable for release, he was not satisfied with the results believing that none of the songs recorded were strong enough. Furthermore, Martin and his assistant, Ron Richards, determined that Pete Best was not suitable to play drums on the band's recordings. But the session and subsequent meeting in the control room did lead to an important decision being made. Rather than picking a lead singer for the group and dubbing them "John Lennon and the Beatles" or "Paul McCartney and the Beatles," Martin decided to "take them as they were, which was a new thing." Although this was an unconventional move for a vocal/instrumental group, Martin realized "I hadn't really heard anything quite like them before."

However, based on the three Lennon-McCartney songs performed at the session, Martin was not convinced the pair could write a hit single. He assigned Ron Richards the task of looking for a song for the group to record that could land them their first hit. Martin knew that the B-side would have to be a Lennon-McCartney tune so that EMI's music publishing firm, Ardmore & Beechwood, would get the publishing rights to at least one of the songs on the disc. With "Love Me Do" being the best of the lot, perhaps it could be the flip side to whatever tune Martin and Richards selected for the group to record. He would not bring the Beatles back to the studio until a suitable song had been found.

During the waning days of July, Martin made his selection, a commercial-sounding tune titled "How Do You Do It?" written by Mitch Murray. An acetate of the song (mistitled "How Do You Do") was sent to Brian at his Whitechapel office along with a directive that the Beatles return to EMI Studios on September 4 to record the song for the A-side of their first single. The Beatles were disappointed in both the song and the news that they were being forced to record a light-sounding pop tune. But, knowing they had no choice, they rearranged the song to give it more of a rock sound.

On September 4, 1962, the Beatles, this time with Ringo Starr on drums, returned to EMI Studios to record their first single. Knowing that Pete Best had been replaced, Martin did not book a session drummer, instead opting to see what Ringo could do. That afternoon (from 2:00 to 5:00 PM), the group, under the supervision of Martin and Richards, rehearsed the following six songs in Studio Three: "How Do You Do It?," "Love Me Do," "P.S. I Love You," "Ask Me Why," "Please Please Me" and "Tip Of My Tongue," all Lennon-McCartney originals except for the song selected by Martin.

The rehearsals gave Martin and Richards a chance to take a deeper look into the group Martin had been forced to sign. This included seeing if the group's new drummer, Ringo, was better adept at handling the precision drumming required in the studio than his predecessor, Pete Best. Unfortunately for Ringo, the pressure got to him, particularly during "Please Please Me," where he played the bass drum and hi-hat with his feet, freeing him to play tambourine with one hand and shake a maraca with the other. It was all a bit much, like he was trying to be a one-man percussion section. Martin also noticed that Ringo couldn't perform one of the basics of drumming—a simple drum roll. In addition, Martin still was not sold on the group's ability to write songs, although he did suggest that the group rework "Please Please Me" by increasing the tempo.

The next order of business was for EMI to get some pictures of the band for promotional use. Dezo Hoffman, a 50-year-old London photographer, dropped by Studio Three and shot pictures of the group performing, plus a wonderful staged photograph of the Beatles and their instruments. The latter image was used for several purposes, both intact and heavily cropped, even divided up into four solo portraits. Unfortunately, George's black eye (obtained in a scuffle with a fan upset at the firing of Pete Best) is clearly visible.

The photo of the Beatles and their instruments was featured on the cover of the British sheet music for the group's first single, "Love Me Do," published by Ardmore & Beechwood. The instruments piled in front of the group include, from left to right, John's Rickenbacker 325 Capri electric guitar (prior to it being painted black), Ringo's Premier drum kit (with maraca and tambourine), George's Gretsch Duo-Jet electric guitar and Paul's Hofner 500/1 "violin" bass guitar.

After the rehearsal and posed photo session, George Martin took the group, along with Brian and road manager Neil Aspinall, to dinner at Alpino, an Italian restaurant on Marylebone High Street, with everyone ordering spaghetti. As they had three months earlier in the control room to Studio Two, Martin and the Beatles hit it off well, with Martin enjoying their sense of humor, and the group being in awe of his tales of making comedy records with the Goons, working with the likes of Peter Sellers, Peter Cook and Spike Milligan.

By 7:00 PM, the Beatles were back at EMI Studios, ready, but reluctant, to record "How Do You Do It?" in Studio Two with George Martin serving as producer. Unlike future early sessions, the recording of the songs was done in mono with the group first laying down an instrumental backing and then superimposing their vocals over a playback of the instrumental track. The afternoon rehearsal paid off, with an acceptable instrumental backing completed in two takes featuring John on a borrowed acoustic guitar, George on lead guitar, Paul on bass and Ringo on drums. John and Paul then overdubbed their lead harmony vocals, and the group added hand claps over the instrumental break. Although some people, including Ron Richards, thought the Beatles deliberately played poorly on the song in an attempt to prevent its release, that does not appear to be the case. While the Beatles lack of enthusiasm is somewhat apparent, their singing and playing are more than competent.

Having completed Martin's initial choice for the A-side, he allowed them to record one of their original compositions, "Love Me Do." This was the song from the group's first session that caught the attention of engineer Norman Smith, leading him to think there might be something to the scrappy-looking group from Liverpool with the strange hair. Although its lyrics are simple and repetitive, the tune is catchy. The presence of harmonica set it apart from the group's other compositions. George Martin selected it for the B-side because he felt it had the most commercial appeal of the Lennon-McCartney compositions he had heard.

John's harmonica playing on the song was heavily influenced by that of Delbert McClinton on Bruce Channel's early 1962 hit "Hey! Baby" (#1 in the U.S. and #2 in the U.K.). Lennon got to meet McClinton two weeks after the group's first EMI session when the Beatles were the top supporting act at a show headlined by Bruce Channel at the Tower Ballroom in New Brighton on June 21. McClinton recalls hanging out with Lennon after the show and jamming with him on harmonica. The experience enabled John to refine his playing on "Love Me Do" and improved his technique.

The recording of the instrumental backing for "Love Me Do," with John on harmonica, George on guitar, Paul on bass and Ringo on drums, did not go smoothly. George had trouble with the tight and hard strings on the borrowed acoustic guitar. John's mouth and lips were tight from blowing the harmonica so many times. Ringo had trouble nailing down his part. Although studio logs no longer exist, it is believed that the group ran through over 15 takes. John and Paul then overdubbed their lead vocals, and the group added hand claps during the song's harmonica solo. The backing track used for the finished master may be an edit of two or more takes. Ringo's difficulties, as well as his manic percussion on "Please Please Me" during rehearsals, did not go unnoticed by Martin and Richards, who would take action to ensure that the next session would not be bogged down by a drummer who might not be ready for the studio.

Both of the songs were mixed for mono by George Martin and Norman Smith at the end of the session, which ran until 11:15 PM, well beyond its scheduled end time of 10:00 PM. Although the plan had been to record four songs, so much time was spent on getting an acceptable instrumental backing track for "Love Me Do" that the group could not work on any additional songs. Martin had acetates cut for each song so that he, Brian Epstein and others could listen to the performances over the next few days.

Before the Beatles left the studio, John Lennon, acting as leader, climbed up the stairs to the control room to let Martin know that the group did not want "How Do You Do It?" on their single. Martin recalled John pleading with him not to release the song, telling the producer that the Beatles could do better. Paul viewed it as a matter of integrity, with the group willing to "live or die" with their own song, "Love Me Do." They recognized that their song wasn't as catchy as the tune Martin forced them to record, but they were concerned they'd be laughed at in Liverpool. They wanted their bluesy song with the harmonica to be their first single.

But seeing as the group was unproven and had no right under their contract to challenge the decisions of their producer, John's request was both audacious and risky. George Martin was having none of it, telling John: "If you write something as good as that song, I'll let you record it, otherwise that's the song that's going out."

However, once again, fate and Ardmore & Beechwood intervened. Sid Coleman and Kim Bennett had pushed for EMI to sign the Beatles so that they could get the publishing rights on the Lennon-McCartney compositions. They let their anger be known of Martin's plan to place "their composition" on the B-side.

Meanwhile, Dick James, who was hoping to obtain the publishing for "How Do You Do It?," dropped by Martin's office and listened to the acetate of the Beatles performance of the song. James was not impressed and let Martin know. When Martin asked him if "How Do You Do It?" could be the flip side of "Love Me Do," James indicated that the songwriter would most likely not allow that to happen.

James was correct in his assessment. Murray refused to have his song serve as the B-side to the Beatles single. Furthermore, he hated what the group had done to his song. Murray felt the song should have a solo vocalist. He did not like the harmonies of John and Paul on the verses or the added "ohh-la-la" on the bridge.

In the end, it worked out well for all involved. James got the publishing and Martin got to record the song with another Brian Epstein-managed act, Gerry and the Pacemakers, who took the song to the top of the charts on April 11, 1963, as their debut single. It remained at number one for three weeks until it was replaced by the Beatles third single, "From Me To You." "How Do You Do It?" made money not only for the songwriter, Mitch Murray, but also Dick James, Brian Epstein and EMI.

As for the Beatles debut single, Martin now had only one side, "Love Me Do," which he viewed as a B-side at best. He would have to issue the song as an A-side paired with whatever else he could get from the Beatles. Martin scheduled the group for a session on September 11 to run from 4:45 to 6:30 PM. Perhaps frustrated by the whole chain of events that took away his potential hit single with the Beatles, Martin delegated the session to Ron Richards.

The Beatles were none the wiser as to why they were summoned back to EMI Studios to record a B-side for "Love Me Do." All they knew was that their debut single would now feature two Lennon-McCartney originals. They thought that George Martin had capitulated to their pleas for "Love Me Do" and respected their desire that "How Do You Do It?" not be issued, making them forever grateful to their A&R man/producer. This time they would not need to borrow an acoustic guitar at their session. John and George had finally received delivery of their Gibson J-160E "Jumbo" acoustic-electric guitars. The band squeezed in a few rehearsals at the Cavern before flying down to London.

Upon arriving at EMI Studio Two, the group was surprised to see a drum kit already set up and manned by an unfamiliar face. Although Ringo's drumming was an improvement over that of Pete Best, neither Martin nor Richards had been satisfied with the drum sound on "Love Me Do." Richards had heard of the difficulties the group had laying down an acceptable backing track for "Love Me Do," and most likely thought that Ringo was at least partially responsible. He wanted his session, which was limited to a little over 100 minutes, to run smoothly. Without consulting or warning the Beatles or their manager, Richards hired Andy White, a reliable studio drummer, to sit in with the band for the session.

The first song recorded on September 11 was "P.S. I Love You," which features Paul on lead vocal and bass, supported by John and George on backing vocals and guitars. Eager to check out their new instruments, John and George played their Jumbo acoustic-electric guitars plugged into their amps. The group was upset with Richards' insistence that Andy White play the drums, but they realized there was nothing they could do about it. For Ringo, it was particularly humiliating, causing him to wonder if he would get the same treatment as his predecessor, Pete Best. Richards recalls that Ringo sat silently in the control booth until Richards thought it best to give the displaced drummer something to do, sending him down to the studio to play the maracas. "He stood next to Andy and the drum microphone picked up his sound." White's rhythm on the wood block and Ringo's maracas give the song a Latin flavor. Unlike their prior session, the group played and sang at the same time. The tenth and final take was used for the finished master.

Having completed their task of recording the B-side for the single, the group turned to the song they had rearranged at Martin's request, "Please Please Me." After a brief rehearsal of the tune, the group was ready to record, once again with Andy White on drums and John and George on their new Jumbos. The song, featuring John and Paul on lead vocals, was played at a much faster tempo than the slow Roy Orbison-sounding song the Beatles had rehearsed the week before. Richards stepped in to clean up the new arrangement. "George was playing the opening phrase over and over and throughout the song. I said, 'For Christ's sake, George, just play it in the gaps!'" Although a little rough around the edges, the acetate cut from the session showed the song's potential.

After getting two tracks on tape, Richards asked the group to record another version of "Love Me Do," this time with Andy White on drums and Ringo relegated to the tambourine (having sat out "Please Please Me"). The song was taken at a slightly faster pace than the September 4 recording. John played harmonica, while George used his new Jumbo and Paul remained on his Hofner bass. The remake took 18 takes to perfect, although many were false starts or breakdowns.

The September 11 session was held to obtain a B-side for the Beatles first single; however, the group was able to complete three songs. Although George Martin was pleased that the band had followed his advice and sped up the tempo for "Please Please Me," he believed the song could be further improved, so he stuck with the plan to issue "Love Me Do" as the A-side with "P.S. I Love You" on the flip side. The version of "Love Me Do" with Ringo on drums ended up on the disc. While this certainly pleased Ringo and the rest of the band, it is not known whether this was a conscious decision on the part of Martin or a mistake. Nonetheless, the Beatles full musical integrity had been preserved on the top side of their debut disc. And although a session drummer played on the B-side, at least it was another song written by members of the group.

Looking back on those early sessions, George Harrison told The Beatles Book: "We still didn't feel really at home in the studios. It was like playing 'cold.' No atmosphere. Nothing to get us excited, like crowd reaction—we just went on and on playing the number over to a handful of technicians and a battery of microphones."

EMI scheduled the Beatles first single for release on October 5, 1962. Unbeknownst to the group, it could have been their only Parlophone release had the single totally bombed (although by this time, George Martin was beginning to realize the group's potential). Under the Beatles contract with Parlophone, the company was required to record a minimum of six songs. And with the September 11 session, this contractual obligation had been completed with "Besame Mucho," "Love Me Do," "P.S. I Love You," "Ask Me Why," "How Do You Do It?" and "Please Please Me."

Sid Coleman and Kim Bennett were delighted that Ardmore & Beechwood would get the publishing to two original compositions by the Beatles. This would also benefit EMI, which owned the company that was an outgrowth of EMI's purchase of Capitol Records, whose publishing companies were Beechwood Music Corporation and Ardmore Music Corporation.

The publishing agreement prepared by Ardmore & Beechwood for the songwriters indicated that the compositions would be credited to "Lennon/McCartney." When Brian met with John and Paul to go over the contract, the decision was made to reverse the credit to "McCartney/Lennon" because the songs were primarily written by Paul. John and Paul would continue their songwriting partnership with each getting an equal 50% share regardless of the amount each contributed, but, at least initially, the person who contributed the most to the song would be listed first.

Although the sheet music for "Love Me Do" (shown on page 207) contains the credit "Written and Composed by McCartney and Lennon," the label copy sent to EMI for the Beatles first single listed the songwriters as "Lennon–McCartney."

EMI prepared approximately 250 promotional copies of the Beatles debut disc for pre-release distribution to selected media and radio stations. These so-called demonstration records had white labels with black print and a large red A on the "Love Me Do" side. The arrival of the disc at Brian's NEMS office should have been a red-letter day for the aspiring manager, but instead, Brian exploded in red-faced rage when he noticed that Paul's last name was misspelled in the songwriters credit as "McArtney." When he called EMI to complain, he was assured that the labels of the commercial copies would have the correct spelling. This failed to calm him down and he curtly replied, "Not the point, journalists and producers and deejays have the wrong name on their copies." While Brian was understandably upset over the spelling error, the mistake made what was destined to be a highly collectible disc even more desirable.

When "Love Me Do" began selling thousands of copies and making a respectable showing on the British charts, George Martin was pleasantly surprised. While he had grown to like the Beatles and thought they might have potential if given the right material to record, he didn't think "Love Me Do" was "all that brilliant." But the song was exceeding expectations and attracting attention in the music business. Martin was now sold and ready to work with the band he was forced to sign.

On November 16, 1962, Martin met with the Beatles and Brian Epstein at EMI House on Manchester Square, London, to discuss the group's upcoming recording session scheduled for November 26. While Martin still believed that "How Do You Do It?" could be a smash hit, he also recognized that the Beatles had no interest in the song, instead wanting to record their original compositions. Nonetheless, he offered them a chance to re-record the song if they so desired. As expected, the group passed, freeing "How Do You Do It?" for other artists seeking a hit the easy way.

Martin agreed with the Beatles that their second single should be "Please Please Me." He knew from the acetate of the group's September 11 recording of the song that it had all the ingredients of a hit. He did, however, suggest that the song be embellished by having John add a harmonica part. The instrument had worked well on "Love Me Do" and would serve as a familiar pathway from the group's first single to the second.

URGENT — **SPECIAL RUSH COPY**

ANOTHER TOP POP!

on

A TOP POP · A TOP POP

Parlophone

DEMONSTRATION RECORD — NOT FOR SALE

ARDMORE & BEECHWOOD

7XCE17144 45   45-R 4949

LOVE ME DO
(Lennon—McArtney)
THE BEATLES

LISTEN NOW PLEASE

As for the disc's B-side, the Beatles selected "Ask Me Why." Although Martin had not been previously impressed with the song, it was good enough to be coupled with "Please Please Me."

Martin also informed the group that Ringo would be the drummer for the session. Ringo and the rest of the group were pleased that there would be no session player on either side of their second single. After discussion, Brian and George Martin selected January 11, 1963, as the release date for the group's all-important second disc. Martin then surprised the group with the news that he wanted to record an LP with the Beatles. Although the extent of discussion regarding the album is not known, Martin envisioned a live album.

On November 26, the Beatles were back at EMI Studio Two to record their second single. The three-hour session was booked from 7:00 to 10:00 PM, although the band arrived an hour early to set-up and rehearse.

After the Beatles rehearsed "Please Please Me" and "Ask Me Why," George Martin asked them to play "Tip Of My Tongue," perhaps wanting to see if the song would be a better choice for the B-side. It wasn't. There was nothing special about the song. Its lyrics were banal and it didn't have the hooks. Paul summed it up this way: "This is pretty much mine, I'm ashamed to say. It sounds like one of these where I tried to work it around the title." John was equally blunt: "Another piece of Paul's garbage—not my garbage."

For the recording session, George Martin was in the control room, joined by balance engineer Norman Smith and a tape operator. Brian Epstein attended, as did reporter Alan Smith of the New Musical Express and Bobby Brown, secretary of the Beatles Fan Club.

Unlike their first September session, the group was recorded onto twin-track tape instead of mono (one-track tape). Rather than first laying down an acceptable instrumental backing for overdubbing of vocals, the group did the songs live, simultaneously playing their instruments and singing as the tape rolled. All the instruments were recorded on one track and the vocals on the other. This enabled George Martin and the engineers to achieve a proper balance of the vocals and instrumental backing. This technique would be used up until the recording of the group's fifth single, "I Want To Hold Your Hand," in October 1963.

The first song recorded was "Please Please Me," which was completed in 15 takes. John, wearing headphones to hear the playback, then overdubbed his harmonica in three takes, with the final take designated number 18. The song is an exciting rocker propelled by superb drumming from Ringo. John and Paul share lead vocals backed by George on the chorus and bridge. After this recording, Martin knew there would be no need for a session drummer for the band. Speaking from the control room of Studio Two, Martin confidently told the group: "Gentlemen, you've just made your first number one record."

Although John flubbed the lyrics during the third verse, it did not matter. It was the excitement of the performance that would make Martin's prediction of the song topping the charts come true. John's error would be fixed with an edit when the single was mixed for mono four days later on November 30. But that was work for another day, so an engineer cut some acetates of Take 18.

After hearing the playback and taking a break in the canteen, the Beatles recorded "Ask Me Why." The band had recorded the song during their first visit to EMI Studios on June 6, 1962. Unlike "Please Please Me," which the Beatles had not yet played in concert, the song had been part of the group's set list for over six months. The group's familiarity with "Ask Me Why" facilitated its quick recording, with the sixth and final take being the master. John sings the lead vocal, backed by Paul and George.

With some studio time remaining, the group then worked on "Tip Of My Tongue." It is not known how many takes were performed. In all likelihood, all of the performances of this song were recorded over without any acetates being cut.

The following morning Brian brought one of his "Please Please Me" acetates to a meeting with Dick James, a music publisher recommended to him by George Martin as an honest London publisher who would work hard to promote the songs. Although Kim Bennett had put considerable effort into plugging "Love Me Do," Martin and Brian thought another publisher would get better results. James responded favorably to "Please Please Me," and impressed Brian with his enthusiasm, sewing up the publishing for the single by quickly lining up a TV appearance for the Beatles with one phone call to his friend Philip Jones, the producer of Thank Your Lucky Stars. The Beatles would mime the song for the cameras on January 13, 1963 for broadcast on the ATV program on Saturday, January 19.

George Martin prepared the label copy for the second Beatles single, naming "Dick James Music Co. Ltd." as the publisher for both songs. For reasons unknown, Martin listed the songwriters credit as "McCartney—Lennon" even though John was the primary composer of the songs. As for the sheet music, "Ask Me Why" has the "McCartney—Lennon" credit found on the record's label, while "Please Please Me" is credited to "John Lennon & Paul McCartney."

How Do You Do It

Recorded: September 4, 1962
Mixed: September 4, 1962 (mono acetate)

Producer: George Martin
Engineers: Norman Smith; tape operator unknown

John: Lead vocal; acoustic guitar; handclaps
Paul: Lead vocal; bass guitar (Hofner); handclaps
George: Lead guitar (Gretsch Duo-Jet); handclaps
Ringo: Drums (Premier kit); handclaps

"How Do You Do It?" was the song that George Martin wanted the Beatles to record for their first single. After the group's initial EMI session on June 6, 1962, Martin did not believe the Beatles were capable of writing a hit single, so he had his assistant, Ron Richards, search for suitable material. Martin selected "How Do You Do It?" and sent a demo of the song to Brian Epstein with instructions that the group learn the song for their upcoming EMI session.

The song was written in early May 1962 by Mitch Murray, a 22-year-old London songwriter whose real name was Lionel Stitcher. Murray told NME: "I was soaking in a hot bath...just sitting there humming to myself when I got an idea for a song." The tune's original title was "How Do You Do What You Do To Me," matching the song's opening line. Murray and fellow tunesmith Barry Mason recorded a demo of the song, along with a tune the pair had written, "Better Luck Next Time," on May 9 at Regent Sounds Studio at 4 Denmark Street, West End, London, backed by the Dave Clark Five, a band from Tottenham, London that would top the U.K. charts in early 1964 with "Glad All Over" and become part of the British Invasion after the Beatles. (The Rolling Stones recorded their first LP and part of their second LP in this small studio. The Beatles initial session for "Fixing A Hole" took place there.) For the demo, Mason sang solo. The duo left the studio with acetates of both songs.

The next day Murray and Mason began pitching their songs, with Decca Records being their first stop. The pair had hopes that one of their songs would be selected for the second single by Brian Poole and the Tremeloes. But producer Mike Smith, who signed the Tremeloes over the Beatles, didn't care for "How Do You Do It?" and passed on the song. Next they targeted Adam Faith, a teen idol singer who had two number one hits with his first Parlophone singles, "What Do You Want?" and "Poor Me," in 1959. By mid-1962, Faith had scored ten top ten hits on Parlophone. The pair met with Faith's manager, Eve Taylor, but alas, she also passed on the songs.

In June, they met with Ron Richards. He liked the songs and played the demos to Dick James, who was interested in obtaining the publishing for the songs. During a late July meeting, Martin told James he had selected the song for his Liverpool group, the Beatles.

The Mason demo of "How Do You Do It?" can be heard on YouTube. It is easy to hear why the Beatles were less than enthusiastic to record the sweet-sounding song. They rearranged it to give it more of a rock sound, adding some guitar breaks and a guitar solo. On September 4, 1962, they laid down an instrumental backing track in two takes with John on acoustic guitar, George on lead guitar, Paul on bass and Ringo on drums. John and Paul then overdubbed their lead harmony vocals, and the group added hand claps over the instrumental break. Although George Martin was pleased with the track, neither Dick James nor Mitch Murray liked what the Beatles had done with the song. As detailed earlier in this chapter, the Beatles recording of the song was not chosen for their debut disc. It was, however, finally issued on *Anthology 1*.

George Martin was ultimately proven right that "How Do You Do It?" was a hit song. His recording of the song for the debut disc by Gerry and the Pacemakers topped the British charts in April 1963. Although released that year in the U.S., the song did not chart until it was reissued in 1964, when it peaked at #9. Martin stayed with Murray for the Pacemakers' second single, "I Like It," which also topped the British charts. Once again, the single did not chart in the U.S upon its release in 1963, but was a #17 hit in 1964.

Murray co-wrote "I'm Telling You Now" with Freddie Garrity of Freddie and the Dreamers, who took the song to #2 in the summer of 1963. The record caught the attention of Dave Dexter at Capitol Records, who issued the single that fall after turning down the Beatles song "She Loves You." The single initially failed to chart, but topped the charts when reissued on Capitol's Tower subsidiary in 1965. Murray also wrote Freddie and the Dreamers' #3 U.K. hit single "You Were Made For Me." Capitol's 1964 single of the song failed to chart, but the reissue on Tower got to #21 the following year.

After teaming up with Peter Callander, Mitch Murray's credits included: "The Ballad Of Bonnie And Clyde" (which Georgie Fame took to the top of the U.K. charts and to #7 in the U.S. in 1968); "Hitchin' A Ride" (Vanity Fare, #16 in the U.K. and #5 in the U.S. in early 1970); "Billy Don't Be A Hero" (a #1 hit in the U.K. for Paper Lace that was covered in the U.S. by Bo Donaldson and the Heywoods, who also took the song to number one); and "The Night Chicago Died" (Paper Lace, #3 in the U.K. and #1 in the U.S.).

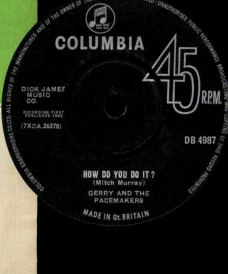

Love Me Do [Single Version]

Recorded: September 4, 1962
Mixed: September 4, 1962 (mono)

Producer: George Martin
Engineers: Norman Smith; tape operator unknown

Paul: Lead vocal; bass guitar (Hofner); handclaps
John: Lead vocal; harmonica; handclaps
George: Acoustic guitar; handclaps
Ringo: Drums (Premier kit); handclaps

"Love Me Do" was the second song recorded by the Beatles at their September 4, 1962 session. The group had previously recorded the tune at their first EMI session on June 6, 1962, with Pete Best on drums. George Martin had been attracted to John's raw harmonica playing on the tune. He made suggestions on the arrangement, directing Paul to sing the "love me do" solo spot previously handled by John and asking them to play the song at a faster tempo. This took away a bit of the blues edge of the song but made it more commercial sounding. The June 6 recording, played at 136 beats per minute ("BPM"), was brought down by Pete's change-of-tempo "skip beat" that made the recording unsuitable for release.

The Beatles first recorded an instrumental backing, this time with Paul on bass, John on harmonica, George on a borrowed acoustic guitar and Ringo on drums. While the backing track for the first song was accomplished in two takes, "Love Me Do" proved much more difficult. Although studio logs for the session no longer exist, the band most likely ran through about 15 takes before George Martin was satisfied. The finished master may be an edit of two or more performances. John and Paul then overdubbed their vocals, while the group added handclaps during the harmonica solo.

Ringo's drumming was a noticeable improvement over that of Pete Best, but he was most likely responsible for some of the band's difficulties in quickly completing an acceptable backing track. John's harmonica playing was more sophisticated than on the June 6 recording. This was due to John gaining tips from Delbert McClinton, who played harmonica on Bruce Channel's "Hey! Baby." The group increased the song's tempo from 136 to 145 BPM.

This version of "Love Me Do" with Ringo Starr on drums was selected for the A-side of the Beatles first single. Thereafter, EMI used the later-recorded version of the song with Andy White on drums. To ensure that this version with Ringo on drums was not mistakenly used, EMI foolishly erased the master tape.

P.S. I Love You

Recorded: September 11, 1962
Mixed: September 11, 1962 (mono); February 25, 1963 (stereo)

Producer: Ron Richards
Engineers: Norman Smith; tape operator unknown

Paul: Lead vocal; bass guitar (Hofner)
John: Backing vocal; acoustic guitar (Gibson J-160E Jumbo)
George: Backing vocal; lead guitar (Gibson J-160E Jumbo)
Ringo: Maracas
Andy White: Drums; wood block

"P.S. I Love You" was the first song recorded during the Beatles second EMI session with Ringo on September 11, 1962. Paul came up with the theme of the song, basing it on a letter to his love, and was its main writer, with John most likely making some minor contributions. The song was written in the spring of 1962 during or in proximity to the Beatles residency at the Star Club in Hamburg.

When the Beatles arrived at EMI Studios, they were told by Ron Richards, who was filling in for George Martin as producer, that Andy White would be the drummer for the session. The group was shocked and disappointed by this development. Ringo became concerned about his future with the band if he were relegated to only playing drums in concert. He felt terrible and blamed George Martin for this indignity, even though it was Ron Richards who had made the decision to hire the session drummer.

Ringo, though sulking, kept his anger in check and was in the control booth with Richards as the group prepared to record the song with Paul on his Hofner bass, John and George on their new Gibson J-160E "Jumbo" acoustic guitars and Andy White on drums. Perhaps motivated by guilt for depriving Ringo from participating in the session, Richards told Ringo to play maracas on the song. Despite the humiliation, Ringo dutifully stood by the drum microphone and shook the maracas.

Paul sang lead on "P.S. I Love You," with John and George adding the song's intricate backing vocals. Unlike the group's first session, the vocals were performed live over the musical backing on twin-track tape. White's rhythm on the wood block and Ringo's maracas give the song a Latin flavor. The group ran through ten takes of the song, with Take 10 being selected for the master. The song was mixed for mono at the end of the session. Although some consideration had been given to making the track the A-side of the Beatles first single, "P.S. I Love You" was relegated to the B-side.

Please Please Me [First Recording]

Recorded: September 11, 1962
Mixed: September 11, 1962 (mono)

Producer: Ron Richards
Engineers: Norman Smith; tape operator unknown

John: Lead vocal; acoustic guitar (Gibson J-160E Jumbo)
Paul: Lead vocal; bass guitar (Hofner)
George: Backing vocal; lead guitar (Gibson J-160E Jumbo)
Andy White: Drums

Although "Please Please Me" would later become the Beatles second single, the group first recorded the song on September 11, 1962, at a session held to obtain the B-side for "Love Me Do." The session was produced by Ron Richards, who booked a session player, Andy White, to replace Ringo on drums.

The Beatles first rehearsed and auditioned "Please Please Me" for George Martin at EMI Studios on the afternoon of September 4, 1962, prior to the group's first proper recording session. Martin was put off by the song's arrangement, finding it "a dreary song" which "was like a Roy Orbison number" with "very slow, bluesy vocals." He suggested they rearrange the song by increasing the tempo and working out tight vocal harmonies.

The group followed Martin's advice, transforming the song into a powerful upbeat rocker. The band's initial recording was made with John on his new Jumbo acoustic guitar, Paul on his Hofner bass, George on his new Jumbo acoustic guitar and Andy White on drums. Ringo did not participate. White's quick drum rolls on the tom-toms leading into the bridge were precisely executed, but seem a bit out of place. Overall his drumming lacks the excitement that Ringo would generate when the song was re-recorded at the session for the group's second single. This initial recording showed the song's potential, but the Beatles and George Martin felt it could be improved. And with Martin aiming for an October release for the group's debut disc, there wasn't time for another recording session. The September 11, 1962 version was released on *Anthology 1*.

John discussed the recording of the song when asked about the group's original compositions during a radio interview recorded on October 27: "Well, we did record another song of our own when we were down there [in London], but it wasn't finished enough. So, you know, we'll take it back next time and see how they like it then." The next time would be on November 26, 1963, and George Martin would love it.

Love Me Do [Album Version]

Recorded: September 11, 1962
Mixed: September 11, 1962 (mono); February 25, 1963 (stereo)

Producer: Ron Richards
Engineers: Norman Smith; tape operator unknown

Paul: Lead vocal; bass guitar (Hofner)
John: Lead vocal; harmonica
George: Acoustic guitar (Gibson J-160E Jumbo)
Ringo: Tambourine
Andy White: Drums

Ron Richards, who was assigned by George Martin to produce the Beatles September 11 session, did not like the drum sound on the September 4 recording of "Love Me Do." So, when studio time was still available after recording "P.S. I Love You" and "Please Please Me," he had the band do a remake of "Love Me Do," but this time with Andy White on drums. Ringo was relegated to the tambourine.

This was the third recording of "Love Me Do" at EMI Studios. When the Beatles rehearsed the song in anticipation of their June 6 session, they envisioned it as a slow number with a blues edge, but George Martin asked the group to increase the tempo to make it more commercial sounding. In the February 9, 1963 Melody Maker, Paul recalled: "When we went to London for the first recording, "Love Me Do" was a slow number like "Halfway To Paradise" [a number three 1961 U.K. hit for Billy Fury, who covered Tony Orlando's U.S. hit], you know, DUM-di-di-di-DUM, but George Martin, our recording manager, suggested we do it faster. I'm glad we did."

Each time the Beatles recorded the song, they played it at a faster tempo, first at 136 BPM for their June 6 session with Pete Best on drums, then at 145 BPM for the September 4 session with Ringo on drums, and finally at 150 BPM with Andy White on drums and Ringo on tambourine. The song's faster pace gives the Album Version recording more of a rock sound. It is easily distinguishable from the Single Version due to the presence of tambourine.

The EMI engineers improved the drum sound for the group's September 11 session, with the kick and snare drum being more prominent. Although the September 4 recording of "Love Me Do" worked well as a standalone single, the September 11 version of the song is more sonically similar not only to "P.S. I Love You," but also to the follow-up single and the tracks recorded on February 11, 1963, for the group's first album. Thus, it is not surprising that George Martin selected the later recording for the *Please Please Me* LP.

Please Please Me

Recorded: November 26, 1962
Mixed: November 26, 1962 (mono); February 25, 1963 (stereo)

Producer: George Martin
Engineers: Norman Smith; tape operator unknown

John: Lead vocal; acoustic guitar (Gibson Jumbo); harmonica
Paul: Lead harmony and backing vocal; bass guitar (Hofner)
George: Backing vocal; lead guitar (Gibson J-160E Jumbo)
Ringo: Drums (Premier kit)

John was inspired to write "Please Please Me" by his early childhood memories of his mother Julia singing the Bing Crosby hit "Please," which topped the U.S. charts for six weeks in 1932 when issued on Brunswick 6394. The song was first issued in the U.K. on Brunswick 1380. John was impressed with the word-play in the song's lyrics, particularly its opening line: "Oh, please lend your little ear to my pleas." He took it one step further with the line "please please me," which first uses the word "please" as a request and then as a verb meaning "to pleasure," giving the song a sexual edge.

John envisioned the tune as a slow ballad in the style of Roy Orbison; however, when George Martin heard the Beatles rehearse the song on September 4, 1962, he recommended that the group increase the tempo and add tight vocal harmonies.

The Beatles first recorded the song on September 11 as a possible B-side to "Love Me Do." The session was produced by Ron Richards, who brought in session drummer Andy White. Fortunately the song was not chosen as the B-side to the Beatles first single, where it almost certainly would have been overlooked.

John discussed how the group kept working on "Please Please Me" in the March 8, 1963 NME: "Our recording manager, George Martin, thought our arrangement was fussy, so we tried to make it simpler. We were getting very tired, though, and we just couldn't seem to get it right. We're conscientious about our work and we don't like to rush things. In the following weeks we went over it again and again. We changed the tempo a little. We altered the words slightly. And we went over the idea of featuring the harmonica, just as we'd done on 'Love Me Do.' By the time the session came around we were so happy with the result, we couldn't get it recorded fast enough."

The Beatles got their chance to remake "Please Please Me" on November 26, 1962. After an hour-long rehearsal, the group recorded the song with John and George once again on their new Gibson Jumbo acoustic-electric guitars, Paul on his Hofner bass and Ringo on drums. The song's extraordinary vocals were recorded simultaneously with the band's instrumental backing. John and Paul perform an Everly Brothers-inspired harmony vocal on the verses. John sings lead on the call-and-response opening lines of the first part of the chorus, with his four "Come on" lines each repeated by Paul and George. For the second part of the chorus, John, Paul and George sing a three-part harmony. John sings lead on the bridge over Paul and George's backing vocals.

George Martin had the group run through 15 takes of the song before he was satisfied with the performance. John, wearing headphones to hear the playback, then overdubbed his harmonica in three takes, with the final take designated number 18.

Four days later, on November 30, George Martin edited the finished master from an unknown number of takes, correcting a vocal flub in the third verse. The song was then mixed for mono. The final result is an exciting rocker vastly superior to the earlier version. With Ringo on drums, the song has more energy. John and Paul's harmonies are more effective, and the addition of harmonica is a nice touch.

Even before he edited and mixed the single, Martin knew he had a hit, telling the group: "Gentlemen, you've just made your first number one record." Ringo's superb drumming also convinced the producer that he would not need a session drummer on the Beatles records. Ringo had, at last, passed the audition.

Ask Me Why

Recorded: November 26, 1962
Mixed: Nov 30, 1962 (mono single); Feb 25, 1963 (mono & stereo)

Producer: George Martin
Engineers: Norman Smith; tape operator unknown

John: Lead vocal; acoustic guitar (Gibson J-160E Jumbo)
Paul: Backing vocal; bass guitar (Hofner)
George: Backing vocal; lead guitar (Gibson J-160E Jumbo)
Ringo: Drums (Premier kit)

"Ask Me Why" was recorded on November 26, 1962, for the B-side to the Beatles second single. After recording and hearing the playback of "Please Please Me" and breaking for tea, the band returned to Studio Two to record "Ask Me Why." The Beatles had recorded the song at their first visit to EMI Studios on June 6, 1962. The take recorded at that session has not been issued.

The Miracles' "What's So Good About Good Bye" inspired John to write "Ask Me Why." The song was written by the Detroit group's lead singer William "Smokey" Robinson and released in the U.S. on Tamla 54053 on December 14, 1961. It peaked at number 35 in the Billboard Hot 100 and at 16 in the magazine's R&B chart. The disc was issued in the U.K. as Fontana H.384 in March 1962. Although "What's So Good About Good Bye" did not chart in England, the Beatles were familiar with the song through manager Brian Epstein's purchase of the disc for his NEMS record store. In his Top Ten Tips column in the April 5, 1962 Mersey Beat, Brian described the single as "double-sided brilliance–a collector's gem." (The flip side of the disc is another Robinson composition, "I've Been Good To You.")

"What's So Good About Good Bye" is the first Motown/Tamla and Smokey Robinson song to influence a Beatles composition. The five-note guitar riff that opens "Ask Me Why" is similar to the four-note guitar motif from the Robinson-penned song. The opening guitar rhythm and riff appears throughout "Ask Me Why." Both songs contain the phrase "tell me why" and reference "misery," but while Smokey laments about a break-up, Lennon is in love. John's line "I can't conceive of any more misery" is a twisting of Smokey's "All I've known is misery." John sings of a happiness that makes him cry, and with her love, he "should never, never, never be blue."

"Ask Me Why" was added to the Beatles stage show during spring 1962. The group's recording of the song before a live audience at Manchester's Playhouse Theatre on June 11 aired four days later on June 15 on the BBC program Here We Go. "Ask Me Why" was the first Lennon-McCartney original to be broadcast. It is on the bootleg collection *The Complete BBC Sessions*. The arrangement is similar to that of the later recorded single, but has Pete Best on drums.

The group's familiarity with "Ask Me Why" facilitated its quick recording, with the sixth and final take being the master. John sings the lead vocal, exquisitely backed by Paul and George. The song features John and George on their Gibson Jumbo guitars, Paul on Hofner bass and Ringo on drums providing an effective Latin beat. The song was mixed for the mono single on November 30, 1962.

Tip Of My Tongue

Recorded: November 26, 1962

Producer: George Martin
Engineers: Norman Smith; tape operator unknown

Paul: Lead vocal; bass guitar (Hofner)
John: Backing vocal; rhythm guitar
George: Backing vocal; lead guitar
Ringo: Drums (Premier kit)

Having studio time remaining after recording the two songs required for the next single, the Beatles recorded an unknown number of takes of a tune written by Paul, "Tip Of My Tongue." Although George Martin told Mersey Beat it was a great number, he added, "we'll have to spend a bit of time giving it a new arrangement. I'm not too happy with it the way it is." Realizing that the song did not measure up to their standards, it was later given to Tommy Quickly, who was also managed by Brian Epstein. When released as a single on Piccadilly 35137 in the summer of 1963, Quickly's version of the song received little airplay and was quickly forgotten.

Apparently the tape of the Beatles EMI recording of the song was erased. If an acetate of this performance was cut, it has not been located. Nor has a demo tape of the song surfaced.

The Please Please Me & With The Beatles Sessions

On February 11, 1963, the Beatles entered EMI Studios on Abbey Road to record songs for inclusion on their debut album. In what is generally acknowledged to be one of the most productive days ever spent in a recording studio, the Beatles recorded 11 high-spirited songs that were standards in their live stage show. Of the ten songs completed for release, four were Lennon-McCartney originals and six were cover versions that are now better known than their original versions. These ten songs, plus four songs recorded for the group's first two singles, became the Beatles first album, which was named *Please Please Me* after the group's hit single.

George Martin first publicly talked of recording a Beatles album shortly after the group's first single, "Love Me Do," became a top-twenty hit. In an interview published in the January 3, 1963 Mersey Beat, Martin revealed: "I'm thinking of recording their first LP at the Cavern, but obviously I'm going to have to come to see the club before I make a decision. If we can't get the right sound we might do the recording somewhere else in Liverpool, or bring an invited audience into the studio in London. They've told me they work better in front of an audience."

He further indicated that the numbers on the disc would probably all be originals, noting that John and Paul had written over a hundred songs, but that had yet to be determined. He expressed concern about coming up with an appropriate name for the album because "LPs need a catchy title if they're going to stand out in the shop window." (Martin came up with *Off The Beatle Track*, but the album was unimaginatively named *Please Please Me* to capitalize on the name recognition of the hit single. Martin later named his first album of orchestrated Beatles songs *Off The Beatle Track*.)

When the group's second single began racing up the charts, Martin felt the need to take action. He recalled: "After the success of 'Please Please Me,' I realized that we had to act very fast to get a long-playing album on the market if we were to cash in on what we had already achieved." He also realized that it would be logistically impossible to record the Beatles in the Cavern with the screaming fans, and that inviting fans to the studio would result in total chaos.

Beginning February 2, 1963, the Beatles were booked for their first nationwide U.K. tour as a supporting act to Helen Shapiro. The final night of the first leg of the tour was a February 10 appearance at the Embassy Cinema in Peterborough. February 11 was a scheduled day off before the group began a series of club appearances on February 12. After checking schedules, George Martin and Brian Epstein determined that the group could do a recording session on February 11 if they could be excused from the February 10 tour date. An arrangement was made for Peter Jay and the Jaywalkers to take the Beatles place on the bill that night.

A few days before the group entered the studio, Norman Jopling interviewed John for a cover story on the band that ran in the February 16, 1963 Record Mirror. Jopling reported that although plans were indefinite for what would be on the Beatles forthcoming album, "Hold Me Tight," "There's A Place" and "My Misery" would be included, along with "I Saw Her Standing There," with George on lead vocals. (Apparently John thought the vocal on Paul's "I Saw Her Standing There" would be handed to George, but in the end George was given the lead vocal on John's composition "Do You Want To Know A Secret.") John told Jopling, "We want to try to make the LP something different. You know, not just all somebody else's songs."

With only a single day available, Martin knew time was an issue. "I asked them what they had which we could record quickly, and the answer was their stage act." This would consist of a mix of Lennon-McCartney original compositions and cover versions of songs by other artists. With the four songs from the group's first two singles slated for the album, the plan was to complete ten new songs to flesh out a 14-song LP, all in one day. Three February 11 recording sessions in Studio Two were booked: 10:00 AM to 1:00 PM; 2:30 to 6:00 PM; and 7:30 to 10:45 PM. It was an ambitious goal, particularly considering that the band had been performing on the road non-stop since returning from Hamburg at the beginning of the year. In addition, the group had been traveling through a brutally frigid winter. All four of the lads were a bit under the weather, with John suffering from a nasty cold. Despite these adverse conditions, the group soldiered on.

The LP was recorded on a twin-track machine. For the most part, the instruments and the vocals were recorded on separate tracks to allow George Martin and the engineers to properly balance the volume of the vocals and instruments when mixing the songs for mono. The songs were recorded live with the group singing and playing their instruments simultaneously. Overdubs appear on only a few of the tracks. Paul played his Hofner bass, and Ringo was on his Premier drum kit for all of the songs. John alternated between his Rickenbacker 325 Capri electric guitar and his Gibson J-160E Jumbo acoustic-electric guitar, while George played either his Gretsch Duo-Jet electric guitar or his Jumbo.

Engineer Norman Smith placed the microphones further from the amplifiers than normal so that they would pick up not only direct sound from the amplifiers, but also the ambient sound of the room. This gave the songs a more raucous sound, resembling what was heard at the group's live performances.

Less than a month after recording their first LP, the Beatles were back at EMI Studios on March 5 to record a pair of new songs for a stand-alone single featuring "From Me To You" and "Thank You Girl." The group recorded both of these songs during a three-hour session starting at 2:30 PM. The Beatles had also hoped to record both "One After 909" and "What Goes On" during an evening session commencing at 7:00 PM, but called it a night after only working on "One After 909." A demo of "What Goes On" shows that the song had different words and melody for the verses. John sings: "How can I conceal/The thrill that I feel/Is our love still real?/Tell me if this is so/I want to know." John and Paul sing the chorus, which is essentially the same, with Everly Brothers–style harmonies.

George Martin and Brian Epstein had devised an ambitious plan for the Beatles to release two albums and four stand-alone singles each year. With the "Please Please Me" and "From Me To You" singles and the group's debut album all coming out during the first few months of 1963, the Beatles were half way there. Martin then booked studio time for the Beatles on July 1, 18 and 30.

The Beatles 7:00 to 10:00 PM session on July 1 was devoted to recording both sides of their next single. The group completed two recently written Lennon-McCartney compositions, "She Loves You" and "I'll Get You."

The remaining July sessions were used to record songs for the band's second album. The July 18 session ran from 7:00 to 10:45 PM. The Beatles recorded cover versions of two Motown/Tamla songs, the Miracles' "You Really Got A Hold On Me" and Barrett Strong's "Money (That's What I Want)," followed by the Donays' "Devil In His Heart" (retitled "Devil In Her Heart") and the Peggy Lee arrangement of "Till There Was You" from *The Music Man*.

July 30 was split between morning and evening sessions. The morning session ran from 10:00 AM to 1:30 PM. During this time the Beatles completed the Marvellettes' "Please Mister Postman" and began work on the first Lennon-McCartney selection for the album, "It Won't Be Long." Before completing the song, the Beatles left EMI Studios to record songs for the August 24th edition of the BBC radio program Saturday Club. The session took place at the Playhouse Theatre in London. The Beatles performed both sides of their yet-to-be-released single, "She Loves You" and "I'll Get You," along with "You Really Got A Hold On Me," "Long Tall Sally," "Glad All Over" and "Twist And Shout."

Then it was back to EMI Studios for a 5:00 to 11:00 PM session. After George Martin overdubbed piano on "Money," the group did a remake of "Till There Was You" and recorded Chuck Berry's "Roll Over Beethoven" with George Harrison on lead vocal. The band then returned to and completed "It Won't Be Long." The session ended with another Lennon-McCartney tune, "All My Loving." The eight songs recorded during these sessions were mixed for mono on August 21.

The Beatles returned to EMI Studios on September 11, recording "I Wanna Be Your Man," "Little Child" and "All I've Got To Do" during the 2:30 to 6:00 PM session, and "Not A Second Time" and "Don't Bother Me" during the 7:00 to 10:15 PM session. The next day the Beatles spent part of the 2:30 to 6:00 PM session recording an open-ended interview for Australian disc jockeys. The band then did a remake of "Hold Me Tight," which had previously been recorded during the session for the *Please Please Me* LP. The 7:00 PM session was extended to 11:30 PM to enable the group to do a remake of "Don't Bother Me" and record additional takes of "Little Child" and "I Wanna Be Your Man." More work was done on "I Wanna Be Your Man" and "Little Child" on October 3 during a 7:00 PM to 10:00 PM session. "I Wanna Be Your Man" was finally completed during a 10:00 AM to 1:00 PM recording and mixing session held on October 23. All of the album's stereo mixes were completed on October 29, except for "Money," which was finished the next day.

The songs for the Beatles fourth single for the year, "I Want To Hold Your Hand" and "This Boy," were recorded on October 17. The session marked the first time the group used a four-track recorder, which enabled them to record a basic backing track on three of the four tracks, leaving a track open to add vocals and/or other instruments. The group also recorded their Christmas fan club disc and an unused take of "You Really Got A Hold On Me" at the session.

I Saw Her Standing There

Recorded: February 11, 1963
Mixed: February 25, 1963 (mono and stereo)

Producer: George Martin
Engineers: Norman Smith; Richard Langham

Paul: Lead vocal; bass guitar (Hofner); handclaps
John: Backing vocal; guitar (Rickenbacker Capri); handclaps
George: Lead guitar (Gretsch Duo-Jet); handclaps
Ringo: Drums (Premier kit); handclaps

The Beatles debut album gets off to a rousing start with Paul's energetic "One, two, three, faaa!" count-in to "I Saw Her Standing There." The song was written primarily by Paul in 1961. Its "boy sees girl at dance and falls for her" story line, complete with booming hearts and dancing through the night, was instantly appealing to teens. According to Paul, the first two lines of the song were originally "She was just seventeen, never been a beauty queen," but John objected and came up with "Well she was just seventeen, you know what I mean." These were words that said nothing, but meant everything to a young mind's imagination.

Paul's lyrics may have been influenced by a pair of songs from the group's stage show repertoire. In Chuck Berry's "Little Queenie," the girl who caught the attention of the singer looks "like a model on the cover to a magazine" (as opposed to Paul's original lyric of a beauty queen) and is "too cute to be a minute over seventeen." Berry sings "she looked at me and sweetly smiled," while Paul sings: "Well she looked at me/And I, I could see/That before too long I'd fall in love with her." Berry sings of "lumps in my throat" and "wiggles in my knees," while Paul sings: "Well my heart went boom." In both songs, the singer thinks dancing will get him the girl. The Coasters' "Young Blood" opens with "I saw her standing on the corner."

"I Saw Her Standing There," which at the time was known as "Seventeen," was the second song recorded during the morning session for the group's first album. From the start, all the ingredients for a classic rocker were present: Paul's exuberant lead vocal backed by John, complete with strategic "woo"s towards the end of the verses; John and George's driving rhythms on guitar and George's exciting solo; Ringo's pounding beat; and Paul's pulsating bass. Paul lifted his bass part from "I'm Talking About You," a 1961 Chuck Berry rocker (issued in the U.K. on Pye International 7N.25100) that was part of the Beatles stage show with John on lead vocal. Similarly, John's rhythm playing uses a pattern frequently used by Berry.

Either of the first two takes were good enough to be released. Take 2 is on the download album *Bootleg Recordings 1963*. The group then ran through three edit pieces before attempting four complete run throughs. Only the ninth and final take was complete. It begins with Paul's energetic count-in that was later edited to the beginning of the finished master. The maxi-single *Free As A Bird*, released in 1995 along with *Anthology 1*, contains the full Take 9.

After breaking for lunch and working on a few other songs, the group returned to "I Saw Her Standing There" to add handclaps onto Take 1. Each overdub take was assigned a new number. After Take 11 breaks down, the boys keep clapping and Paul says: "We have to keep Britain tidier." After the tape was rewound, they perfected the handclaps on Take 12, which was used as the finished master.

"I Saw Her Standing There" had been part of the Beatles stage show since 1962. The first known recording is on a crude tape known as the Cavern Rehearsal tape, which was most likely made in early December 1962 to demo songs for the LP and Dick James. This version of the song has John on harmonica, giving it an R&B edge. (James arranged for R&B singer Duffy Power to record the song on February 20, 1963, backed by the Graham Bond Quartet, whose members included Jack Bruce and Ginger Baker.) The song is on the *Live At The Star Club* LP recorded in Hamburg, Germany in late 1962.

After the group recorded "I Saw Her Standing There" for their first LP, they performed the song 11 times for BBC radio, including a live broadcast on the March 16, 1963 Saturday Club. This was the weekend before the album's release and was part of its promotion. The group's October 20, 1963 recording of the song is on *Live At The BBC*. A live performance of the song broadcast on Sveriges Radio in Sweden on November 11, 1963, is on *Anthology 1*.

The Beatles performed "I Saw Her Standing There" numerous times on television, including an October 20, 1963 broadcast on the Swedish program Drop In. This performance is included on Volume 2 of the *Anthology* video. The group played the song during its February 9 and 16, 1964 Ed Sullivan Show appearances. The Beatles ripped through a high-energy performance of the song at their Washington Coliseum concert, which appears on Volume 3 of the *Anthology* video and on *The First U.S. Visit*.

"I Saw Her Standing There" is a great rock song that was included in most Beatles concerts from late 1962 through mid-1964. Several live performances from their 1964 European and Australian tours were recorded. By the time the Beatles began their American tour in August 1964, the song was no longer part of the stage show.

Misery

Recorded: February 11, 1963; piano overdub on February 20
Mixed: February 25, 1963 (mono and stereo)

Producer: George Martin
Engineers: Norman Smith; Richard Langham

John: Lead vocal; rhythm guitar (Gibson J-160E Jumbo)
Paul: Lead vocal; bass guitar (Hofner)
George: Backing vocal, lead guitar (Gibson J-160E Jumbo)
Ringo: Drums (Premier kit)
George Martin: Piano (Steinway Music Room Model B Grand)

The album's second track, "Misery," is another John Lennon-Paul McCartney composition. It was started on January 26, 1963, backstage before the Beatles show at King's Hall, Stoke-on-Trent, Staffordshire. The song was primarily written by John. Tony Bramwell was present that evening and recalls John and Paul getting stuck on one of the lines and receiving an assist from Allan Clarke and Graham Nash of the Hollies. According to Bramwell, "John and Paul were desperate to get it finished" because they wanted to get it ready for Helen Shapiro, who they would soon be touring with. The song was finished shortly thereafter at Paul's 20 Forthlin Road home.

Brian Epstein learned early on that the songwriting of John and Paul was an important asset. After all, the pair's original compositions recorded during the Decca session led to a meeting with Sid Coleman, general manager of EMI's Ardmore & Beechwood music publishing company. This in turn led to the group obtaining a recording contract with EMI's Parlophone label. Brian believed that having established stars record songs written by John and Paul would enhance the group's reputation. Thus, he encouraged the group's tunesmiths to write songs for other artists.

Their first assignment was to write a song for Helen Shapiro, a British singer who, at the age of 14, recorded the hit singles "Don't Treat Me Like A Child" (#3 in May 1961), "You Don't Know" (#1 in August 1961) and "Walkin' Back To Happiness" (#1 in October 1961). She also had a number two hit with "Tell Me What He Said" in March 1962. Shapiro recorded for EMI's Columbia label and was produced by Norrie Paramor, who served as her recording manager.

The Beatles were part of a package tour headlined by Shapiro, then 16, that was to begin on February 2, 1963. John and Paul wrote the song for Shapiro to record at her upcoming Nashville session. In the March 1, 1963 NME, Paul told Alan Smith: "We've called it 'Misery,' but it isn't as slow as it sounds. It moves along at quite a steady pace and we think Helen will make a pretty good job of it." A demo tape of the song was sent to Norrie Paramor, but he did not think a song titled "Misery" was suitable for the young star who had hit it big with the upbeat "Walking Back To Happiness."

The song was then offered to another artist on the tour, Kenny Lynch, a black British singer who had a top ten hit with a cover of the Drifters' "Up On The Roof" in January 1963. Lynch would become the first non-Beatle to record a Lennon-McCartney song.

"Misery" was the last song recorded during the afternoon session. It opens with a slowly strummed guitar chord, followed by John and Paul singing: "The world is treating me bad, misery." The song about lost love then proceeds at a medium pace. The pair sing most of the song in unison, only harmonizing on the word "misery." They also use a "sh" sound rather than that of an "s" to sing "shend her back to me." The instrumental backing has John and George on their Jumbo guitars, Paul on his Hofner and Ringo on his Premier kit.

The group completed the song in 11 takes. Take 1 was complete, but the next four broke down with flubbed lyrics. Takes 6 and 7 were complete, while Takes 8-10 were breakdowns. George initially played an arpeggio of descending notes on the bridge before it was decided to have him just play rhythm on the final two takes. On Take 6, Ringo tried a busy sounding drum fill on the bridge that was not played again. Takes 1 and 7 are on *Bootleg Recordings 1963*.

The best performance, Take 11, was recorded with the tape speed at 30 ips (inches per second), which was twice the normal speed of 15 ips. This was done to facilitate George Martin's piano overdub, which took the place of Harrison's lead lines. Martin's part was completed in four takes on February 20.

The Beatles performed "Misery" seven times for BBC radio. The first two broadcasts, the March 12, 1963 Here We Go and the live March 16, 1963 Saturday Club, predate the album's release.

Kenny Lynch's recording of "Misery" was issued as HMV POP 1136 on March 15, 1963, a week ahead of the *Please Please Me* LP. Lynch changed the lyrics from a third-person account to a direct conversation with his lover, opening with "You've been treating me bad, misery," and further singing "I've lost you now, I'm sure/I won't see you no more." Lynch is backed by an orchestra conducted by Harry Robinson. The disc received a favorable review from Keith Fordyce in the March 15 NME, but failed to chart. Fordyce wrote: "Kenny solos and self-duets excellently and the song, in fact, is very attractive with a strong melody and medium-pace beat." Fordyce failed to mention that the song was written by Lennon and McCartney.

Teenager Helen Shapiro graced the cover of the souvenir program sold during her February 1963 package tour that included the Beatles. After her recording manager Norrie Paramor turned down the Lennon-McCartney song "Misery," it was offered to fellow tourmate Kenny Lynch. EMI's HMV (His Master's Voice) label released Lynch's recording of the song as HMV POP 1136 on March 15, 1963.

Anna (Go To Him)

Recorded: February 11, 1963
Mixed: February 25, 1963 (mono and stereo)

Producer: George Martin
Engineers: Norman Smith; Richard Langham

John: Lead vocal; acoustic guitar (Gibson J-160E Jumbo)
Paul: Backing vocal; bass guitar (Hofner)
George: Backing vocal; lead guitar (Gretsch Duo-Jet)
Ringo: Drums (Premier kit)

"Anna (Go To Him)" was written and first recorded by Arthur Alexander, a black musician and songwriter from Alabama, whose soulful vocals influenced many sixties soul singers. His recording of "Anna" features Floyd Cramer on piano playing the lead pattern. The track also contains strings. Released in America on Dot 16387 on September 17, 1962, Alexander's recording of the song was a number 68 pop and number ten R&B hit in 1962. The song was released in the U.K. on London 45-HLD 9641 in December 1962.

John idolized Alexander, so it is not surprising that the Beatles recorded one of his songs on their debut LP. The group's 1962 repertoire included three more of his recordings: "Where Have You Been All My Life," "A Shot Of Rhythm And Blues" and "Soldier Of Love." The band recorded the latter two songs for the BBC. Both are on the album *Live At The BBC*.

The Beatles recorded "Anna," misidentified on the session recording sheet as "Hannah," as the second song in the evening session. The track was completed in three takes (the first two being false starts). The recording is highlighted by John's passionate lead vocal, which has a greater sense of urgency than Alexander's version. By this time in the session, John's vocal chords were showing signs of strain. George handles Floyd's piano part on guitar, while Ringo's drums are similar to that of the single, particularly with his use of the hi-hat. The Beatles perform the song at a slightly slower tempo than Alexander's recording (110 BPM as opposed to 114 BPM). George discussed the song in the *Anthology* book: "Arthur Alexander used a peculiar drum pattern, which we tried to copy; but we couldn't quite do it, so in the end we invented something quite bizarre but equally original. A lot of the time we tried to copy things but wouldn't be able to, and so we'd end up with our own versions."

The group performed "Anna" twice on their BBC radio show, Pop Go The Beatles—first on June 25, 1963, and again on August 27, 1963. The latter performance is on *On Air - Live At The BBC Volume 2*.

Chains

Recorded: February 11, 1963
Mixed: February 25, 1963 (mono and stereo)

Producer: George Martin
Engineers: Norman Smith; Richard Langham

George: Lead vocal; lead guitar (Gretsch Duo-Jet)
John: Backing vocal; guitar (Rickenbacker Capri); harmonica
Paul: Backing vocal; bass guitar (Hofner)
Ringo: Drums (Premier kit)

The Beatles showed their fondness for American girl groups by including three songs originally recorded by girl groups on their first album. The first of these songs, "Chains," was recorded by the Cookies, a trio of black female vocalists from New York that went through numerous lineup changes. The single features Ethel "Earl-Jean" McCrea on lead vocals, backed by Margaret Ross and Dorothy Jones. Eva Boyd, who performed as Little Eva, sang on the chorus. The Cookies added their backing vocals to many songs by other recording artists, including Little Eva's number one U.S. hit "The Loco-Motion," which peaked at number two in the U.K. (Earl-Jean's later recording of "I'm Into Something Good" charted at number 38 in the U.S. during the summer of 1964. Herman's Hermits scored their first U.K. hit and only U.K. chart-topper with a cover version of the song, which peaked at number 13 in the States.)

"Chains" was written by the Brill Building songwriting team of Gerry Goffin and Carole King, who also produced the session. When released on Dimension 1002 on October 22, 1962, the song peaked at number 17. The song was released in the U.K. on London 45-HLU 9634 in December 1962. Record Retailer charted the single for one week at number 50 in January 1963. George purchased the single at Brian Epstein's NEMS record store.

The Beatles recorded "Chains" as the fourth song in the evening session. The song was completed in four takes, with George, John and Paul singing a three-part harmony on the verses, and George singing solo on the bridge (although the Cookies single and the group's first BBC performance has backing vocals.) George and John are on electric guitars, Paul is on bass, and Ringo is on drums. John adds harmonica during the song's introduction. The group performed "Chains" four times for BBC radio. The first performance on the January 25, 1963 Here We Go predates the recording of the album. The Beatles third BBC performance, broadcast on the June 25, 1963 Pop Go The Beatles, is on *On Air - Live At The BBC Volume 2*.

Boys

Recorded: February 11, 1963
Mixed: February 25, 1963 (mono and stereo)

Producer: George Martin
Engineers: Norman Smith; Richard Langham

Ringo: Lead vocal; drums (Premier kit)
John: Backing vocal; guitar (Rickenbacker Capri)
Paul: Backing vocal; shouts; bass guitar (Hofner)
George: Backing vocal; lead guitar (Gretsch Duo-Jet)

"Boys" was first recorded by the Shirelles, a group of four black teenage girls from Passaic, New Jersey, who had numerous hits in the early sixties that helped define the girl-group sound. The song was written by Luther Dixon, who produced the group, and Wes Farrell. Although not a hit, the song came to the attention of the Beatles as the flip side of "Will You Love Me Tomorrow," a number one single in the U.S. on Scepter 1211, and a number three British hit on EMI's Top Rank label (JAR-540) in early 1961.

The Beatles admired the Shirelles, with three of the group's songs in their repertoire: "Will You Love Me Tomorrow," "Boys" and "Baby It's You." Prior to Ringo joining the band, Pete Best sang lead on what Paul described as one of the highlights of the group's stage show. Ringo had sung lead on the song when he was with Rory Storm and the Hurricanes, so he had no problem taking over.

The Beatles recorded "Boys" in one explosive take as the third song in the evening session. While the Shirelles' version of the song has a moderate tempo and sensual R&B groove, the Beatles version of "Boys" is an all-out rocker. Knowing that the microphone recording Ringo's lead vocal would pick up a significant amount of sound from the drums, engineer Norman Smith elected to record the drums on the vocal track. Thus, the stereo mix of the song has the guitars and bass on the left channel, and Ringo's lead vocal and drums, along with the backing vocals, on the right.

Ringo lays down a driving beat, keeping it simple as he sings, but providing exciting fills between lines and particularly during George's guitar solo. John and Paul play the same eight-note pattern in lock step throughout, while George adds chords and lead notes filling in for the piano present on the Shirelles' single. Harrison's impressive solo incorporates elements of rockabilly and the blues.

Although Ringo has a limited baritone range, his singing is spot on, with his rough-sounding voice melding perfectly with the song's wild but controlled backing. John, Paul and George supply the "bop shoo wop, bop bop shoo wop" and "yeah, yeah boys" backing vocals. Ringo introduces George's solo with an "Alright George," while Paul adds exciting shouts and howls there and onward.

The group recorded "Boys" seven times for BBC radio. The June 17, 1963 recording of the song was broadcast on the June 25 Pop Go The Beatles. This performance is on the "Baby It's You" maxi-single issued on March 20, 1995, and is also on On Air - Live At The BBC Volume 2. The group also recorded "Boys" at IBC Studios for lip-syncing on the TV special Around The Beatles. This recording was not used for the show, but was later released on Anthology 1. The group made a film recording of the song before a live audience at Granville Studio in London for broadcast on the October 3, 1964 Shindig, a popular American teen-oriented show.

"Boys" was Ringo's featured song during the Beatles 1964 American tour. The song is on the 1977 album The Beatles At The Hollywood Bowl (and its 2016 remix Live At The Hollywood Bowl).

Baby It's You

Recorded: February 11, 1963; celeste overdub on February 20
Mixed: February 25, 1963 (mono and stereo)

Producer: George Martin
Engineers: Norman Smith; Richard Langham

John: Lead vocal; rhythm guitar (Gibson J-160E Jumbo)
Paul: Backing vocal; bass guitar (Hofner)
George: Backing vocal; lead guitar (Gibson J-160E Jumbo)
Ringo: Drums (Premier kit)
George Martin: Celeste (Schiedmayer)

"Baby It's You" was the second Shirelles song appearing on the Beatles debut LP. The song was written by Burt Bacharach, Mack David and Shirelles producer Luther Dixon (under the pseudonym of Barney Williams). It was initially titled "I'll Cherish You," but Dixon reworked the lyrics and added the "cheat, cheat" refrain. Bacharach prepared a backing track for the song, which included the songwriter on backing vocals. His male voice can clearly be heard on the "sha la la la la" refrains. Shirley Owens added her lead vocal to the track, becoming the only member of the Shirelles to sing on the song.

The single was issued in the U.S. on Scepter 1227 and was a number eight pop and number three R&B hit in 1961. It was released in the U.K. on Top Rank JAR-601, but did not chart. Its distinctive percussion, passionate vocals and memorable "sha la la la la" refrain make it one of the best girl group songs ever recorded.

The Beatles recorded "Baby It's You" as the fifth and next-to-last song of the evening session. John handles the emotional lead vocal on the Beatles version of song, which closely follows the Shirelles' superb original rendition. It was recorded in three takes (Take 2 being a false start). Paul and George supply the "Sha la la la la" backing vocals. The backing track has John and George on their Jumbos, Paul on his Hofner bass and Ringo on drums. On February 20, George Martin superimposed celeste over the song's instrumental break in four takes. A celeste (also known as a celesta) is a keyboard-operated instrument whose keys are connected to hammers that strike a set of metal plates suspended over wooden resonators.

The group performed the song twice for the BBC. The June 1, 1963 recording was broadcast on the June 11 Pop Go The Beatles and appears on *Live At The BBC*. The song is the title track of a four-song maxi-single issued a few months after the album in April 1995. The song became a surprise hit, peaking at number seven in the U.K. and at 67 in the U.S.

Do You Want To Know A Secret

Recorded: February 11, 1963
Mixed: February 25, 1963 (mono and stereo)

Producer: George Martin
Engineers: Norman Smith; Richard Langham

George: Lead vocal; lead guitar (Gibson J-160E Jumbo)
John: Backing vocal; rhythm guitar (Gibson J-160E Jumbo)
Paul: Backing vocal; bass guitar (Hofner)
Ringo: Drums (Premier kit); drum sticks

"Do You Want To Know A Secret" was primarily written by John shortly after his marriage to Cynthia. Its inspiration came from a song John's mother sang to him from the 1937 Walt Disney animated film, *Snow White And The Seven Dwarfs*. Early in the film, Snow White sings to the doves, "Wanna know a secret? Promise not to tell?" (The song, "I'm Wishing," was written by Larry Morey and Frank Churchill.) The music for "Do You Want To Know A Secret" was based on "I Really Love You" by the Stereos, an American R&B/doo wop group who had a number 29 hit with the song in 1961. The single was issued in the U.K. on 45-MGM-1143, but did not chart. The song was written by the Stereos' tenor singer, Leroy Swearingen. George recorded the song for his 1982 album *Gone Troppo*.

John made a demo of "Do You Want To Know A Secret" for Billy J. Kramer, who later recorded it with the Dakotas at EMI Studios on March 21, 1963. George Martin served as producer and overdubbed piano. Kramer recalls that on the demo John apologizes for the poor sound quality, but states that he is in the quietest room in the building. John proves his point by flushing the toilet. Kramer's recording was issued as a single on Parlophone R 5023. It peaked at number two, unable to pass the Beatles "From Me To You."

The Beatles recorded "Do You Want To Know A Secret" as the second song of the afternoon session in six takes (four complete) with George on lead vocal backed by he and John on their Jumbos, Paul on his Hofner bass and Ringo on drums. John and Paul then overdubbed their "do dah do" backing vocals, while Ringo tapped his drum sticks onto Take 6 in two takes. The first, Take 7, is on *Bootleg Recordings 1963*. It has the "do dah do" backing vocals throughout.

The Beatles recorded the song six times for the BBC, including a March 6, 1963 live performance at Manchester's Playhouse Theatre broadcast March 12 on Here We Go prior to the album's release. The Beatles sixth BBC performance, broadcast on the July 30, 1963 Pop Go The Beatles, is on *On Air - Live At The BBC Volume 2*.

A Taste Of Honey

Recorded: February 11, 1963
Mixed: February 25, 1963 (mono and stereo)

Producer: George Martin
Engineers: Norman Smith; Richard Langham

Paul: Lead vocals; bass guitar (Hofner)
John: Backing vocal; acoustic guitar (Gibson J-160E Jumbo)
George: Backing vocal; lead guitar (Gretsch Duo-Jet)
Ringo: Drums (Premier kit)

A Taste Of Honey, a dramatic play written by Shelagh Delaney, a 19-year-old British woman, premiered at London's Theatre Royal Stratford East on May 27, 1958. The song "A Taste Of Honey" was written by Bobby Scott and Ric Marlow as a recurring instrumental theme for the Broadway adaptation of the British play, which opened in 1960 at the Biltmore Theater. The song was first released as an instrumental on Bobby Scott's album *A Taste Of Honey*. The first vocal version of the song was issued by Billy Dee Williams, who played the part of "The Boy" in the Broadway show. The tune came to the Beatles attention through Lenny Welch's recording of the song released in America on Cadence 1428 on September 17, 1962, and in the U.K. on London 45-HLA 9601. The Beatles added the song to their stage show shortly after the release of Welch's British single. An instrumental of the song by British clarinetist Acker Bilk charted in the U.K. in January 1963, peaking at number 16.

"A Taste Of Honey" was the first song recorded by the Beatles during the afternoon session. The basic track, with Paul on lead vocal supported by John and George, was completed in five takes (including breakdowns on Takes 2 and 3). The instrumental backing has George on his Duo-Jet, John on his Jumbo, Paul on his Hofner bass and Ringo on drums. John provides a ska rhythm for the song's bridge. After the group recorded "Do You Want To Know A Secret," Paul double-tracked his lead vocal on the bridge. This was completed in two takes, with his second vocal treated heavily with echo. The first overdub, Track 2, Take 6, is on *Bootleg Recordings 1963*.

The Beatles performed the song, along with "Love Me Do," on October 29, 1962, for broadcast on the November 2 Granada TV show People And Places. The group recorded the song six times for the BBC. The first performance, recorded for the October 26, 1962, Here We Go, predates the *Please Please Me* LP. *Live At The BBC* contains the July 10, 1963 recording, which was broadcast on the July 23 Pop Go The Beatles.

There's A Place

Recorded: February 11, 1963
Mixed: February 25, 1963 (mono and stereo)

Producer: George Martin
Engineers: Norman Smith; Richard Langham

John: Lead vocal; rhythm guitar (Gibson J-160E Jumbo); harmonica
Paul: Lead vocal; bass guitar (Hofner)
George: Backing vocal; lead guitar (Gretsch Duo-Jet)
Ringo: Drums (Premier kit)

The Lennon-McCartney song "There's A Place" was written primarily by John, who described it as "my attempt at a sort of Motown black thing, but it says the usual Lennon things: 'In my mind there's no sorrow.' It's all in your mind." The song goes beyond being a simple love song; it is John's first song with reflective lyrics, opening with: "There, there's a place/Where I can go/When I feel low/When I feel blue/And it's my mind/And there's no time/When I'm alone." It predates another reflective song, the Beach Boys' "In My Room," written by Brian Wilson and Gary Usher, which opens with: "There's a world where I can go/Tell my secrets to/In my room."

"There's A Place" was the first song recorded by the Beatles at their February 11, 1963 session. The basic track was completed in ten takes (including three false starts). John and Paul sing the song together in harmony, with John soloing on the line "When I'm alone." He also solos on the first and third lines of the bridge, with Paul and George singing the response. The instrumental backing has George on his Duo-Jet playing lead notes (including his harmonic lines at the beginning and end of the song) and chords, John playing chords on his Jumbo, Paul on his Hofner bass and Ringo on his Premier drum kit. Ringo supplies a steady beat and throws in exciting drum fills going into the bridge and at the end of the song. Takes 5, 6, 8 and 9 are on *Bootleg Recordings 1963*.

The Beatles returned to the song in the afternoon session for John to superimpose his harmonica onto Take 10. This was accomplished in three takes (including a false start on the middle take). Each take was given a number that was preceded by "Track 2" to designate it was an overdub. The final take was called Track 2, Take 13.

The group performed the song three times for the BBC, including a live performance on July 17, 1963, in front of an audience at the Playhouse Theatre in London. The Beatles third BBC performance, broadcast on the September 3, 1963 Pop Go The Beatles, is on *On Air - Live At The BBC Volume 2*.

Twist And Shout

Recorded: February 11, 1963
Mixed: February 25, 1963 (mono and stereo)

Producer: George Martin
Engineers: Norman Smith; Richard Langham

John: Lead vocal; rhythm guitar (Gibson J-160E Jumbo)
Paul: Backing vocal; bass guitar (Hofner)
George: Backing vocal; lead guitar (Jumbo; possibly Duo-Jet)
Ringo: Drums (Premier kit)

The album's closing track was also the last song recorded at the session. Although the group had been in the studio for 12 hours, and John's voice was all but gone, one more song was needed to complete the album. During a break in the canteen, it was decided to record one of the more popular rockers from the band's stage show, "Twist And Shout." Journalist Alan Smith reported in the July 19, 1963 NME that he was present at EMI Studios towards the end of the session and that he suggested the group record the song, which he had heard the Beatles perform on the BBC radio program The Talent Spot on December 4, 1962.

"Twist And Shout" was written by Phil Medley and Bert Berns, who used the name Bert Russell for his writer's credit on the song. It was originally recorded by the Top Notes in 1961 at a session produced by Phil Spector. Although Spector would gain notoriety in the early sixties for his "wall of sound," his handling of the song is weak. Bert Berns was disappointed with the recording, believing that Spector had ruined his song.

Relegated in the States to the B-side of a Top Notes single that flopped on Atlantic 2115, "Twist And Shout" would have remained unknown but for Berns' belief in the song. When recorded by the Isley Brothers and released in the U.S. on Wand 124 in mid-1962, the song became a number 17 pop and number two R&B hit. It was this version of the song (released in the U.K. on Stateside SS 112) that caught the attention of the Beatles, who added the tune to their stage show. The song appears on *Live At The Star Club*, which was recorded in late 1962.

After the canteen break, the group returned to Studio Two. John, shirtless and revived by biscuits and gargling milk, gamely strapped on his guitar, stepped up to the microphone and belted out the song with an incredible intensity that all but destroyed his vocal cords. Paul and George supplied effective backing vocals. The band, propelled by Ringo's steady beat, laid down a flawless instrumental backing with John and George on their Jumbos and Paul on his trusty Hofner bass. With this remarkable single take, the Beatles had recorded one of the greatest rock 'n' roll performances of all time. Although a second take was recorded, it was never considered for release as John's voice was totally shot from the first rendition.

At the end of the session, the group went upstairs to hear the playback. According to Tony Barrow, John's vocal cords were bleeding, as evidenced by the red blood mixed with milk in John's glass.

The Beatles recorded "Twist And Shout" nine times for BBC radio. The group's sixth BBC performance, broadcast on the August 6, 1963 Pop Go The Beatles, is on *On Air - Live At The BBC Volume 2*. The Beatles performed the song at several iconic events, including their debut on the London Palladium show, the Royal Variety Performance, the Washington Coliseum and The Ed Sullivan Show. The group also opened up several 1964 and 1965 concerts with a shortened version of the song.

Mixing, Banding and Mastering

On February 20, nine days after the February 11 recording session, George Martin superimposed piano onto "Misery" and celeste onto "Baby It's You." Stuart Eltham and Geoff Emerick served as engineers. That same day Martin determined the running order for the LP and prepared the text for the labels (known as label copy).

Martin thought it was important to open and close the album with a "potboiler," a tune that boiled over with excitement. He selected the original composition "I Saw Her Standing There" to get the program off to a rousing start, and "Twist And Shout" to end things with a bang. Both sides of the group's current hit single were placed at the end of Side 1, with "Please Please Me" selected as the closer. The second side opened with both sides of the band's first single, with the hit "Love Me Do" placed in the opening slot. The running order of three tracks on Side 1 unintentionally gave the S&M message: "Anna Chains Boys."

In addition to the ten songs completed for the LP, the Beatles had recorded another original tune, "Hold Me Tight," at the start of the evening session. Martin was not pleased with how the song was progressing, and with time running out and needing five more songs, he had the group move on. The Beatles would return to "Hold Me Tight" for their second album. Although the press reported that the group recorded a cover of Little Eva's "Keep Your Hands Off My Baby," the song is not listed on the Recording Sheets for the session.

In preparing the label copy, Martin credited the original compositions to "(McCartney-Lennon)" and listed the publisher of these songs as Dick James Music, except for "Love Me Do" and "P.S. I Love You," which were published by Ardmore & Beechwood.

At the time Martin prepared the label copy, he was unaware that Dick James was negotiating a new publishing arrangement for the Beatles. On February 22, James established Northern Songs Ltd. to publish the group's original compositions. The ownership of the company was most likely just over 50% to Dick James Music, 20% to Paul McCartney, 20% to John Lennon and just under 10% to NEMS Enterprises. It was a clever deal by James. By giving John and Paul an ownership interest in Northern Songs, he encouraged the two songwriters to enter into a long-term deal with the company. After learning of this, Martin changed the label copy for "I Saw Her Standing There," "Misery," "Do You Want To Know A Secret" and "There's A Place" to show Northern Songs Ltd. as publisher. However, the change was too late for the initial pressings of the LP.

The album was mixed for mono and stereo on February 25, with Martin assisted by engineers Norman Smith and A.B. Lincoln. Prior to mixing the tracks, Martin took Paul's exciting "One, two, three, faaa!" count-in from Take 9 of "I Saw Her Standing There" and edited it to the start of Take 12 of the song. Most of the songs were first given mono mixes. Although "Ask Me Why" had been mixed for the mono single, the song was given a new mono mix.

The instruments and the vocals were recorded on separate tracks to allow for the proper mixing of vocals and instruments for a mono master. This made it difficult to produce a balanced stereo mix. In the early sixties, the emphasis for pop and rock records was on mono, with the stereo mix being an afterthought or mere accommodation to satisfy the record company's marketing department. Martin viewed stereo as being for hi-fi freaks and insisted that the early Beatles recordings were never intended to be heard in stereo.

The stereo mix of "Please Please Me" proved problematic. The single was edited from multiple takes, but engineers could only locate the tape with the later takes of the song, most likely those with the harmonica overdubs. The stereo master consists of an edit of Takes 16, 17 and 18, whereas the single contains some edits from earlier takes. The most noticeable difference between the mono and stereo versions is the flubbed lyrics in the final verse coming out of the middle eight that is only in the stereo version. In addition, Paul's bass part varies between the two versions.

As for the tracks from the September 1962 sessions, Martin decided to use the later version of "Love Me Do" with Andy White on drums and Ringo on tambourine. This was most likely done because the remake of "Love Me Do" was more sonically similar to the other tracks on the album. To ensure that the earlier take would not be used by mistake, the tape was foolishly discarded.

Because the two-track tapes from the September sessions were either lost or recorded over, it was not possible to create true stereo mixes of "Love Me Do" and "P.S. I Love You." In keeping with the industry practice of the time that all songs on a stereo LP should sound like stereo, fake stereo mixes of the songs were prepared for the stereo album by transferring the mono songs to a two-track machine and then lowering the treble to enhance the bass in one channel and lowering the bass to tweak the treble in the other.

After the songs were banded in their proper running order, mono and stereo masters were cut at EMI Studios. Due to a calibration issue with the cutting lathe, the mono master was cut at too fast a speed. Each song is about one second faster than it should be.

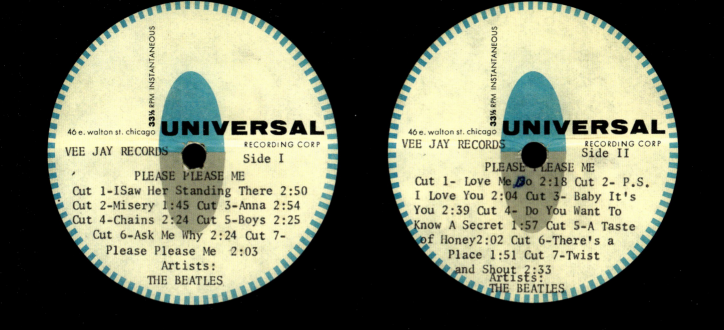

Mastering of *Introducing The Beatles*

Vee-Jay Records received a copy of the master tape for the *Please Please Me* album from EMI in April or early May 1963. The company hired Universal Recording Corporation to cut a mono reference acetate of the entire LP shortly thereafter. The acetate has Paul's entire "One, two, three, faaa!" count-in at the start of the LP.

Prior to Universal cutting masters for the album, Vee-Jay decided to trim two songs from the record's 14-track lineup. While British LPs typically had 14 songs, American albums normally had 12. This was due to the different way publishing royalties were calculated in the two countries. In the U.K., the royalties owed by a record company for an album was a fixed amount regardless of the number of songs on the LP. Each publisher received a percentage of the royalties based on the number of songs it had on the disc. However, in the U.S., a mechanical license fee was paid for each song. In the sixties, this fee was normally two cents per song. Record companies could save four cents per album by having 12 rather than 14 songs. Because "Please Please Me" and "Ask Me Why" had already been issued by Vee-Jay as a single that did not sell particularly well, the company decided to drop the two songs from its Beatles LP. With "Please Please Me" not being on the album, Vee-Jay needed a new title for the disc. As the Beatles were relatively unknown in America, Vee-Jay decided to name the album *Introducing The Beatles*.

Engineer Roger Anfinsen prepared mono and stereo masters for the album at Universal in late June 1963. Either on his own or following instructions from Vee-Jay, Anfinsen edited most of Paul's count-in at the beginning of the tape, perhaps thinking that it did not belong on the album. Thus, both the mono and stereo versions of *Introducing The Beatles* open with Paul shouting "Faaa!"

The mono and stereo lacquers were then sent by Universal via Air Express to Audio Matrix, Inc. in the Bronx, New York. Audio Matrix prepared the metal parts (masters, mothers and stampers) to press the albums, with the stereo parts made on June 28 and the mono parts the following day. The stereo metal parts were sent to The American Record Pressing Co. in Owosso, Michigan ("ARP") and Monarch Record Manufacturing Co. in Los Angeles, California. The mono metal parts were sent to ARP, Monarch and Southern Plastics in Nashville, Tennessee. Although plans called for a summer release, these factories would not begin pressing albums for Vee-Jay until January 1964.

Beechwood Music, at the behest of Capitol Records, obtained an injunction prohibiting Vee-Jay from manufacturing and selling records that contained the songs "Love Me Do" and "P.S. I Love You." In response, Vee-Jay had Universal cut lacquers of the album dropping those two songs, replacing them with "Please Please Me" and "Ask Me Why." The first stereo lacquers were cut on January 24, 1964. The initial mono lacquers were cut on February 6, 1964.

From Me To You

Recorded: March 5, 1963
Edited and mixed: March 14, 1963 (mono and stereo)

Producer: George Martin
Engineers: Norman Smith; Richard Langham

John: Lead vocal; rhythm guitar (Gibson J-160E Jumbo); harmonica
Paul: Lead vocal; bass guitar (Hofner)
George: Lead guitar (Gibson J-160E Jumbo)
Ringo: Drums (Premier kit)

Three weeks after the February 11, 1963 marathon recording session that produced ten tracks for the *Please Please Me* album, the Beatles were back at EMI Studios on March 5, 1963, to record their third single. The band had barely recovered from the throat troubles stemming from the earlier recording session and the strain of singing songs like "Twist And Shout" night after night. In the April 19, 1963 NME, John told Alan Smith that throat sweets had kept them going, adding: "Just lately things have been getting better. But my voice wasn't the same for a long time after. Every time I swallowed it was like sandpaper. We sang for 12 hours, almost non-stop. We had colds and we were concerned how it would affect the record. And by the end of the day, all we wanted to do was drink pints of milk."

John then elaborated on the group's anxiety over how their sore throats might have damaged the album: "You know, waiting to hear that LP played back was one of our most worrying experiences. We're perfectionists. If it had come out any old way, we'd have wanted to do it all over again. As it happens, we were very happy with the result–or to put it more eloquently, dead chuffed!"

But for the Beatles, they were on a roll and there would be no rest for the weary. The success of the "Please Please Me" single had prompted George Martin to request a pair of songs for a followup disc. Martin recalled: "I was always saying to the Beatles 'I want another hit, come on, give me another hit' and they always responded. 'From Me To You,' 'She Loves You,' 'I Want To Hold Your Hand.' Right from the earliest days they never failed."

John and Paul showed up with two new songs for the session, "From Me To You" and "Thank You Girl." At this stage of their career, George Martin would come down to the floor of Studio 2 and have John and Paul audition the songs before the recording began. In his autobiography *All You Need Is Ears*, Martin detailed the process: "I would meet them in the studio to hear a new number. I would perch myself on a high stool, and John and Paul would stand around me with their acoustic guitars and play and sing it—usually without Ringo or George, unless George joined in on the harmony. Then I would make suggestions to improve it, and we'd try it again. That's what is known in the business as a 'head arrangement,' and we didn't move out of that pattern until the end of what I call the first era. That was the era that lasted through 'Love Me Do,' 'Please Please Me,' 'From Me To You,' 'She Loves You' and 'I Want To Hold Your Hand,' which were the first batch of recordings."

"From Me To You" was written by John and Paul during the Helen Shapiro tour on February 28, 1963, a mere five days before the recording session. John told Alan Smith how the song came about in the April 19 NME: "We were having a lot of laughs the night Paul and I wrote 'From Me To You.' I remember we were on the coach, traveling from York to Shrewsbury. We'd already written 'Thank You Girl' as a follow-up to 'Please Please Me.' This new number was to be the 'B' side. Anyway, there we were, not taking ourselves seriously. Just fooling about on the guitar. This went on a while. Then we began to get a good melody line and we really started to work at it. Before that journey was over, we'd completed the lyric, everything. We were so pleased we knew we had to make it the 'A' side."

John explained the inspiration for the song to Smith in the May 10, 1963 NME: "What puzzled us was why we'd thought of a name like 'From Me To You.' In fact, it had me thinking until only recently, when I picked up the NME to see how we were doing on the charts. Then I realized–we'd got the inspiration from reading a copy on the coach! Paul and I had been talking about one of the letters in the [magazine's] 'From You To Us' [readers] column."

That same issue Paul responded to Smith's comment that all of the Beatles hit compositions contained the words "me" or "you" in the title: "We didn't plan it that way. It just happened. Still I suppose putting 'me' or 'you' into a song helps its chances of success a lot. People can identify themselves with it." As for their ease of writing songs, Paul added: "We have such a fairly easy job thinking up tunes, we used to worry whether we were copying from someone else. Then we realized that it was probably because they had such a simple melody. These days, if we think up a tune very quickly we know we've got a hit!"

John later claimed that the song's first line was his and that the song was "far bluesier when we wrote it." Paul remembered being "very pleased with the middle eight because there was a strange chord in it, and it went into a minor: 'I've got arms that long…'"

"From Me To You" has John and Paul on lead and harmony vocals backed by John and George on their Gibson J-160E Jumbo acoustic-electric guitars, Paul on his Hofner bass, Ringo on drums and John on overdubbed harmonica. The session tape shows that the Beatles were not completely over their throat issues at the time the song was recorded. After the engineer announces "Take 1," Paul coughs. When John exhorts him to "Come on," Paul gives his "One, two, three" count-in at a slightly sluggish pace, causing the tempo of the song to be slower than in the later takes. The performance breaks down towards the end of the verse following the bridge, with Paul asking "What happened?" After George Martin responds from the control room "You tell me what happened," Paul says, "Well I just thought I heard you talking actually," that he thought he heard a whistle indicating to stop. When the engineer announces "Take 2," Paul says, "Sorry, oh, ready," and clears his throat. George Martin instructs the band "From the top again," and Paul counts in at a faster pace, initiating an increase in tempo from that of the first take. As the song comes to a close, Paul says to one of his band mates, "Aaaa, you missed the ending." At this time in the song's development, George solos on the introduction and end bits and plays a lead line between verses that would be dropped by the final performance. Also, the song has no instrumental break.

Takes 3 and 4 were completed, with the latter take performed at a slightly faster pace for a running time of just over 1:45. Before the group moved on to the fifth take, George Martin instructed the boys to add an instrumental break to lengthen the song. After the engineer announces "Five," the group is still discussing the change, with John saying: "Yeah, but do the first bit, but not the second bit he says." When Martin asks, "Are you with us?," John inquires: "George is to play the first bit of instrumental, isn't he?," to which Martin replies, "Right." This performance adds an instrumental break following the verse coming out of the first bridge. George does not play a solo here, although John and Paul sing their "from me" and "to you" refrains that will follow George's lead lines and John's harmonica once added. Take 6 is a false start, followed quickly by Take 7, which was the best of the completed performances. Takes 1, 2 and 5 are on *Bootleg Recordings 1963*.

After taking time to record "Thank You Girl," the Beatles returned to "From Me To You" to add embellishments suggested by Martin. Track 2, Take 8 added the "da da da da da dun dun dah" vocals over the song's introduction, John's harmonica and George's lead guitar notes in tandem with additional bass notes by Paul to the instrumental break, and John's harmonica over the song's ending. George Martin then set up six attempted edit pieces. The first appears to be a tape edit of the song's introduction and instrumental break, with John adding harmonica over the song's opening instrumental bars. Additional edit pieces had the boys humming or using falsetto voices on the introduction. Neither was used.

George Martin edited and mixed "From Me To You" for mono and stereo on March 14. Although only a mono mix was needed for the single, Martin did a stereo mix in case the song was to be included on the Beatles second LP. These edits consisted primarily of Take 8, with John's harmonica added to the song's introduction, perhaps from the first edit piece, continuing the tradition of opening a Beatles single with harmonica. Because the 1966 stereo remix made for *A Collection Of Beatles Oldies* does not contain harmonica on the introduction, it was most likely made straight from Take 8.

The Beatles made numerous radio and TV appearances during April 1963 to promote their new single. On April 3, the group performed "From Me To You" in front of a live teenage audience at the Playhouse Theatre in London for BBC radio's Easy Beat program. The show aired on April 7, four days before the single's release. On April 9 the group lip-synced the song on the ITV program Tuesday Rendezvous. Four days later the Beatles performed both sides of the single for The 625 Show, a BBC TV program, which was broadcast on April 16. The group's third appearance on Thank Your Lucky Stars, taped on April 14 and broadcast on April 20, had the band mime "From Me To You." On April 16, the group mimed the song for Granada Television's People And Places program.

The Beatles recorded "From Me To You" 14 times for 16 BBC broadcasts, making it the most performed Beatles song for the BBC. The group adapted the song to serve as the theme for their radio show From Us To You. *Live At The BBC* contains a version of "From Us To You" recorded on February 28, 1964. *On Air - Live At The BBC Volume 2* has the group's October 16, 1963 recording of the song.

The Beatles continued performing "From Me To You" into 1964. *Anthology 1* contains the group's October 24, 1963 performance of the song taped in Stockholm, Sweden for November 11 broadcast on Sveriges Radio. The Beatles performed "From Me To You" during several of their famous appearances, including the October 13 edition of Val Parnell's Sunday Night At The London Palladium, the November 4, 1963 Royal Variety Show, their first U.S. concert at the Washington Coliseum on February 11, 1964, and their second Ed Sullivan Show on February 16, 1964.

Thank You Girl

Recorded: March 5, 1963
Edited and mixed: March 13, 1963 (mono and stereo)

Producer: George Martin
Engineers: Norman Smith; Richard Langham

John: Lead vocal; rhythm guitar (Gibson J-160E Jumbo); harmonica
Paul: Lead vocal; bass guitar (Hofner)
George: Lead guitar (Gibson J-160E Jumbo)
Ringo: Drums (Premier kit)

As was the case with "From Me To You," "Thank You Girl" was written by John and Paul during the Helen Shapiro tour for the group's third single. Paul admitted that the song was a show of gratitude to their fans: "We knew that if we wrote a song called 'Thank You Girl' that a lot of the girls who wrote us fan letters would take it as a genuine thank you. So a lot of our songs were directly addressed to the fans." In Barry Miles' *Many Years From Now*, Paul added that the song "was pretty much co-written but there might have been a slight leaning towards me with the 'thank you, girl' thing, it sounds a bit like me, trying to appease the mob."

"Thank You Girl" was intended to be the A-side until "From Me To You" relegated it to the B-side. But "Thank You Girl" is not a B-grade song. From the song's powerful introduction led by Ringo's pounding floor tom-tom drums to John and Paul's exciting vocals and catchy melody line to John's wailing harmonica, "Thank You Girl" is a great rocker.

The song has the same lineup as its A-side: John and Paul on lead and harmony vocals backed by John and George on their Gibson J-160E "Jumbo" acoustic-electric guitars, Paul on his Hofner bass, Ringo on drums and John on overdubbed harmonica.

At the time the song was recorded, it was known as "Thank You Little Girl." The first take was a complete performance with a fade-out ending that had Ringo playing it straight and simple. Realizing the song needed an ending as exciting as its introduction, Ringo was instructed to close out the song with active drums fills alternating with John and Paul's "Oh, oh, oh" refrains. Before Take 2, John tells the drummer: "Just fill it however you can, Ringo." After two quick false starts, the group completes Take 4 with Ringo adding some tentative fills during the song's fade-out ending. Ringo's drumming is better at the end of Take 5, but John's voice cracks before the drum fills get going. Takes 1 and 5 are included on *Bootleg Recordings 1963*.

Take 6 is a solid performance of the main part of the song. Rather than fade out the ending, the group hammers out a "one-two-three-four, one-two-three-four, stop" similar to the song's pounding introduction. Although Ringo's drumming is solid, Paul fails to sing the third "Oh" in the first set of the ending refrains, while John comes in early during the second set and Paul lets out a scream. The duo's vocal errors mar what otherwise would have been a performance suitable for release.

George Martin was satisfied with all of Take 6 except for the ending, which clearly needed additional work. Rather than having the boys take it from the top again, Martin decided to go with Take 6 as the basic track for the master, but have the group record an edit piece for the song's tricky ending. This would enable the band to fully concentrate on getting it right. Each of the seven attempts at the edit piece was given a separate take number. The vocals recorded during the edit pieces were treated with echo.

Of the first few edit piece attempts, Take 7 quickly breaks down, Take 8 is decent and Take 9 is marred by Ringo being a bit off at the start. John then talks about changing the guitar parts to help keep Ringo on the beat, but Take 10 is still a bit off and Take 11 breaks down. The band comes close on the next try before finally nailing the ending on Take 13, with Ringo flawlessly pounding out the complex drum fills, and John and Paul perfecting their vocal refrains.

Prior to editing and mixing the song, George Martin decided that "Thank You Girl" would benefit from the addition of harmonica. Although John had yet to recover from his nasty cold and was forced to miss four of the group's concert appearances, he arrived at Abbey Road on the morning of March 13 to overdub harmonica over Takes 6 and 13. These takes were numbered 14-28. Martin, assisted by engineers Norman Smith and Geoff Emerick, then edited the finished master from Takes 6, 13, 17, 20, 21 and 23.

The mono mix has the harmonica at the song's introduction, following the bridge and at the start of the song's ending. The stereo mix makes more effective use of John's harmonica, placing the instrument at those three places plus twice in the bridge (doubling with the "way that you do" refrain and filling in the gap after "good to be true") and during the song's final measures.

The Beatles performed "Thank You Girl" for BBC television program The 625 Show broadcast on April 16. They also performed the song three times for BBC radio. *Live At The BBC* contains the June 19, 1963 performance before a live audience at the Playhouse Theatre, which was broadcast on the June 23 Easy Beat program.

One After 909

Recorded: March 5, 1963
Edited and mixed in 1995 for *Anthology 1*

Producer: George Martin
Engineers: Norman Smith; Richard Langham

John: Lead vocal; rhythm guitar (Gibson J-160E Jumbo)
Paul: Lead vocal; bass guitar (Hofner)
George: Lead guitar (Gretsch Duo-Jet)
Ringo: Drums (Premier kit)

After completing both sides of their third single during the March 5 afternoon session, the group returned to Studio 2 for an evening session booked from 7:00 to 10:00 PM. Although the Beatles planned on recording two more Lennon-McCartney originals, "One After 909" and "What Goes On," the session ended prior to the worn-out group starting on the latter song.

John wrote "One After 909" (initially called "The One After 909") sometime around early 1960. Cynthia Powell, who he would later marry, recalls helping John with some of the words while they were sitting in The Jacaranda club in Liverpool. In Miles' *Many Years From Now*, Paul recalled: "It's not a great song but it's a favorite of mine because it has great memories for me of John and I trying to write a bluesy freight-train song. There were a lot of those songs at the time, like 'Midnight Special,' 'Freight Train' and 'Rock Island Line,' so this was the 'One After 909,' she got the one after it!" The three songs referenced by Paul were released as skiffle singles in the U.K. The line "Come on baby don't be cold as ice" most likely came to John from Elvis Presley's "Treat Me Nice" in which Elvis sings: "If you don't want me to be cold as ice/Treat me nice."

John, Paul and George recorded "One After 909" at Percy Phillips' home studio in Kensington shortly after the song was written. Unfortunately the acetate has not yet surfaced and most likely never will. There is a poor quality tape of the song made in mid-1960 at Paul's house on a borrowed Grundig tape recorder. John and Paul sing the verses in harmony. A Cavern rehearsal tape from early December 1962 contains two takes of the song. George's solos are sub-par and John flubs the lyrics on one of the takes.

The Beatles were tired and frustrated when they tackled the song during the March 5 evening session. John and Paul harmonize on the verses, while John sings solo on the bridge. John plays Chuck Berry–style guitar. On Take 1, Paul had trouble playing the song without a plectrum (pick), causing John to stop the song during the second verse and ask, "What are you doing? You're out of your mind." Take 2 is complete, but George's guitar solo is off. As the song ends, John asks, "What kind of solo was that?" Take 3 runs through the bridge, when John stops playing and once again asks Paul, "What are you doing?" Paul explains, "It's murder, I can't do it. I can't keep up." When John inquires as to why he isn't using a plectrum, Paul say he hasn't got one. On Take 4, George plays a decent solo, but John comes in too early with his vocal. With the group obviously tired, Martin instructs that band to begin Take 5 shortly before Harrison's solo so he can edit the first part of Take 4 with Take 5 to obtain a master. However, no additional work was done on the song.

Takes 1 and 2 are included on *Bootleg Recordings 1963*, while *Anthology 1* has a sequence containing bits of Takes 3, 4 and 5, as well as an edit of Takes 4 and 5 to form a complete version of the song as Martin intended. The Beatles returned to the song during the *Get Back* sessions, including it on the *Let It Be* album.

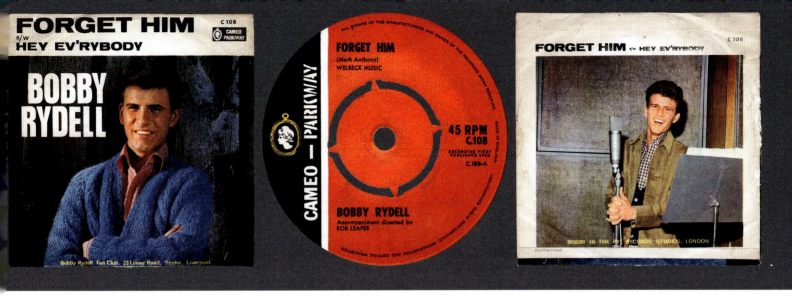

She Loves You

Recorded: July 1, 1963
Edited and mixed: July 4, 1963

Producer: George Martin
Engineers: Norman Smith; Geoff Emerick

John: Lead vocal; rhythm guitar (Gibson J-160E Jumbo)
Paul: Lead vocal; bass guitar (Hofner)
George: Backing vocal; lead guitar (Gretsch Country Gentleman)
Ringo: Drums (Ludwig kit)

The Beatles returned to EMI Studios on July 1, 1963, to record their fourth single during sessions booked from 2:30 to 5:30 PM and 7:00 to 10:00 PM. Although some questioned whether it was as good as their previous release, "She Loves You" holds the distinction of being the Beatles biggest selling single in the U.K. It is the song that best conjures up images of Beatlemania. From Ringo's thundering floor tom drum opening to the final "yeah, yeah, yeah, yeah," "She Loves You" is two minutes and 18 seconds of pure excitement.

The Beatles performed "She Loves You" during their pivotal October 13, 1963 appearance on Val Parnell's Sunday Night At The London Palladium, which was seen by over 15 million people throughout the U.K. The bedlam caused by the group both inside and outside the theatre caught the attention of British news editors, who elevated the Beatles from a successful entertainment act to a national news phenomenon. The Daily Mirror described the mass hysteria as "Beatlemania!" Three weeks later the group performed the song before British royalty at the Royal Variety Show. When the Beatles were filmed in front of hundreds of screaming fans at the Scalla Theatre for the frenzied concert scene at the end of their first film, A Hard Day's Night, the song chosen to conclude the madness and define Beatlemania was "She Loves You." As seen in the film, teenage girls screamed each time the boys shook their heads as they shouted "Oooo" in falsetto unison leading into the chorus.

The song's inspiration came from an unlikely source. In his 2022 book The Lyrics, Paul recalled: "One idea that lay behind 'She Loves You' was the song by Bobby Rydell called 'Forget Him,' which was based on the call-and-response structure. That's how it started out. The idea was that one person would sing, 'She loves you,' and the other ones would answer, 'Yeah, yeah, yeah.'"

Bobby Rydell was the antithesis of the rock 'n' roll rebels that inspired the Beatles. Rydell was a clean-cut American singer/actor teen idol. He recorded "Forget Him," written by Tony Hatch under the pseudonym Mark Anthony, at a Hatch-produced London session at Pye Studios, complete with brass and a female chorus. The song was released first in the U.K., entering the Record Retailer chart at number 50 on May 25, 1963, while "From Me To You" was in its sixth week at number one. The disc charted for 14 weeks with a peak at number 13. The single was not released in the U.S. until October 1963, entering the Billboard Hot 100 on November 9, charting for 16 weeks with a peak at number 4 on January 18, 1964, the same week "I Want To Hold Your Hand" entered the chart at number 45. Bobby Rydell was part of the Frankie Avalon, Fabian, Bobby Vee, Bobby Vinton crew that made the Beatles cringe at the thought of being billed below them on an American package tour.

The initial plan of having a "Yeah, yeah, yeah" refrain serve as an answer to the lead singer's "She loves you" was discarded. Paul recalls: "We decided that was a crummy idea as it was, but at least we then had the idea for a song called 'She Loves You.'"

239

The Beatles recorded their fourth single, "She Loves You" c/w "I'll Get You," on July 1, 1963, at EMI Studios on Abbey Road, St. John's Wood, London. British photographer Terry O'Neill attended the session. In addition to taking posed shots in the studio's outside garden area, O'Neill was given access to the actual recording session in Studio No. 2. The above image shows John, Paul and George running through their new songs for producer George Martin and music publisher Dick James (left, with glasses). All appear to be in good spirits, with the boys ready to record what Martin and James were expecting to be another number one hit. The image on the following page shows Ringo and George during the recording of one of the songs. Ringo is on his new 1963 Ludwig Downbeat drum kit with black oyster pearl shells. His bass drum is adorned with the newly designed Beatles "drop T" logo. The overhead boom microphone for Ringo's drums is an STC 4038. The floor mic for his bass drum is an STC 4033-A. George is playing his Gretsch Country Gentleman guitar for the first time on a Beatles recording. John and George's Vox AC30 amplifiers are visible left and right, with John's amp (left) miked with a Neumann KM 54.

Although there are some musical and lyrical similarities between "Forget Him" and "She Loves You," the songs are quite different. "Forget Him" is a pop song typical of the era, while "She Loves You" is pure rock 'n' roll, with fresh and exciting ideas. In the former song, the singer's message is a warning to a girl that her boyfriend doesn't love her or care: "Little girl, he's never dreaming of you/He'll break your heart, you wait and see." The singer then gives her advice: "So don't you cry now, just tell him goodbye now/Forget him and please come home to me."

For "She Loves You," Paul took a new approach for him as he explained in Miles' *Many Years From Now*: "I suppose the most interesting thing about it was that it was a message song, it was someone bringing a message. It wasn't us anymore, it was moving off the 'I love you, girl' or 'Love me do,' it was third person, which was a shift away." In the song, the message is telling the guy that the girl he thought he lost still cares about him: "You think you've lost your love/Well I saw her yesterday/It's you she's thinkin' of/And she told me what to say/She says she loves you." He is also given advice: "Pride can hurt you too/Apologize to her."

There are conflicting stories as to when John and Paul began writing "She Loves You." Beatles lore has held that the pair began the song on June 26, 1963, while the Beatles were staying at Turk's Hotel in Newcastle-upon-Tyne for an engagement at the Majestic Ballroom. However, Paul and others tell the story of John and Paul working on one of their hit singles on the bus during their tour with Roy Orbison, which ran from May 18 to June 9, 1963. Although Paul identifies the song as "From Me To You," that is not possible because that song was recorded over two months earlier on March 5. Thus, if a hit single was written on the Orbison tour, it had to be "She Loves You."

Regardless of when the song was started, John and Paul made significant progress on "She Loves You" in Newcastle on June 26. The song was completed the following evening at the McCartney home on Forthlin Road. After the duo played the song for Paul's dad, the elder McCartney suggested that they replace the "yeah, yeah, yeah" refrain with "yes, yes, yes." Fortunately they didn't follow his advice, and "yeah, yeah, yeah" became the catch phrase of Beatlemania.

"She Loves You" was recorded at EMI's Studio Two on July 1, 1963. Because the master tape of the day's session was either lost or recorded over, details of the recording session are not known. The song's instrumental backing consists of John playing his Jumbo acoustic-electric guitar, George on his new Gretsch Country Gentleman electric guitar, Paul playing his Hofner bass and Ringo on his new Ludwig drum kit. John and Paul handle the lead vocal, with George adding his voice on the second and fourth lines of each verse and on the chorus. At the suggestion of George Martin, the song begins with the chorus rather than a verse. Martin believed in powerful openings, and would make the same suggestion for a later single, "Can't Buy Me Love." The song's concluding G sixth chord was unusual for rock 'n' roll, although it was frequently used in jazz and big band recordings. Although Martin was initially against its use, fearing it was too old-fashioned and would be associated with Glenn Miller and the Andrews Sisters, the Beatles held their ground and Martin capitulated.

The EMI engineers have vivid memories of the session that produced the Beatles biggest hit to date. Norman Smith recalled seeing the lyrics on a music stand while he was setting up the microphones. "I thought I'll just have a quick look. 'She loves you, yeah, yeah, yeah. She loves you, yeah, yeah, yeah.' I thought, oh my God, what a lyric! This is going to be the one that I do not like. But when they started singing it—bang, wow, terrific, I was up at the mixer dancing around."

Geoff Emerick remembers the day hysterical fans invaded EMI Studios. That summer, girls camped out by the studio on Abbey Road hoping to catch a glimpse of their heroes. On the day of the July 1 session, the Beatles arrived early to pose for pictures in the alleyway behind the studio. This attracted a larger than usual gathering of fans as word spread. Some of the girls climbed on the top of the walls surrounding the studio to get a better view. The Beatles waved and smiled back.

Emerick recalls John entering the studio and joking about the "barbarians storming the walls." As the engineer was moving a microphone, Beatles roadies Mal Evans and Neil Aspinall burst in shouting "Fans!" One teenage girl burst through the door and headed for Ringo, who was behind his drum kit. The roadies managed to capture her and escort her out of the studio. Neil explained that dozens of rabid fans had overpowered the police, broke through the outside door and were running around the building in search of the Beatles. Emerick recalls, "Curious, I poked my head out the door and what I saw astounded, amazed and even frightened me…but it also made me burst out in laughter. Scores of hysterical screaming girls were racing down the corridors chased by a handful of out-of-breath beleaguered London bobbies…John, Paul and George [were] running around the studio imitating the girls."

Emerick has no doubt that "the excitement of the day helped spark a new level of energy in the group's playing. "She Loves You" was a fantastic song, with a powerhouse beat and a relentless hook. Norman Smith and I agreed it was destined to be a hit. There was a level of intensity in that performance that I had not heard before and have rarely heard since. I still judge that single to be one of the most exciting performances of the Beatles entire career."

The records pertaining to the mixing of "She Loves You" are missing, along with the tape. The song was edited from an unknown number of takes and edit pieces, and mixed for mono on July 4. The names of the engineers who assisted George Martin are not known.

The Beatles promoted "She Loves You" with TV and radio appearances. On August 14, the group performed the song for Granada TV's north-area news magazine program Scene At 6:30 for broadcast on August 19. On August 18, the group mimed the single and its flip side, "I'll Get You," for ABC Television's Lucky Stars (Summer Spin) for broadcast on August 24, the day after the disc's release. On August 23, they mimed "She Loves You" for broadcast that evening on Southern Television's Day By Day. On September 1, the group lip-synced "She Loves You" for September 7 broadcast on the ABC variety show Big Night Out. On October 4, the Beatles made their debut on Ready, Steady, Go! miming both sides of the single.

The group played "She Loves You" on their first two Ed Sullivan Show appearances and included the song in all of their 1964 U.S. concerts. The Beatles recorded "She Loves You" several times for BBC radio. "She Loves You" was broadcast on Pop Goes The Beatles on August 13, 20 and 27 and on September 10 and 24. It was also broadcast on Saturday Club on August 24, October 5 and December 21, Easy Beat on October 20, The Ken Dodd Show on November 3 and From Us To You on December 26. The October 5 Saturday Club broadcast is on *On Air - Live At The BBC Volume 2*.

I'll Get You

Recorded: July 1, 1963
Edited and mixed: July 4, 1963

Producer: George Martin
Engineers: Norman Smith; Geoff Emerick

John: Lead vocal; rhythm guitar (Jumbo); harmonica; handclaps
Paul: Lead vocal; bass guitar (Hofner); handclaps
George: Backing vocal; lead guitar (Country Gentleman); handclaps
Ringo: Drums (Ludwig kit)

The single's flip side, "I'll Get You," is another true Lennon-McCartney collaboration that was originally titled "Get You In The End." It was written in mid-June at the Menlove Avenue home of John's Aunt Mimi. The Beatles planned on making the song the A-side to their next single, but relegated it to the B-side after John and Paul finished writing "She Loves You."

"I'll Get You" was recorded during the same July 1 session as "She Loves You." The instrumental backing features John on his Jumbo acoustic-electric guitar, George on his Gretsch Country Gentleman, Paul on his Hofner bass and Ringo on his Ludwig drum kit. John overdubbed harmonica, and he, Paul and George add handclaps. John and Paul sang the lead vocals, in unison and in harmony at times. George provided backing harmony vocals.

The song opens with a series of "oh yeah"s accompanied by Paul's bass, John's harmonica and handclaps. This is followed by Ringo's drum roll leading into the line "Imagine I'm in love with you." The "oh yeah"s may have made their way into the Beatles music through the Marvellettes' 1961 hit "Please Mister Postman," which the group added to its stage show in 1961 and recorded for its second album, *With The Beatles*. Their second single used the phrase in its chorus, "Please please me, oh yeah, like I please you." In "I'll Get You," the "oh yeah" introduction and recurring refrain is one of the song's strongest hooks.

The song's bridge has multiple errors. John and Paul sing the first line together as "Well, there's gonna be a time," but on the second line Paul sings "When I'm gonna change your mind," while John sings "When I'm gonna make you mine." At the start of the third line, John, Paul and George start at different times, with John and Paul correctly singing "So you might as well resign yourself to me," while George mistakenly starts with "So I might as well...." Although George Martin was most likely aware of the mistakes, it was the performance that mattered. For this reason, it is a great pop rock song, and the gaffes only add to its charm.

The Beatles performed "I'll Get You" on television and radio appearances to promote their new single "She Loves You." On August 18, the group mimed both sides of the single for ABC Television's Lucky Stars (Summer Spin) for broadcast on August 24, the day after the disc's release. The group made their debut on Ready, Steady, Go! miming both sides of the single on October 4. "I'll Get You" was broadcast on Pop Goes The Beatles on August 13 and September 3 and 10, as well as on Saturday Club on August 24 and October 5. The latter performance is on *On Air - Live At The BBC Volume 2*.

The sessions for the Beatles second album began at EMI Studios on July 18, 1963. British fashion photographer Norman Parkinson shadowed the group on September 12, 1963. In addition to taking a series of iconic portraits of the group, Parkinson was able to capture the Beatles rehearsing and recording in Studio 2 during the band's evening session, which ran from 7:00 to 11:30. During this session, the Beatles recorded a remake of George's "Don't Bother Me" (pages 248 and 249), "Little Child" (pages 250 and 251) and "I Wanna Be Your Man" (pages 256 and 257). The image shown left is of Paul working out his piano part for "Little Child" under the watchful eye of George Martin, with John wailing along on harmonica and George playing guitar. The above image shows George Martin in the upstairs control room of Studio No. 2 overlooking the recording area for the musicians. Engineer Norman Smith is shown lower right at the EMI REED.37 mixing console.

It Won't Be Long

Recorded: July 30, 1963
Edited and mixed: August 21 (mono); October 29 (stereo mix)

Producer: George Martin
Engineers: Norman Smith; Richard Langham

John: Lead vocals; rhythm guitar (Rickenbacker Capri)
Paul: Backing vocal; bass guitar (Hofner)
George: Backing vocal; lead guitar (Gretsch Country Gentleman)
Ringo: Drums (Ludwig kit)

The Beatles second British LP, *With The Beatles*, opens with "It Won't Be Long," which was the first Lennon-McCartney original recorded for the album. John began writing the song in July as the follow-up single to "She Loves You," which had yet to be released. Like "She Loves You," the song opens with its chorus, which makes prominent use of "yeah"s. In addition, the song employs call-and-response patterned vocals utilizing "yeah"s, an idea that had been considered for "She Loves You" before being discarded. But here, it makes an effective hook to start and carry the chorus. After John sings "It won't be long, yeah," Paul and George respond with "Yeah," quickly followed by two rounds of call-and-response "yeah"s. After this entire pattern is repeated, John sings "It won't be long, yeah, till I belong to you."

Once again, John works double-meaning wordplay into the lyrics as he had done with "Please Please Me" when he sings "Please please me, oh yeah, like I please you." This time it is in the line "It won't be long, yeah, till I belong to you." Although John considered this to be his song, he was most likely assisted by Paul after he started the song on his own.

The Beatles began recording "It Won't Be Long" during the 10:00 AM to 1:30 PM session on July 30 after completing "Please Mister Postman." The rocker opens with an energetic chorus full of trademark "yeah"s before moving to a catchy guitar riff and a passionate lead vocal by John on the verses and bridge. Paul and George supply backing vocals. The instrumental backing is John on his Rickenbacker Capri, Paul on his Hofner bass, George on his Gretsch Country Gentleman guitar and Ringo on his Ludwig drum kit. The group recorded ten takes of the song during this session before heading to the Playhouse Theatre in London to record songs for the August 24th edition of the BBC radio program Saturday Club.

Work resumed on the song in the evening session after the group recorded "Till There Was You" and "Roll Over Beethoven."

George Martin and the group agreed that Take 7 was the best of the performances from the earlier session. George overdubbed his lead guitar riff, Paul added bass in the same places to reinforce the riff and John double-tracked his lead vocal over Take 7 during seven takes designated Track 2, Takes 11-17, with Take 17 selected as the best. The group then recorded six edit pieces of the song's ending, designated Takes 18-23.

The song was edited and mixed for mono on August 21 with Norman Smith and Geoff Emerick assisting George Martin. Take 17 served as the basic track, with edit piece Take 21 used for the ending. This crew, along with an additional engineer whose initials are B.T., mixed the song for stereo from the same edit on October 29.

While "It Won't Be Long" would have been a great concert song, the Beatles never performed it live or recorded it for the BBC. They did, however, lip-sync the song on the March 20, 1964 edition of Ready, Steady, Go!

Although the song was not issued as a single, George Martin thought "It Won't Be Long" was worthy of being the potboiler opener for the Beatles all-important second album. Had the song been released as a single, it very likely would have been a huge hit.

All I've Got To Do

Recorded: September 11, 1963
Mixed: September 30 (mono); October 29 (stereo)

Producer: George Martin
Engineers: Norman Smith; Richard Langham

John: Lead vocal; rhythm guitar (Gibson J-160E Jumbo)
Paul: Backing vocal; bass guitar (Hofner)
George: Backing vocal; lead guitar (Gretsch Country Gentleman)
Ringo: Drums (Ludwig kit)

"All I've Got To Do" was written by John, who described the song as another attempt to "do" [imitate] Smokey Robinson. Because the song opens with a strummed chord as does the Miracles' "(You Can) Depend On Me," it has been written that John's song is inspired by "Depend On Me." However, that may not be the case. Although "Depend On Me" was issued in the U.S. in the fall of 1959, it was not issued in the U.K. on a single. Its first British release came in July 1963 when Oriole Records issued the group's first album, *Hi We're The Miracles* (Oriole PS 40044), which contains the song.

While it is possible John heard "Depend On Me" on the Oriole LP, his inspiration may have once again been "What's So Good About

Good Bye," which previously inspired "Ask Me Why." The start-and-stop rhythms of "All I've Got To Do" more closely resemble "What's So Good About Good Bye" and even "You Really Got A Hold On Me" than the steady doo-wop stylings of "Depend On Me."

Although it has been reported that John wrote the song in 1961, that is most likely not the case. There is no record of the group performing the song prior to the recording session. The group did not perform the song in concert or for the BBC as part of its promotion of the *With The Beatles* LP.

"All I've Got To Do" was recorded as the third and final song of the 2:30 to 6:00 PM session on September 11. The group ran through 14 takes, eight of which were incomplete. Take 14 was determined to be the best and was enhanced with overdubs to form Take 15.

The moderate-paced song opens with a jazz-sounding chord (E11#5) setting the stage for John's passionate and soulful vocal. Paul and George provide backing vocals, with McCartney alternating between singing in unison and in harmony with Lennon. Harrison's backing vocals are limited to the bridge. John is on his Gibson J-160E Jumbo, while George plays his Gretsch Country Gentleman. Paul, on his trusty Hofner bass, plays "bass chords" rather than single notes on the first part of the verses. Ringo, on his Ludwig kit, makes sparse but effective use of his hi-hat. The song ends with John and Paul humming in harmony during the fade-out. "All I've Got To Do" has a catchy melody and demonstrates how the Beatles were able to incorporate influences of other artists, in this case Smokey Robinson, into their original compositions.

Martin, Norman Smith and Geoff Emerick mixed the song for mono on September 30. The stereo mix was made on October 29.

All My Loving

Recorded: July 30, 1963
Mixed: August 21 (mono); October 29 (stereo)

Producer: George Martin
Engineers: Norman Smith; Richard Langham

Paul: Lead vocals; bass guitar (Hofner)
John: Backing vocal; rhythm guitar (Rickenbacker Capri)
George: Backing vocal; lead guitar (Gretsch Country Gentleman)
Ringo: Drums (Ludwig kit)

"All My Loving" was written by Paul during the first part of the group's tour with Roy Orbison, which began on May 18, 1963. According to Paul, it was the first song where he wrote the words before the music. In Miles' *Many Years From Now,* Paul explained: "We were on a tour bus going to a gig and so I started with the words. I had in mind a little country and western song.... We arrived at the gig and I remember being in one of these big backstage areas and there was a piano there so I'd got my instrument. I didn't have a guitar, it was probably with our road manager, and I remember working the tune out to it on the piano. It was a good show song, it worked well live." The song was most likely inspired by Jane Asher, who Paul had recently met on April 18 at the Royal Albert Hall.

The song's opening melody line is very similar to a brief set of notes and chords in "Kathy's Waltz," a track on the 1959 album *Time Out* by the Dave Brubeck Quartet. At the song's 1:02 mark, Brubeck plays a melody line on piano where you can sing-along with "Close you eyes and I'll kiss you, to-" before Brubeck shifts to backing a flute solo. Whether Paul was inspired by or subconsciously nicked Brubeck's brief melody line when he composed "All My Loving" on piano is not known. It may just be a fascinating coincidence.

The Beatles recorded "All My Loving" at the end of the same July 30 session that produced "It Won't Be Long." The song opens with Paul's lead vocal, which is quickly accompanied by its exciting, fast-paced instrumental backing, dominated by John's high-speed churning rhythm guitar on his Rickenbacker Capri and Paul's walking bass part on his Hofner. George plays a rockabilly-influenced guitar solo on his Gretsch Country Gentleman during the instrumental break. Ringo's steady rock drumming has a bit of jazzy swing to it. John and George provide backing vocals during the "All my loving, I will send to you, all my loving, darling I'll be true" refrains.

The group completed the basic track in ten takes, with at least two takes being false starts. The number 5 was skipped, so the final and best take was actually numbered Take 11. Paul then recorded a harmony part over his previously recorded vocal during the final verse onto Take 11. This was accomplished in three takes designated as Track 2, Takes 12 through 14, with the final take serving as the master. The song was mixed for mono on August 21 and for stereo on October 29. When "All My Loving" was performed in concert, George sang the harmony part that had been double-tracked by Paul on the studio version of the song.

Although none of the tracks on *With The Beatles* were released as singles in the U.K., "All My Loving" was viewed by many as the album's standout song. EMI selected "All My Loving" for the title track of the Beatles fourth EP, which topped the EP charts for eight weeks in 1964.

John considered "All My Loving" to be a "damn good piece of work," hinting that he wished he had written it himself. In his Playboy interview, John rightly added: "I play a pretty mean guitar in back." Paul agreed with John's assessment, stating in his book *The Lyrics*: "The thing that strikes me about the 'All My Loving' recording is John's guitar part; he's playing the chords as triplets. That was a last-minute idea, and it transforms the whole thing, giving it momentum. The song is obviously about someone leaving to go on a trip, and that driving rhythm of John's echoes the feeling of travel and motion. It sounds like a car's wheels on the motorway, which, if you can believe it, had only really become a thing in the U.K. at the end of the fifties. But, it was often like that when we were recording. One of us would come up with that little magic thing. It allowed the song to become what it needed to be."

The Beatles performed "All My Loving" three times for the BBC. The third performance, which was recorded at the Piccadilly Theatre in London on February 28, 1964, and aired on the March 30 From Us To You program, is included on *Live At The BBC*.

"All My Loving" was the first song performed by the Beatles on their first Ed Sullivan Show appearance. This historic performance is on Volume 3 of the *Anthology* video and *The First U.S. Visit*. The audio portion of the broadcast is included on *Anthology 1*. The group's performance of the song on the second Sullivan Show appears on *The First U.S. Visit* video. Volume 3 of the *Anthology* video contains the first part of the June 17, 1964 Melbourne performance.

"All My Loving" was part of the Beatles stage show from late 1963 through all of 1964. *The Beatles At The Hollywood Bowl* includes the group's August 23, 1964 performance, which is also included in black and white film on Volume 4 of the *Anthology* video.

Don't Bother Me

Recorded: September 11 and 12, 1963
Mixed: September 30 (mono); October 29 (stereo)

Producer: George Martin
Engineers: Norman Smith; Richard Langham

George: Lead vocals; lead guitar (Gretsch Country Gentleman)
John: Rhythm guitar (Rickenbacker Capri); tambourine
Paul: Bass guitar (Hofner); claves (or woodblock)
Ringo: Drums (Ludwig kit); doumbek (Arabian bongo drum)

George's "Don't Bother Me" was his first solo composition recorded by the Beatles. Harrison says he wrote the song as an exercise to see if he could write a song. It was written in a hotel in Bournemouth, Hampshire, during the group's August 19-24, 1963 engagement at the Gaumont Cinema. Harrison recalls, "I was sick in bed—maybe that's why it turned out to be 'Don't Bother Me.'"

He previously received co-songwriter's credit for Paul's 1958 song "In Spite Of All The Danger," where his contribution was limited to creating the song's two guitar solos. This early recording made its public debut on *Anthology 1*. He co-wrote an instrumental with John titled "Cry For A Shadow," which was recorded by the Beatles in Hamburg in June 1961. But "Don't Bother Me" was George's first attempt at writing a song on his own.

The group first recorded the song towards the end of the evening session on September 11, 1963. The session was attended by Melody Maker's Chris Roberts, who wrote about it in the magazine's September 28 issue. After completing one of John's songs ["Not A Second Time"], John told George Harrison: "It's your turn now. I'm looking forward to this." John ran his guitar through a fuzz box and was knocked out by the new sound, but George Martin didn't like it. Harrison then asked: "Can we have a compressor on this guitar? We might try to get a sort of organ sound." A compressor was then brought into the control room. Recording Sheets show that four takes were recorded, with the fourth being the best. Takes 5-7 apparently consisted of overdubs onto Take 4. The tape from this session is missing and was most likely recorded over.

Neither the Beatles nor George Martin were satisfied with the results, so they returned to "Don't Bother Me" the following day, this time recording the song at the beginning of the evening session. Fashion photographer Norman Parkinson shot George singing the song (shown right). The group started from scratch, with the remake designated Take 10. The basic track consists of George singing and playing his Gretsch Country Gentleman backed by John on his Rickenbacker Capri (through a compressor, giving it a dark tone), Paul on his Hofner bass and Ringo on drums. The band's initial attempt at the remake, Take 10, is an excellent performance. Towards the end of the song George can be heard singing "Oh yeah, rock 'n' roll now." Takes 11 and 12 were false starts, while Take 13 was designated the best. The number 14 was skipped when the overdubs began with Take 15. George double-tracked his vocal, while the other Beatles added the following percussion: John on tambourine, Paul on claves (or woodblock) and Ringo on a loose-skinned Arabian bongo drum. Take 15 was deemed the best. The song was mixed for mono on September 30 and for stereo on October 29.

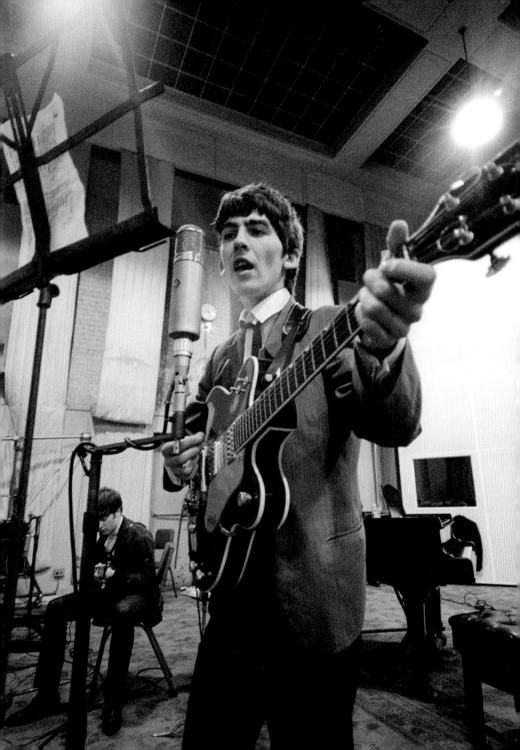

Little Child

Recorded: September 11 & 12 and October 3, 1963
Mixed: October 23 (mono); October 29 (stereo)

Producer: George Martin
Engineers: Norman Smith; Richard Langham

John: Lead vocals; rhythm guitar (Rickenbacker Capri); harmonica
Paul: Lead vocals; bass guitar (Hofner); piano
George: Lead guitar (Gretsch Country Gentleman)
Ringo: Drums (Ludwig kit)

"Little Child" was described by John as a knockoff between the two composers: "'Little Child' was another effort of Paul and I to write a song for somebody. It was probably Ringo." In Miles' *Many Years From Now*, Paul was equally dismissive of the song: "'Little Child' was a work job. Certain songs were inspirational and you just followed that. Certain other songs were, 'Right, come on, two hours, song for Ringo for the album.'" In this case, the song was originally intended to serve as Ringo's lead vocal contribution to the group's second British album; however, the drummer was not comfortable with the song, instead opting to sing lead on "I Wanna Be Your Man."

In *Many Years From Now*, Paul described what it was like writing for Ringo: "[The songs] had to be fairly simple...he didn't have a large vocal range but he could handle things with good *con brio* and *spirito* if they were nice and simple. It had to be something he could get behind. If he couldn't mentally picture it, you were in trouble." Ringo didn't feel comfortable with the song, so it was up to the composers to handle the vocals.

Paul indicated that part of the song's melody line came from a song sung by British actor/folk singer Elton Hayes in the 1952 RKO-Walt Disney British Productions film *The Story Of Robin Hood*. In the movie, Hayes plays the part of Alan-a-Dale, a wandering minstrel who joins Robin Hood's Merry Men. As Robin woos Maid Marian, the minstrel sings the song "Whistle My Love," which was released as a 78 RPM single by Elton Hayes on Parlophone R 3509. In *Many Years From Now*, Paul explained: "I nicked a bit of the melody from one of [Hayes'] tunes, 'I'm so sad and lonely,' that little bit came from a line: '*Whistle, my love*, and I will come to thee, *I'll always find you*.' It's actually not the same tune, but in my mind it was a quote from Elton Hayes." John and Paul's "Little Child" turns it into "I'm so sad and lonely/Baby take a chance with me."

The Beatles recorded two takes of "Little Child" during the afternoon session of September 11. This was preceded by one take of "I Wanna Be Your Man." It is possible that Ringo sang lead on both songs that day to determine which one would be best suited for his lead vocal on the album. As the tape no longer exists, we may never know if that is the case.

The group returned to "Little Child" the following evening after completing the remake of "Don't Bother Me." The basic track was recorded in Takes 3-7, with Take 7 being the best. These takes most likely consisted of John and Paul singing in unison on most of the song (although John's voice is clearly more dominant) and harmony on the line "I'm so sad and lonely." The vocals are backed by George on his Gretsch Country Gentleman (and possibly John on his Rickenbacker Capri, although it is hard to tell because the guitars are not featured in the mix), Paul on his Hofner bass and Ringo on drums. Norman Parkinson attended the session and took pictures of George Martin and the boys working out the song's arrangement (page 244) and of John overdubbing his harmonica (shown left).

John overdubbed his wild bluesy harmonica onto Takes 8-13, with Take 13 being the best. Paul superimposed piano onto Take 13 in Takes 14 and 15, with Take 15 being the best. This was Paul's first piano playing on a Beatles recording. Apparently not satisfied with John's harmonica solo, three edit pieces were recorded as Takes 16-18 to get an improved harmonica solo from John. The best edit piece, Take 18, has both Paul's piano and bass. Thus, Paul most likely overdubbed piano onto the final edit piece.

An edit and mono mix of the song was made on September 30 from Take 15 for the body of the song and Take 18 for the middle eight featuring John's harmonica solo. The edit piece has a totally different sound than the body of the song.

On October 3, John and Paul double-tracked their "Come on, come on, come on" vocals to the September 30 edit of "Little Child." These takes were numbered 19-21, with Take 21 deemed the best. Oddly, when the song was remixed for mono on October 23, the mix was once again made from Takes 15 and 18. The stereo mix, made on October 29, used Take 21, so it has the additional double-tracked "Come on, come on, come on" vocals not present on the mono mix.

Although John and Paul considered "Little Child" nothing more than a "work job," the finished product is quite impressive. The infectious rocker has many of the ingredients of past hits, including "come on"s, "oh yeah"s and John's wailing harmonica, this time introducing the song and being featured throughout. The song holds its own with the other tracks on *With The Beatles* and still holds up today as a classic example of a spirited sixties rocker.

Till There Was You

Recorded: July 18 & 30, 1963
Mixed: August 21 (mono); October 29 (stereo)

Producer: George Martin
Engineers: Norman Smith; Richard Langham

Paul: Lead vocal; bass guitar (Hofner)
John: Rhythm guitar (Gibson J-160E Jumbo)
George: Lead guitar (Jose Ramirez nylon-stringed acoustic guitar)
Ringo: Bongos

As detailed in the earlier Decca Sessions chapter, the Beatles added "Till There Was You" to their set list in 1961. Their arrangement of the song from *The Music Man* is based on Peggy Lee's rendition, which was pulled from her 1960 album *Latin A La Lee* and released as a single in the U.K. in 1961. The Beatles performed "Till There Was You" three times for the BBC before recording the song at an EMI session.

The Beatles first attempt at "Till There Was You" took place at the end of the first session for the group's second album on the evening of July 18. The band recorded three takes of the song, two of which were complete. Although the tape from the session no longer exists, the backing to Paul's solo vocal most likely consisted of George on his Country Gentleman, John on his Rickenbacker Capri or Gibson Jumbo, Paul on his Hofner bass and Ringo on his Ludwig drum kit. These performances most likely sounded like the group's earlier recordings of the song for the BBC. *On Air - Live At The BBC Volume 2* contains the Beatles July 10 performance of the song that was broadcast on the July 30 Pop Go The Beatles.

Neither the Beatles nor George Martin were satisfied with the recordings of "Till There Was You" from the July 18 session, so they returned to the song on the evening of July 30. At George Martin's suggestion, the remake was to have an acoustic sound, with John on his Gibson J-160E Jumbo acoustic/electric guitar and George on a José Ramirez nylon-stringed classical acoustic guitar. Both guitars were directly miked rather than being played through their Vox amplifiers. Ringo abandoned his drum kit for bongos. Paul's Hofner bass was the song's only electric instrument. The Beatles recorded Takes 4-8, with Take 8 selected as the best. There were no overdubs. George expertly handled the song's jazzy lead fills and solo. McCartney's soaring vocal performance is noteworthy not only for its beauty, but also for his pronunciation of the word "saw" as "sar" in the line "But I never sar them winging, no I never sar them at all."

The Beatles performed the song four more times for the BBC after the EMI session. Apple's *Live At The BBC* includes the group's final BBC recording of the tune from the February 28, 1964 session that aired on From Us To You on March 30. "Till There Was You" was used to charm the audiences of two of the Beatles most important and famous television appearances. It was one of four songs played by the group at the November 4, 1963 Royal Variety Show. This performance is included on both the *Anthology* video and *Anthology 1*. The tune was the second song performed by the band on their Ed Sullivan Show debut. For curious elder Americans seeing (and perhaps hearing) the group for the first time, the ballad brought them a certain level of comfort towards the four long-haired boys from Liverpool. The Ed Sullivan performance appears on *The First U.S. Visit*. The song remained part of the Beatles stage show through mid-1964. Recorded live performances include the February 11, 1964 Washington Coliseum show and three later Australian concerts from June.

Please Mister Postman

Recorded: July 30, 1963
Mixed: August 21 (mono); October 29 (stereo)

Producer: George Martin
Engineers: Norman Smith; Richard Langham

John: Lead vocals; rhythm guitar (Rickenbacker Capri); handclaps
Paul: Backing vocal; bass guitar (Hofner); handclaps
George: Backing vocal; lead guitar (Country Gentleman); handclaps
Ringo: Drums (Ludwig kit)

"Please Mr. Postman" (identified on the Beatles album cover and label as "Please Mister Postman") was originally recorded by the Motown girl group the Marvelettes and released on August 21, 1961, on Tamla 54046. The song spent 23 weeks in the Billboard Hot 100, including one week at the top. It also spent 23 weeks on the Billboard Hot R&B Sides chart, including seven weeks at number one. The single was released in the U.K. on Fontana H 355, but did not chart. Although credited on the album jacket and label to "Holland," the tune was co-written by Marvelette Georgia Dobbins along with William Garrett, Brian Holland, Robert Bateman and Freddie Gorman. Marvin Gaye played drums on the track. The song's "oh yeah" vocal ad-libs may have been the source of the "oh yeah" and "yeah" vocal refrains that dominate Lennon-McCartney songs such as "I'll Get You," "She Loves You" and "It Won't Be Long."

The Beatles added "Please Mr. Postman" to their stage show in 1961 and played the song for their very first BBC performance. This was taped before a live audience at the Playhouse Theatre in Manchester on March 7, 1962, for broadcast the following day on Teenager's Turn—Here We Go. Pete Best was on drums. The group next recorded the song for the BBC at Studio Two, Aeolian Hall in London on July 10, 1963, for broadcast on the July 30 Pop Go The Beatles. At that time, the song opened with a three-note riff played by George (copied from the piano part on the Marvelettes single), that ran throughout the song. The group also worked out a doo-wop style hard ending to replace the single's fade-out.

The Beatles opened the morning session on July 30 with two takes of "Please Mister Postman." The track featured John on lead vocal, with backing vocals from Paul and George. The instrumental backing has John on his Rickenbacker Capri, George on his Gretsch Country Gentleman, Paul on his Hofner bass and Ringo on drums. For Track 2, Take 3, John double-tracked his vocal onto Take 2. Although the tape from this session no longer exists, a tape of a monitor mix confirms that the song's arrangement was similar to that of the BBC performance.

After listening to the playback, the group rearranged the song by scaling back George's lead guitar and reworking the intro by dropping the guitar riff and bass, and adding hi-hat. The group recorded four takes, with the final Take 7 selected as the best. John doubled-tracked his vocal while the group added hand claps for the introduction onto Take 7 in two takes, with Take 9 becoming the master. From the opening tap of Ringo's hi-hat to the "Deliva de letta, de soona de betta" vocal line and Paul's scream during the fade-out, this graceful rocker is one of the group's most memorable cover songs.

As with many of the album's tracks, the song was mixed for mono on August 21 and for stereo on October 29. The Beatles third and final BBC performance of "Please Mister Postman" was broadcast on the March 30, 1964 From Us To You. The group lip-synced the song on February 23, 1964, as part of their six-song set for the British ITV network show Big Night Out. This performance appears on Volume 2 of the *Anthology* video.

Roll Over Beethoven

Recorded: July 30, 1963
Edited and mixed: August 21 (mono); October 29 (stereo mix)

Producer: George Martin
Engineers: Norman Smith; Richard Langham

George: Lead vocals; lead guitar (Gretsch Country Gentleman)
John: Rhythm guitar (Rickenbacker Capri); handclaps
Paul: Bass guitar (Hofner); handclaps
Ringo: Drums (Ludwig kit); handclaps

"Roll Over Beethoven" was written and originally recorded by American singer/guitarist Chuck Berry and released on Chess 1626. Berry's classic rocker entered the Billboard charts on June 9, 1956, peaking at number two on the R&B chart and at 29 on the pop chart. It was issued in the U.K. on London 45-HLU 8428, but did not chart.

The song was one of 12 Chuck Berry songs performed by the Beatles, with the group adding the rocker to their stage show back in their Quarrymen days when the emphasis shifted from skiffle to rock 'n' roll. Although John originally handled the lead vocal, George took over the song in 1961. It was one of nine Chuck Berry songs that the Beatles performed for the BBC, the most by any other artist.

The Beatles performed "Roll Over Beethoven" in Hamburg, Germany during the 1962 Christmas holiday season. The song is on *Live At The Star-Club*, which was released in America in June 1977.

"Roll Over Beethoven" was recorded during the July 30 evening session. The lineup features George on lead vocal and lead guitar on his Country Gentleman, John on his Rickenbacker, Paul on his Hofner bass and Ringo on his Ludwig drum kit. The group ran through five takes, with Takes 1 and 3 quickly breaking down. Take 5 was deemed the best. George then doubled-tracked his vocal while the others provided handclaps onto Take 5. This was accomplished in two takes, with the first breaking down and Take 7 being the best. The song's final chord was then recorded an edit piece.

The master is an edit of Take 7 and edit piece Take 8. This was accomplished on August 21, with the mono mix made later that same day. The track was mixed for stereo on October 29.

The Beatles performed "Roll Over Beethoven" seven times for the BBC, including two performances that predate the July 30, 1963 EMI session. The August 1 recording aired on the September 3 Pop Go The Beatles, predating the album's release. It is on the *On Air - Live At The BBC Volume 2* collection. *Live At The BBC* contains the performance broadcast on the March 30, 1964 From Us To You. *Anthology 1* contains a high-energy version of the tune recorded on October 24, 1963, for broadcast on Sweden's Sveriges Radio on November 11. The group also recorded "Roll Over Beethoven" at IBC Studios in London on April 19, 1964, for lip-syncing on the TV special, Around The Beatles, which was broadcast nine days later.

The Beatles boldly opened their first American concert at the Washington Coliseum with the song. The group's spirited August 23, 1964 performance of the rocker is on *Live At The Hollywood Bowl*.

Hold Me Tight

Recorded: September 12, 1963
Edited and mixed: September 30 (mono); October 29 (stereo)

Producer: George Martin
Engineers: Norman Smith; Richard Langham

Paul: Lead vocals; bass guitar (Hofner); handclaps
John: Backing vocals; rhythm guitar (Rickenbacker); handclaps
George: Backing vocals; lead guitar (Country Gentleman); handclaps
Ringo: Drums (Ludwig kit); handclaps

"Hold Me Tight" is a Lennon-McCartney original that was written in the front parlor of Paul's Forthlin Road home. Paul was the primary contributor of the song, which was viewed by him as a "work song" and a "failed attempt at a single which then became an acceptable album filler." He said it was inspired by the Shirelles.

The Beatles first recorded the song at the February 11, 1963 marathon session for their first album. Although the tape no longer exists, the Recording Sheet indicates that the group recorded nine takes of the song, with only Takes 2, 6 and 9 being complete. Take 9 was deemed the best. This was followed by four edit piece takes, with Take 13 marked as the best. Although an edit of Takes 9 and 13 could have been made, this was never done, most likely because George Martin and the Beatles thought the performance was not up to par. This view is supported by the Beatles knocking out "Twist And Shout" as the eleventh song at the end of the session whose goal was to produce ten acceptable tracks to flesh out an album. The personnel were probably Paul and John on lead vocals backed by George on his Gretsch Duo-Jet, John on his Rickenbacker Capri, Paul on his Hofner bass and Ringo on drums.

Although Norman Joplin had speculated in the February 16 Record Mirror that "Hold Me Tight" might be the Beatles next single and quoted John as saying that the song had a "good catchy riff," the Beatles did not consider recording the song at their next session on March 5. Instead they recorded "From Me To You," "Thank You Girl" and "One After 909," with "What Goes On" as part of their plan had they not grown too tired to get to it.

The Beatles returned to "Hold Me Tight" during the afternoon session of September 12. The first take, which was incomplete, was ultimately numbered Take 20. Take 21 was complete and is on *Bootleg Recordings 1963*. Takes 22 and 23 quickly broke down, causing Paul to say: "Ah, bloody hell." Take 24 was complete and deemed the best. These takes have Paul on lead vocal backed by John and George only on the second part of the verses. The instrumental backing consists of John on his Rickenbacker Capri, George on his Country Gentleman, Paul on his Hofner bass and Ringo on drums. The overdubs have Paul double-tracking his lead vocal, John and George adding more backing vocals, and the entire band clapping hands throughout the song. Track 2, Take 25 was a false start, while Takes 26 and 29 were complete.

The song was edited and mixed for mono on September 30 at a session with George Martin assisted by Norman Smith and Geoff Emerick. The mono mix is from an edit of Takes 26 and 29. The stereo mix, made on October 29 with the same crew plus B.T., appears to be from a different edit.

You Really Got A Hold On Me

Recorded: July 18, 1963
Edited and mixed: August 21 (mono); October 29 (stereo)

Producer: George Martin
Engineers: Norman Smith; Richard Langham

John: Lead vocal; rhythm guitar (Rickenbacker Capri)
George: Lead vocal; lead guitar (Country Gentleman)
Paul: Backing vocal; bass guitar (Hofner)
Ringo: Drums (Ludwig kit)
George Martin: Piano (Steinway B)

"You Really Got A Hold On Me" by the Miracles was the first song recorded by the Beatles during the first session for their second LP. The session began at 7:00 PM on July 18, 1963. Although the group had a couple of original compositions ready to go, they felt more comfortable starting the session with songs from their stage show. That same evening they also completed Barrett Strong's "Money (That's What I Want)" and the Donays' "Devil In His Heart."

The song, titled "You've Really Got A Hold On Me" on the American pressings of the single, was written by the Miracles' lead singer, William "Smokey" Robinson, while on a business trip in New York. It was inspired by Sam Cooke's "Bring It On Home To Me," which was sung as a duet by Cooke and Lou Rawls. Smokey produced "You've Really Got A Hold On Me" at an October 16, 1962 session, singing harmony with fellow Miracle Bobby Rogers. The song was released as the B-side to Smokey's "Happy Landing" on Tamla 54073 on November 9, 1962. When disc jockeys flipped the disc, the ballad charted for 16 weeks, peaking at number eight in the Billboard Hot 100. It topped the Billboard Hot R&B Singles chart.

The song was released in the U.K. on Oriole 45-CBA 1795 in January 1963 as part of its TAMLA series. The label prominently displays the word "American" below the Oriole logo and lists the song's title as "You Really Got A Hold On Me." EMI would use this title on the album's cover and label. The British single did not chart.

The Beatles recorded five takes of the song, with Takes 1, 4 and 5 being complete. Take 5 was deemed the best. John sings the lead with a passionate soulful voice, joined by George on the lower harmony parts. Paul sings on the refrains and is part of a three-part harmony on the "Hold me" repeated lines. John plays the rhythm guitar part on his Rickenbacker Capri, while George dutifully copies Miracles' guitarist Marv Tarplin's lead lines. Paul's bass on his Hofner outshines that of James Jamerson of the Funk Brothers, Motown's top-notch session group. Ringo swings along on drums.

George Martin overdubbed his piano onto Take 5 as Track 2, Takes 6 and 7. Takes 8-10 were vocal overdubs on the word "baby" towards the end. Take 11 was an edit piece of the song's opening piano. The song was edited from Takes 7, 10 and 11, and mixed for mono on August 21 and stereo on October 29. The Beatles attempted one take of the song on EMI's four-track recorder on October 17.

The Beatles recorded the song four times for BBC radio, including a May 24, 1963 session that predates the EMI session. The July 30, 1963 recording, which was broadcast August 24 on Saturday Club, is on Live At The BBC. The group's October 24, 1963 performance of the song for Sweden's Sveriges Radio is included on Anthology 1. The Let It Be film contains a joyous segment of the band playing the song with Billy Preston on organ. John's passionate vocal on the album version of the song shows his admiration for Smokey, who influenced several of the Beatles early recordings.

I Wanna Be Your Man

Recorded: September 11, 12 & 30, 1963 and October 3 & 23, 1963
Mixed: October 23 (mono); stereo (October 29)

Producer: George Martin
Engineers: Norman Smith; Richard Langham (September 11 & 12) & Geoff Emerick (September 30)

Ringo: Lead vocal; drums (Ludwig kit); maracas
John: Backing vocal; guitar (Rickenbacker Capri)
Paul: Backing vocal; bass guitar (Hofner); handclaps
George: Lead guitar (Gretsch Country Gentleman)
George Martin: Organ (Hammond RT-3) [probably]

Because Ringo was uncomfortable singing "Little Child" for his vocal spotlight on the group's second album, John and Paul had to provide him with another song. While on tour in 1963, John had read something in a newspaper that gave him an idea for a song title, "I Wanna Be Your Man." However, John credits Paul with coming up with the bit: "I wanna be your lover, baby. I wanna be your man." The words were very simple, but that was the idea. In Miles' *Many Years From Now*, Paul recalled: "We often used to say to people, the words don't really matter, people don't listen to words, it's the sound they listen to. So 'I Wanna Be Your Man' was to try and give Ringo something like 'Boys;' an up-tempo song he could sing from the drums. So again it had to be very simple." The song remained unfinished until fate stepped in.

On September 10, 1963, John and Paul attended a Variety Club awards luncheon at London's Savoy Hotel. Afterwards they ran into the Rolling Stones' manager, Andrew Oldham, who lamented that his group was having trouble coming up with a follow-up to their debut single, a cover of Chuck Berry's "Come On." They told Oldham that they had an unfinished R&B tune that was sure to be a hit. At Oldham's request, John and Paul dropped by a Stones rehearsal and played the unfinished song for them. When the Stones expressed interest in recording the tune, John and Paul went off into another room to complete the song. After a few minutes, they returned with the finished product.

This incident was significant for two reasons. First, it gave the Stones their next single. On October 7, 1963, the band recorded a hard-driving, bluesy version of the song, complete with Bill Wyman's frantic bass, Brian Jones' jarring slide guitar and Mick Jagger's snarling vocal. "I Wanna Be Your Man" became a number 12 hit in England. In addition, the encounter with John and Paul showed the Stones and their manager that writing songs wasn't that difficult. Volume 2 of the *Anthology* video contains a clip of the Stones performing the song live on the BBC.

The day after their encounter with the Stones, John and Paul presented Ringo with the finished song. After attempting only one take of "I Wanna Be Your Man" on September 11, the Beatles returned to the song at the end of the next day's evening session with Ringo singing lead and playing drums backed by John on his Rickenbacker Capri, George on his Gretsch Country Gentleman and Paul on his Hofner bass. Pictures of the session taken by Norman Parkinson show Paul in front of Ringo's drum kit encouraging and singing off-mic with the drummer. If these pictures are of recorded takes rather than rehearsals, it means Ringo sang solo that night. The Beatles recorded Takes 2 through 7, with Take 7 deemed the best. The group then called it a night.

During a September 30 mixing session held without the Beatles, George Martin superimposed Hammond organ onto Take 7. These takes, numbered 8-13, were most likely not used. On October 3, John and Paul added their backing vocals and Ringo overdubbed maracas onto Take 7 during Takes 14 and 15. Tambourine was added to Take 15 on October 23. Organ was superimposed on either October 3 or 23, most likely played by George Martin, although Tony Barrow's liner notes credit John.

The Beatles version of the song is an all-out rocker with a totally different feel than the Rolling Stones' single. After George starts things off by bending a guitar string, the rest of the band jumps in, led by Ringo's limited but effective voice. John and Paul help flesh out the vocal sound, and George provides energetic lead guitar and an effective solo.

The Beatles recorded "I Wanna Be Your Man" twice for the BBC. *Live At The BBC* contains the performance broadcast on the March 30, 1964 From Us To You. The group recorded the song at IBC studios for lip-syncing on the TV special, *Around The Beatles*. This audio is on *Anthology 1*. Volume 2 of the *Anthology* video contains a partial clip of the group lip-syncing the song.

Ringo sang "I Wanna Be Your Man" at the Beatles February 11, 1964 Washington Coliseum concert. The rocker was played during many of the group's 1965 and 1966 concerts, including the 1965 Hollywood Bowl shows. The Japanese laserdisc *The Beatles Concert at Budokan 1966* contains the June 30 performance in color. The Beatles played "I Wanna Be Your Man" at their last concert on August 29, 1966, at Candlestick Park.

Devil In Her Heart

Recorded: July 18, 1963
Mixed: August 21 (mono); October 29 (stereo)

Producer: George Martin
Engineers: Norman Smith; Richard Langham

George: Lead vocals; lead guitar (Gretsch Country Gentleman)
John: Backing vocal; rhythm guitar (Rickenbacker Capri)
Paul: Backing vocal; bass guitar (Hofner)
Ringo: Drums (Ludwig kit); maracas

George handles the lead vocal on "Devil In Her Heart," a cover version of "Devil In His Heart" by the Donays, a little-known girl group from the Detroit area. The group consisted of Yvonne Allen (lead singer), Michelle Ray and sisters Janice and Amy Gwenn. After impressing a talent scout with their performance of the Marvelettes' "Please Mr. Postman" at a high school talent show, the teenage girls obtained management, which led to some concert dates in the Detroit area. Although Motown's Berry Gordy showed some interest in the group, they signed with one of Gordy's competitors, Correc-Tone Recording, Inc. The girls recorded a pair of songs written by Richard Drapkin, "Bad Boy" (not the Larry Williams song recorded by the Beatles) and "Devil In His Heart." The songs were leased to Brent Records, a New York label associated with Bob Shad's Time Records. The single's A-side, "Bad Boy," got respectable air play in Detroit when it was released in August 1962, but sales were poor and the record did not chart. The girls' parents were against them touring to promote the single, wanting them to finish high school. The group broke up and never recorded again.

That would have been the end of the story, but in September 1962, a British label, Oriole Records, issued a trio of singles licensed from the Tamla/Motown labels, Mary Wells' "You Beat Me To The Punch," the Contours' "Do You Love Me" and the Marvelettes' "Beachwood 4-5789." That same month the company released Hugh Montenegro's "Dark Eyes," licensed from Time Records. All four discs were pressed with "Oriole American" labels. Then, in October, Oriole American released a pair of singles from Time's sister label, Brent Records: the instrumental "Watermelon Walk" by the Five Counts; and "Bad Boy" by the Donays. None of those records charted in the U.K.

So how did the Beatles end up recording a B-side to a disc that did not chart in America or in Great Britain? George Harrison explains: "Brian had a policy at NEMS of buying at least one copy of every record that was released. Consequently he had records that weren't hits in Britain, weren't even hits in America. Before we were going to a gig, we'd meet in the record store, after it had shut, and we'd search the racks like ferrets to see what new ones were there… 'Devil In Her Heart' and Barrett Strong's 'Money' were records we'd picked up and played in the shop and thought were interesting."

As it turns out, "Devil In His Heart" was released on October 5, 1962, the same day as "Love Me Do." For a group of young lads ferreting through the record racks for hidden gems pressed in vinyl, the disc would have been irresistible. While "The Donays" would have meant nothing to the boys, the word "American" surely caught their attention. And the song's Latin flavor sealed the deal. At the time, the group was fascinated with Latin rhythms, as evidenced by their own "P.S. I Love You," the flip side of their brand new single, and songs like "Besame Mucho." George claimed the Donays' song, and the Beatles quickly added the tune to their stage show with gender-altered lyrics and title as "Devil In Her Heart."

The Beatles recorded "Devil In Her Heart" as the third song during their first session for the album on July 18, 1963. The group did three takes (including one false start) for the basic track, which featured George on lead vocal supported by John and Paul's backing vocals. The track has George on his Country Gentleman, John on his Rickenbacker Capri, Paul on his Hofner bass and Ringo on drums. The first two overdub takes were false starts. With Take 6, George double-tracked his lead vocal and Ringo added maracas.

The song begins with Ringo's drums, quickly followed by George's lead guitar harmony lines. John and Paul sing a warning in harmony, with George answering with a denial. After a repeat of this pattern, George sings the verses double-tracked with John and Paul "Ahh"-ing in the background. The last line of each verse is sung in three-part harmony. George re-sang a punch-in vocal for the line "But her eyes they tantalize" to correct a sour note. George's lead guitar and Ringo's samba beat give the song a Latin American flavor.

Two days prior to the EMI session, the Beatles recorded the tune during a marathon BBC session during which 17 songs were recorded. This BBC version aired on August 20 on Pop Go The Beatles. Although not included on *Live At The BBC*, this performance is on the *Baby It's You* maxi-single. The group also recorded the song on September 3, 1963, for broadcast on the September 24 Pop Go The Beatles. This is on *On Air-Live At The BBC Volume 2*. The group romped through a rough take of the song during the *Get Back* project on January 7, 1969, between workouts of "Don't Let Me Down."

Not A Second Time

Recorded: September 11, 1963
Mixed: September 30 (mono); October 29 (stereo)

Producer: George Martin
Engineers: Norman Smith; Richard Langham

John: Lead vocals; rhythm guitar (Gibson J-160E Jumbo)
George: Lead guitar (Gibson J-160E Jumbo)
Paul: Bass guitar (Hofner)
Ringo: Drums (Ludwig kit)
George Martin: Piano (Steinway B)

"Not A Second Time" is one of two songs on *With The Beatles* that was written entirely by John, the other being "All I've Got To Do." And, like that song, it was a case of John, in his own words, "writing a Smokey Robinson." In fact, the song can be viewed as the opposite or a follow-up to Smokey's "You've Really Got A Hold On Me," which is also on the album. Smokey is trapped in a relationship, singing "I don't like you, but I love you," but he admits "I want to split now, I just can't quit now/You really got a hold on me." John has been betrayed and doesn't want to get burned again. She made him cry, but now she's back again. He sings: "And now you've changed your mind/I see no reason to change mine." He knows it's through and he won't fall for the "same old line." John makes it clear: "You hurt me then/You're back again/No, no, no, not a second time."

The song was recorded at the start of the evening session on September 11. It took five takes to get the basic track of John's lead vocal backed by he and George on their Gibson Jumbo acoustic-electric guitars, Paul on his Hofner bass and Ringo on drums. On Track 2, Takes 6-9, John double-tracked his vocal and George Martin superimposed simple but elegant piano, including a solo played over the song's refrain. Towards the end of the song, John's double-tracking is exposed when one voice sings "no, no, no" while the other sings "not a second time." It's a nice touch that may have been an error. Take 9 was mixed for mono on September 30 and for stereo on October 29. George's guitar is buried in the mix, leading some to believe he did not participate in the recording.

In an article on the Beatles music appearing in the December 27, 1963 edition of the prestigious London newspaper, The Times, music critic William Mann compared the "Aeolian cadence" at the end of "Not A Second Time" to the chord progression that ends Mahler's "Song Of The Earth." And Beatles fans thought it was just another great rock song.

Money (That's What I Want)

Recorded: July 18 & 30, 1963; September 30, 1963
Edited and mixed: August 21 (mono); October 30 (stereo)

Producer: George Martin
Engineers: Norman Smith; Richard Langham

John: Lead vocal; rhythm guitar (Rickenbacker Capri); handclaps
Paul: Backing vocal; bass guitar (Hofner); handclaps
George: Backing vocal; lead guitar (Country Gentleman); handclaps
Ringo: Drums (Ludwig kit); handclaps
George Martin: Piano (Steinway B)

As detailed in the earlier Decca Sessions chapter, the Beatles added Barrett Strong's "Money (That's What I Want)" to their set list in 1960. George Martin selected "Money" to be the all-important closing statement for *With The Beatles*, a decision consistent with his placement of "Twist And Shout" as the final track on the group's first LP. Both songs are rousing rockers with a scorching lead vocal from John augmented by Paul and George's exciting backing vocals, complete with shouts and "Oooo"s. The backing track is dominated by Ringo's pounding beat on tom-toms and George Martin's relentless piano. While John's vocal on the Decca recording is tentative, here he lets it rip. The growth in the band's musical abilities and confidence in 18 months between the two recordings is remarkable.

"Money" was the second song recorded for the album on July 18. The basic track was recorded in five takes (1, 3 and 4 were false starts), with Take 5 the best. John plays his Rickenbacker Capri, George is on his Country Gentleman, Paul is on his Hofner bass and Ringo is on drums. Take 6 was an edit piece on the piano introduction with Ringo tapping his drum sticks. Take 7 had George Martin overdub piano for an intro and throughout the entire song onto Take 5. Handclaps were also added during Take 7.

On August 21, George Martin, assisted by Norman Smith and Geoff Emerick, edited Takes 6 and 7 and then made a mono mix of the song. On September 30, Martin overdubbed more piano onto Take 7; however, none of these takes appear to have been used. The song was initially mixed for stereo on October 29. The following day, Martin made two separate mono mixes, which were then run through separate channels that were mixed to form a stereo mix.

The band's October 1963 performance for Sweden's Sveriges Radio is on *Anthology 1*. The December 26, 1963 broadcast on The Beatles Say From Us To You is on *On Air-Live At The BBC Volume 2*. The group returned to the song during the *Get Back* sessions.

Editing, Mixing, Banding and Mastering

By September 12, nearly all of the songs for *With The Beatles* had been completed, although some tracks received fine-tuning on September 30 and October 3 and 17. Most of the songs were mixed for mono during sessions held on August 21, September 30 and October 23. Edits were performed on those days for the songs that required editing. All of the songs were mixed for stereo on October 29, with "Money" getting a special remix the following day.

By October 4, George Martin had determined the running order for the album's tracks. The label copy sheet indicates that the album's cover had been submitted and that Tony Barrow would be writing the liner notes for the back cover. The publishing for Beatles originals was listed as Northern Songs, and all John and Paul compositions were credited to "Lennon–McCartney." The banding of the tracks (placing the songs in their final running order on the master tape) was done in early November. The mono and stereo masters were cut at EMI Studios on November 4 and forwarded to EMI's factory in Hayes, Middlesex, England.

Because the entire LP was recorded on a two-track recorder, nearly all of the songs on the stereo album have the same drastic stereo separation as the first LP with music on the left and vocals on the right, although musical introductions and solos were often on the left side as well.

Banding and Mastering of *Meet The Beatles!*

Capitol received tape copies of the Beatles recordings in late November or early December 1963. The company wanted rockers on both sides of its first Beatles single, so "I Saw Her Standing There" was substituted for "This Boy" as the flip of "I Want To Hold Your Hand." Capitol decided to base its first Beatles album on the group's most current LP, *With The Beatles*. It changed the title to *Meet The Beatles!* and programmed a 12-song LP. The record opens with both sides of the Capitol single "I Want To Hold Your Hand" and "I Saw Her Standing There" followed by the U.K. B-side "This Boy." The remaining tracks keep the running order of *With The Beatles*, starting with "It Won't Be Long," but drop all covers songs except for "Till There Was You." The tape for the album was assembled on December 18.

On December 19, 1963, Maurice Long made a proof reference dub (shown above with the group's name spelled as "BEATTLES" with two "T"s) for the stereo version of *Meet The Beatles!* The lacquer masters were cut later that same day by Hal Muhonen.

The mono version of the album was mastered by Billy Smith on December 19. Capitol used the same mono mixes for "I Want To Hold Your Hand" and "This Boy" as the single. All other songs on the album are fold-down mixes from the stereo tapes. These Type B Mono mixes were made by Lee Minkler on December 19. Capitol believed it could achieve a fuller sound from the stereo masters.

I Want To Hold Your Hand

Recorded: October 17, 1963
Mixed: October 21 (mono and stereo)

Producer: George Martin
Engineers: Norman Smith; Richard Langham

John: Lead vocal; rhythm guitar (Rickenbacker Capri); handclaps
Paul: Backing vocal; bass guitar (Hofner); handclaps
George: Backing vocal; lead guitar (Rickenbacker 420 and Gretsch Country Gentleman); handclaps
Ringo: Drums (Ludwig kit); handclaps

"I Want To Hold Your Hand" was recorded as the A-side to a stand-alone single to be issued contemporaneously with the Beatles second LP, *With The Beatles*. The single was actually released on November 29, 1963, a week after the album. This delay may have been due to the unexpected resurgence of sales of "She Loves You" following the group's London Palladium and Royal Variety Show television appearances (see page 32).

John and Paul wrote "I Want To Hold Your Hand" in the cellar of the Asher residence on Wimpole Street in London. Paul was then dating Jane Asher and spending much of his time at her parents' house while in London. According to John: "We wrote a lot of stuff together, one-on-one, eyeball to eyeball. Like in 'I Want To Hold Your Hand,' I remember when we got the chord that made the song. We were in Jane Asher's house, downstairs in the cellar playing on the piano at the same time. And we had, 'Oh you-u-u… got that something…' And Paul hits this chord and I turn to him and say, 'That's it!' I said, 'Do that again!' In those days, we really used to absolutely write like that – both playing into each other's nose." This would be one of the last times the pair worked together to create an entire song. Future songs would be written primarily by one individual, with the other making suggestions and contributions of varying degrees.

It has been speculated that "I Want To Hold Your Hand" was written specifically for the American market. And while Brian Epstein may have requested that the group come up with a song that would be well suited for American audiences, there is no evidence that John and Paul wrote the song with that in mind. The fact that the song sounded different than their prior singles does not prove it was tailored for the U.S. Each successive Beatles single sounded different than its predecessor. John and Paul were most likely just looking to write another great single; however, "I Want To Hold Your Hand" was the song that became the Beatles first U.S. hit.

The Beatles recorded "I Want To Hold Your Hand" during an October 17, 1963 session at EMI's Studio Two. The session marked the first time the group used a four-track recorder. Although EMI had purchased a Telefunken M10 four-track recorder in 1960, its use was restricted primarily to classical recordings. The company did not think pop or rock music was worthy of the advanced technology and the increased costs associated with its use. But the success of "She Loves You" and the group's growing need for additional tracks allowed George Martin to demand the use of the four-track for the Beatles recordings.

This significantly expanded what the group could do in the studio. For these early sessions with the four-track, the group's performance would typically be recorded live over three tracks spread as follows: (1) rhythm guitar, bass and drums; (2) lead guitar; and (3) vocals. The fourth track would then be used for overdubs, which often included double-tracked vocals, percussion and additional guitar. As the group's arrangements got more complex, they often reduced or bounced down the three recorded tracks to one or two tracks on another tape, leaving the remaining tracks open for multiple overdubs. EMI engineer Ken Townsend summed it up: "It made the studios into much more of a workshop."

The four-track also gave the group more flexibility during the recording process. For example, George could concentrate on a basic rhythm guitar part during the live recording of the song and then later overdub the tricky guitar parts onto an unused track. The four tracks were also helpful during mixing since each track could be equalized, compressed and given echo separately. Having instruments and vocals spread over four tracks also provided more options when it came time to make a stereo mix. Future stereo mixes would no longer be restricted to vocals on one channel and instruments on the other.

The October 17 session began with the group recording dialog for "The Beatles' Christmas Record," which would become the first in a series of annual Christmas messages issued as flexi discs by the Beatles Fan Club from 1963 through 1969. A vinyl LP of all previous Christmas messages sent to members in 1970 after the group broke up. The Beatles took a break from the task to try a remake of the first song recorded for the album, "You Really Got A Hold On Me." Apparently this version of the song was not superior to the earlier recording, so it was not chosen for the album. It has yet to be released. After completing the Christmas dialog, the group returned to the main task at hand—recording their next single.

"I Want To Hold Your Hand" was completed in 17 takes with the four-track most likely used as follows: (1) John's Rickenbacker Capri, Paul's newly purchased 1963 Hofner 500/1 violin-shaped bass (replacing his well-worn 1961 model) and Ringo's drums; (2) George's recently purchased Rickenbacker 420; (3) John and Paul's vocals; and (4) overdubs, including handclaps and notes played by George on his Gretsch Country Gentleman. John's guitar is heavily compressed with an Altec RS124 Compressor and an EMI RS114 Limiter, making it sound like an organ. Studio logs indicate that after two false starts, the group ran through nine complete takes, with five breakdowns mixed in. It all came together for Take 17, the best. The group then overdubbed handclaps and George's guitar onto Take 17. The song was mixed on October 21 for mono and stereo.

Although no outtakes of the song have been released, a few bits of studio banter and playing are included on Volume 2 of the *Anthology* video in a chapter titled "Voice Clips From Abbey Road Studios." They show Paul in charge. Before Take 4, John says: "Do it slower." Paul disagrees and commands: "No! Sssh! Play it from the beginning. One, two, three." Prior to Take 9, Paul gives Ringo instructions: "Keep your bit dead, Ringo!" After John makes a suggestion, Paul shoots it down: "No. The first one, loud, attack. The second one not so loud. Just try it."

The song's powerful opening phrase is repeated three times. This pattern returns at the end of the middle eight when John and Paul sing "I can't hide, I can't hide, I can't hide." John picked up this idea from a French album of experimental music, where a phrase was repeated as if the record had stuck with a repeating skip. The song is taken at a slower pace than the group's earlier singles.

The Beatles promoted their new single with a series of TV and radio performances. On November 25, the group mimed the song for the November 27 Granada TV show Late Scene Extra. On December 15, the group mimed "I Want To Hold Your Hand" and three other songs for the December 21 Thank Your Lucky Stars. On December 17, the Beatles recorded both sides of the single for BBC Radio's December 21 Saturday Club. The next day they recorded "I Want To Hold Your Hand" for the December 26 broadcast of From Us To You. This performance is on *On Air - Live At The BBC Volume 2*. The band later recorded another performance of the song for the February 15, 1964 Saturday Club. The Beatles opened up their January 12, 1964 appearance on Val Parnell's Sunday Night at the London Palladium with "I Want To Hold Your Hand" and played the song on all three February 1964 Ed Sullivan Show appearances.

This Boy

Recorded: October 17, 1963
Mixed: October 21 (mono); November 10, 1966 (stereo)

Producer: George Martin
Engineers: Norman Smith; Richard Langham

John: Lead and backing vocals; rhythm guitar (Gibson Jumbo)
Paul: Backing vocals; bass guitar (Hofner)
George: Backing vocals; rhythm guitar (Gibson Jumbo); over-dubbed lead guitar (Gretsch Country Gentleman)
Ringo: Drums (Ludwig kit)

"This Boy" is a beautiful ballad written by John (possibly with an assist from Paul). According to John: "Just my attempt at writing one of those three-part harmony Smokey Robinson songs. Nothing in the lyrics; just sound and harmony." Although inspired by Smokey Robinson songs such as "You Really Got A Hold On Me" and "I've Been Good To You" (the B-side to "What's So Good About Good Bye," which influenced "Ask Me Why"), the song also incorporates elements found in the Teddy Bears' "To Know Him Is To Love Him." Both songs have a three-part harmony and a slow 12/8 meter. The Beatles added the song to their stage show, changing its gender to "To Know Her Is To Love Her."

The group took 15 takes to obtain a suitable performance of "This Boy" with the instruments and vocals most likely spread across the four tracks as follows: (1) John's Jumbo guitar, Paul's Hofner bass and Ringo's drums; (2) George's Jumbo guitar; and (3) vocals by John, Paul and George. Some of the earlier takes had a guitar solo in the middle eight and a full ending. John and George play differing but complementary rhythm guitar parts, Paul adds a melodic bass line and Ringo provides his usual excellent drumming primarily using his hi-hat. John, Paul and George sing in three-part harmony during the verses. John solos on the bridge, backed by Paul and George. Two more takes were needed to complete overdubs onto the fourth track. One pass had John, Paul and George adding backing vocals to the bridge, while another had John double-tracking his lead vocal on the bridge. On one of these takes, George added octave lead guitar on his Gretsch Country Gentleman during the song's fade-out ending. The song was mixed for mono on October 21. The finished master is an edit of Takes 15 and 17.

The Beatles mimed "This Boy" for the December 20 Granada TV show Scene At 6.30. The group's BBC recording of the song for the December 21 Saturday Club is on *On Air - Live At The BBC Volume 2*.

The Beatles, sharing a single microphone, performed "This Boy" on Val Parnell's Sunday Night at the London Palladium on January 12, 1964 (shown above). They also played the song on the February 16, 1964 Ed Sullivan Show and as part of their February 11, 1964 concert at the Washington Coliseum.

VISIT
www.beatle.net
for more books by Bruce Spizer

SUBSCRIBE TO BRUCE'S EMAIL LIST
FOR EXCLUSIVE BEATLES ARTICLES AND CONTENT

THE BEATLES ALBUM SERIES

AVAILABLE IN DIGITAL, HARD COVER AND SPECIAL COLLECTOR'S EDITIONS

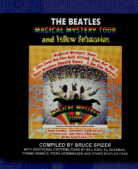
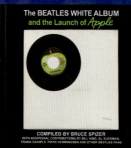
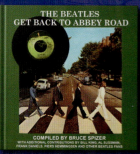

ORIGINAL SERIES: DIGITAL EDITIONS, FIRST EDITION HARDCOVER AND SPECIAL COLLECTOR'S EDITIONS

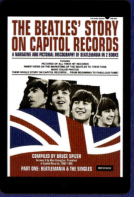

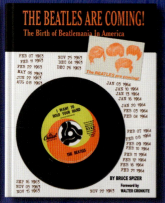
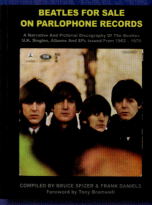

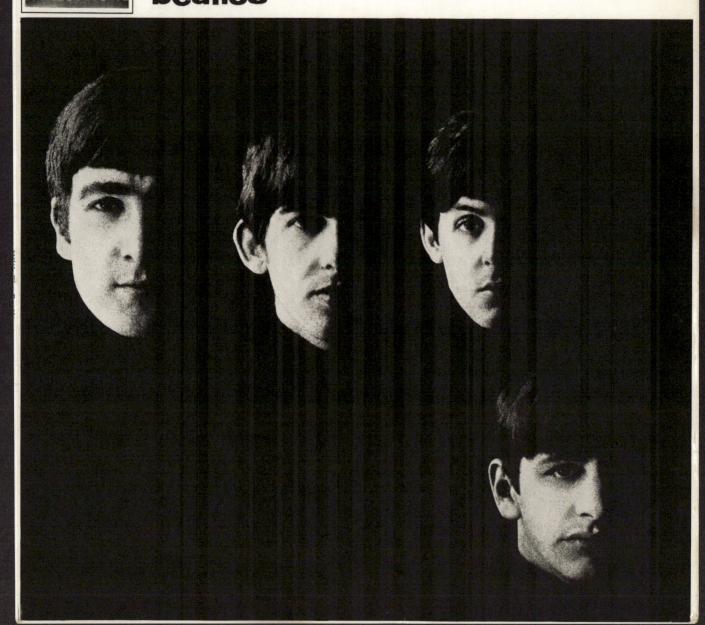